OV

FASTI

BOOK IV

EDITED BY

ELAINE FANTHAM

Giger Professor of Latin,
Princeton University

CAMBRIDGE
UNIVERSITY PRESS

CAMBRIDGE UNIVERSITY PRESS
Cambridge, New York, Melbourne, Madrid, Cape Town, Singapore, São Paulo

Cambridge University Press
The Edinburgh Building, Cambridge CB2 2RU, UK

Published in the United States of America by Cambridge University Press, New York

www.cambridge.org
Information on this title: www.cambridge.org/9780521445382

First published 1998

A catalogue record for this publication is available from the British Library

Library of Congress Cataloguing in Publication data

Ovid, 43 BC – 17 or 18 AD
[Fasti. Book 4]
Fasti. Book IV/Ovid; edited by Elaine Fantham.
p. cm. – (Cambridge Greek and Latin classics)
Introd. and commentary in English; text in Latin.
Includes bibliographical references and index.
ISBN 0 521 44538 8 (hardback) ISBN 0 521 44996 0 (paperback)
1. Rome – Religious life and customs – Poetry. 2. Didactic poetry,
Latin – History and criticism. 3. Ovid, 43 BC – 17 or 18 AD
Fasti. 4. Rites and ceremonies – Rome – Poetry. 5. Didactic poetry,
Latin. 6. Calendar – Rome – Poetry. I. Fantham, Elaine.
II. Title. III. Series.
PA6519.F6A4 1998
871′.01 – dc21 97-13724 CIP

ISBN-13 978-0-521-44538-2 hardback
ISBN-10 0-521-44538-8 hardback

ISBN-13 978-0-521-44996-0 paperback
ISBN-10 0-521-44996-0 paperback

Transferred to digital printing 2005

CAMBRIDGE GREEK AND LATIN CLASSICS

1(*a*) Venus (Genetrix)

1(*b*) Aeneas

2 Venus Verticordia

3 Cybele

4 Ceres

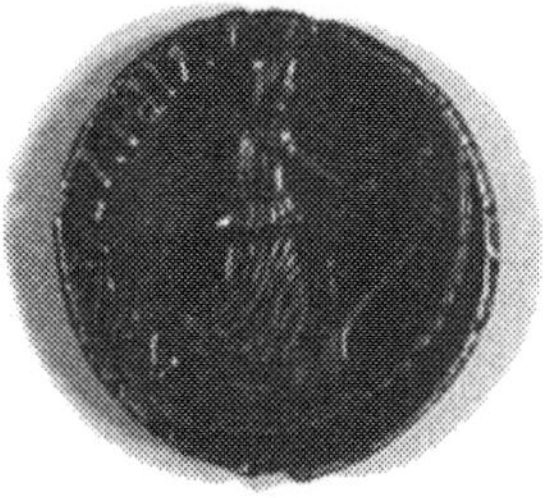

5 Ceres

6 Ceres

7 Flora

The cults of *Fasti* IV on Roman coins (for a full description see p. vi).

CONTENTS

DETAILS OF FRONTISPIECE

The cults of *Fasti* IV on Roman coins

1. Denarius of C. Iulius Caesar (47–46 BC), Crawford, *RRC* 458/1.
   (*a*) Obverse: Diademed head of Venus (Genetrix) r.
   (*b*) Reverse: Aeneas walking l., carrying Anchises and Palladium.
2. Denarius of M. Cordius Rufus (*c.* 46 BC), Crawford, *RRC* 463/1b. Reverse: Venus Verticordia standing l., holding scales and sceptre; Cupid on her shoulder.
3. Denarius of C. Fabius Hadrianus (*c.* 102 BC), Crawford, *RRC* 322/1b. Reverse: Veiled and turreted head of Cybele, r.
4. Denarius of C. Memmius (*c.* 56 BC), Crawford 427/2. Reverse: Ceres seated r. MEMMIVS AED CERIALIA PRIMVS FECIT.
5. Denarius of C. Vibius Pansa (*c.* 48 BC), Crawford, *RRC* 449/2. Reverse: Ceres walking with two outstretched torches, plough before. (Cf. C. Vibius Pansa (*c.* 90 BC) Ceres with two torches and pig, Crawford, *RRC* 342/3b.)
6. Denarius of M. Volteius (*c.* 78 BC), Crawford, *RRC* 385/3. Reverse: Ceres in chariot drawn by two serpents. (Cf. C. Vibius Pansa (*c.* 48 BC), Crawford, *RRC* 449/3a.)
7. Denarius of C. Servilius (*c.* 57 BC), Crawford, *RRC* 423/1. Reverse: head of Flora r., with flower and lituus behind. FLORAL PRIMVS.

PREFACE

Ovid's *Fasti* has been the centre of increasingly vigorous literary and historical study since 1978, but despite the flood of stimulating articles and monographs, there has been no English language commentary on any part of the text since Frazer's five splendid volumes published in 1929. This commentary on book IV is intended to make one of the most interesting months of Ovid's calendar available for undergraduate and graduate study. As far as possible I have incorporated the ideas and approaches of recent discussions on Augustan monuments and ideology, on the Augustan public calendar and on both early and Augustan religious practice.

The bulk of my research for this commentary was made possible by leave granted by Princeton University in 1994–5: during that time I was privileged to be the guest of the Department of Classics and Archaeology at the University of New England, Australia, and the Dipartimento di Filologia Latina, University of Pisa. The American Academy graciously awarded me a residency for October to December 1994: there the Librarian Christina Huemer and her staff made research a delight, and the Professor in Charge Malcolm Bell enabled me to walk the ground that Ovid trod and understand where I was standing. In 1995 and again in summer 1996 Pembroke College Cambridge generously welcomed me as a Visiting Scholar, and the Cambridge University Faculty of Classics offered me use of its library and enjoyment of its seminars. There and elsewhere I have profited from the kindness of scholars ready to let me see their unpublished work and discuss problems informally: in particular Sandro Barchiesi, Mary Beard, Dennis Feeney, Philip Hardie, Stephen Hinds, Richard Hunter, Richard King, Carole Newlands, John Miller, and Peter Wiseman have generously shared their writings and ideas. I cannot thank them enough, and only hope I have not wasted or distorted their thought. Ted Kenney has been both patient and kind beyond his editorial duties, and I thank him for the many occasions when I have delighted in his wit and learning. Perhaps authors do not always appreciate just how much they owe to the quality of their copy-editors. I was exceptionally fortunate to benefit from the superb scholarship and meticulous editing of Susan

Moore, and I would like to express my heartfelt thanks to her not just for her skills, but also for her patience and forbearance.

Besides a sincere appreciation of the skill and tact of Pauline Hire and the staff at Cambridge University Press I would like here to express a different kind of thanks, to my graduate students. The adventurous and versatile 1995 *Fasti*-Class – Al, Andrew, Andromache, Ed, Jesse, Kasha, Katharina, Lara, Peter and Paolo – were a continuing stimulus. Their discussions and individual research enlivened and improved my reading of the poem with the fun of chasing ideas and links of thought. Among the senior graduates Grant Parker's impeccable scholarship helped me to set my manuscript in better order and submit a cleaner text. I would like to dedicate this commentary to them all and to their futures as Classical scholars.

Princeton / Cambridge 1996 Elaine Fantham

ABBREVIATIONS AND REFERENCES

Except where the omission might give rise to ambiguity the name of the work is omitted from references to Ovid's *Fasti* (to be distinguished from the Roman public calendar, *fasti* lower case). Likewise the name of Ovid is omitted before references to his works. Other works are cited as in the *Oxford Latin Dictionary* except as indicated below. Journals are cited with the abbreviations of *L'Année Philologique* except where these may not be easily recognized.

(Ovid)	*AA*	*Ars amatoria*
	Am.	*Amores*
	Ex P.	*Epistulae ex Ponto*
	F.	*Fasti*
	Her.	*Heroides*
	Med. fac.	*Medicamina faciei femineae*
	Met.	*Metamorphoses*
	Rem.	*Remedia amoris*
	Tr.	*Tristia*
Virg.	*Aen.*	*Aeneid*
	Ecl.	*Eclogues*
	Georg.	*Georgics*

ANRW (eds.) H. Temporini and W. Haase, *Aufstieg und Niedergang der römischen Welt.* Berlin–New York 1972–

CHCL *Cambridge history of classical literature.* Vol. II, Cambridge 1982; vol. I, Cambridge 1985

CIL *Corpus inscriptionum Latinarum.* Berlin 1863–

G–L B. W. Gildersleeve and G. Lodge, *Gildersleeve's Latin Grammar.* London 1960

GLK (ed.) H. Keil, *Grammatici Latini*, 8 vols. Leipzig 1857–70, repr. 1961

HE (eds.) A. S. F. Gow and D. L. Page, *The Greek anthology: Hellenistic epigrams*, 2 vols. Cambridge 1965

HRR (ed.) H. Peter, *Historicorum Romanorum reliquiae.* vols I and II. Stuttgart 1967

H–S	J. B. Hofmann and A. Szantyr, *Lateinische Syntax und Stylistik.* Munich 1965
K–S	R. Kühner and C. Stegmann, *Ausführliche Grammatik der lateinischen Sprache* 3. Auflage, ed. A. Thierfelder, 2 vols. Leverkusen 1955
LALE	R. Maltby, *A lexicon of ancient Latin etymologies.* Liverpool 1993
LCL	Loeb Classical Library. Cambridge, MA
LEV	M. Platnauer, *Latin elegiac verse.* Cambridge 1951
N–W	F. Neue and C. Wagener, *Formenlehre der lateinischen Sprache* 3. Auflage, 4 vols. Leipzig–Berlin 1892–1905
OLD	(ed.) P. G. W. Glare, *Oxford Latin dictionary.* Oxford 1982
RE	(eds.) A. Pauly, G. Wissowa and W. Kroll, *Real-Encyclopädie der classischen Altertumswissenschaft.* Stuttgart 1893–
RK	G. Wissowa, *Religion und Kultus der Römer.* Munich 1902
RRC	M. H. Crawford, *Roman republican coinage.* Cambridge 1975
RVV	*Religionsgeschichtliche Versuchen und Vorarbeiten.* Giessen, 1903–
SH	(eds.) H. Lloyd-Jones and P. Parsons, *Supplementum Hellenisticum.* Berlin and New York 1983
TLL	*Thesaurus linguae Latinae.* Munich 1900–

INTRODUCTION

1. THE *FASTI* IN ITS HISTORICAL CONTEXT

By February of 2 BC, when Augustus finally consented to accept the title of *Pater Patriae* celebrated in *Fasti* 2.131–44, Ovid was forty years old. He was renowned as a love poet, author of three books of ostensibly autobiographical *Amores*, a collection of love letters from Penelope and a range of abandoned heroines, and a tragedy based on the deserted Medea's child murders. In his latest work, the *Ars amatoria* (advice to lovers), he brought together seduction and dynastic politics as he celebrated the departure of the young prince Gaius Caesar's expedition to secure the submission of Rome's enemy Parthia by war or diplomacy, and anticipated the prince's triumphant return as a future occasion for amatory encounters. But neither Gaius nor his younger brother and co-heir Lucius Caesar lived to return. By AD 4, Augustus had no other potential heir than his stepson Tiberius, a man of Ovid's own age but of very different temperament, hardened by campaigning and embittered by dynastic in-fighting. This year opened the last unhappy phase of Augustus' forty-two years as Princeps, marked by famine, rebellion and the military disaster of Quintilius Varus' three legions annihilated by a Roman-trained German prince in AD 9. On the domestic front the family scandal which caused the exile of Augustus' daughter Julia for adultery in 2 BC was renewed by the fate of her daughter. In AD 8 the younger Julia was relegated to the island of Trimerus for adultery with D. Silanus, her husband was executed for conspiracy and her child exposed to die. Soon after came the shock of Ovid's relegation by the emperor's private decree to remote Tomis on the NW coast of the Black Sea.

In *Tristia* II, the extended self-defence which Ovid addressed to Augustus from Tomis, he responds to condemnation of his *Ars amatoria* in part by defending its moral harmlessness, in part by citing as examples of his new 'serious' poetry his *Fasti* (549–52), the tragedy *Medea* and the *Metamorphoses* (555–62). Of the *Metamorphoses* – a history of transformation from the beginning of the universe *in tua ... tempora* – Ovid claims that the Princeps need only read it to recognize how he has been the poet's inspiration for his loyal celebration of Augustus and his house: *quantum dederis mihi pectoris ipse | quoque fauore animi teque tuosque canam* (*Tr.* 2.561–2). Of the *Fasti* he speaks more briefly:

sex ego Fastorum scripsi totidemque libellos
cumque suo finem mense uolumen habet,[1]
idque tuo nuper scriptum sub nomine, Caesar,
et tibi sacratum sors mea rupit opus. (2.549–52)

Since the *Metamorphoses* was virtually complete by AD 8, it seems reasonable to assume that Ovid began working on both major poems soon after the publication of the last amatory books, *Ars amatoria* 3 and *Remedia*, in AD 1, if not before. Ovid claims to have written twice six books of the *Fasti* (*sex ... totidemque*), but adds that *sors mea* (disgrace and exile) has broken off his work. There is no trace of any text of the six books that would have covered the second half of the year, and scholars agree that *scripsi* must be special pleading. Indeed Ovid's forward references to events like the August Consualia (*Fasti* 3.199–200; but the rape had already been covered in *AA* 1) and anticipation of the defeat of the Fabii (moved from July back to 13 February: 2.195–242) may imply that he had decided quite early to forgo the pleasure of celebrating the months of Julius and Augustus: probably there was never even a partial draft of the later books. The false claim of completion could be simple self-extenuation, or a malicious ploy to make Augustus feel responsible for the loss of the part of the work that would have done him most honour. Internal evidence, the reference to Augustus' restoration of the temple of Cybele in AD 3 (4.348, see Commentary), shows that Ovid reached book IV after that year; the lack of any specific datable allusions between AD 3 and the principate of Tiberius may, but need not, suggest that the poet did no more work on the *Fasti* after that year. Sir Ronald Syme has placed more stress on negative evidence: he argues from the omission of the anniversary of Tiberius' adoption on 26 January AD 4, that Ovid was so aware of Tiberius' hostility that he ceased to work

[1] This line echoes the ending of *Fasti* 1, *cumque suo finem mense libellus habet*, 724.

on the *Fasti* from the time of Tiberius' adoption; but this assumes rapid composition of the extant six books, followed by abandonment. Ultimately little can be inferred from this or from other omissions.[2]

Echoes and cross-references between *Fasti* and *Metamorphoses* suggest that Ovid was working simultaneously on the two poems even while composing the last 'Italian' books of *Metamorphoses*,[3] which makes it most unlikely that Ovid had finished with either work much before AD 8. But if we consider that no poet is ever ready to call his work finished, Ovid's claim that exile had broken off the work, used to excuse him from completing the poetic year, may have been as true for the six books of *Fasti*, conceived as a coherent composite poem, as it was for the *Metamorphoses*.

What is clear is that the exiled poet returned to the *Fasti* after the death of Augustus in AD 14 and composed a new dedication, not to Tiberius but to his older heir, the crown prince Germanicus.[4] Germanicus, son of Tiberius' dead brother Drusus, had inherited his father's popularity; he was married to Agrippina, daughter of Agrippa and the now exiled Julia, and he seems to have been a poet, author of an adaptation (rather than a translation) of Aratus' *Phaenomena*. Ovid might hope for both sympathy and influence from Germanicus, the more so if the coincidence of Ovid's relegation with the exile of Germanicus' wife's sister, the younger Julia, occurred because Ovid was an associate of the 'Julians', that is Julia and her children. We need not assume he was an accessory to their political and dynastic intrigues against Tiberius.[5]

Whatever his motive, Ovid remodelled the first book, adding homage to Germanicus' expected triumph (285–8), to Tiberius and Livia (531–6) and quite probably reworking at least part of the

[2] Syme (1978). See now Herbert-Brown (1994) 215–33.

[3] See Hinds (1987) and Bömer (1988) 207–21.

[4] At the time when Augustus adopted Tiberius in AD 4 he had required Tiberius to adopt his orphaned nephew Germanicus along with his own (slightly younger) son Nero Drusus, thus attempting to control the succession at one remove.

[5] On Germanicus' *Aratea* and his relationship with Ovid see Fantham (1986) 243–81; his authorship of the *Aratea* is disputed by Herbert-Brown (1994) 173–212.

Carmenta/Evander narrative.[6] Did he remodel other parts of the poem? Bömer and many before him[7] have seen 2.3–18 as the original dedication to Augustus, now moved into a parallel position to the new Germanicus proem. And there can be no doubt that 4.81–4, perhaps with some of its immediate context (see Commentary on 81–4 and 87), is addressed to Germanicus from exile. Other additions cannot be proved, but there are a significant number of innovative phrases common to the *Fasti* and the exilic corpus (see index s.v. 'exile'): probability is in favour of further, now undetectable, changes. With this in mind I have included in the Commentary all linguistic or thematic evidence that might argue for rewriting in Ovid's last years of exile.

2. GENRE

(i) *Problems of genre and generic history. Epic and elegy: elegy as 'not epic'*

What kind of elegy was the *Fasti*? We can guess Ovid's sense of innovation from two important excerpts from *Fasti* book II: first the supposed original dedication to Augustus:

> nunc primum *uelis, elegi, maioribus itis*:
> *exiguum*, memini, nuper eratis *opus*.
> ipse ego uos habui faciles in amore ministros
> cum *lusit numeris* prima iuuenta *suis*.
> idem sacra cano signataque tempora fastis:
> ecquis ad haec illinc crederet esse uiam?
> haec mea militia est, ferimus quae possumus arma. (2.3–9)

> at tua prosequimur studioso pectore, Caesar,
> nomina, per titulos ingredimurque tuos. (2.15–16)

A hundred lines later, the poet shifts to a higher gear for the first Augustan anniversary of the month, 5 February, when Augustus

[6] Compare her consolation to Evander for his exile 1.479–96. See Fantham (1992a) for this and other allusions to Evander which would be more pointed if composed by the poet in exile.

[7] The first serious consideration of the *Fasti* for dating of the original text and verses added in this second edition can be found in Merkel (1841) ccliv–cclxvii.

finally accepted the title of *Pater Patriae*:

> nunc mihi mille sonos quoque est memoratus Achilles
> uellem, Maeonide, pectus inesse tuum,
> dum canimus sacras *alterno carmine* Nonas.
> maximus hic fastis accumulatur honos.
> *deficit ingenium, maioraque uiribus urgent,*
> haec mihi *praecipuo* est *ore* canenda dies.
> quid uolui demens *elegis imponere tantum*
> *ponderis? heroi* res erat ista *pedis*. (2.119–26)

Both passages express the poet's fears that he will not rise to the dignity of his material, first the rites and occasions marked in the public *Fasti*, and then (anticipated by 2.15–16 *tua nomina ... titulosque tuos*) the Very Important Occasion of Augustus' most valued title. In both passages he blames his sense of inadequacy on his choice of metre (*elegi*) and in 2.126 contrasts the grander powers of *heroi ... pedis*. What is this all about?

Alan Cameron has recently claimed with some justification that 'the key respect in which the *Fasti* outstrip Ovid's earlier work ... is in their treatment of the honours of Augustus',[8] and demonstrated a tradition in Augustan poetry of associating the grand style with the emerging post-Callimachean genre of Panegyric, a poetic genre not normally recognized by modern critics.

Thus with *uelis ... maioribus* Ovid invokes the standard image of the poem as a ship voyaging on high seas[9] to suggest the undertaking of too great and dangerous a task, and belittles his *elegi* as a petty or tiny work. *Exiguus*, unlike its near-synonym *tenuis*, denotes smallness without compensating delicacy: it first occurs of elegy in Horace, *AP* 77 *exiguos elegos*; cf. *F.* 6.22 *exiguos ... modos*, *Tr.* 2.532, *Ex P.* 3.4.5 *est opus exiguum uestrisque paratibus impar.*[10] In 2.5–6, the idea of elegiac verses

[8] Cameron (1995) 470.

[9] For this image compare 4.18 *dum licet et spirant flamina, nauis eat* with commentary. In the Germanicus proem Ovid adopts the alternative image of the poet as charioteer: 1.25 *uates rege uatis habenas.*

[10] Contrast *leuis* at *Am.* 2.1.21, 3.1.41, *Tr.* 2.331–2 *numeris leuioribus aptus | sim satis, in paruos sufficiamque modos*, *Ex P.* 4.5.1, *mollis* at *Tr.* 2.307 *nec tamen est facinus uersus euoluere molles*, 349 *delicias et mollia carmina*, *Ex P.* 3.4.85–6 *ferre etiam molles*

as adaptable slaves and go-betweens (*ministri*) gives to *lusit* a double sense, alluding to both the erotic sport of Ovid's youth and his poetic play *numeris . . . suis* in the metre appropriate to youth. *Ludere* too, from Catullus on, signified poetry as divertissement, light, but not necessarily erotic poetry such as Catullus composed with Calvus (Cat. 50.2) or Virgil and his shepherds set to music (*Ecl.* 1.10, 6.1). But the association with youth recalls Virgil's distancing, as poet of the *Georgics*, from his own youthful *Bucolics*: *Georg.* 4.565–6 *carmina qui lusi pastorum, audaxque iuuenta | . . . cecini.* Ovid, the *tenerorum lusor amorum* of *Tr.* 4.10.1, associates *ludere* with his early amatory elegy in *Am.* 3.1.27, *Rem.* 379–80, *Tr.* 1.9.61–2, 2.223 *lusibus . . . ineptis*, 330, 3.1.7; so *F.* 2.6 is recalled in 4.9 *quae decuit primis sine crimine lusimus annis* (see 4.9n.).

In the second excerpt, Ovid openly invokes the model of Homer's *Iliad* and the topos of the many mouths with which Homer prefaced his catalogue of ships (*Il.* 2.489 calls for only ten mouths!) to stress that his theme is a hero (that is a man of divine ancestry, destined to become a god) and requires the voice and pace, that is, the style (*praecipuo . . . ore*[11]) and metre (*heroi . . . pedis*[12]), of epic. It is too great for the strength (*maiora . . . uiribus*[13]) and too weighty (*urgent, ponderis*[14]) for elegy, with its alternation of the hexameter with the catalectic effect of the pentameter.[15]

elegi tam uasta triumphi | pondera disparibus non potuere rotis; more implicitly critical is *Am.* 3.15.19 *imbelles elegi.*

[11] For this use of *os* compare Virg. *Georg.* 3.294 *magno nunc ore sonandum,* Hor. *Sat.* 1.4.43–4 *os | magna sonaturum,* Propertius 2.10.10 quoted below, *Am.* 3.1.64 *iam nunc contracto magnus in ore sonus, Rem.* 382 *Cydippe non est oris, Homere, tui, Tr.* 2.73–4 *te celebrant alii quanto decet ore, tuasque | ingenio laudes uberiore canunt.* See also R. F. Thomas, *AJP* 99 (1978) 447–50, esp. 448.

[12] *TLL* VI 3.2665 cites for *herous* of epic content Prop. 2.1.18, 3.3.16; then *Tr.* 4.10.47, Mart. 3.20.6, Quint. 10.1.88 of Ovid *lasciuus quidem in herois*; Pliny, *Ep.* 7.4.3; of epic metre, *Am.* 2.17.21–2 *apte | iungitur herous cum breuiore modo.* But in practice it is difficult to exclude the metrical sense from several of the first group of examples.

[13] For *uires* often combined with *ingenium*, cf. Prop. 2.10.5 and 9 quoted below, *Ex P.* 3.3.33–4 *forsitan exiguas aliquas tamen arcus et ignes | ingenii uires comminuere mei*, 3.4.11–13 and 79 *ut desint uires, tamen est laudanda uoluntas.*

[14] Cf. *Ex P.* 3.4.85–6.

[15] I apply 'catalectic' here to the braking effect of the single long syllable at the half-line and syllaba anceps at the line-end. But given the coincidence of

All these phrases are characteristic of the language used by Ovid and Propertius before him to mark the relative status of their own composition in elegiac couplets and epic hexameters, but that status is in fact as much a cause for pride as for modesty, and the opposition has a long history. This first section will discuss only elegy's response to epic, as defined by the form (continuous hexameters) and content of Homer, treated by Greek and Roman alike as the earliest and most authoritative type of poetry. In this respect it is the *Iliad*, not the less military *Odyssey*, that dominates the imagination of those who invoke Homer.

The early Greek elegists, however, do not seem to have spent time justifying or defining their own genre against the standard of epic. Indeed Callinus and Tyrtaeus wrote 'public' elegy exhorting young men into battle or commemorating military exploits, and in the sixth century Solon used elegy to explain his political principles and exhort the Athenians to reconciliation and co-operation. Theognis of Megara and Phocylides of Miletus used the elegy chiefly for moral and social advice, whether at symposia or in a wider context. As banqueting poetry elegy takes a more private form, but it seems that the first personal and amatory elegist had already appeared in the seventh century: Mimnermus of Colophon certainly composed poems about warriors (poems 13, 14 *Elegy and Iambus* vol. 1, LCL) but far more survives of his laments at ageing and the loss of love (1–3, 5, 11). He may have been exceptional, since the later Hermesianax and third-century Callimachus (*Aitia* fr. 1 below) and Posidippus (*Anth. Pal.* 12.168) all appeal to him as precedent. So when Horace in the *Ars poetica* defines the contents of the elegiac metre, he seems to fuse elegy like that of Mimnermus with epigram in his claim:

uersibus impariter iunctis querimonia primum,
post etiam inclusa est uoti sententia compos.
quis tamen exiguos elegos emiserit auctor
grammatici certant et adhuc sub iudice lis est. (75–8)

the first two and a half feet of hexameter and pentameter, the effect is not felt until the initial dactyl of the second half of the pentameter, e.g. *conueniente* in *Am.* 1.1.2 discussed below.

Yet he has done so in overt contrast with the epic of Homer:

> res gestae regumque ducumque et tristia bella
> quo scribi possent numero, monstrauit Homerus. (73–4)

But Horace is using terms of theme and scale as no archaic Greek seems to have done. It was the poet and critic Callimachus of Cyrene who polarized the relationship between the genres. Like many before him he wrote epigrams in elegiac metre, but he also returned to the archaic model of composing longer elegies. He even composed one hymn (Hymn 5: see section 2(iii)) in elegiac metre, but it is in the programmatic introduction to his composite work, the *Aitia*, that he articulates what is represented as a defence of elegy but is clearly an attack:

> The Telchines, who are ignorant and no friends of the Muse, grumble at my poetry because I did not complete one continuous poem of many thousands of lines on ... kings or heroes, but like a child I unroll a short tale, though the decades of my years are not few. And this is what I say to the Telchines ... Poems are sweeter for being short. Begone, you jealous brood of envy! From now on judge poetry by the canons of art and not by the Persian chain: and do not look to me for a song loudly resounding. Thundering is not my style. That belongs to Zeus. For when I first placed a writing tablet on my knees, Lycian Apollo said to me ...: 'Poet, feed the sacrificial offering to be as fat as possible, but my friend, keep your muse slim.' (*Aitia* fr. 1. Pfeiffer 1–7, 16–24)

Callimachus' attack is directed not so much against epic as against long poems, whether the uninspired *cyclica*, the post-Homeric epics, here identified by their content 'kings and heroes', or long elegiac compositions: he finds Mimnermus' shorter poems superior to the extended book entitled Nanno.[16] But in turn Callimachus' manifesto is received with some difference of emphasis by Roman elegiac (and lyric) poets when they take up the defence of their chosen genre. For

[16] See A. Cameron, 'Genre and style in Callimachus', *TAPA* 122 (1992) 305–12, and (1995) ch.10; P. E. Knox, *Ovid's Metamorphoses and the traditions of Augustan poetry* (Cambridge 1986) 10.

them Callimachus' rejection of the long poem is seen specifically as rejection of heroic epic defined by content (warfare) and his distaste for thundering is made more prominent as a rejection of epic style.[17]

(*ii*) *Cross-fertilizing the genre: the Hellenistic elegists*

It has become customary to point to the antecedents of the *Fasti* in Propertius' fourth book of elegies, in which the poet set out to present this kind of material, and to recognize the overwhelming influence of Callimachus' *Aitia* as a model for the treatment of patriotic or religious themes by Propertius and Tibullus (2.5) and by Ovid in his calendar poem. But Latinists often pass over the broader tradition of Hellenistic elegy, and there are enough affinities between the *Fasti* and other works by Callimachus and his contemporaries and successors to justify a selective survey of other known Alexandrian elegiac poetry.

Three older contemporaries of Callimachus wrote elegy, but only Philetas, by the refined qualities of poetry that was already lost by the time of Quintilian, if not of the Augustans,[18] won a place in the canon of four elegists, with Callimachus and the earlier Callinus and Mimnermus. Callimachus in his introduction to the *Aitia* mentions respectfully Philetas' elegiac poem *Demeter*. Three fragments (1–3 *Collectanea Alexandrina* ed. Powell) express the goddess's weariness and grief at the loss of her daughter, a theme matching the traditional image of elegy as lament, and a situation Ovid will treat in *Fasti* IV. His pupil Hermesianax seems to have followed the model of the fourth-century Antimachus in composing a collection of elegies around a beloved, Leontion: two of his romances are summarized in

[17] Cf. P. E. Knox 71n., *GRBS* 26 (1985) 28: 'The Callimachean ban on epic verse appears to have been largely the invention of Augustan poets, a clever adaptation of the Callimachean program prescribing short finely wrought poems to the special needs of their own time.'

[18] Bulloch, *CHCL* I 544 notes the implications of Quintilian 10.1.58; Philetas is paired with Callimachus by Propertius in 2.34.31 and 3.1.1 (cf. 3.3.52) and by Ovid, *AA* 3.329, *Rem.* 759–60, but given no separate attention. For his probable influence in *Georgics* IV and a reconstruction of bucolic elements in his poetry see R. F. Thomas, 'The old man revisited', *Materiali e Discussioni* 29 (1992) 35–70.

Parthenius' *Erotica pathemata* (5 and 22), composed as a handbook for Cornelius Gallus to set either as elegy or epyllion.[19] Athenaeus preserves 98 lines from book III (fr. 7 Powell), recounting in Hesiodic catalogue form the love sorrows of poets from Orpheus through to Philetas: this is followed by a less plausible list of the supposed loves of philosophers.[20] Ἔρωτες ἢ καλοί, the chief work of Phanocles, a slightly older contemporary of Callimachus, treated the passions of gods and heroes for beautiful boys: a longer excerpt (fr. 1 Powell) on the death of Orpheus compares in content (if not in quality) with Orpheus' death in *Metamorphoses* XI. The triviality of these erotic catalogues helps to explain Callimachus' objections to extended elegy.

A more interesting figure is Callimachus' pupil, the poet and scientist Eratosthenes, who wrote both *epos* and elegy. His highly imaginative hymn to Hermes (in hexameters, the traditional metre of hymns) describes the god's precocious childhood and his skills, and culminates in a celestial vision of the universe, which influenced both Virgil (*Georg.* 1.231–44) and Ovid (*Met.* 1.45–51). But his narrative poem *Erigone* (frr. 22–7 Powell) was in elegiacs: it told the sad tale of the first human to make wine, Icarius, killed by drunken guests who thought he had poisoned them, and the suicide of his daughter Erigone and her dog Maira; all three were raised to the sky as stars (see 4.939 *canis Icarius* and n.).

The tragic poet Alexander of Aetolia, last of the minor elegists, worked both at Alexandria (where he organized the Ptolemaic collection of tragic texts) and at the Macedonian court of Antigonus Gonatas in Pella. His long elegiac poem *Apollo* presented a series of tragic love stories in the form of prophecy by Apollo himself: it is significant for students of Latin poetry that Parthenius quotes this extensively in *Erotica pathemata* 14. As Parthenius also derives stories from Hermesianax and Phanocles, Gallus and others may well have used the romantic tales of these lesser poets without reading their texts. Alexander's *Mousai* seems more sophisticated: the few fragments suggest that it too was a catalogue poem, but one voicing criticisms of his predecessors.

An anonymous elegiac papyrus (*SH* 961) offers a new 'genre' since

[19] The preface of Parthenius speaks of ἔπη καὶ ἐλεγείας.

[20] Powell fr.7.79ff., or consult Gulick's translation at Athenaeus 13 597b (LCL).

it seems to be an epithalamium for queen Arsinoe. In *Callimachus and his critics* Cameron isolates different types of elegy before Callimachus in separate discussion[21] but shows that *epithalamia*, *epikedia* and *epinikia* are all types of 'occasional' elegy which offer scope for hymnic or panegyrical elements.

Only one of Callimachus' hymns, the splendid *Bath of Pallas* (Hymn 5) is elegiac, but this has prompted scholars to ask whether he has precedents, and why he chose to depart from the standard hexameter form. Both Cameron and R. L. Hunter have reviewed the evidence for elegiac hymns, citing the recent papyrus discovery of Simonides' elegiac hymn to Achilles and Crates' elegiac, if parodic, hymn to Euteleia (*SH* 361).[22] But Hunter has also drawn attention to the apparent discrepancy between the bulk of surviving Alexandrian texts and the conception of *flebilis elegia* that prevails in Roman histories of the genre. Did Alexandrian critics think elegy particularly adapted to laments? It is adopted by Euripides, *Andr.* 103–16 for Andromache's lament: Hunter points to Heracleitus, mourned by Callimachus (*HE* 34 = Call. *Epigr.* 2 Pf.), and called ἐλεγείας ποιητής. The title of his poetry book, *Nightingales*, alludes to the lament of Procne for Itys, which is prominent in Chariclo's lament for her blinded son in Callimachus' Hymn 5 (85–94). There the climax of the hymnic narrative is Athena's pity, the ἐλεεινόν which Heinze singled out as distinctive of elegiac narrative.[23]

(*iii*) *Callimachus' Hymn 5 and* Aitia *as a precedent for* Fasti

Hymn 5, the only complete Callimachean elegiac text (apart from the epigrams), combines first-person 'mimetic' participation in a cult act with a narrative whose length and richness parallel some of the

[21] See his preliminary discussion (1995) 149–53, but also 289–91 on 'panegyrical elegy' (highly relevant to *Fasti*), 312–15 on narrative elegy, and 380–6 on 'Hesiodic catalogue elegy'.

[22] Cameron (1995) 151, Hunter (1992) 9–34: the metrical discussion occupies pp. 18–22.

[23] Heinze (1960) 308–82, here 322. Although the discovery of more papyri since his original study has increased knowledge of the structure of the *Aitia*, enabling the scholars cited below to go beyond Heinze's comments, Heinze still offers (371–92) superb insights into the influence of both the *Aitia* and Hellenistic 'epyllion' on the Roman elegists.

best writing in the *Fasti*.[24] Hunter speaks of Callimachus' experimentation with the boundaries between 'hymn' and 'narrative'. But how shall we classify the beginning?

> Come forth all you bath-attendants of Pallas: I have heard the sacred horse whinnying and the goddess has come. Hurry, now, hurry, fair daughters of Pelasgos!

Like an officiating priest or master of ceremonies, the poet seems to address the celebrants directly, calling them out, because he has heard noises indicating that the goddess is at hand. As in a dramatic monologue his words have to inform the readers whom he is addressing and tell what is happening, but even so his words leap another ontological gap: they imply the identification of the conventional ξόανον, object of the washing ritual, with the goddess herself, so that the rite organized by humans is presented as a divine epiphany.[25] In the first fifty-six lines of the hymn, between exhortations to the attendants (1–4, 13–14) and to the goddess herself (invoked at 33–4, 43–4 and 55–6), the poet-priest alternates signs of the coming divine appearance (complete with the horses that pull her wagon) with miniature flashbacks of the great myths: her victory over the giants (5–11), and her participation in the contest of the three goddesses before Paris (which is made to seem a triumph: 15–32).[26] Only in the last few lines does he introduce an urgent warning: 'But be sure you do not see the goddess: it is fatal to see her unless she wishes to be seen!'

This warning, repressing the eager excitement that has preceded, leads into the central myth of the hymn, the story at once terrible and consolatory, of a different kind of bath, and the punishment of

[24] See now the illuminating discussion of the hymns by Haslam (1993) 113–25 (esp. 122–5) and M. Depew 57–79 of the same volume.

[25] As Hunter (1992) points out, 'there is no other evidence for such a ritual, but it is of a familiar type'. None the less he notes (p. 14) that scholars should at least consider the possibility that the rite is invented. A similar problem arises in the lack of documentary evidence for the washing of Venus described by Ovid at 4.134–44: is it pure invention in emulation of Callimachus or has he moulded a private ceremony to resemble the Greek poet's account?

[26] In this and other 'poetic glosses' comic realism may enter, as with Athene's athletic preparation for the contest.

Teiresias, who involuntarily came upon the goddess bathing. But in contrast with the urgency of the opening running commentary, the poet slows pace as he enters his myth, and the poem turns into distanced narrative.

Teiresias' mother Chariclo is introduced over ten lines as Athene's favourite companion, with whom she travelled to many sites of Boeotia and Greece – all named. The moment of crisis approaches as the noon heat possesses the mountain, and in its stillness (repeated with new phrasing after 2 lines) they begin to bathe, when young Teiresias comes to the brook to drink, sees the goddess's body and is blinded: pain and shock strike him dumb, but the action is all over in eight lines. From now on (80–130) speech takes over, but speech formally introduced as in Homeric narrative. The goddess denounces him for seeing what is unlawful (τὰ μὴ θεμιτά) and his mother cries out in terrible lament, reproaching Athene with the severity of his punishment for an unintended blunder (85–92).

The goddess expresses pity (95–6) and in a speech occupying a quarter of the hymn (97–130) explains that she does not want to blind mere children, but cannot control the decrees of Kronos: and before the movement of personal compensation such as we have met in, for example, Artemis' final speech to Hippolytus, inserts a prophetic account of the worse penalty that will wait Actaeon and the greater grief of his mother when he comes upon Artemis bathing (107–18). Only then does she comfort mother and son with her undertaking to give Teiresias enhanced hearing so that he may know the ways of birds, and the stick of a respected seer and long years of health. Thus this episode has been both the ruin and the exaltation of the future prophet.

Two groups of six lines act as epilogue: reacting to the story the poet-priest confirms the validity of Athena's decisions and the power she received from her birth from Zeus's head, then turns back to the ceremony. Addressing the bath-attendants he hails the approaching goddess with a wish for her blessing and her return to all her people.

Scholars disagree on the religiosity of the hymns: Haslam insists 'we are not supposed to "believe" in them', 'they are literary texts'.[27] Others affirm various degrees of seriousness: Fraser speaks of a

[27] Haslam (1993) 123, 125.

'genuine sense of the mystery and power of the divine',[28] whereas Bulloch, noting that elegy is 'a common medium ... more appropriate for incidental than high poetry' sees Callimachus' introduction of ordinary detail into the heroic subject matter of *Aitia* and some of the hymns as aiming at 'a new realism'.[29] Hunter, who cautions against assuming that the human sympathy for Teiresias' innocence and Chariclo's pain implies a secular rather than a religious outlook, recognizes that 'we cannot evaluate the religious content of the hymns without careful identification of various levels of humour and irony in mythic narrative'.[30] The constantly shifting tone and pace of the whole hymn is perhaps the most important and indefinable of many features which are not only characteristic of Ovid, but a systematic feature of the *Fasti.*[31]

To consider first the 'mimetic' aspects shared by the hymn and the *Fasti*, the poet addresses the human participants in ritual three times in *Fasti* IV, the first of which, the bathing ceremony of Venus in 133–70, has many features that adapt and imitate this particular hymn (see Commentary); compare also the poet's presentation of the procession of Cybele (future tense yields to present and the direct command *spectate, Quirites* 187). In the same way he instructs the shepherds and people at the Parilia in 731–46: cf. *F.* 1.663–72, 695–6.[32] When Callimachus inserts the cautionary tale of Teiresias, he opens with a warning to the people and a disclaimer: 'This is not my story, but other men's.' So Ovid distances himself from the tale of Cronos (4.203–4 *pro magno teste uetustas | creditur*) and his similar compressed

[28] *Ptolemaic Alexandria* (Oxford 1972) 662.

[29] A. Bulloch, *CHCL* I 559 and 564: cf. also the more extensive argument in 'The future of a Hellenistic allusion: some observations on Callimachus and religion', *Mus. Helv.* 41 (1984) 209–25.

[30] Hunter (1992) 31, 33.

[31] Haslam (1993) is particularly good at catching aspects of Callimachus' obtrusive stylization, 'the way he poses an enigma in order to solve it', his intertextuality and his pervasive irony. These are features also characteristic of Ovid, but I will argue that the frequent irony of *Metamorphoses* is generally absent from *Fasti.*

[32] This pose as Master of Ceremonies enters Roman poetry with Catullus' epithalamium (61) and is a common feature in Tibullus, especially 2.1, and Propertius, notably 4.6.

tale of Attis' offence and punishment 4.223–42), like Callimachus' narrative, includes several (brief) snatches of speech (227–8, 235, 240–1): it differs chiefly in being presented as *aition* for the castration of the Galli, whereas Callimachus does not tell the story of Teiresias as *aition* of the Argive ceremony, which goes unexplained. Callimachus' list of places visited by Athena with Chariclo has its equivalent in the travel catalogues at 4.277–91, 467–80, 563–72; his lingering description of the setting of the drama (Hymn 5, lines 71–4) finds counterparts in e.g. 4.425–30, or 3.13–20, 295–8, 357–60. Ovid's tale of Demeter, like that of Chariclo, ends in expostulation (4.587–96) and divine prophecy and consolation of the mother (598–604) as the innocent and unwilling Persephone is both penalized and compensated. And the direct Homeric quotation in Athene's forecast of Teiresias' continued intelligence in the afterlife (Hymn 5, line 128) finds a parallel when Ovid's Mars, arguing before Jupiter for Romulus' deification (2.487), cites Jupiter's promise from Ennius' *Annales*.

Other features, like the parenthetic stage directions ('I hear the screeching of axle-pins' Hymn 5, line 15) or the systematic classification of birds into 'the well-omened, those who fly aimlessly, and those whose wings are not good' (Hymn 5, lines 123–4) are common features of Ovidian narrative technique in the *Metamorphoses* also.

The *Fasti* contains both prayers and hymnic elements (e.g. the aretalogy or list of benefactions of Ceres, 4.399–416), and its alternation of narrative and dialogue may have more in common with the mood of the dramatic hymns, in view of its involvement with actual Roman gods and cult practice,[33] than with the objectively reported antiquities and curiosities of Callimachus' major elegiac work, the *Aitia*. But the *Aitia* was an extraordinary landmark in the evolution of the poetry-book or 'collective poem', without which a composition like the *Fasti* would have been inconceivable.

The pity is that our knowledge is drawn almost entirely from

[33] Hymns 2 to Apollo and 6 to Demeter are also relevant: although they are in conventional hexameters, they are presented mimetically as epiphanies, with an embedded myth to illustrate the god's terrible power.

disconnected papyri of the text or of its commentators.[34] No section of the text is complete, but since the recent publication of the 'Victoria Berenices' study of individual parts can be amplified by a better understanding of the poem's final edition.[35]

The *Aitia* is bound together by its common interest in the causes or origins of communities, their customs and rituals, and its material is drawn from all over the Greek world and from named sources, mostly prose writers of histories and 'Problems'. It seems that the separate investigations of the first two books were held together by the framework of a continuing conversation between the poet and the Muses, within which (as in fr. 7.19–20, fr. 43.56 and 84, *SH* 238.5) one Muse would end a tale and the poet open a new query, answered by her or another another Muse, or even the poet himself. Successive subjects may be linked, as in the explanations of elements of obscenity and abuse common to the ritual of Apollo Aigletes on Anaphe, associated with the Argonauts, and the sacrifice to Heracles at Lindos, or that sacrifice and a different story of Heraclean greed, the encounter of Heracles and Theiodamus. Within the continuing exchange between poet and Muses, however, are embedded reports of conversations held by Callimachus at symposia, such as his catalogue of the cities of Sicily and their foundation myths. Probably the newly published programmatic passages *SH* 239 and 253 belong to the same context and closed book II, thus matching the programmatic dream-sequence in which Callimachus first imagines himself meeting the muses like Hesiod tending his sheep on Helicon, and then prays to the Graces for beauty and charm in his poetry.

In contrast, the various poems of books III to IV are not bound by an over-arching conversation; the Muses seem to play no part: in-

[34] Besides scholia on individual lines, the commentators' διηγήσεις quote the openings of successive poems as *lemmata* and summarize their content: but no διηγήσεις have been found for most of book I or any of book II.

[35] The following treatment draws on Bulloch, *CHCL* I 553–62: P. J. Parsons, 'Victoria Berenices', *ZPE* 25 (1977) 1–49, and three papers by M. A. Harder, 'Aspects of the structure of Callimachus' *Aitia*', *Hellenistica Groningana* I (Groningen 1993) 99–110, 'Callimachus and the Muses: some aspects of narrative technique in *Aitia* bks. 1 and 2', *Prometheus* 14 (1988) 1–14, and 'Untrodden paths: where do they lead?', *HSCP* 93 (1990) 287–309. Cameron (1995) 104–32 now disputes the hypothesis of a second edition of *Aitia*.

stead Callimachus uses two celebratory works for the Cyrenaean Queen Berenice to frame the books, beginning book III with her team's victory in the Nemean chariot race and ending book IV with the 'lock of Berenice'. This poem was composed to honour the naming of a previously unnamed star-cluster after the lock of hair which Berenice had dedicated in the temple of Aphrodite for the safe return of her brother-husband Ptolemy Euergetes from campaigning. Both these poems were written in response to royal occasions, and can be dated after 245 BC, in Callimachus' old age. But there are more associative links. Like a Pindaric ode the Nemean victory poem tells how Heracles founded the Nemean games after killing the Nemean lion, and describes his visit to Molorchus, the creator of a singular mousetrap. Book III probably ended with a feat of another victor in the Games, the boxer Euthycles (frr. 84–5), and as Harder has argued, book IV exhibits ring composition, repeating in more or less reverse order allusions to Androgeus (bk I frr. 3–7.18; bk 4 fr. 103), the Argonauts (bk I fr. 7.19–21; bk IV frr. 108–9) and as epilogue a treatment of the Muses also involving the Graces, and alluding to Hesiod: the signing off, or *sphragis*, is a farewell to both the Muses and Zeus with good wishes for the royal dynasty (bk I frr. 1–2; bk IV fr. 112).[36]

Most scholars now believe that it was only for the later edition, combining the continuous books I–II with the collection of separate poems in books III–IV, that Callimachus composed the polemical introduction replying to the pseudonymous Telchines: thus the first version of the *Aitia* would have presented a very different appearance to its readers. Within the poem Callimachus has a more whimsical persona: he uses many thematic starting-points, such as the statue of Apollo with whom he exchanges question and answer (fr. 114.1–15), the tomb of Simonides from which the old poet himself speaks to Callimachus (and his readers): for a narrative poet he is

[36] P. E. Knox, 'The epilogue to the *Aitia*', *GRBS* 26 (1985) 69–75 shows that this must have been composed as epilogue to the original 2-book edition involved with the Muses, and transferred by Callimachus to the end of IV when he added books III–IV to make the new edition. Knox (n.21) appropriately compares Ovid's transference of his Augustus Proem from the opening of *Fasti* I to *Fasti* II when he composed the new dedication to Germanicus.

remarkably self-conscious, prefacing tales with 'and then the fancy took me' (fr. 1a.19–23, Add. fr. 31b) and intruding into the narrative: the poet adopts many devices to 'interfere with his own story', in the romance of Acontius and Cydippe (fr. 75) apostrophizing the lover Acontius at beginning and end, starting to tell a tale about the first mating of Zeus and Hera, and checking himself, attributing part of the story to others ('and then they say that ...') and changing the point of view or focalizer of the story like a director shifting his camera.

It has been suggested that when Callimachus writes about religion in this way he is not necessarily writing religious poetry, nor indeed 'patriotic' poetry except as being generically Greek. These antiquarian curiosities could hardly have been a source of sentiment or pride to his cosmopolitan audience in the immigrant community of Alexandria. This detachment seems one of the most important differences between Callimachus' poetry and that of his Roman admirers.[37] Rome dominated the Mediterranean, and her language had spread with her culture to exclude other Italic languages that could be compared to the artificial and archaizing Ionic and Doric dialects of Callimachus. The work of his Roman admirers like Propertius and Ovid must have exploited local cults and monuments to appeal to their public through the familiar rather than the bizarre.

(*iv*) *Blending the genres: the contribution of hexameter poetry*

Just as many of the Alexandrian elegiac poets we have considered also wrote narrative poems in hexameters, so Callimachus was famous for one hexameter narrative, a single book of about two thousand lines, called *Hecale* after its protagonist. This too survives only in fragments, but its sentimental focus, not on the hero Theseus and his contest with the bull of Marathon, but on the impoverished old woman who generously feeds him and tells him her life-story, was to

[37] Denis Feeney notes (*per litteras*) how Callimachus echoes Hesiod's encounter with the muses on Helicon, but for Callimachus this is purely a dream. On the 'diachronic gulf' or 'rupture' between Callimachus and early Greek poetry see Peter Bing, *The well-read Muse* (Leiden 1988) 50–90.

influence both Virgil and Ovid: at the same time the resemblance of this story to what is known of Heracles' elegiac visit to Molorchus in the *Aitia* confirms the cross-fertilization of genres in Hellenistic poetry. Ovid creates his Baucis and Philemon in *Metamorphoses* VIII in emulation of Hecale, and takes over into book II the complex structure of digressionary tales told by transformed birds as part of the Callimachean text.[38]

Hellenistic art was fascinated by age, and by country poverty, and just as Theocritus' *Bucolics* were adapted by Virgil to create a new Latin genre, so the domestic scenes of the *Hecale* influence the *Georgics* and the *Fasti*. In *Fasti* IV the farmer of Carseoli (4.691–708) and the shepherd's prayer (4.735–82) reflect the new interest in details of rural life: it is under the influence of Callimachus that Ovid turns King Celeus of Eleusis, in the tale of Demeter's wanderings based on the Homeric hymn, into a poor peasant with a simple diet (4.508–46).

One other form of Hellenistic poetry played its part in the Roman inheritance, didactic: not, that is, practical instruction in a τέχνη like hunting or equitation, but versified learning. The astronomical learning of Aratus of Soli's *Phaenomena*, beloved by Roman translators from Cicero to Germanicus, was adapted by Virgil in *Georg.* 1.351–463, and apparently translated by Ovid (some fragments survive). Aratus' constellations are described, not inscribed in a calendar, with dates of their risings and settings; but memories of his text contribute to the (very inaccurate) astronomical component in the *Fasti*. A century later (around 150 BC) Nicander adapted into verse studies of snakes and cures for snake-bite (*Alexipharmaka*), and his lost *Geourgika* on plants was known to Virgil. Directly or indirectly Ovid used his mythological work, *Heteroioumena*, a collection of transformation tales; but the only strictly 'didactic' poetry that directly influenced either *Metamorphoses* or *Fasti* is the Roman didactic of Lucretius and Virgil.

[38] A. S. Hollis, *Callimachus: Hecale* (Oxford 1990) 339–40 argues that the poem was well over 1,000 lines. The raven of this epic (also introduced into *Metamorphoses* book II) seems to have recounted ancient Athenian customs comparable to the material of *Fasti*. See Alison Keith, *The play of fictions* (Ann Arbor 1992).

We know very little of writers in elegiac metre at Rome before Catullus,[39] but Catullus, for all his reverence of Callimachus, chose to write narrative poetry in hexameters: although he used elegiacs for personal poems of love and hate, for translating Callimachus' elegiac 'Lock of Berenice' (poem 66) and for an apparently detached if abusive narrative (poem 67), his 'Wedding of Peleus and Thetis' (64) is composed in epic metre and combines with the exquisite celebration of their marriage the embedded narrative of Ariadne (full of emotional and highly elegiac speech), a more heroic or Homeric section of praises of the future Achilles,[40] and a Hesiodic denunciation of the evils of contemporary society.

Catullus' friend Calvus wrote both narrative hexameters (the *Io*, frr. 9–14 Courtney, but only isolated hexameters survive) and elegy, while Helvius Cinna, despite the influence of Parthenius,[41] composed his *Zmyrna* in hexameters (cf. frr. 6–8 Courtney, of which 6 is two consecutive lines).

(*v*) *The transformations of Roman elegy*

With the emergence of Augustus as leader, poets writing in elegiac and other personal genres like bucolic or lyric often adopt the device of *recusatio*, a polite mode of declining or postponing epic celebration, as being beyond their skill or delicate voices, while offering homage in miniature to the Princeps or a lesser patron. Thus Virgil 'excuses' himself to Varus in *Ecl.* 6.3–4 (*cum canerem reges et proelia, Cynthius aurem | uellit*), Horace makes his demurral to Agrippa (*Odes* 1.6) or to Augustus himself (*Odes* 4.15) even in an ode which does the great man honour. Propertius goes further. Once (2.10), he actually represents himself straining to rise to the theme of Augustus' victories:

sed tempus lustrare aliis Helicona choreis,
  et campum Haemonio iam dare tempus equo.

[39] See now Courtney (1993) 70–1 for Aedituus, Licinus and Catulus.

[40] It has even been called a hymn, but hymns usually honour and are addressed to deities.

[41] Parthenius himself composed both in narrative hexameters (he cites six consecutive lines about Byblis in *Erotica pathemata* 11.3 = *SH* 646) and elegiacs (*SH* 640).

iam libet et fortes memorare ad proelia turmas
et Romana mei dicere castra ducis.
quod si deficiant uires, audacia certe
laus erit: in magnis et uoluisse sat est. (2.10.1–6)

surge, anime, ex humili; iam carmina *sumite uires*
Pierides, *magni* nunc erit *oris* opus. (2.10.9–10)

In other elegies he invokes Callimachus to show he is unfit to celebrate Augustus or Maecenas in the grand style:[42]

quod mihi si tantum, Maecenas, fata dedissent
ut possem heroas ducere in arma manus ... (2.1.17–18)

bellaque resque tui memorarem Caesaris, et tu
Caesare sub magno cura secunda fores. (2.1.25–6)

sed neque Phlegraeos Iouis Enceladique tumultus
intonet angusto pectore Callimachus,
nec mea conueniunt *duro* praecordia uersu
Caesaris in Phrygios condere nomen auos. (2.1.39–42)

The poetry of *arma*, 'battle' (cf. Prop. 3.1.7 *a ualeat Phoebum quicunque moratur in armis*), is associated with everything harsh and grim. Ponticus the epic poet is told he must abandon his *arma ... fraternae tristia militiae* (1.7.2) and *tristes ... libelli* (1.9.13), because love needs elegy and gentle songs: *plus in amore ualet Mimnermi uersus Homero: | carmina mansuetus lenia quaerit amor* (1.9.11–12). Homer is still the great model of the poet who immortalized Troy (Prop. 3.1.25–34, cf. *Am.* 1.15.9–10). But Roman epic, typified by Ennius (Prop. 3.3.6–12) is harsh and shaggy,[43] always identified with *arma*: thus Prop. 2.34.61–4 conjures up the *Aeneid* by evoking the battle of Actium and Augustus' fleet, the arms of Aeneas and the city walls of Lavinium. The contrast

[42] Not epic celebration, perhaps, but shorter hexameter panegyric: so Cameron argues persuasively, (1995) 354–87. In this he differs from W. Wimmel, *Kallimachos in Rom*, *Hermes Einzelschriften* 16, (Wiesbaden 1960). See also C. O. Brink, *Horace on poetry* III (Cambridge 1982) 257–9, 267.

[43] Cf. Prop. 4.1.61 *Ennius hirsuta cingat sua dicta corona*, and *Tr.* 2.259 *nihil est hirsutius illis.*

between Virgilian epic and elegy is brought out by an epigram of Domitius Marsus, lamenting the death of Tibullus:

te quoque Vergilio comitem non aequa, Tibulle,
  mors iuuenem campos misit ad Elysios,
ne foret *aut elegis molles qui fleret amores*
  aut caneret *forti regia bella pede.* (Marsus 7 Courtney)

Ovid inherits and develops all these associations; the opposition, epic = *arma* vs. elegy = *amor*, is now fixed, so that the first words of Ovid's *Amores*, earliest of his compositions, begin as an epic with appropriate theme and metre:

arma graui numero uiolentaque bella parabam
  edere, materia ...

but when the second line reveals itself a pentameter

... conueniente modis

it turns out to be Cupid's fault:

par erat inferior uersus: risisse Cupido
  dicitur atque unum surripuisse pedem. (*Am.* 1.1.1–4)

The second (or weaker?) line had been equal. *Impar* (cf. *Am.* 3.1.37, *Tr.* 2.220 *imparibus ... modis*) and *dispar* (*Ex P.* 2.5.1, *Ibis* 344) denoting 'uneven', 'unequal', also denote 'unfit', as in *impar congressus Achilli* (*Aen.* 1.475) or even 'lopsided', as in the joking chariot metaphor for Ovid's elegy *disparibus ... rotis* (*Ex P.* 3.4.86). He will play repeatedly on elegy's crippled status, as with the clubfoot Muse of *Am.* 3.1.8. and 10 (*et puto, pes illi longior alter erat* | ... *et pedibus uitium causa decoris erat*), a poem which affects an inferiority complex about elegy *not* in relation to epic, but to tragedy. While Ovid remains a poet of love elegy this sense of the metre's limitations persists, but usually in response to perceived pressure to glorify warfare as the proper theme of his verse. He does not openly challenge, but plays along with the assumption that celebrating Augustus' military successes is the best use of a poet's talent, as military service is the best use of his citizen youth and strength: hence the paradox of *Am.* 1.9.1 *militat omnis amans et habet sua castra Cupido*; hence too the claim in *Fasti* 2.9 *haec mea mili-*

tia est; ferimus quae possumus arma. At times he avoids the real issue of writing contemporary epic by claiming failed attempts to treat the allegorically related triumph of Jupiter over the Giants. Both in his early love poetry (*Am.* 2.1.11–18) and his defence (*Tr.* 2.333–4) Ovid solemnly claims that he had tried to compose a Hesiodic *Gigantomachia*, but was forced to recognize his limitations. He knew very well that the issue for Augustus went beyond a poet's literary or aesthetic preferences for small private themes, or the modest diction of the self-contained elegiac distich. The Princeps wanted praise from his poets in the terms that Romans would understand.

Propertius, with this in mind, tactfully addresses Rome, rather than the emperor: *multi, Roma, tuas laudes annalibus addent | qui finem imperii Bactra futura canent* (3.1.15–16). Horace, Augustus' contemporary and trusted supporter, answered more direct imperial pressure by claiming that Virgil and Varius could do epic justice to the Princeps' victories (*Ep.* 2.1.245–7), whereas he, Horace, would only discredit them by his inadequacy: *sed neque paruum | carmen maiestas recipit tua, nec meus audet | rem temptare pudor quam uires ferre recusent* (257–9). Ovid learnt much from Horace's later poetry, both from this Letter to Augustus and the last book of Odes, and in his defence written from exile he echoes this demurral: *Tr.* 2.73–4 *te celebrant alii quanto decet ore, tuasque | ingenio laudes uberiore canunt.*[44]

When Roman elegy departed from its central concern with love and (to a far lesser extent) friendship, it was to follow Callimachus' model. *Amor* not *arma*, but if not *amor*, what should an elegist celebrate? Propertius in his third book (3.4) seriously considered poetry about the heavenly bodies and the causes of natural phenomena like thunder and eclipses – material treated by Lucretius in the hexameters of books v and vi. But he is already beginning to experiment with other themes: the hymn to Bacchus (3.17), satirical treatment of greed in society, and the threat posed to Rome by Cleopatra (3.11, cf. 2.16). With its echoes of Actium 3.11 pointed the way to national celebration and his 'mimetic' anniversary hymn of 4.6, but what Propertius formally took as his theme for book iv was a kind of

[44] See A. Barchiesi, 'Insegnare ad Augusto', *Materiali e Discussioni* 31 (1994) 149–84, and (1994) 20ff.

Roman *aitia*: *sacra diesque ... et cognomina prisca locorum* (4.1.69). This is demonstrated in 4.6 and four other elegies of the collection: 4.2, the talking statue of Vertumnus explains his origin and powers; 4.4, Tarpeia's betrayal of the Capitoline citadel from love of the Sabine king Titus Tatius; 4.9, Hercules' defeat of Cacus, his intrusion into the all-female rites of the Bona Dea, and exclusion of women from the cult and altar (*Ara Maxima*) which he founded; and 4.10, the *spolia opima* awarded to Romulus for killing King Acron in single combat and to Cossus for defeating a Gallic chief.[45]

So he has honoured *sacra* and *cognomina*, but the only *dies* overtly celebrated is the anniversary of Actium, and the poet turns his focus away from public rejoicing to an esoteric gathering in the temple of Apollo Palatinus[46] and a Callimachean evocation of Caesar's and Apollo's victory. Critics construe the composition of book IV, in which the other five elegies (3, 5, 7, 8, and 11) are concerned with Cynthia and women's life and love, as a mark of failure, or perhaps early death, and read the second part of the introductory poem, in which Propertius is warned off national poetry and sent back to love-elegy, as a veiled confession. The relative weakness of the shortest and last-placed aetiological elegy, 4.10, supports this possibility, but given the ingenious symmetry of the book around the pivotal 4.6, it is also quite possible that Propertius wanted to balance the themes of his youth and his maturity in this way.

None the less the key to this new aetiological poetry may well be *sacra*, as Puelma stressed in his discussion of Callimachus' influence at Rome.[47] *Sacra*, cult and rites, provide a more dignified theme, requiring a higher tone than *Amor* (Puelma calls it *tenuitas sublimis*) and respond to the need for patriotic commitment without submitting the poet to the distasteful tedium of *arma*, contemporary, no longer

[45] On the relationship of *Fasti* to Propertius book IV see the introduction and opening chapter of Miller (1991) and on Propertius' adaptation of Callimachean techniques, H. S. Pillinger, *HSCP* 73 (1969) 168–99.

[46] Cf. 2.31, ostensibly concerned with a missed rendezvous, but really with evoking the new temple and its porticoes.

[47] M. Puelma, 'Die Aitien des Kallimachos als Vorbild der römischen Amores-Elegie', *Mus. Helv.* 39 (1992) 221–46, 285–304; discussion of *sacra* 295–303.

heroic, warfare. Thus Propertius and Tibullus take on the loftier name of *Vates* only for their celebratory sacral poems.[48]

Ovid includes an example of *sacra* near the end of his third book of *Amores* (the Faliscan rite of 3.13), and another elegy, 3.10, with its treatment of Ceres' cult and mythology, shows how he is developing the mythical associations of his personal situation into poetry in its own right.[49]

When he set about making Roman religious festivals the subject of his elegiac *Fasti*, Ovid saw this as a chance to reconcile his poetic tastes with a more congenial way of showing his patriotism and loyalty to the Emperor and his dynasty. After 13 BC Augustus no longer went on campaign but won his victories by proxy: on the other hand he was now continuously present in Rome, and continued unabated his concern with the restoration of morality and religion, both in cult and in monuments. Both ancestral religion and new national and dynastic monuments offered scope for Ovid's art, and he declares them his subject: *Caesaris arma canant alii: nos Caesaris aras | et quoscunque sacris addidit ille dies* (1.13–14). In planning the *Fasti*, Ovid showed his recognition that both the potential of elegy and the nature of didactic poetry had changed, and could be developed so as to encompass large 'patriotic' themes without straining or falsifying his talent. He is ready, then, to embark on a new kind of elegy, largely concerned with *sacra*, but with a formal framework and sequence determined not by his fancy but by the Roman year.

3. THEMES

(*i*) *Ovid's material and sources for the* Fasti

Tempora cum causis Latium digesta per annum
  lapsaque sub terras ortaque *signa* canam ...
sacra recognosces annalibus eruta priscis. (*Fasti* 1.1–2, 7)

[48] Prop. 2.10.19, 4.6.1 and 10, Tib. 2.5.114 only. But neither calls himself *Vates* in his hymns (Prop. 3.17 and Tib. 1.7). Ovid less scrupulously claims the title even in amatory elegy.

[49] We can see a precedent for Ovid's protests at the chastity required by the rites of Ceres/Demeter in Propertius' exploitation of the myth of Io/Isis to reproach the goddess with his mistress's unwanted chastity in 2.33.

(*a*) *Tempora*

The opening word of *Fasti* 1 covers many different kinds of 'time' or 'occasion', which together constitute the poem's formal theme. But the phases of nature, the lunar and solar year and their seasons, play a secondary role to the time units devised by man; the praises of spring in 4.125–32 are a rewriting of 1.150–60, but little systematic attention is paid to winter or approaching summer.

On the other hand the Romulean year of ten months is explained with its possible origins in 1.27–38, and again in 3.99–125 with some added justifications for decimal reckoning. Initially the months were (like our moon-ths) lunar: as Ovid says, *luna regit menses* (3.883). But they were poorly coordinated with the solar year. A first adjustment was the twelve-month year of Numa (1.43–4, cf. 3.152–5) which still ran five days short of the solar cycle, and this discrepancy was remedied by *ad hoc* 'intercalation' of supplementary days at the end of every second or sometimes third year.[50] The Roman official year seems to have begun on 1 March, like the cult year: the bare claim in 1.39–40 is argued in 3.135–50 before it is reiterated in 4.25–8 and 130. It is in March, too, that Ovid acknowledges Caesar's reform of the old calendar on the basis of observations by his astronomer Sosigenes. Caesar established the real duration of the solar year, or as Ovid puts it, *moras solis, quibus in sua signa rediret* (the periods within which the sun returns to his proper signs) as 'three hundred and sixty five days and a fifth' (3.164). The fifth is of course an error, for a quarter, the product no doubt of Roman inclusive reckoning, and Augustus made the necessary correction in 8 BC when it was realized that the leap-day had been introduced every third year instead of every fourth.[51]

[50] See now J. Rüpke, *Kalender und Öffentlichkeit: die Geschichte der Representation und religiöse Qualifikation von Zeit in Rom* (Berlin–New York 1995). He accepts Ovid's claim (*F.* 2.47–54) that the Decemviri of 450 (whose new laws included intercalation) may have moved February from after December to its position between January and March.

[51] A more detailed account is given by Macrobius, *Saturnalia* 1.12.5 and 38 for the Romulean year, 1.13.1–6 for Numa's twelve-month year and the system of intercalation, 1.14.1–12 for Caesar's calendar and his adjustments to the individual months, and 1.14.13–14 for the error corrected by Augustus in 8 BC when he suspended the addition of a leap-day until AD 8.

The days themselves, however, had different civil and religious characters, and Ovid includes in his introductory material of book I *uariorum iura dierum* (45) 'the entitlements of different days', defining the main categories of days in public life. The name *Fasti* itself was a plural originally denoting *dies fasti*, the days on which it was *fas*, 'right', to conduct legal business, and Ovid contrasts the *nefastus* on which the magistrate could not utter the three words '*do, dico, addico*', 'I grant, declare and adjudge.' In the inscribed calendars every date in the year was recorded as N, *nefastus*, if no legal hearings were permitted, or either F, *fastus* or C, *comitialis*. On a day that was *comitialis* assemblies could be held, and presumably this would suspend the holding of lawcourts, but the relationship of lawcourt and senate hearings to actual assemblies was a practical rather than a ritual distinction.[52] There were other patterns: for example the day after each of the named days marking the phases of the moon, Kalends, Nones (usually 5th, but 7th of March, May, July, October) and Ides (usually 13th, but 15th in the four months named above) was deemed 'black' or ill-omened, and no festivals or other religious and public acts took place. Again, festivals (*dies festi*) were *feriati*, that is no public business could be undertaken; they were thus N, *nefasti*, though in no sense negative or ill-omened.

After 1.45–62 Ovid does not discuss this classification again, and there is nothing in the text of *Fasti* IV to remind the reader of each day's civil status. But inscribed Roman calendars, including the *Fasti Praenestini* drawn up by the imperial grammarian Verrius Flaccus, whose work Ovid consulted, show that in April very few days indeed were available for legal business.[53] The 1st and 2nd were *fasti*; the

[52] Ovid also mentions the eight-day cycle of the *nundinae* or market days on which originally (cf. Macrobius, *Sat.* 1.16.28–36) no courts could be held: but this restriction was dropped for practical reasons. The headings inserted in the text at 4.133, 165, 179 etc., reproduce the nundinal letter, the holy days KAL, NON, or EID (where applicable) and status letter (N, F, C, NP etc.) as listed in Roman calendars. The meaning of NP is uncertain, but 1 March, all Ides, and most *feriae* (in April the 13th, 15th, 19th, 21st and 25th) are NP. See Michels (1967) 68–9.

[53] On Verrius Flaccus' work for the *Fasti Praenestini* see Mommsen in *CIL* I pp. 285,313 etc., Bömer, *Fasti* I 18ff. and R. A. Kaster, *Suetonius: De grammaticis et rhetoribus* (Oxford 1995) 194–6.

3rd and 4th *comitiales*, so if there was no assembly they too could be used; but from the 5th to the 10th the games of the Great Mother made the days *feriati*, and so unusable by the courts; from the 11th on, days are *nefasti* for business either in their own right (like the *postriduanus* 14 April) or because of the festivals, the Fordicidia, Cerialia, Parilia. Only with the Vinalia of 23 April is there a *dies fastus*, and although 24 and 26–30 April are marked *comitiales* and so available for business in the absence of an assembly, the Robigalia of 25 April again counts as a public holiday and is marked as *nefastus*.[54]

Thus in his discussion of types of days Macrobius, like Ovid (1.49–53), distinguishes working days (*profesti*) from *festi* and *intercisi*, the days on which business was suspended during the morning offering, and renewed until a further suspension for the burning of the offering. *Festi dis dicati sunt*, he explains, *profesti hominibus ob administrandam rem priuatam publicamque concessi* (*Sat.* 1.16.20). *Festi* included sacrifices, feasts (*epulae*) games and holidays. But he adds an important further classification: public holidays, *feriae*, are either fixed (*statiuae*) or movable (*conceptiuae*),[55] *imperatiuae* or *nundinae*. *Imperatiuae*, 'command' holidays, introduce an important feature of Augustan public life. Like earlier authorities (the senate in the republic) Augustus might assign a day or days to *supplicationes* for a victory, or the dedication of an altar. These holidays would initially be *imperatiuae*, but they would only reach the written calendar if the *princeps* went a step further and secured from the senate the order to celebrate the continuing anniversaries of this occasion. At this point presumably the *feriae* would no longer be *imperatiuae* but *statiuae*. It was the most conspicuous aspect of the calendar changes during Augustus' rule that such personal and dynastic anniversaries were celebrated as public holidays. April has relatively few; 4.377–86 records Caesar's

[54] Again the fullest source is probably Macrobius, *Sat.* 1.16 1–30; on *postriduani* see 1.15.22 and 16.21; on *nundinae* originally N but subsequently made *fastae* 1.16.30. For a full scholarly discussion see Michels (1967) 22–54, summarized in Herbert-Brown (1994) 15–22.

[55] Varying from year to year, these cannot be included in an inscribed calendar and Ovid warns his reader not to expect them in his record, except that he offers a celebration of the year's first movable feast, the *sementiua* or Sowing Festival, in 1.657–704.

victory over Juba (and the republican rump) at Thapsus on 6 April; 4.673–6 honours 16 April as the anniversary of Octavian's first *salutatio* as *imperator*. Other months such as January and the newly baptized August had six or seven such anniversaries to celebrate.

The real 'original' holidays are listed by Varro with their etymologies in *De lingua Latina*: for April he explains in turn (*LL* 6.15–16) Megalensia, Cerialia, Fordicidia, Parilia, Vinalia and Robigalia. Ovid will offer these etymologies and more, and to these we will return under the next rubric, *causae*.

(*b*) Causae: *aetiology and origins*

Long before Ovid's time Romans had become conscious of their calendar, and with the earliest known figure to record the days must have come also the first exegete, however summary, of their origins in religion or national achievement. This seems to have been Fulvius Nobilior, victor over Ambracia in 189, and patron of the poet Ennius. According to Macrobius, Fulvius compiled *fasti* and deposited them or more likely set them up (*posuit*) in the new temple of Hercules and the Muses which he had vowed – the temple which ends Ovid's sixth and last book (6.799–812). Others like the little-known L. Cincius and Granius Licinius composed studies on the calendar; but essentially the first detailed research arises with Varro, not just in *De lingua Latina* and *De re rustica* which have survived, but in his *Antiquitates rerum diuinarum*, much of which was concerned with rituals and their occasions. We do not know when this work was compiled, but the others date after Caesar's reforms of 46 BC and may well have been stimulated by them, as were the many inscribed public calendars of the next thirty years.

Suetonius, *De grammaticis* 17 reports that Verrius Flaccus, a younger contemporary of Varro who lived on to the reign of Tiberius, was tutor to Augustus' grandsons. At some time after his charges had left him for military commands he began researches for the new calendar that would be erected around AD 10 on the curved walls of an exedra containing his statue in the forum of Praeneste, his home town. The calendar itself was excavated in instalments and can best be studied in Degrassi's *Inscriptiones Italiae* XIII 2, where the fragments belonging to each month are drawn and their contents transcribed and supplemented on opposite pages. But there is further evidence for Roman cult in the surviving abridgement by Sextus Pompeius Festus[56] of Verrius' glossary *De uerborum significatu.*

Many Roman festivals reflected the natural arable and pastoral year, and Ovid seizes on their origins in the needs of shepherd and farmer. But their rituals could be obscure, and long before the Augustan age syncretism had overlaid the lost or fading Roman origins of cult practice with Greek mythology. Thus when Ovid came to associate festival ritual with explanations of its form, he might find conflicting explanations in Greek mythology and Roman legend, and one challenge to his skill lay in reconciling them. Schilling[57] has shown how Ovid's Parilia narrative offers as explanations for the bonfire ritual both the firing of their discarded shepherd huts by Romulus' new citizens and Aeneas' flight from burning Troy,[58] but it is not easy to apply the firm distinction between history and myth which he makes the basis of Ovid's threefold treatment of holy days. I have preferred to keep Ovid's own distinction of *causae* and *sacra.*

Such explanations in the *Fasti* usually develop Verrius' material: where the poet diverges from known comments of Varro or Verrius, he may have preferred a rejected explanation for its imaginative or ideological appeal, as in his choice of etymology for *Aprilis* as from Aphrodite, rather than *aperire* (see Commentary), or his insistence on Venus' role in the Vinalia.

Etymology was important to Callimachus, Ovid's model, and even more important to the Romans. Thus Ovid prefaces each month in the *Fasti* with a discussion of its name's etymology, whether from a god like Janus or Mars or Juno, or from less obvious derivations. Not only Ovid but Ennius, Lucretius and all the Augustan poets play

[56] And further abridgement by Paulus Diaconus: in some cases only this survives. Festus and where necessary Paulus (= Paul, *Fest.*) will be cited from *Sexti Pompei Festi De uerborum significatu quae supersunt cum Pauli Epitome,* ed. W. M. Lindsay (Leipzig 1913).

[57] 'Ovide, poète des Fastes' (1979: 1–10) and 'Ovide, interprète de la religion romaine' (ibid.: 11–23). Schilling argues that Ovid usually analyses his festivals from three points of view, first describing the rite, then locating them in Roman history, and offering an explanation based on myth.

[58] *F.* 4.783–805. But he could have included the allusion to Phaethon and Deucalion at 793–4, both more mythical than Aeneas!

on words because they hold or recognize the belief that a word's form expresses the nature of what it describes. It is poets, even more than formal antiquarians and grammarians, who fill R. Maltby's recent *Lexicon of ancient Latin etymologies* (Leeds 1993).[59]

(c) Sacra

In *F.* 1.7 Ovid promised his imperial dedicatee *sacra recognosces*, and at 2.7 and 6.8 declared his theme as *sacra cano*. For a long time scholars drew their picture of traditional Roman religion primarily from the *Fasti*.[60] More recently we have come to think that Ovid, though not ignorant, was both selective and inventive in his presentation of deities and their cult. At the same time the study of comparative religion has increased interpretive conflict among students of early Roman religion, and the strong disagreement of otherwise respected scholars has made it seem rash to embrace particular theories.[61] Denis Feeney's study of religion in Roman literature brings out a further distinction, between the questions to be asked when considering religious behaviour in a society, and questions appropriate to interpreting religion as expressed in poetry and other imaginative texts.[62]

Rome's major festivals were marked by lavish public displays, like

[59] On Ovidian exploitation of etymology see the discussions of J. C. McKeown, *Ovid: Amores* (Liverpool 1987) I 45–61, and O'Hara (1996a) 96–102, and (1996b).

[60] Besides Warde Fowler (1908) compare his *Religious experience of the Roman people* (London 1911) and C. Bailey's *Phases in the religion of ancient Rome* (Oxford 1932).

[61] The best general guide to early Roman religion is now North (1989) 573–624. On problems arising from the more theoretical and mutually conflicting work of Wagenvoort and Dumézil see North (1989) 581–2. This commentary owes much to works by Beard, Liebeschuetz, Scheid and Weinstock listed in the bibliography, as well as the *Notes complémentaires* of Schilling's Budé edition of the *Fasti*. Wissowa (1912) is still invaluable for details and sources of specific cults.

[62] Feeney (1998). Feeney considers the treatment of religion in Roman poetry under the categories of 'belief', 'myth', 'divinity' and 'ritual'. *Fasti* is central to his discussion of literary representation of ritual, but all of his categories are reflected in Ovid's writing and essential to our understanding of the poem.

the *ludi scaenici* and *circenses* (*Fasti* IV marks the *scaena* (188), *pompa*,[63] and Circus games (389–92) in honour of Cybele and of Ceres (679–82) and heralds the *scaenici* of Flora (946), to be described in the following month).

But these were not religious acts in the strict sense, as were the acts of purification, prayer and sacrifice that fill the *Fasti*. Thus in February, named after the *februa* or purifying agents, the poet illustrates the range of materials used for *lustratio*, to expiate offences and purge the worshippers (*piamina*, *purgamina* 2.19): wool, the salted meal used to clean houses or dress sacrificial victims, branches of laurel and other trees (2.19–36). The more complex ingredients used for the Parilia of 21 April include water, laurel branches and sulphur to fumigate the sheep pens and ritually obtained ash from the blood and tail of the October *equus* (sacrificed six months previously) and the sacrificial embryos from the Fordicidia of 15 April, mixed with a base of ash from beanstalks (4.725–6 and 731–4). In Roman life everything, citizens, houses, fields (cf. 1.669 = Tib. 2.1.17–18), city walls, had to be purified at designated times, and Rome's citizen army had to be purified both before campaigning and after to eliminate the pollution of slaughter.[64] The ritual bathing of the images of Venus and Cybele (4.135–8, 337–40) is both a purification and a preparation for a divine *pompa*.

Prayer was either private or public, but a king's utterance was somehow both. Among royal prayers in book IV are Romulus' founding prayer to Jupiter (827–32) and Numa's plea to Faunus after incubation: typically Ovid concentrates on the king's ritual preparation (abstinence from sex, and removal of his rings, twice sprinkling the head with water and covering his brow with beech leaves (4.655–8) but omits his words (660 *adorato per sua uerba deo*). Before Claudia Quinta's prayer to Cybele she loosens her hair, sprinkles her head three times with running water from the Tiber, and kneels as a suppliant (4.316–18). In composing the words of prayers, whether of the

[63] Not the notorious procession of the goddess and her Phrygian eunuch priests described in 4.181–6, but the ceremonial parade through the Circus of images of the gods also described in *Amores* 3.2.

[64] Festus 104 Lindsay cites the wearing of laurel as triumphal processions entered the city to purify the soldiers *a caede humana*.

Flamen Quirinalis to Robigo (4.911–32) or in the poet's own person to Ceres and Tellus (1.675–94), Ovid combines ritual language with free invention. The fullest example is the shepherd's extended prayer to Pales, in which the poet surveys the incidental hazards of pastoral life to expiate possible offences against Pales, the nymphs, Diana and Pan (4.747–62) and asks for the health and fertility of his flock (763–76). A playful imagined prayer to Mercury combines correct ritual acts (5.675–80) with an unscrupulous plea for profitable cheating (681–90).

But as its name (*sacra facere*[65]) implies, the most important procedure in Roman religion was sacrifice, public or private. Sacrifice was partly related to means, partly to the requirements of the deity: thus in his excursus on blood sacrifice (1.319–443) Ovid claims that before incense, myrrh and costly spices were imported the earliest offerings were of salted spelt meal (*far ... et puri lucida mica salis*) with the fragrance of laurel and local foliage (*herba Sabina, uerbenae* (1.338, 343).[66] This is followed by a rationalizing history of the adoption of animal sacrifice,[67] justified by the animals' alleged offences against the gods. Greek myth (like the Old Testament) told of the goat's offences against Dionysus, by eating the tender vines, and the pig's sins against Demeter by rooting up the corn (*F.* 1.349–61, so also Varro, *RR* 1.2.19 and *Georg.* 2.380–1 on goat sacrifice, Varro, *RR* 2.4.9 on pigs). Keeping in mind the *Suouetaurilia*, the most important public sacrifice of a boar, ram and bull, to Jupiter, Ovid protests the innocence of sheep and oxen (1.362), citing the story of Aristaeus' *Bougonia* from *Georgics* IV to explain the ox-sacrifice, and hypothesizing that sheep had offended by eating sacred herbs: *poscit ouem fatum: uerbenas improba carpsit* (1.381): in quest of novelty he lists also sacrifices

[65] *Sacra facere* (passive *fieri*): *F.* 1.530, 618, 627, 2.528, 572, 682, 3.809, etc. The rarer *sacrificare* is found only at 3.850 and 4.414 below, and once in *Met.* 14.84. A similar pattern limits *sacrificus* to *Met.* 12.249, 13.590, 15.483; *F.* 1.130, 6.803.

[66] Cf. Horace, *Odes* 3.23.20 on Phidyle's rustic offering *farre pio et saliente mica*: the entire Ode is predicated on contrasting simple offerings with expensive sacrifice.

[67] The treatment in *F.* 1.347–456 accepts and justifies blood sacrifice, in contrast to the previous denunciation by Pythagoras at *Met.* 15.48–140, and the traditional protest at the sacrifice of plough oxen (see 413–16n.).

of horse, deer, dog, donkey (391, with an *aition*, 392–440) and birds, punished for their mythical role as informants on divine misbehaviour (441–50).

Ovid clearly had studied the meaning of these acts of killing, and depicts the behaviour of the public slave (1.319 *succinctus ... minister*) striking the victim with the ritual knife (327 *culter*) from behind; he evokes the ritual cry *agone?* as an etymological explanation of the Agonalia (1.322).[68] The victim had to co-operate in what was in effect a ritual execution, by nodding (Plut. *Qu. conv.* 729F) or kneeling in mark of submission: hence the typical evocation of the flight or collapse of the sacrificial bull as a *dirum omen* (Tac. *H.* 3.56) in *Aen.* 2.223–4 and later epic. After the sacrifice the *exta* were reserved for the gods (cf. 4.670, and Remus' offence in consuming the ritually prepared *exta* at 2.363–4, 373–4) but the other meat was distributed to human participants. Exceptions to this pattern are the bloodless and wineless sacrifice of millet cakes, milk and unfermented *sapa* to Pales (4.743–6) and some animal sacrifices mentioned above: just as the October horse and pregnant heifer of the Fordicidia were not eaten (4.670–1, 725–6, 733–4) so the dog sacrificed to Robigo (or in the *Augurium canarium:* see 933n.) was not for human consumption.

Along with prescribed acts, there are hints throughout *Fasti* of prescribed dress (619–20, 658, the towel of 933) and human or divine food, cheese curds seasoned with herbs (*moretum*) for Cybele 368–72, millet cakes for Pales 743–4, honey-cakes (*liba*) for Bacchus 3.733–6. But Jupiter, not Bacchus, received the dedication of the first grape juice from the vintage, explained by Ovid through the *aition* of Aeneas' vow of *proxima musta* in return for victory (888). Just as sacrifice was properly the offering to the god of animals which formed the staple food of the group, so the offering of the *musta* represented *primitiae*, the first and best share for the god.

From these *aitia* of ritual and sacrifice, and from more loosely associated episodes of Rome's early history Ovid has provided a deliberately fragmented narrative, largely based on Livy, so as to cover the evolution of the city itself. But festivals could originate in other

[68] For *agone* cf. Varro, *LL* 6.12, Festus 9 Lindsay, Sen. *Contr.* 2.3.19 and Plut. *Qu. Conv.* 729F. The ritual order to kill was *hoc age* (cited with Greek translation by Plut. *Numa* 14, *Coriol.* 25).

kinds of crisis. Portents and plagues, droughts and other kinds of sterility offered immediate cause for the introduction of new cults or new rituals in old cults, and in book IV occasion the fetching of Cybele from Pergamum and Numa's new ritual of the Fordicidia. Vows and dedications of temples provide more anniversaries recorded in the public *fasti* and explained by the poet; there are typical minimal entries for the temples of Jupiter Victor and Libertas on 13 April (4.625–80) and Aeneas' legendary vow to Jupiter (893–4) is only the most famous of many historical vows by commanders in return for success in battle.

Yet Ovid does not let himself be bound by attested rituals. On other occasions, such as the Cerialia, he can completely pass over the Roman cult and historical origins of the festival in favour of the mythical cause of the original Greek rituals imitated by Rome. Far from being an obstacle, exegesis is Ovid's licence: the different conceptions of cause offer a glittering variety of treatments and themes.

(*d*) Signa: *astronomy and myth in service to the calendar*

The first pentameter of the *Fasti*, *lapsaque sub terras ortaque signa canam*, is as important as the preceding hexameter: Ovid is combining Greek astronomy with his Roman festivals.[69] Although he knew and had translated Aratus' *Phaenomena* describing the constellations, Ovid could hardly have related this to his stellar calendar. Aratus dealt with celestial space, not time: he did not report the times of rising and setting of the stars, and if he had, these times for Alexandria would have been incorrect for the sky over Rome. Again Eratosthenes, both scientist and poet, wrote of the myths associated with the constellations, in which Ariadne's crown or Callisto or Arion's dolphin were turned by the gods to stars to rescue or honour the mortal protégé.[70] Early poets like Hesiod had mentioned the risings and settings of stars as signals for the farmer's calendar, and star-

[69] See J. Rüpke, 'Ovids Kalenderkommentar: Zur Gattung der libri Fastorum', *Antike u. Abendland* 40 (1994), who notes (129) that astronomical entries do not belong in the Roman calendar.

[70] See C. Robert, ed., *Eratosthenis katasterismoi* (Berlin 1878), which combines an abridgement of the lost text with other evidence from scholia on Aratus and Hyginus.

appearances are reported in the Roman imperial agricultural writers Columella and Pliny the elder (*Natural history* book XVIII). After Caesar's calendar came into force there was a standard dating (based on astronomical tables) of the apparent rising and setting of the major stars, both for their morning and their evening appearances in the sky. And yet even the sources used by Columella and Pliny are sometimes wrong, while Ovid himself is wildly inaccurate. He brought the stars into his calendar for their mythical associations, and in the process might confuse their rising with their setting, or a morning appearance with one in the evening, or mention them quite out of season.[71]

Among the seven constellations mentioned in April, for instance, it is true that the sun passes from Aries into Taurus around 20 April (4.713–20) but the supposed setting of Aries on 24 April (4.903) corresponds to no phase of that constellation, and the alleged rising of the Dogstar is three months too early. When Ovid speaks of the Pleiades setting in the morning of 2 April, he has confused it with their evening setting (8 April); he shares with Columella the assigning of the morning setting of Scorpio to 1 April (4.163–4), early, even allowing for the slow setting of this large constellation; but then he is almost right with the evening setting of Orion on 9 April (387–8), and of the Hyades on 17 April (4.678–9). It is noticeable that Ovid inserts star observations on days without other anniversaries: he may indeed be looking for a star myth to enliven or punctuate between major festivals: but neither he nor his readers were likely to check the sky. These notices are a decorative relic of a pre-calendar world.

(*ii*) *The structure of book IV: combination and variation*

While each book of the month in the *Fasti* is self-contained, O. has linked the books together through their proems. Thus the dedicatory proem or opening discussion of the etymology of each month will relate to at least one other proem: similarity of design and content pairs the proems of books I and II, III and IV, and V and VI. In addi-

[71] This judgement and the statements that follow depend on the detailed examination of J. Ideler, 'Über den astronomischen Theil der *Fasti* des Ovid', *Abhandl. d. Hist.-Phil. Kl. d. Königl. Akad. d. Wissenschaften* (Berlin 1822–3).

tion, since the fourth book begins what may be called the second half of the *Fasti*, its proem recalls that of book I, dealing with both the content of the poem (4.11–12 = 1.1–2) and the poetics of the new genre; its dedication to Venus in turn leads Ovid to evoke his apparent renunciation of love elegy in the earlier programmatic closure of *Amores* 3.15, and elements of the recantatory *Remedia amoris*. The pairing of book IV with book III, based on the antithetical partnership of Mars and Venus as patrons of their months, is expressed through the form of Ovid's opening appeal to the deity and recalled explicitly and implicitly as late as 133 (see Commentary on 57–8, 129–30 and 133).

From the summary of entries (pp. 53–4) it can be seen that the preliminary account of Venus' patronage and role as Julian ancestress (19–132) is followed by a group of short entries (some only four lines), introducing the poet's interview with Cybele and Erato at and about the Megalensia (179–372); this is the first of three extended panels. Similar groups of shorter entries contrast with the other major panels: the hymn to Ceres and narrative of her search for Proserpina (393–620) and the double (and inseparable) celebration of Parilia and *urbis origo* (721–862). There is balance, rather than symmetry: thus the centre of the book's 954 lines occurs in the early phase of Ceres' search, but the Parilia panel does not correspond symmetrically to the Megalensia. Indeed the structure and contents of the three panels differ: the Megalensia is a mixture of Greek and Asiatic myths, Roman historical legend, and ritual details: the Cerialia omits description of ritual in favour of a Greek hymn, combining praise of Ceres as cultural benefactress with the myth of her quest for Persephone.[72] Only the two-part Parilia / *urbis origo* is entirely Roman. Only 18 of the thirty days have their own entries: 1, 2, 4 and 5 April (the Nones); 6, 9, 10, 12 and 13 April (the Ides); 14, 15, 17, 19, 20, 21, 23, 25 and 28 April.

Within this composite structure L. Braun has noted patterns linking or framing separate units to create a sense of symmetry.[73] Thus the

[72] It is indicative that she is even called Persephone by both poet and goddess-mother (483, 485, 591), except at 587.

[73] Braun (1981): his conception of the organization of book IV is given in tabular form at 2373. I have diverged slightly from it in my account of the relationships between entries after Mutina.

celebration of Venus Verticordia on 1 April (133–62) is thematically related to the celebration of Erycina on 23 April (863–76). Julian military celebrations occur at 377–86 (Thapsus) and 625–8 (Mutina) each with a weather warning: they are disposed symmetrically near the 1/3 and 2/3 mark. We note that the second is echoed by the consequence of Mutina, Octavian's first salutation a day later, and so might see the last Julian (non-military) celebration of Palatine Vesta in 949–54 as completing this pattern.

Another pattern based on the actual sequence of Roman *ludi* links the last days of both Megalensia and Cerialia with their *ludi in circo* (389–92, 679–712). Ritual ingredients link the Fordicidia (629–72) with the Parilia (721–806), at which the ashes of the Fordicidia offerings were distributed for the lustration of men and beast. Ovid himself seems to have constructed the strange episode of the fox of Carseoli in order to parallel the sacrifice of red canine victims (foxes, dogs) to avert harm to the crops, which link the last day of the Cerialia (679–712) and the Robigalia (905–42), while his inclusion of extensive (and original) prayers to stand for the actual prayers to Pales and Robigo links Parilia and Robigalia. Within this last third of the month with its many rituals one can also see poetically constructed symmetry between the bonds with Jupiter established by Rome's pre-founder and her founder: first by Romulus' auspices and prayer (807–32) then by Aeneas' vow (877–900); in moving from Numa's Fordicidia to Romulus' founding to Aeneas' victory the poem is retracing history. These symmetries are more felt than identified, and throughout the varying sequence of rituals, games, dedications and legends contrasted with recurring evocations of the stars, they produce an Alexandrian *poikilia* which could be illustrated from any of the six months of Ovid's poem.

(*iii*) *Augustan ideology: the poet and his readers*

Augustus' constitutional innovations and domestic moral and religious reforms have long been familiar from his own autobiographical testament, the *Res gestae*, and from the poetry written by Horace and Virgil, above all from *Odes* I–III and from the *Aeneid*. But these works were composed in the first decade of the principate: even when we add the representation of Augustus and Augustan order in

Horace's *Carmen saeculare*, and *Odes* IV, it does not carry much beyond 13 BC. From Horace's death in 8 BC, there are no contemporary witnesses except Ovid to the changing political and social scene during the fifteen years before AD 8, when he was relegated to Tomis. The pattern of later evidence from the elder Seneca to Tacitus suggests that Augustus' own authority became more rigid, but we do not know how attitudes may have changed towards him, or towards the monuments and institutions he used to publicize first his grandsons, then his heir by default, Tiberius. But recent archaeological discoveries and scholarship have thrown new light on the way Augustus made himself and his family conspicuous by the coordination on the Campus Martius of the Ara Pacis (dedicated 9 BC), the Mausoleum erected by the emperor for himself and his descendants, and the great sundial or Horologium, whose gnomon, an obelisk from conquered Egypt, would cast its shadow directly on both altar and Mausoleum on the Princeps' birthday (23 September, the autumn equinox) each year.[74] Further attention was drawn to the Julian dynasty by the decorative programme of the Forum Augusti and temple of Mars Ultor: on the temple pediment Mars was flanked by Venus, as ancestress of the dynasty, and Fortuna (as Ovid would put it in *Tr.* 2.296 *stat Venus Vltori iuncta, uir ante fores*). On either side of the forum a row of statues of the Julii, traced from their ancestor Aeneas, with honorific inscriptions, was faced by a row of other generals including Romulus.[75]

As both Zanker and Wallace Hadrill demonstrate, Augustus' appropriation of public space was matched by his appropriation of

[74] E. Buchner, *Die Sonnenuhr des Augustus* (Mainz 1982). But his claims have been powerfully challenged by F. Schütz, 'Die Sonnenuhr des Augustus?', *Gymnasium* 77 (1990) 432–57. For a plan and discussion of the Augustan Campus Martius see Zanker (1988) fig. 114 p. 140, F. Coarelli, *Guida Archeologica di Roma* (Milan 1974) 268. Originally close to the Horologium, the Altar of Peace was moved to its present position not far from the Mausoleum by the Tiber in 1938. After the Horologium was covered over in antiquity the Gnomon-Obelisk too was dismantled and moved to its present position in Piazza Montecitorio.

[75] On the *Forum Augustum* see Zanker (1988) 201–15 and plan fig. 149 p. 194; on the dynastic symbolism of Venus and Mars, and the problem of its possible impropriety see Zanker (1988) 195–20.

public time.[76] The old republican calendar was now filled by the new anniversaries of his victories and public acts and those of his father Julius Caesar, as well as family celebrations, *festa domestica*. Approximately fifty Julian festivals or commemorations had been added to the public *fasti* by Augustus' death, and most of these are to be found in the *Fasti Praenestini* of Ovid's scholar friend Verrius Flaccus.

When Ovid set out to compose his calendar poem he must have known that this would entail celebrating these anniversaries as they occurred, and it was surely at least part of his purpose to do so. The issue is not so much whether he realized a need to please the emperor, as the very nature of the poem, which was modelled on Callimachus' *Aitia*, with its component of praise poetry or encomium.[77] If the Augustan regime was more humourless, more moralistic and more conscious of its dignity than young Ptolemy Euergetes and his queen, Ovid himself understood that his commemoration of Augustus, and where appropriate of Livia, should not risk causing offence by playfulness out of season. Thus a recent study of the poet's treatment of Augustus and his family in the *Fasti* has found not only tactful but even ideologically supportive treatment of the emperor's new roles, such as *Pontifex Maximus* and *Pater Patriae*.[78]

It seems that Ovid was successful in presenting an image of the emperor and the cults he associated with the dynasty that would please Augustus. But more than one scholar has found what seem to be troubling implications in the text. In a wider study of Ovid's poetry Stephen Hinds has suggested that Ovid, a known master of language and word-play, wrote in terms which permitted the orthodox Augustan reader to accept imperial encomium at its face value, but invited the radical or dissenting reader to see contradictions and dishonesties in the official titles and actions.[79] Hinds has since re-

[76] Zanker (1988) 114–18, Wallace-Hadrill, (1987).

[77] See Miller's judicious introduction (1991) 1–7: more recent publications on this topic are considered more fully than is appropriate here in this writer's review article on Barchiesi (1994) and Herbert-Brown (1994), *CP* 91 (1996); also 'Rewriting and rereading the *Fasti*: Ovid, Augustus and recent Classical scholarship', *Antichthon* 29 (1995) 42–59.

[78] Herbert-Brown (1994).

[79] (1987b) 4–31.

inforced his case by a major study of two Augustan icons, Mars and Romulus, as they are treated in the *Fasti*.[80] Ovid had won fame by carrying a banner as poet of *amor* opposed to *arma*: there is no doubt that in the *Fasti* he presents early Roman militarism and Romulus, its embodiment, as primitive. How far would this offend Augustus? Romulus, the city's first founder, was *Pater Patriae*, as was Augustus; but if the poet treats Romulus unfavourably, when comparing him with Augustus, and recalls the offences of the fratricide whose name Octavian had declined when he chose the title of 'Augustus' twenty-five years earlier in 27 BC, need this have offended? Romulus was prominent as Aeneas' counterpart in both the *Forum Augustum* and Augustus' funeral procession: but both the forum *elogia* and the procession included Pompey.

Other voices have cited further elements in the poem which seem to imply dissent from if not criticism of official values. Alessandro Barchiesi's recent study starts from Ovid's past as love elegist – his opposition of *arma* and *amor* – and his future as exile, surveying his treatment of Augustus and his ideology after AD 8.[81] Barchiesi's method is to examine carefully a series of passages in *Fasti* where the poet's language provokes the suspicious reader to question Augustan innovations: for example Augustus' conversion of the twin *Lares Praestites*, honoured on 1 May, into a trinity with his own *genius* represented between them (5.129–48), and the transference of their worship to the first day of August, the Princeps' own month. Some of Barchiesi's examples certainly go against humane or Christian values: thus in honouring the temple of Mars Ultor, the poet gives to the Princeps a speech opening *Mars ades et satia scelerato sanguine ferrum* (5.575), whereas Ovid's own address to Mars at 3.1–2 opens by asking Mars to disarm. Modern readers are offended by demands for vengeance and bloodshed. How many of Ovid's readers would find this morally reprehensible? Perhaps the strongest case for an element of protest in the poem is made by Dennis Feeney, who draws attention to the theme of enforced silence that recurs in the *Fasti*, whose very title derives from permission to speak.[82] But Feeney himself

[80] Hinds (1992) 89–141. [81] Barchiesi (1994) 5–36. [82] Feeney (1991).

raises seriously the possibility that these features spring from Ovid's reworking of the poem in exile. Thus the *Fasti* could have begun as a poem of loyal praise, and changed its nature when the poet's lot was changed. Certainly anyone who approaches *Fasti*, like Barchiesi's readers, by considering *Tristia* II, also addressed to Augustus, but composed from exile in AD 9 or 10, will find the same aspects of Augustan ideology and dynastic cult treated with an edge of bitterness; but this is no reason for assuming the same tone in *Fasti*.

The issue is an important one, in part because it surely calls Ovid's good faith into question. Centuries of readers have accepted the poem as an act of celebration, both national and Augustan. Indeed none of these scholars is suggesting that the *Fasti* is a poem of systematic dissent, composed in order to show up the emperor's hypocrisy (or other sins), or sneer at official behaviour for those in the know. But given Ovid's earlier career, given his gift for maximizing the subtlety and allusivity of language, we must assume he envisaged the alternative readings of his text which have been pointed to by Hinds and Barchiesi. Some of the text's ambiguous potential no doubt springs from the heart, expressing the poet's discomfort with aspects of what he had set out to celebrate: some critical implications may have been written into his text by the poet in embittered exile. But others may exist only for those who in their distaste for Augustan autocracy look for dissidence in the poet they admire, so that they can continue to respect him. I have tried to be objective, but readers of *Fasti* and of the present commentary should consult these modern studies and decide for themselves how each passage is to be interpreted.

4. STYLE

(*i*) *Diction and narrative technique*

Both the end-stopped, self-contained form of the elegiac distich and its generic tradition as the voice of personal poetry favoured a simple style, nearer to elegant conversation than to the grand solemnity of epic. Ovid's amatory elegy is rich in dialogue, and conveys the impression that the poet himself is speaking, whether in the dramatic monologues of *Amores* 1.11, 2.7 and 8, etc., or in the didactic mode of the *Ars*. The *Fasti* also offer naturalistic conversation, whether between Ovid and his interlocutors or in the dramatic speeches of his narrative sections. But connoisseurs of Ovidian wit will find the subject matter offers little scope for the paradoxes and plays of language which delight them in the amatory exchange of earlier elegy. Besides etymological word play, however, there are three puns in book IV: between the standard emotional and less expected literal sense of *mota est* (327, contrast 15, 729), *micae salientis* used of the *mola salsa* in 409 (as in Horace, *Odes* 2.23.20 evoking *sal* through *salire*), and *telis*, blending literal *telae* with metaphorical *tela* in 699. The sexual incidents of *Fasti* are wordless rapes, and instead of amatory dialogue, the aetiological aspect of Ovid's enquiries means that many exchanges are explanatory, even didactic. In contrast the dramatic speeches of the longer narratives often have the pathos which Heinze showed was the generic inheritance of elegy.[83]

At another level this poem about religion is rich in prayers (cf. 319–24, 747–76, 826–32, 911–32) and hymn-like passages (91–132, 397–408) to which we may add the solemn celebration of imperial glory (949–54). The third major component of the *Fasti* is narrative, whether humble vignettes like the farmer and the fox (691–708) or historical and mythical sequences like the coming of Cybele (249–348) and Demeter's quest for Persephone (417–618), diversified by catalogues and punctuated by fast-moving dialogue.

Each of these 'modes' has its stylistic features: dialogue has the urgency and ellipsis of ordinary speech (4.5 *scis dea ... de uulnere*, 4.269 *ipsa peti uolui; ne sit mora; mitte uolentem*), or can rise to the high tone of an oracle (259–60 *Mater abest: Matrem iubeo, Romane, requiras. | cum ueniet, casta est accipienda manu*, cf. 665–6) or the emotive rhetoric of an angry Ceres (587–96): it can also subside into the more prosaic structures of explanation.

Prosaic elements are more often matters of idiom than of diction. As is usual in poetry parataxis predominates, suggesting relationships by asyndeta and avoiding subordination by the skilful use of tense. Thus 141–5 presents by means of five main verbs (*siccabat*, *uiderunt*, *sensit*, *texit*, *tuta fuit*) what prose might have wrapped up in a period: *dea, cum sensisset satyros ... se uidisse dum rorantes capillos in litore siccaret*

[83] Cf. 240–1, 447, 455–66nn. and on Heinze, n. 23 above.

[*siccat?*] *corpora opposita myrto tegendo se tutam seruauit*; parentheses avoid subordination in e.g. 358–9 *cum dea, sensit enim,* | . . . *inquit*, 412 *parua bonae Cereri, sint modo casta, placent*, and the complex sequence at 936–8 *turpiaque obscenae (uidimus) exta canis.* | *tum mihi 'cur detur sacris noua uictima quaeris?'* | *(quaesieram) 'causam percipe' flamen ait.* Typically *si*-clauses in future conditional sentences are replaced by imperatives (271–2 *proficiscere* . . . | *nostra eris*, 731–2 *i pete* . . . *suffimen ab ara,* | *Vesta dabit, Vestae munere purus eris*), and there are multiple forms of command: jussive subjunctive (*parcas, sinas*, 911, 914), *ne* + present imperative (922, 931 *neue noce, ne uiola Cererem*, described by G–L §270 as 'poetic or colloquial'), and periphrases (204 *parce mouere*, 247 *moneas precor*, 151–2 *nec pigeat* . . . | *sumere*). Other colloquial features are idioms of place and time (e.g. 399 *postmodo*, only found once in *Met.*, 775 *ad annum*, 843, 889 *nec mora*) and the casual use of abl. for duration of time (505 *multis diebus*).

Colloquial dialogue employs indefinite pronouns and relative clauses (7 *numquid* . . . *reliqui*, 9 *quae decuit* . . . *lusimus*, 85 *sunt qui* . . . *uelint* (229–30 *desinit esse* | *quod fuit* is a pointed euphemism)) and links clauses by prepositional phrases (351–2, 587 *de quo*, 381 *sub quo*, 422 *in quibus*, 524 *e quibus*). The narratives use prosaic connecting relatives in abl. abs., 159 *quibus ordine factis*, and temporal connectives, 497 *quo simul ac uenit*. Explanations entail reported questions (140, 145, 194, 350, 353, 357, etc. *cur, quare*) answered by causal clauses (26, 41, 87, 171, 177, 196, 355, 535 etc. *quod, quia*). The *aition* has its own vocabulary: *unde* is answered by 352 *inde*, 494 *hinc*, 786 *idcirco* and the signals 352 *mos* . . . *manet*, 494, 504 *nunc quoque*, 709 *monimenta manent*.

These conversational features might be called negative; positive ornaments such as coinages, visual or honorific epithets and figured diction belong rather to narrative or ritual or solemn speech. However, one linguistic device peculiar to Ovid jumps the gap between narrative and speech; book IV contains two positive instances and one negative. At 838 *'sint'que 'Celer, curae'* and 848 *'sic'que 'meos muros transeat hostis'*, narrative -*que* is attached to Romulus' first words, *sint* and *sic* (cf. 5.394 *'uir'que ait 'his armis, armaque digna uiro!'*). Similarly at 597–8 *factumque excusat amore,* | *'nec gener est nobis ille pudendus' ait* modern editors must compromise on punctuation, since *nec* fuses the narrative copula *et* into the spoken *non* of *non* . . . *pudendus*.

Generally Ovid's prayers are economical with archaic or ritual diction: they use only basic religious terms such as *supplex*, *luere* (319, 322), *adesse*, *auspex* (1, 828; 830), *quae precor eueniant* (775), *uota soluere* (932), and create their effect of litany more by patterning through anaphoric recall of the goddess, using *tu* or *illa* (91, 95–7, 759–60, 913–15), or anaphora of conjunctions (*si*, *ne*, *nec*, *nunc*).

Another figure of repetition also found outside prayer is polyptoton (the repetition of a word in different inflexion): 324 *et castas casta sequere manus*, 372 *cognoscat priscos ut dea prisca cibos*, 924 *quodque potest alios perdere, perde prior*. Ovid delights in parallelism and antithesis: thus the prayer to Pales is full of binary phrases paired by sound: 747 *pecori pariter pecorisque magistris*, 749 *sacro paui sediue sub arbore sacra*, 768 *quaeque lauent artus quaeque bibantur aquae*.

Narrative and catalogue features

With the larger scale of narrative comes ornament familiar from epic models: only in narrative and its associated catalogues do we find abundant 'poetic' epithets and imagery.

Typical of epic are compound adjective formations; those not found before Ovid are marked with an asterisk: 561 *aliger*, 68 *clauiger**, 388 *ensifer*, 467 *herbifer**, 715 *laniger* (found as early as Ennius), 252 *sacrifer**, 531 *soporifer*, 219, 224 *turrifer/ger*,[84] 569 *turilegus**, 501 *bimaris**, 185 *semimas**, 752 *semicaper**, 746 *siluicola*, 400 *magnificus*, 408 *pacificus*.[85] Ovid also favours formations in *-osus*: 367 *herbosus*, 300 *limosus*, 815 *nemorosus*, 392 *uentosus*, or *-eus*: 498, 578 *aequoreus* (a favourite), 656 *fagineus*, 121, 374, 780 *niueus* (a common poetic substitute for *albus*, *candidus*), 135, 917 *marmoreus*.

Ovid readily creates verbal nouns in *-men*: 163 *acumen*, 325 *conamen*, 835 *fundamen*, 211 *imitamen*, 731 *suffimen*: these, together with 'poetic' plurals such as 143 *corpora*, 169 *nomina*, etc., contribute to dactylic

[84] As with many other adjs. in *-fer* or *-ger*, MSS waver between forms in both 219 and 224. See however Commentary on 219 for arguments in favour of retaining both forms in the one passage.

[85] See Commentary for detailed comment on separate words. Some are innovations of *Fasti* absent from *Met.*, but this list takes its cue from Kenney (1973) 117–53.

rhythm. He is more conservative in choice of verbs: notable are 919 *incalfacere*, 755 *degrandinare* (agricultural?), 202 *indolescere* (medical), and 414 *sacrificare* imported from prose usage. More often solemn effects are achieved by locutions like 317–18 *uultus ... figit ... edit ... sonos*, 484 *nomen ... ciet*, 488 *gressus tulit*, 518 *dicta refert*.

Another source of exotic ornament is the patronymics and periphrases which stand for persons and places: Venus is *Cytherea* (673), her son Aeneas *Cythereïus* (195), her myrtle *Cytheriacus* (15); dawn is *Pallantias* (373). Other Greek derivatives occur with variants: contrast *Atlantis* of Maia in 31, with *Atlanteas* of her and her sisters, coined to create a dispondaic ending to the hexameter in 3.105; contrast also 285 *Pelopeïdas* with 3.83 six-syllabled *Pelopeïades*. Particularly favoured are pentasyllabic forms in ∪∪–∪× or ∪–∪∪× that lighten and colour the hexameter: some like 405 *Chalybeïa*, 873 *Arethusidas*, are unique. Other innovative forms appeal for their Greek sounds: cf. from the Sicilian narrative 420 *Trinacris*, 467 *Amenana*, 472 *Symaetheas*, 475 *Tauromenumque*, 499 *Zanclaea Charybdis* and the coined patronymic 479 *Peloriades*.

Imagery is not characteristic of elegy: apart from the programmatic imagery of the poem as ship (18, 729), there are some legal metaphors (90 *iniecta uindicat ... manu*, 320–3 *sub certa condicione* followed by *damnas*, *iudice*, *crimen*, *pignora*, 589–90 *iniuria ... commissi*, cf. 596 *emendet*) and two striking physical images (846 *deuorat*, 923 *amplectere*). Full similes occur only to frame the catalogue of Ceres' Sicilian travels in her quest for Persephone (457–86) which is cited here to illustrate this and other highly wrought figures. Ceres' search is launched by two pathetic similes:

> mentis inops rapitur, *quales audire solemus*
> *Threïcias fusis Maenades ire comis.*
> *ut uitulo mugit sua mater ab ubere rapto*
> *et quaerit fetus per nemus omne suos,*
> sic dea nec retinet gemitus, et concita cursu
> fertur ... (457–62)

Both are traditional (the first marked as such by *audire solemus*) and Ovid has neatly set narrative and image in chiastic arrangement moving from *rapitur* to the rushing Bacchante, but from the Lucretian acoustic simile of the lowing cow to Ceres' unrestrained groans. It is difficult not to see humour in the pathetic excess of the language, as in the headlong quest which follows.

Lines 467–80 elaborate the catalogue of places, first near, then far across the whole of Sicily, with every kind of figure, from simple anaphora, as in 468, 469 *praeterit*, 479 *iamque ... iamque*, to apostrophe 468, 470 (cf. 462) and polysyndeton. From 471 to 479 every line except 477 is linked by *-que*, and 475–6 pile up five places:

> Himera*que et* Didymen Acraganta*que* Tauromenum*que*
> sacrarum*que* Mylas pascua laeta boum.

Here the exotic Greek names and terminations are rounded off with a Lucretian/Virgilian echo (*pabula laeta*, Lucr. 1.14, 2.875, *Georg.* 4.509). To close the catalogue after 480 the poet invokes a universalizing *quacumque ingreditur* and another simile – again traditional and echoing a famous Virgilian simile of elegiac lament: as Orpheus mourned Eurydice (*Georg.* 4.511–12, 515 *qualis populea maerens Philomela sub umbra | amissos queritur fetus ... et maestis late loca questibus implet*), so Ceres laments Persephone with the same liquid elegiac sounds *l*, *m*, *r*:

> ... mise*r*is *l*oca cuncta que*rell*is
> im*pl*et, ut a*m*issu*m* cu*m* ge*m*it a*l*es Ityn. (481–2)

This leads into the last and most highly patterned of four passages (the others are 4.135–7, 215–17, 331–3) with multiple sound and word patterning between successive distichs:

> perque uices modo '*Persephone*!' modo '*filia*!' clamat,
> clamat *et alternis nomen utrumque* ciet.
> sed neque *Persephone* Cererem nec *filia* matrem
> audit, *et alternis nomen utrumque* perit. (483–6)

Besides the repetitions in the same *sedes* from distich to distich the paired *modo* is answered by paired *neque*, *clamat* is repeated in anadiplosis (echo within the same clause) and the four parallel verbs *clamat*, *ciet*, *audit*, *perit* correspond. But the pathos is partly countered by the poetic self-consciousness which draws attention by the twice repeated *alternis* to the alternation of hexameter and pentameter which defines elegiac form.[86]

The special qualities of such elegiac narrative were first isolated and analysed by Richard Heinze:[87] constant shifting of pace and change of time or location (cf. 454, 489, 495, 549), catalogues, snatches of dialogue, explanatory parentheses and stage directions (455, 513, 517, 521, 539, 586) and the insertion of 'alienating' reference to the author's own time and process of writing (507, 535–5, 573–4). Within the confines of the distich Ovid can expand to create a resting-point:

> *tota domus* laeta est, hoc est materque paterque
> nataque: tres illi *tota* fuere *domus*.[88] (543–4)

(reinforced by the repetition of the first hemistich in the last) or a sense of rapid action:

> hanc uidet et uisam patruus uelociter aufert
> regnaque caeruleis in sua portat equis. (445–6)

The alternation of movement and rest, like speech and action, patterns of sound and visual effect, produces a narrative as varied and urgent, if less measured, than Ovid's or Virgil's hexameters. Here however direct comparison with the Ceres–Persephone narrative of *Metamorphoses* can be misleading just because that tale has been given the artifices and digressions of the professional rhapsode.

(*ii*) *Versification*

Technically there is no innovation to note in Ovid's adaptation of elegiac metre to its new genre. He shows the same skill in varying

[86] See Hinds (1987) 119–20.

[87] See n. 22 above.

[88] The framing partial 'echo' creates an effect of closure. The full echo occurs at 365–6; cf. 2.235–6. Platnauer, *LEV* 34 lists four other examples of this pattern in Ovid and a whole epigram of Martial, 9.97, framed by *rumpitur inuidia* opening and closing each couplet.

the division of the distich. The most fragmented hexameter conveys Attis' dementia at 4.235:

> et modo 'tolle faces', 'remoue' modo 'uerbera' clamat

but elsewhere speech is often interlaced with copulas as in

> 'sic'que 'meos muros transeat hostis', ait (848)

Ovid can use enjambment to run over the hexameter into the first foot of the pentameter, but seldom overruns the distich. Platnauer (*LEV* 29–32) notes the expressive exception at 357–9, where the Muse anticipates Ovid's question, but misses the deliberately transitional sequence at 801–5 (see Commentary).

The treatment of the verse-end in the six books of *Fasti* is relatively free. Of the eight hexameters with spondaic fifth feet, six end in Greek quadrisyllabic names, one in the Roman name *Collatini* (2.787), one with hiatus before a trisyllabic ending *caelifero Atlante* (5.83). The only spondaic ending in book IV, *Hellespontum* (567), is conventional in Ovid but not attested earlier.[89] There are no deviations from the disyllabic pentameter ending in this book, but the final quadrisyllables *fluminibus* at 5.582, *funeribus* at 6.660 both deliberately recall Propertian models.

It is worth mentioning that internal pentameter rhyme, commonly produced by agreement of epithet and noun at the end of each hemistich, varies in frequency over *Fasti* IV. First occurring at 10 *nunc teritur nostris area maior equis*, it is found only eight times before the Cybele narrative begins in 179, but twenty times between 179 and 372, often in groups of successive pentameters, and twenty-one times in the Ceres narrative between 417 and 619. These match the Ovidian average of 20% cited by Platnauer, so that it would be the non-narrative section that was anomalous.

5. THE TEXT

The textual tradition of *Fasti* is separate from that of *Metamorphoses*, as of the amatory and exile poems. Although over 170 manuscripts

[89] See 567n. for fuller listing and comment.

survive, the tradition can be almost completely reconstructed from five manuscripts, representing three branches:

A, the tenth-century Vaticanus Reginensis 1709, which ends at 5.24;
U, the eleventh-century Vaticanus Latinus 3262, slightly inferior in accuracy to A; and the family
Z, consisting of three MSS:
- **I,** the tenth-century fragmentum Ilfeldense, containing only parts of books II and III, and 4.317–814;
- **G,** the eleventh-century Bruxellensis 5369–73 starting at 1.505;
- **M,** Oxoniensis Bodleianus Auct.F.4.25, the fifteenth-century Mazarinianus, used and annotated by Nicolaas Heinsius.

Where A, U and Z survive but offer divergent readings agreement between two of the three branches is likely to represent the paradosis; after 5.25, the A tradition can be reconstituted from three secondary MSS.

To read Heinsius' collation and comments in the Mazarinianus and his annotations in Pieter Burman's Variorum edition (Amsterdam 1727) is a revelation of how much the text of the *Fasti* owes to this extraordinary scholar.[90] Relatively little improvement was made to the text by the nineteenth-century editions of W. Weber (1833), and R. Merkel. But Merkel's enormous learning enriched understanding of the *Fasti* in other ways, prefacing his 1841 edition with almost 300 pages of encyclopaedic argument covering the Roman calendar, the problems of astronomy and Ovid's later revision of book I and other parts of the poem. It was Merkel who in his second Teubner edition (1850–2) first divided and headed the text by individual days, preceding each day with an Arabic numeral identifying its modern date and a brief version of its Roman calendar entry: the present text follows the practice for the reader's convenience. Among more recent editions, such as H. Peter (3rd edn

[90] On Nicolaas Heinsius' editorial practice and principles see Kenney (1974) 59–73. The 34 manuscripts collated by Heinsius towards his revision of his father Daniel's 1629–30 text for his own edition of 1658–61 have now all been identified by E. H. Alton, *Hermathena* 45 (1929) 119–51 and M. D. Reeve, *Rheinisches Museum* 117 (1974) 133–66; 119 (1976) 65–78. For a complete catalogue of the *Fasti* MSS see D. E. W. Wormell and E. Courtney, *BICS* 24 (1977) 37–63.

1889), Landi–Castiglioni (1960), Frazer (1929), Bömer (1957–8) and now the Budé of R. Schilling (vol. I, 1992, vol. II, 1994), Frazer, Bömer and Schilling have been valuable chiefly for their contributions to interpreting the poem's religious and anthropological content.

This text depends on the apparatus criticus of the recent Teubner text of E. H. Alton, D. E. W. Wormell and E. Courtney (1978, revised 1985), but in view of the arguments of J. B. Hall (*Proceedings of the African Classical Association* 16 (1982) 68–75) for horizontal contamination of the 'primary' MSS and the preservation of authentic readings in the 'vulgares', a number of their readings preferred by Heinsius and other early editors have been reinstated.

Bömer and the new Teubner offer different conventions of spelling and punctuation. This edition punctuates less heavily than Alton–Wormell–Courtney, and observes different conventions of orthography, writing consonantal *u*, even before vocalic *u* (as in *uultus*), and prepositional compounds according to the norms suggested by Buck in *CR* 13 (1899) 116–18, 156–67.[91]

[91] As a convenience it marks with a diaeresis vowels standing as separate syllables in Greek names.

A tabular list is appended of places where readings differ significantly from either Bömer or A–W–C.

Fasti IV	Bömer	Alton–Wormell–Courtney	Fantham
12	canam	cano	cano
17	subito causae	causae subito	subito causae
20	quo tenearis	quod tuearis	quo tenearis
21	origine	imagine	imagine
24	tuos	tuos	suos
26	nascenti	nascendi	nascendi
27	repertam	receptam	receptam
55	patruo	patrui	patrui
85	adit	abit	abit
115	secundo	secundi	secundi
211	priscique manent	priscique manent	patrem, priscique
279	rapax	capax	rapax
286	Veneris	Veneris	Veneri
338	ab amne	in amne	ab amne
349	quaero	quaeram	quaeram
388	ensiger	ensifer	ensifer
421	ea	ea	ibi
428	umidus	uuidus	uuidus
440	rhoien	rhoean	rhoean
452	clamat	clamant	clamant
457	ut quas	quales	quales
479	Peloriaden	Peloriadem	Peloriaden
480	prima	prima	trina
500	Nisaei	Nisei	Nisei
507	fors	sors	sors
525	quaeris	quaeris	quereris
562	alifero	aligero	aligero
613	nisi pactus	pactus nisi	pactus nisi
627	sit licet	scilicet	sit licet
686	umida	obuia	obuia
709	dicere certa	†dicere certam†	†dicere certam†
724	facta	festa	facta
726	casta	tosta	tosta
741	maris rores	mares oleas	maris rores
881	adoptat	adorat	adoptat
942	fiat	fiat	pereat

SUMMARY OF OVID'S APRIL CALENDAR ENTRIES

1–18	Invocation to Venus.
19–132	Address to Caesar. 23–57 Romulus' naming of the month in honour of his ancestress; the Trojan descent of Aeneas, and the Alban kings. 63–80 April's Greek etymology from *aphros* and the Greek settlement of Italy. (81–4 personal lament.) 85–132 etymology from *aperire*; spring; Venus as goddess of fertility, civilization, Troy and Rome (117–24) and spring.
133–64	**1 April KALENDS.** Bathing of Venus. Feast of Fortuna Virilis, Venus Verticordia. Scorpio sets.
165–78	**2 April** Pleiades rise (link with Troy).
179–372	**4 April Megalensia.** Interview with Erato (including 195–214 birth of Jupiter; 221–44 castration of Attis; 247–348 coming of Cybele to Rome and Claudia's vindication).
373–6	**5 April NONES.** Dedication of Fortuna Publica.
377–86	**6 April** Games; anniversary of Thapsus. Libra setting.
387–8	**7 April** End of Games; Orion sets.
389–92	**10 April** Circus Procession.
393–620	**12 April** Games for Ceres. 393–416 hymn in her praise. 417–620 rape of Persephone. 417–55 flower-gathering, and rape. 455–501 Ceres' search in Sicily. 502–60 Ceres at Eleusis; blessing of Triptolemus. 561–613 renewed search and appeal to Jupiter. 614–20 the divided year.
621–4	**13 April IDES.** Dedication of temple of Jupiter Victor, Atria Libertatis.
625–8	**14 April** Augustan victory and salutation of Mutina.
629–75	**15 April Fordicidia.** Numa's consultation of Faunus; sacrifice of pregnant heifer.
677–8	**17 April** Setting of Hyades.

679–712 **19 April Cerealia.** Circus games. Release of foxes.

713–20 **20 April** Sun passes from sign of ram to sign of bull.

721–862 **21 April Parilia.** Fire-leaping, fumigation, shepherds' prayer and offering. Meaning of fires. 801–58 Romulus' foundation of Rome; death and burial of Remus. 859–62 poet's prayer for Rome.

863–900 **23 April Vinalia.** 863–77 Venus Erycina ad portam Collinam; 878–900 war of Latins and Rutuli. Mezentius' demand for vintage; Aeneas' vow to Jupiter and victory.

901–42 **25 April Robigalia.** Dogstar rises. Prayer of Flamen Quirinalis; dog sacrifice and its causes.

943–54 **28 April Floralia** (postponed). Dedication by Augustus of Palatine Vesta; Palatine triad of Apollo, Vesta, Augustus.

P. OVIDI NASONIS
FASTORVM
LIBER QVARTVS

P. OVIDI NASONIS
FASTORVM LIBER QVARTVS

'Alma faue,' dixi 'geminorum mater Amorum';
ad uatem uultus rettulit illa suos:
'quid tibi' ait 'mecum? certe maiora canebas.
num uetus in molli pectore uulnus habes?'
'scis, dea,' respondi 'de uulnere.' risit, et aether
protinus ex illa parte serenus erat.
'saucius an sanus numquid tua signa reliqui?
tu mihi propositum, tu mihi semper opus.
quae decuit primis sine crimine lusimus annis;
nunc teritur nostris area maior equis.
tempora cum causis annalibus eruta priscis
lapsaque sub terras ortaque signa cano.
uenimus ad quartum, quo tu celeberrima mense:
et uatem et mensem scis, Venus, esse tuos.'
mota Cytheriaca leuiter mea tempora myrto
contigit et 'coeptum perfice' dixit 'opus.'
sensimus, et subito causae patuere dierum:
dum licet et spirant flamina, nauis eat.

Si qua tamen pars te de fastis tangere debet,
Caesar, in Aprili quo tenearis habes:
hic ad te magna descendit imagine mensis
et fit adoptiua nobilitate tuus.
hoc pater Iliades, cum longum scriberet annum,
uidit et auctores rettulit ipse suos:
utque fero Marti primam dedit ordine sortem
quod sibi nascendi proxima causa fuit,
sic Venerem gradibus multis in gente receptam
alterius uoluit mensis habere locum;
principiumque sui generis reuolutaque quaerens
saecula, cognatos uenit adusque deos.

Dardanon Electra nesciret Atlantide natum
  scilicet, Electran concubuisse Ioui?
huius Ericthonius, Tros est generatus ab illo,
  Assaracon creat hic, Assaracusque Capyn;
proximus Anchises, cum quo commune parentis
  non dedignata est nomen habere Venus:
hinc satus Aeneas: pietas spectata per ignes
  sacra patremque umeris, altera sacra, tulit.
uenimus ad felix aliquando nomen Iuli,
  unde domus Teucros Iulia tangit auos.
Postumus hinc, qui quod siluis fuit ortus in altis
  Siluius in Latia gente uocatus erat.
isque, Latine, tibi pater est; subit Alba Latinum;
  proximus est titulis Epytus, Alba, tuis.
ille dedit Capyi repetita uocabula Troiae
  et tuus est idem, Calpete, factus auus.
cumque patris regnum post hunc Tiberinus haberet,
  dicitur in Tuscae gurgite mersus aquae.
iam tamen Agrippam natum Remulumque nepotem
  uiderat: in Remulum fulmina missa ferunt.
uenit Auentinus post hos, locus unde uocatur,
  mons quoque; post illum tradita regna Procae.
quem sequitur duri Numitor germanus Amuli;
  Ilia cum Lauso de Numitore sati:
ense cadit patrui Lausus; placet Ilia Marti,
  teque parit, gemino iuncte Quirine Remo.
ille suos semper Venerem Martemque parentes
  dixit, et emeruit uocis habere fidem:
neue secuturi possent nescire nepotes,
  tempora dis generis continuata dedit.

Sed Veneris mensem Graio sermone notatum
  auguror: a spumis est dea dicta maris.
nec tibi sit mirum Graeco rem nomine dici;
  Itala nam tellus Graecia maior erat.

uenerat Euander plena cum classe suorum
uenerat Alcides, Graius uterque genus
(hospes Auentinis armentum pauit in herbis
clauiger, et tanto est Albula pota deo),
dux quoque Neritius; testes Laestrygones exstant
et quod adhuc Circes nomina litus habet;
et iam Telegoni, iam moenia Tiburis udi
stabant, Argolicae quod posuere manus.
uenerat Atridae fatis agitatus Halaesus,
a quo se dictam terra Falisca putat.
adice Troianae suasorem Antenora pacis,
et generum Oeniden, Apule Daune, tuum.
serus ab Iliacis, et post Antenora, flammis
attulit Aeneas in loca nostra deos.
huius erat Solymus Phrygia comes unus ab Ida
a quo Sulmonis moenia nomen habent,
Sulmonis gelidi, patriae, Germanice, nostrae.
me miserum, Scythico quam procul illa solo est!
ergo ego tam longe –sed supprime, Musa, querellas;
non tibi sunt maesta sacra canenda lyra.

Quo non Liuor abit? sunt qui tibi mensis honorem
eripuisse uelint inuideantque, Venus.
nam, quia uer aperit tunc omnia densaque cedit
frigoris asperitas fetaque terra patet,
Aprilem memorant ab aperto tempore dictum
quem Venus iniecta uindicat alma manu.
illa quidem totum dignissima temperat orbem,
illa tenet nullo regna minora deo,
iuraque dat caelo, terrae, natalibus undis,
perque suos initus continet omne genus.
illa deos omnes (longum est numerare) creauit,
illa satis causas arboribusque dedit,
illa rudes animos hominum contraxit in unum,
et docuit iungi cum pare quemque sua.

quid genus omne creat uolucrum nisi blanda uoluptas?
nec coeant pecudes, si leuis absit amor.
cum mare trux aries cornu decertat, at idem
frontem dilectae laedere parcit ouis;
deposita sequitur taurus feritate iuuencam,
quem toti saltus, quem nemus omne, tremit;
uis eadem lato quodcumque sub aequore uiuit
seruat et innumeris piscibus implet aquas.
prima feros habitus homini detraxit: ab illa
uenerunt cultus mundaque cura sui.
primus amans carmen uigilatum nocte negata
dicitur ad clausas concinuisse fores,
eloquiumque fuit duram exorare puellam,
proque sua causa quisque disertus erat.
mille per hanc artes motae; studioque placendi,
quae latuere prius, multa reperta ferunt.
hanc quisquam titulo mensis spoliare secundi
audeat? a nobis sit furor iste procul.
quid quod ubique potens templisque frequentibus aucta,
urbe tamen nostra ius dea maius habet?
pro Troia, Romane, tua Venus arma ferebat,
cum gemuit teneram cuspide laesa manum;
caelestesque duas Troiano iudice uicit
(a, nolim uictas hoc meminisse deas!),
Assaracique nurus dicta est, ut scilicet olim
magnus Iuleos Caesar haberet auos.
nec Veneri tempus, quam uer, erat aptius ullum:
uere nitent terrae, uere remissus ager;
nunc herbae rupta tellure cacumina tollunt,
nunc tumido gemmas cortice palmes agit.
et formosa Venus formoso tempore digna est,
utque solet Marti continuata suo est.
uere monet curuas materna per aequora puppes
ire nec hibernas iam timuisse minas.

C KAL F (1 April)

Rite deam colitis, Latiae matresque nurusque
et uos, quis uittae longaque uestis abest.
aurea marmoreo redimicula demite collo,
demite diuitias: tota lauanda dea est.
aurea siccato redimicula reddite collo:
nunc alii flores, nunc noua danda rosa est.
uos quoque sub uiridi myrto iubet ipsa lauari:
causaque cur iubeat, discite, certa subest.
litore siccabat rorantes nuda capillos:
uiderunt satyri, turba proterua, deam.
sensit et opposita texit sua corpora myrto:
tuta fuit facto, uosque referre iubet.
discite nunc quare Fortunae tura Virili
detis eo, gelida qui locus umet aqua.
accipit ille locus posito uelamine cunctas
et uitium nudi corporis omne uidet;
ut tegat hoc celetque uiros, Fortuna Virilis
praestat, et hoc paruo ture rogata facit.
nec pigeat tritum niueo cum lacte papauer
sumere et expressis mella liquata fauis:
cum primum cupido Venus est deducta marito,
hoc bibit; ex illo tempore nupta fuit.
supplicibus uerbis illam placate: sub illa
et forma et mores et bona fama manet.
Roma pudicitia proauorum tempore lapsa est:
Cumaeam, ueteres, consuluistis anum.
templa iubet fieri Veneri: quibus ordine factis
inde Venus uerso nomina corde tenet.
semper ad Aeneadas placido, pulcherrima, uultu
respice, totque tuas, diua, tuere nurus.

Dum loquor, elatae metuendus acumine caudae
Scorpios in uirides praecipitatur aquas.

D F (2 April)

Nox ubi transierit, caelumque rubescere primo
coeperit, et tactae rore querentur aues,
semustamque facem uigilata nocte uiator
ponet, et ad solitum rusticus ibit opus,
Pliades incipient umeros releuare paternos,
quae septem dici, sex tamen esse solent:
seu quod in amplexum sex hinc uenere deorum,
(nam Steropen Marti concubuisse ferunt,
Neptuno Alcyonen et te, formosa Celaeno,
Maian et Electran Taygetenque Ioui),
septima mortali Merope tibi, Sisyphe, nupsit;
paenitet, et facti sola pudore latet:
siue quod Electra Troiae spectare ruinas
non tulit, ante oculos opposuitque manum.

E C F C (3, 4 April)

Ter sine perpetuo caelum uersetur in axe,
ter iungat Titan terque resoluat equos,
protinus inflexo Berecyntia tibia cornu
flabit et Idaeae festa parentis erunt.
ibunt semimares et inania tympana tundent,
aeraque tinnitus aere repulsa dabunt;
ipsa sedens molli comitum ceruice feretur
urbis per medias exululata uias.
scaena sonat, ludique uocant: spectate, Quirites,
et fora Marte suo litigiosa uacent.
quaerere multa libet, sed me sonus aeris acuti
terret et horrendo lotos adunca sono.
'da, dea, quem sciter.' doctas Cybeleïa neptes
uidit et has curae iussit adesse meae.
'pandite mandati memores, Heliconis alumnae,
gaudeat assiduo cur dea Magna sono.'

sic ego. sic Erato (mensis Cythereïus illi
cessit, quod teneri nomen amoris habet):
'reddita Saturno sors haec erat: "optime regum,
a nato sceptris excutiere tuis."
ille suam metuens, ut quaeque erat edita, prolem
deuorat, immersam uisceribusque tenet.
saepe Rhea questa est totiens fecunda nec umquam
mater, et indoluit fertilitate sua.
Iuppiter ortus erat (pro magno teste uetustas
creditur; acceptam parce mouere fidem):
ueste latens saxum caelesti gutture sedit:
sic genitor fatis decipiendus erat.
ardua iamdudum resonat tinnitibus Ide
tutus ut infanti uagiat ore puer.
pars clipeos sudibus, galeas pars tundit inanes:
hoc Curetes habent, hoc Corybantes opus.
res latuit patrem, priscique imitamina facti
aera deae comites raucaque terga mouent.
cymbala pro galeis, pro scutis tympana pulsant:
tibia dat Phrygios, ut dedit ante, modos.'
desierat; coepi: 'cur huic genus acre leonum
praebent insolitas ad iuga curua iubas?'
desieram; coepit: 'feritas mollita per illam
creditur: id curru testificata suo est.'
'at cur turrifera caput est onerata corona?
an primis turres urbibus illa dedit?'
adnuit. 'unde uenit' dixi 'sua membra secandi
impetus?' ut tacui, Pieris orsa loqui:
'Phryx puer in siluis, facie spectabilis, Attis
turrigeram casto uinxit amore deam;
hunc sibi seruari uoluit, sua templa tueri,
et dixit "semper fac puer esse uelis."
ille fidem iussis dedit et "si mentiar" inquit
"ultima qua fallam sit Venus illa mihi."

fallit, et in nympha Sagaritide desinit esse
quod fuit: hinc poenas exigit ira deae.
Naida uulneribus succidit in arbore factis,
illa perit: fatum Naidos arbor erat;
hic furit, et credens thalami procumbere tectum
effugit et cursu Dindyma summa petit.
et modo "tolle faces", "remoue" modo "uerbera" clamat,
saepe Palaestinas iurat adesse deas.
ille etiam saxo corpus laniauit acuto,
longaque in immundo puluere tracta coma est,
uoxque fuit "merui: meritas do sanguine poenas:
a, pereant partes quae nocuere mihi!
a, pereant!" dicebat adhuc: onus inguinis aufert,
nullaque sunt subito signa relicta uiri.
uenit in exemplum furor hic, mollesque ministri
caedunt iactatis uilia membra comis.'
talibus Aoniae facunda uoce Camenae
reddita quaesiti causa furoris erat.
'hoc quoque, dux operis, moneas, precor, unde petita
uenerit: an nostra semper in urbe fuit?'
'Dindymon et Cybelen et amoenam fontibus Iden
semper et Iliacas Mater amauit opes:
cum Troiam Aeneas Italos portaret in agros,
est dea sacriferas paena secuta rates,
sed nondum fatis Latio sua numina posci
senserat, adsuetis substiteratque locis.
post, ut Roma potens opibus iam saecula quinque
uidit et edomito sustulit orbe caput,
carminis Euboici fatalia uerba sacerdos
inspicit; inspectum tale fuissse ferunt:
"Mater abest: Matrem iubeo, Romane, requiras.
cum ueniet, casta est accipienda manu."
obscurae sortis patres ambagibus errant,
quaeue parens absit, quoue petenda loco.
consulitur Paean, "diuum"que "arcessite Matrem"
inquit: "in Idaeo est inuenienda iugo."

mittuntur proceres. Phrygiae tum sceptra tenebat
Attalus; Ausoniis rem negat ille uiris.
mira canam: longo tremuit cum murmure tellus,
et sic est adytis diua locuta suis:
"ipsa peti uolui; ne sit mora; mitte uolentem.
dignus Roma locus quo deus omnis eat."
ille soni terrore pauens "proficiscere!" dixit:
"nostra eris: in Phrygios Roma refertur auos."
protinus innumerae caedunt pineta secures
illa quibus fugiens Phryx pius usus erat,
mille manus coeunt, et picta coloribus ustis
caelestum Matrem concaua puppis habet.
illa sui per aquas fertur tutissima nati,
longaque Phrixeae stagna sororis adit,
Rhoeteumque rapax Sigeaque litora transit,
et Tenedum et ueteres Eëtionis opes.
Cyclades excipiunt, Lesbo post terga relicta,
quaeque Carysteis frangitur unda uadis;
transit et Icarium, lapsas ubi perdidit alas
Icarus, et uastae nomina fecit aquae.
tum laeua Creten, dextra Pelopeïdas undas
deserit, et Veneri sacra Cythera petit.
hinc mare Trinacrium, candens ubi tinguere ferrum
Brontes et Steropes Acmonidesque solent,
aequoraque Afra legit, Sardoaque regna sinistris
respicit a remis, Ausoniamque tenet.
ostia contigerat, qua se Tiberinus in altum
diuidit et campo liberiore natat:
omnis eques mixtaque grauis cum plebe senatus
obuius ad Tusci fluminis ora uenit.
procedunt pariter matres nataeque nurusque
quaeque colunt sanctos uirginitate focos.
sedula fune uiri contento bracchia lassant:
uix subit aduersas hospita nauis aquas.
sicca diu fuerat tellus, sitis usserat herbas:
sedit limoso pressa carina uado.

quisquis adest operi, plus quam pro parte laborat,
adiuuat et fortes uoce sonante manus:
illa uelut medio stabilis sedet insula ponto;
attoniti monstro stantque pauentque uiri.
Claudia Quinta genus Clauso referebat ab alto
(nec facies impar nobilitate fuit),
casta quidem, sed non et credita: rumor iniquus
laeserat, et falsi criminis acta rea est.
cultus et ornatis uarie prodisse capillis
obfuit ad rigidos promptaque lingua senes.
conscia mens recti famae mendacia risit,
sed nos in uitium credula turba sumus.
haec ubi castarum processit ab agmine matrum
et manibus puram fluminis hausit aquam,
ter caput inrorat, ter tollit in aethera palmas
(quicumque aspiciunt, mente carere putant)
summissoque genu uultus in imagine diuae
figit, et hos edit crine iacente sonos:
"supplicis alma, tuae, genetrix fecunda deorum,
accipe sub certa condicione preces.
casta negor: si tu damnas, meruisse fatebor;
morte luam poenas iudice uicta dea;
sed si crimen abest, tu nostrae pignora uitae
re dabis, et castas casta sequere manus."
dixit, et exiguo funem conamine traxit;
mira, sed et scaena testificata loquor:
mota dea est, sequiturque ducem laudatque sequendo;
index laetitiae fertur ad astra sonus.
fluminis ad flexum ueniunt (Tiberina priores
Atria dixerunt), unde sinister abit.
nox aderat: querno religant in stipite funem,
dantque leui somno corpora functa cibo.
lux aderat: querno soluunt a stipite funem,
ante tamen posito tura dedere foco,

ante coronarunt puppem, sine labe iuuencam
mactarunt operum coniugiique rudem.
est locus, in Tiberim qua lubricus influit Almo
et nomen magno perdit ab amne minor.
illic purpurea canus cum ueste sacerdos
Almonis dominam sacraque lauit aquis.
exululant comites, furiosaque tibia flatur,
et feriunt molles taurea terga manus.
Claudia praecedit laeto celeberrima uultu,
credita uix tandem teste pudica dea;
ipsa sedens plaustro porta est inuecta Capena:
sparguntur iunctae flore recente boues.
Nasica accepit; templi non perstitit auctor:
Augustus nunc est, ante Metellus erat.'

Substitit hic Erato, mora fit, si cetera quaeram.
'dic' inquam 'parua cur stipe quaerat opes?'
'contulit aes populus de quo delubra Metellus
fecit' ait; 'dandae mos stipis inde manet.'
cur uicibus factis ineant conuiuia, quaero,
tum magis indictas concelebrentque dapes.
'quod bene mutarit sedem Berecyntia' dixit
'captant mutatis sedibus omen idem.'
institeram, quare primi Megalesia ludi
urbe forent nostra, cum dea (sensit enim)
'illa deos' inquit 'peperit: cessere parenti,
principiumque dati Mater honoris habet.'
'cur igitur Gallos qui se excidere uocamus,
cum tanto a Phrygia Gallica distet humus?'
'inter' ait 'uiridem Cybelen altasque Celaenas
amnis it insana, nomine Gallus, aqua.
qui bibit inde furit: procul hinc discedite, quis est
cura bonae mentis: qui bibit inde, furit.'
'non pudet herbosum' dixi 'posuisse moretum
in dominae mensis? an sua causa subest?'

'lacte mero ueteres usi narrantur et herbis,
sponte sua siquas terra ferebat' ait;
'candidus elisae miscetur caseus herbae,
cognoscat priscos ut dea prisca cibos.'

G NON N (5 April)

Postera cum caelo motis Pallantias astris
fulserit, et niueos Luna leuarit equos,
qui dicet 'quondam sacrata est colle Quirini
hac Fortuna die Publica', uerus erit.

H NP A N B N (6–8 April)

Tertia lux (memini) ludis erat, ac mihi quidam
spectanti senior continuusque loco
'haec' ait 'illa dies, Libycis qua Caesar in oris
perfida magnanimi contudit arma Iubae.
dux mihi Caesar erat, sub quo meruisse tribunus
glorior: officio praefuit ille meo.
hanc ego militia sedem, tu pace parasti,
inter bis quinos usus honore uiros.'
plura locuturi subito seducimur imbre:
pendula caelestes Libra mouebat aquas.

C N (9 April)

Ante tamen quam summa dies spectacula sistat
ensifer Orion aequore mersus erit.

D N (10 April)

Proxima uictricem cum Romam inspexerit Eos
et dederit Phoebo stella fugata locum,

Circus erit pompa celeber numeroque deorum,
   primaque uentosis palma petetur equis.

E N F N (11, 12 April)

Hinc Cereris ludi: non est opus indice causae;
   sponte deae munus promeritumque patet.
panis erat primis uirides mortalibus herbae
   quas tellus nullo sollicitante dabat;
et modo carpebant uiuax e caespite gramen,
   nunc epulae tenera fronde cacumen erant.
postmodo glans nota est; bene erat iam glande reperta,
   duraque magnificas quercus habebat opes.
prima Ceres homine ad meliora alimenta uocato
   mutauit glandes utiliore cibo.
illa iugo tauros collum praebere coegit;
   tum primum soles eruta uidit humus.
aes erat in pretio, Chalybeïa massa latebat:
   eheu, perpetuo debuit illa tegi.
pace Ceres laeta est; et uos orate, coloni,
   perpetuam pacem pacificumque ducem.
farra deae micaeque licet salientis honorem
   detis et in ueteres turea grana focos;
et, si tura aberunt, unctas accendite taedas:
   parua bonae Cereri, sint modo casta, placent.
a boue succincti cultros remouete ministri:
   bos aret; ignauam sacrificate suem.
apta iugo ceruix non est ferienda securi;
   uiuat et in dura saepe laboret humo.

Exigit ipse locus raptus ut uirginis edam:
   plura recognosces, pauca docendus eris.
terra tribus scopulis uastum procurrit in aequor
   Trinacris, a positu nomen adepta loci,

grata domus Cereri: multas ibi possidet urbes,
   in quibus est culto fertilis Henna solo.
frigida caelestum matres Arethusa uocarat:
   uenerat ad sacras et dea flaua dapes.
filia, consuetis ut erat comitata puellis,
   errabat nudo per sua prata pede.
ualle sub umbrosa locus est aspergine multa
   uuidus ex alto desilientis aquae.
tot fuerant illic, quot habet natura, colores
   pictaque dissimili flore nitebat humus.
quam simul aspexit, 'comites, accedite' dixit
   'et mecum plenos flore referte sinus.'
praeda puellares animos prolectat inanis,
   et non sentitur sedulitate labor.
haec implet lento calathos e uimine nexos,
   haec gremium, laxos degrauat illa sinus;
illa legit calthas, huic sunt uiolaria curae,
   illa papauereas subsecat ungue comas;
has, hyacinthe, tenes; illas, amaranthe, moraris;
   pars thyma, pars rhoean et meliloton amat;
plurima lecta rosa est, sunt et sine nomine flores;
   ipsa crocos tenues liliaque alba legit.
carpendi studio paulatim longius itur,
   et dominam casu nulla secuta comes.
hanc uidet et uisam patruus uelociter aufert
   regnaque caeruleis in sua portat equis.
illa quidem clamabat 'io, carissima mater,
   auferor!' ipsa suos absciderātque sinus;
panditur interea Diti uia, namque diurnum
   lumen inadsueti uix patiuntur equi.
at chorus aequalis, cumulatae flore ministrae
   'Persephone' clamant 'ad tua dona ueni.'
ut clamata silet, montes ululatibus implent,
   et feriunt maesta pectora nuda manu.
attonita est plangore Ceres (modo uenerat Hennam),
   nec mora, 'me miseram! filia' dixit 'ubi es?'

mentis inops rapitur, quales audire solemus
  Threicias fusis maenadas ire comis.
ut uitulo mugit sua mater ab ubere rapto
  et quaerit fetus per nemus omne suos,
sic dea nec retinet gemitus, et concita cursu
  fertur, et e campis incipit, Henna, tuis.
inde puellaris nacta est uestigia plantae
  et pressam noto pondere uidit humum;
forsitan illa dies erroris summa fuisset,
  si non turbassent signa reperta sues.
iamque Leontinos Amenanaque flumina cursu
  praeterit et ripas, herbifer Aci, tuas;
praeterit et Cyanen et fontes lenis Anapi
  et te, uerticibus non adeunde Gela.
liquerat Ortygien Megareaque Pantagienque,
  quaque Symaetheas accipit aequor aquas,
antraque Cyclopum positis exusta caminis,
  quique locus curuae nomina falcis habet,
Himeraque et Didymen Acragantaque Tauromenumque,
  sacrarumque Mylas pascua laeta boum;
hinc Camerinan adit Thapsonque et Heloria Tempe,
  quaque iacet Zephyro semper apertus Eryx.
iamque Peloriaden Lilybaeaque, iamque Pachynon
  lustrarat, terrae cornua trina suae:
quacumque ingreditur, miseris loca cuncta querellis
  implet, ut amissum cum gemit ales Ityn.
perque uices modo 'Persephone!' modo 'filia!' clamat,
  clamat et alternis nomen utrumque ciet;
sed neque Persephone Cererem nec filia matrem
  audit, et alternis nomen utrumque perit;
unaque, pastorem uidisset an arua colentem,
  uox erat 'hac gressus ecqua puella tulit?'
iam color unus inest rebus tenebrisque teguntur
  omnia, iam uigiles conticuere canes:
alta iacet uasti super ora Typhoëos Aetne,
  cuius anhelatis ignibus ardet humus;

illic accendit geminas pro lampade pinus:
  hinc Cereris sacris nunc quoque taeda datur.
est specus exesi structura pumicis asper,
  non homini regio, non adeunda ferae:
quo simul ac uenit, frenatos curribus angues
  iungit et aequoreas sicca pererrat aquas.
effugit et Syrtes, et te, Zanclaea Charybdi,
  et uos, Nisei, naufraga monstra, canes
Hadriacumque patens late bimaremque Corinthum:
  sic uenit ad portus, Attica terra, tuos.
hic primum sedit gelido maestissima saxo:
  illud Cecropidae nunc quoque triste uocant.
sub Ioue durauit multis immota diebus,
  et lunae patiens et pluuialis aquae.
sors sua cuique loco est: quod nunc Cerialis Eleusin
  dicitur, hoc Celei rura fuere senis.
ille domum glandes excussaque mora rubetis
  portat et arsuris arida ligna focis.
filia parua duas redigebat monte capellas,
  et tener in cunis filius aeger erat.
'mater' ait uirgo (mota est dea nomine matris),
  'quid facis in solis incomitata locis?'
perstitit et senior, quamuis onus urget, et orat
  tecta suae subeat quantulacumque casae.
illa negat (simularat anum mitraque capillos
  presserat); instanti talia dicta refert:
'sospes eas semperque parens: mihi filia rapta est.
  heu melior quanto sors tua sorte mea est!'
dixit, et ut lacrimae (neque enim lacrimare deorum est)
  decidit in tepidos lucida gutta sinus.
flent pariter molles animis uirgoque senexque;
  e quibus haec iusti uerba fuere senis:
'sic tibi, quam raptam quereris, sit filia sospes:
  surge, nec exiguae despice tecta casae.'

cui dea, 'duc' inquit; 'scisti qua cogere posses',
  seque leuat saxo subsequiturque senem.
dux comiti narrat quam sit sibi filius aeger,
  nec capiat somnos inuigiletque malis.
illa soporiferum, paruos initura penates,
  colligit agresti lene papauer humo.
dum legit, oblito fertur gustasse palato
  longamque imprudens exsoluisse famem:
quae quia principio posuit ieiunia noctis,
  tempus habent mystae sidera uisa cibi.
limen ut intrauit, luctus uidet omnia plena;
  iam spes in puero nulla salutis erat.
matre salutata (mater Metanira uocatur)
  iungere dignata est os puerile suo.
pallor abit, subitasque uident in corpore uires:
  tantus caelesti uenit ab ore uigor.
tota domus laeta est, hoc est, materque paterque
  nataque: tres illi tota fuere domus.
mox epulas ponunt, liquefacta coagula lacte
  pomaque et in ceris aurea mella suis.
abstinet alma Ceres, somnique papauera causas
  dat tibi cum tepido lacte bibenda, puer.
noctis erat medium placidique silentia somni:
  Triptolemum gremio sustulit illa suo,
terque manu permulsit eum, tria carmina dixit,
  carmina mortali non referenda sono,
inque foco corpus pueri uiuente fauilla,
  obruit, humanum purget ut ignis onus.
excutitur somno stulte pia mater, et amens
  'quid facis?' exclamat, membraque ab igne rapit.
cui dea, 'dum non es' dixit 'scelerata fuisti:
  inrita materno sunt mea dona metu.
iste quidem mortalis erit; sed primus arabit
  et seret et culta praemia tollet humo.'

dixit, et egrediens nubem trahit, inque dracones
  transit et aligero tollitur axe Ceres.
Sunion expositum Piraeaque tuta recessu
  linquit et in dextrum quae iacet ora latus;
hinc init Aegaeum, quo Cycladas aspicit omnes,
  Ioniumque rapax Icariumque legit,
perque urbes Asiae longum petit Hellespontum,
  diuersumque locis alta pererrat iter.
nam modo turilegos Arabas, modo despicit Indos;
  hinc Libys, hinc Meroë siccaque terra subest;
nunc adit Hesperios, Rhenum Rhodanumque Padumque
  teque, future parens, Thybri, potentis aquae.
quo feror? immensum est erratas dicere terras:
  praeteritus Cereri nullus in orbe locus.
errat et in caelo, liquidique immunia ponti
  adloquitur gelido proxima signa polo:
'Parrhasides stellae, namque omnia nosse potestis,
  aequoreas numquam cum subeatis aquas,
Persephonen natam miserae monstrate parenti.'
  dixerat. huic Helice talia verba refert:
'crimine nox uacua est; Solem de uirgine rapta
  consule, qui late facta diurna uidet.'
Sol aditus 'quam quaeris', ait 'ne uana labores,
  nupta Iouis fratri tertia regna tenet.'
questa diu secum, sic est affata Tonantem
  (maximaque in uultu signa dolentis erant):
'si memor es de quo mihi sit Proserpina nata,
  dimidium curae debet habere tuae.
orbe pererrato sola est iniuria facti
  cognita: commissi praemia raptor habet.
at neque Persephone digna est praedone marito,
  nec gener hoc nobis more parandus erat.
quid grauius uictore Gyge captiua tulissem
  quam nunc te caeli sceptra tenente tuli?

uerum impune ferat, nos haec patiemur inultae;
reddat et emendet facta priora nouis.'
Iuppiter hanc lenit, factumque excusat amore,
'nec gener est nobis ille pudendus' ait.
non ego nobilior: posita est mihi regia caelo,
possidet alter aquas, alter inane chaos.
sed si forte tibi non est mutabile pectus,
statque semel iuncti rumpere uincla tori,
hoc quoque temptemus, siquidem ieiuna remansit;
si minus, inferni coniugis uxor erit.'
Tartara iussus adit sumptis Caducifer alis
speque redit citius uisaque certa refert:
'rapta tribus' dixit 'soluit ieiunia granis,
Punica quae lento cortice poma tegunt.'
non secus indoluit quam si modo rapta fuisset
maesta parens, longa uixque refecta mora est.
atque ita 'nec nobis caelum est habitabile' dixit;
'Taenaria recipi me quoque ualle iube.'
et factura fuit, pactus nisi Iuppiter esset
bis tribus ut caelo mensibus illa foret.
tum demum uultumque Ceres animumque recepit,
imposuitque suae spicea serta comae;
largaque prouenit cessatis messis in aruis,
et uix congestas area cepit opes.

Alba decent Cererem: uestes Cerialibus albas
sumite: nunc pulli uelleris usus abest.

G EID NP (13 April)

Occupat Apriles Idus cognomine Victor
Iuppiter: hac illi sunt data templa die.

hac quoque, ni fallor, populo dignissima nostro
atria Libertas coepit habere sua.

H N (14 April)

Luce secutura tutos pete, nauita, portus:
uentus ab occasu grandine mixtus erit.
sit licet ut fuerit, tamen hac Mutinensia Caesar
grandine militia perculit arma sua.

A FORD NP B N (15, 16 April)

Tertia post Veneris cum lux surrexerit Idus,
pontifices, forda sacra litate boue.
forda ferens bos est fecundaque dicta ferendo:
hinc etiam fetus nomen habere putant.
nunc grauidum pecus est, grauidae quoque semine terrae:
Telluri plenae uictima plena datur.
pars cadit arce Iouis, ter denas curia uaccas
accipit et largo sparsa cruore madet.
ast ubi uisceribus uitulos rapuere ministri,
sectaque fumosis exta dedere focis,
igne cremat uitulos quae natu maxima Virgo est,
luce Palis populos purget ut ille cinis.
rege Numa, fructu non respondente labori,
inrita decepti uota colentis erant.
nam modo siccus erat gelidis Aquilonibus annus,
nunc ager adsidua luxuriabat aqua;
saepe Ceres primis dominum fallebat in herbis,
et leuis obsesso stabat auena solo,
et pecus ante diem partus edebat acerbos
agnaque nascendo saepe necabat ouem.
silua uetus nullaque diu uiolata securi
stabat, Maenalio sacra relicta deo:

ille dabat tacitis animo responsa quieto
noctibus; hic geminas rex Numa mactat oues.
prima cadit Fauno, leni cadit altera Somno;
sternitur in duro uellus utrumque solo.
bis caput intonsum fontana spargitur unda,
bis sua faginea tempora fronde premit.
usus abest Veneris, nec fas animalia mensis
ponere, nec digitis anulus ullus inest;
ueste rudi tectus supra noua uellera corpus
ponit, adorato per sua uerba deo.
interea placidam redimita papauere frontem
Nox uenit, et secum somnia nigra trahit;
Faunus adest, ouiumque premens pede uellera duro
edidit a dextro talia uerba toro:
'morte boum tibi, rex, Tellus placanda duarum:
det sacris animas una iuuenca duas.'
excutitur terrore quies; Numa uisa reuoluit,
et secum ambages caecaque iussa refert.
expedit errantem nemori gratissima coniunx
et dixit 'grauidae posceris exta bouis.'
exta bouis grauidae dantur; fecundior annus
prouenit, et fructum terra pecusque ferunt.

Hanc quondam Cytherea diem properantius ire
iussit et admissos praecipitauit equos,
ut titulum imperii cum primum luce sequenti
Augusto iuueni prospera bella darent.

C N D N (17, 18 April)

Sed iam praeteritas quartus tibi Lucifer Idus
respicit: hac Hyades Dorida nocte tenent.

E CER NP (19 April)

Tertia post Hyadas cum lux erit orta remotas,
carcere partitos Circus habebit equos.
cur igitur missae uinctis ardentia taedis
terga ferant uolpes causa docenda mihi est.
frigida Carseolis nec oliuis apta ferendis
terra, sed ad segetes ingeniosus ager;
hac ego Paelignos, natalia rura, petebam,
parua, sed adsiduis obuia semper aquis.
hospitis antiqui solitas intrauimus aedes;
dempserat emeritis iam iuga Phoebus equis.
is mihi multa quidem, sed et haec narrare solebat
unde meum praesens instrueretur opus:
'hoc' ait 'in campo' (campumque ostendit) 'habebat
rus breue cum duro parca colona uiro.
ille suam peragebat humum, siue usus aratri,
seu curuae falcis, siue bidentis erat;
haec modo uerrebat stantem tibicine uillam,
nunc matris plumis oua fouenda dabat.
aut uirides maluas aut fungos colligit albos
aut humilem grato calfacit igne focum;
et tamen adsiduis exercet bracchia telis,
aduersusque minas frigoris arma parat.
filius huius erat primo lasciuus in aeuo,
addideratque annos ad dua lustra duos.
is capit extremi uolpem conualle salicti:
abstulerat multas illa cohortis aues.
captiuam stipula fenoque inuoluit et ignes
admouet: urentes effugit illa manus;
qua fugit, incendit uestitos messibus agros:
damnosis uires ignibus aura dabat.
factum abiit, monimenta manent: nam †dicere certam†
nunc quoque lex uolpem Carseolana uetat,

utque luat poenas, gens haec Cerialibus ardet,
quoque modo segetes perdidit ipsa perit.'

F N (20 April)

Proxima cum ueniet terras uisura patentes
Memnonis in roseis lutea mater equis,
de duce lanigeri pecoris, qui prodidit Hellen
sol abit: egresso uictima maior adest.
uacca sit an taurus non est cognoscere promptum:
pars prior apparet, posteriora latent.
seu tamen est taurus siue est hoc femina signum,
Iunone inuita munus amoris habet.

G PAR NP (21 April)

Nox abiit, oriturque Aurora: Parilia poscor;
non poscor frustra, si fauet alma Pales.
alma Pales, faueas pastoria sacra canenti,
prosequor officio si tua facta meo.
certe ego de uitulo cinerem stipulasque fabales
saepe tuli plena, februa tosta, manu;
certe ego transilui positas ter in ordine flammas,
udaque roratas laurea misit aquas.
mota dea est, operique fauet. naualibus exit
puppis; habent uentos iam mea uela suos.
i, pete uirginea, populus, suffimen ab ara;
Vesta dabit, Vestae munere purus eris.
sanguis equi suffimen erit uitulique fauilla,
tertia res durae culmen inane fabae.
pastor, oues saturas ad prima crepuscula lustra:
unda prius spargat, uirgaque uerrat humum;

frondibus et fixis decorentur ouilia ramis
et tegat ornatas longa corona fores.
caerulei fiant puro de sulpure fumi,
tactaque fumanti sulpure balet ouis.
ure maris rores taedamque herbasque Sabinas,
et crepet in mediis laurus adusta focis;
libaque de milio milii fiscella sequatur:
rustica praecipue est hoc dea laeta cibo.
adde dapes mulctramque suas, dapibusque resectis
siluicolam tepido lacte precare Palem.
'consule' dic 'pecori pariter pecorisque magistris:
effugiat stabulis noxa repulsa meis.
siue sacro paui sediue sub arbore sacra,
pabulaque e bustis inscia carpsit ouis;
si nemus intraui uetitum, nostrisue fugatae
sunt oculis nymphae semicaperque deus;
si mea falx ramo lucum spoliauit opaco,
unde data est aegrae fiscina frondis oui,
da ueniam culpae: nec dum degrandinat, obsit
agresti fano supposuisse pecus.
nec noceat turbasse lacus: ignoscite, nymphae,
mota quod obscuras ungula fecit aquas.
tu, dea, pro nobis fontes fontanaque placa
numina, tu sparsos per nemus omne deos.
nec Dryadas nec nos uideamus labra Dianae
nec Faunum, medio cum premit arua die.
pelle procul morbos; ualeant hominesque gregesque,
et ualeant uigiles, prouida turba, canes.
neue minus multos redigam quam mane fuerunt,
neue gemam referens uellera rapta lupo.
absit iniqua fames: herbae frondesque supersint,
quaeque lauent artus quaeque bibantur aquae.
ubera plena premam, referat mihi caseus aera,
dentque uiam liquido uimina rara sero;

sitque salax aries, conceptaque semina coniunx
reddat, et in stabulo multa sit agna meo;
lanaque proueniat nullas laesura puellas,
mollis et ad teneras quamlibet apta manus.
quae precor eueniant, et nos faciamus ad annum
pastorum dominae grandia liba Pali.'
his dea placanda est: haec tu conuersus ad ortus
dic quater et uiuo perlue rore manus.
tum licet apposita, ueluti cratere, camella
lac niueum potes purpureamque sapam;
moxque per ardentes stipulae crepitantis aceruos
traicias celeri strenua membra pede.
expositus mos est; moris mihi restat origo:
turba facit dubium coeptaque nostra tenet.
omnia purgat edax ignis uitiumque metallis
excoquit: idcirco cum duce purgat oues?
an, quia cunctarum contraria semina rerum
sunt duo discordes, ignis et unda, dei,
iunxerunt elementa patres, aptumque putarunt
ignibus et sparsa tangere corpus aqua?
an, quod in his uitae causa est, haec perdidit exul,
his noua fit coniunx, haec duo magna putant?
uix equidem credo: sunt qui Phaëthonta referri
credant et nimias Deucalionis aquas.
pars quoque, cum saxis pastores saxa feribant,
scintillam subito prosiluisse ferunt:
prima quidem periit, stipulis excepta secunda est:
hoc argumentum flamma Parilis habet?
an magis hunc morem pietas Aeneïa fecit
innocuum uicto cui dedit ignis iter?
num tamen est uero propius, cum condita Roma est,
transferri iussos in noua tecta Lares,
mutantesque domum tectis agrestibus ignem
et cessaturae supposuisse casae,

per flammas saluisse pecus, saluisse colonos?
quod fit natali nunc quoque, Roma, tuo.
ipse locum casus uati facit: urbis origo
uenit, ades factis, magne Quirine, tuis.
iam luerat poenas frater Numitoris, et omne
pastorum gemino sub duce uulgus erat;
contrahere agrestes et moenia ponere utrique
conuenit: ambigitur moenia ponat uter.
'nil opus est' dixit 'certamine' Romulus 'ullo;
magna fides auium est: experiamur aues.'
res placet: alter init nemorosi saxa Palati;
alter Auentinum mane cacumen init.
sex Remus, hic uolucres bix sex uidet ordine: pacto
statur, et arbitrium Romulus urbis habet.
apta dies legitur qua moenia signet aratro:
sacra Palis suberant; inde mouetur opus.
fossa fit ad solidum, fruges iaciuntur in ima
et de uicino terra petita solo;
fossa repletur humo, plenaeque imponitur ara,
et nouus accenso fungitur igne focus.
inde premens stiuam designat moenia sulco;
alba iugum niueo cum boue uacca tulit.
uox fuit haec regis: 'condenti, Iuppiter, urbem,
et genitor Mauors Vestaque mater, ades,
quosque pium est adhibere deos, aduertite cuncti:
auspicibus uobis hoc mihi surgat opus.
longa sit huic aetas dominaeque potentia terrae,
sitque sub hac oriens occiduusque dies.'
ille precabatur, tonitru dedit omina laeuo
Iuppiter, et laeuo fulmina missa polo.
augurio laeti iaciunt fundamina ciues,
et nouus exiguo tempore murus erat.
hoc Celer urget opus, quem Romulus ipse uocarat,
'sint'que 'Celer, curae' dixerat 'ista tuae,
neue quis aut muros aut factam uomere fossam
transeat; audentem talia dede neci.'

quod Remus ignorans humiles contemnere muros
coepit et 'his populus' dicere 'tutus erit?'
nec mora, transiluit: rutro Celer occupat ausum;
ille premit duram sanguinolentus humum.
haec ubi rex didicit, lacrimas introrsus obortas
deuorat et clausum pectore uulnus habet.
flere palam non uult exemplaque fortia seruat,
'sic'que 'meos muros transeat hostis' ait.
dat tamen exsequias; nec iam suspendere fletum
sustinet, et pietas dissimulata patet;
osculaque applicuit posito suprema feretro
atque ait 'inuito frater adempte, uale',
arsurosque artus unxit: fecere quod ille,
Faustulus et maestas Acca soluta comas.
tum iuuenem nondum facti fleuere Quirites;
ultima plorato subdita flamma rogo est.
urbs oritur (quis tunc hoc ulli credere posset?)
uictorem terris impositura pedem.
cuncta regas et sis magno sub Caesare semper,
saepe etiam plures nominis huius habe;
et quotiens steteris domito sublimis in orbe,
omnia sint umeris inferiora tuis.

H N A VIN FP (22, 23 April)

Dicta Pales nobis: idem Vinalia dicam.
una tamen media est inter utramque dies.
numina, uulgares, Veneris celebrate puellae:
multa professarum quaestibus apta Venus.
poscite ture dato formam populique fauorem,
poscite blanditias dignaque uerba ioco;
cumque sua dominae date grata sisymbria myrto
tectaque composita iuncea uincla rosa.
templa frequentari Collinae proxima portae
nunc decet; a Siculo nomina colle tenent,

utque Syracusas Arethusidas abstulit armis
   Claudius et bello te quoque cepit, Eryx,
carmine uiuacis Venus est translata Sibyllae,
   inque suae stirpis maluit urbe coli.
cur igitur Veneris festum Vinalia dicant
   quaeritis, et quare sit Iouis ista dies?
Turnus an Aeneas Latiae gener esset Amatae
   bellum erat: Etruscas Turnus adoptat opes.
clarus erat sumptisque ferox Mezentius armis,
   et uel equo magnus uel pede maior erat;
quem Rutuli Turnusque suis adsciscere temptat
   partibus. haec contra dux ita Tuscus ait:
'stat mihi non paruo uirtus mea: uulnera testor
   armaque, quae sparsi sanguine saepe meo.
qui petis auxilium, non grandia diuide mecum
   praemia, de lacubus proxima musta tuis.
nulla mora est operae: uestrum est dare, uincere nostrum.
   quam uelit Aeneas ista negata mihi!'
adnuerant Rutuli. Mezentius induit arma,
   induit Aeneas adloquiturque Iouem:
'hostica Tyrrheno uota est uindemia regi:
   Iuppiter, e Latio palmite musta feres.'
uota ualent meliora: cadit Mezentius ingens
   atque indignanti pectore plangit humum.
uenerat Autumnus calcatis sordidus uuis:
   redduntur merito debita uina Ioui.
dicta dies hinc est Vinalia: Iuppiter illa
   uindicat et festis gaudet inesse suis.

B C   C ROB NP   (24, 25 April)

Sex ubi, quae restant, luces Aprilis habebit,
   in medio cursu tempora ueris erunt,

et frustra pecudem quaeres Athamantidos Helles,
signaque dant imbres, exoriturque Canis.
hac mihi Nomento Romam cum luce redirem,
obstitit in media candida turba uia:
flamen in antiquae lucum Robiginis ibat,
exta canis flammis, exta daturus ouis.
protinus accessi, ritus ne nescius essem;
edidit haec flamen uerba, Quirine, tuus:
'aspera Robigo, parcas Cerialibus herbis,
et tremat in summa leue cacumen humo.
tu sata sideribus caeli nutrita secundi
crescere, dum fiant falcibus apta, sinas.
uis tua non leuis est: quae tu frumenta notasti,
maestus in amissis illa colonus habet;
nec uenti tantum Cereri nocuere nec imbres,
nec sic marmoreo pallet adusta gelu,
quantum si culmos Titan incalfacit udos:
tum locus est irae, diua timenda, tuae.
parce, precor, scabrasque manus a messibus aufer,
neue noce cultis; posse nocere sat est.
nec teneras segetes, sed durum amplectere ferrum,
quodque potest alios perdere perde prior.
utilius gladios et tela nocentia carpes:
nil opus est illis: otia mundus agit.
sarcula nunc durusque bidens et uomer aduncus,
ruris opes, niteant; inquinet arma situs,
conatusque aliquis uagina ducere ferrum
adstrictum longa sentiat esse mora.
at tu ne uiola Cererem, semperque colonus
absenti possit soluere uota tibi.'
dixerat; a dextra uillis mantele solutis
cumque meri patera turis acerra fuit.
tura focis uinumque dedit fibrasque bidentis
turpiaque obscenae (uidimus) exta canis.

tum mihi 'cur detur sacris noua uictima quaeris?'
(quaesieram) 'causam percipe' flamen ait.
'est Canis, Icarium dicunt, quo sidere moto
tosta sitit tellus praecipiturque seges.
pro cane sidereo canis hic imponitur arae,
et quare pereat nil nisi nomen habet.'

D F E C F NP G C H C
(26–30 April)

Cum Phrygis Assaraci Tithonia fratre relicto
sustulit immenso ter iubar orbe suum,
mille uenit uariis florum dea nexa coronis:
scaena ioci morem liberioris habet.
exit et in Maias sacrum Florale Kalendas:
tunc repetam, nunc me grandius urget opus.
aufer, Vesta, diem! cognati Vesta recepta est
limine; sic iusti constituere patres.
Phoebus habet partem: Vestae pars altera cessit:
quod superest illis, tertius ipse tenet.
state Palatinae laurus, praetextaque quercu
stet domus: aeternos tres habet una deos.

COMMENTARY

1–18

The eighteen lines of proem to the fourth book of the *Fasti*, which opens the second quarter of the year (or second half of O.'s six-month poem), are designed to recall but mark with significant differences both the proem of book 1, composed to introduce the whole year, and the proem of the preceding month of March, addressed to Venus' consort, Mars, joint ancestor of Romulus and protector of his people.

Thus 4.11–12 repeats the opening couplet of book 1, indicating the contents of the *Fasti*, with two changes: the future *canam* of 1.2 has become present *cano*, since O. is now in progress through the year, and the second half of 4.11 substitutes the corresponding part of 1.7 *annalibus eruta priscis* for the reference in 1.1 to the Latin calendar year. It is now the occasions, *tempora*, not the rituals, *sacra*, that are described as retrieved from ancient annals.

But while the proem to book 1, in its re-edited version, was dedicated to the mortal prince and patron Germanicus (and answered by the proemiac address to *Caesar* in book II) the proems to books III and IV are addressed to the gods after whom, as O. will argue, the months are named. Mars, the mythical father of Romulus, won apotheosis for his son (2.481–90, imitating the treatment of the same deification in Ennius, *Annales* 1), but Venus' link with Romulus was more obscure; although she had been the consort of Mars, by whom she gave birth to Amor (Cupid), the ancestry of Romulus had to be traced through her mortal son Aeneas, whose descendant Ilia was impregnated by Mars to produce the twins Romulus and Remus. It is above all as mother of Aeneas and ancestress of the Julian house that Venus became important to Roman theology in the age of Julius Caesar and his adopted son Augustus.

O. had opened the proem of book III with a direct invocation of Mars: *bellice* ... | *Mars, ades* and urged the warrior god to set aside his warlike (*bellice*) mood and be at leisure to enjoy *ingenuae artes*. The address to Venus presents a different problem. For she had been O.'s patroness in all his past career of love poetry. Yet, just as he imagined Mars asking (3.3) *quid sit cum Marte poetae*, Venus will answer his appeal *alma faue* with a half-hostile (4.3) *quid tibi ... mecum?*

Why is she hostile? She herself explains immediately. O. had been planning to sing *maiora*, poetry on 'higher' themes. And if O.'s former readers did not recognize this allusion to his valediction to Venus in the last poem of the *Amores* (3.15), they should certainly have done so, for *Fasti* 4.1, appealing to Venus as *geminorum mater Amorum*, clearly echoes *Am.* 3.15.1 *quaere nouum uatem, tenerorum mater Amorum*. O. is now appealing to the goddess he so churlishly dismissed. Hence, too, the self-reference as *uates* in line 2. Venus now turns back her gaze to the poet who had left her. His reply will be protestations of loyalty whose very language (4.7 *numquid tua signa reliqui?*) recalls his former dismissal: *Am.* 3.15.15–16 *puerique parens Amathusia culti, | aurea de campo uellite signa meo.*

The text will reveal O.'s relationship with Venus as very different from his dialogues with other gods, with Janus, Mars, or even Cybele at 4.191. This reported dialogue (the perfect *dixi* sets the exchange in the past) has an intimacy which leaves things half said but understood, and O. wins a smile from the goddess with the briefest of allusions to his old wounds of love (4.5). He can then follow up his beguiling allusion to their shared past with a rephrasing of his reformed poetic goals that demonstrates Venus' importance to his new purpose (4.10–14) and wins from her a gesture of endorsement (the touch with her myrtle branch 4.15) and the command to complete (*perfice*) his undertaking. Venus' touch magically opens up the mysterious knowledge O. needs for his task (4.17 *subito causae patuere dierum*) and he launches the next phase of his poetic voyage while the going is good.

This brief glance back at O.'s love poetry raises many questions. Many of his readers had relished precisely the erotic irresponsibility of his old poetry which he was now trying to disclaim. But whereas inside the *Fasti* O. represents his change of theme and tone for the new patriotic elegy as an offence against Venus for which he must make amends, outside the poem O.'s old themes of extra-marital love, especially when he turned from description in the *Amores* to prescription in the *Ars amatoria*, had caused offence to Augustus. It is more than likely that O. was made to realize this, and began the

Fasti hoping to honour the Princeps and make amendment for his past advocacy of sex for pleasure, and love as a way of life.

So the very lines which inside the dialogue are designed to win back the goodwill of Venus, must also look over O.'s shoulder at their possible effect on his august reader: line 9 *primis sine crimine lusimus annis* extenuates his frivolous love poetry as the product of his youth, a time of legitimate wild oats (but O. was over 40 when the *Ars amatoria* appeared); lines 10–14 indicate to both Venus and Augustus that the poet is now invoking the goddess, not for her erotic assistance, but because the approaching month does her honour. A detailed consideration of the discussion of April which follows will show how ingenious is O.'s wording in line 13 *quo tu celeberrima mense*: for he cannot affirm categorically that the month is named after the goddess, but his unfolding narrative will show her important role in both the natural and cultural activities of April. The Venus that will be honoured in book IV is a far more significant power, for the *gens Iulia*, for Rome and for all Nature, than the love-goddess of O's amatory elegy. (See Miller (1991) 29–34, Barchiesi (1994) 45–51, Herbert-Brown (1994) 86–95.)

1 'Alma, faue: *alma*, 'nurturing', is an epithet that can be applied to more than one goddess: to Cybele, mother of the gods, *alma Cybebe, alma parens Idaea deum* in *Aen.* 10.220 and 252; cf. *F.* 4.319 *alma ... genetrix fecunda deorum*; to Ceres, *alma Ceres* in *Georg.* 1.7, cf. 547 below; even to Pales, as in 722. But the precedent of Lucretius' opening invocation, to *Aeneadum genetrix ... alma Venus* (1.1–2) and Virgil's allusion to *alma Venus* at *Aen.* 1.618, 10.332, or Aeneas' address to his mother as *alma parens* in *Aen.* 2.664 (cf. 591), might increase the reader's expectation that the addressee would be Venus. In his defence to Augustus, *Tr.* 2.261, O. refers to Lucretius' poem by its opening words *Aeneadum genetrix* and suggests provocatively that the innnocent reader might ask *Aeneadum genetrix unde sit alma Venus.* O. repeats the epithet at 4.90 below.

'geminorum mater Amorum': the two Loves are most probably a reference to *Amor* (Affection) and *Cupido* (Desire), not the Platonic *Eros* and *Anteros.* Given the representation of Venus with two cupids on a coin of one of Julius Caesar's kinsmen in 94 or 90 BC, and O.'s preoccupation with the Julian Venus from line 19 onwards, we should not exclude reference to a contemporary cult image familiar to O.'s readers but now lost (cf. Wlosok (1975a) 172–85, (1975b) 514–23). Here the duality is specific, distinct from the usual collective of *Erotes* as in Catullus 3.1 (*lugete, o Veneres Cupidinesque*). In all other allusions to *Amores* O. has the indefinite plural: *Am.* 3.15.1 *tenerorum mater Amorum* (*tenerorum lusor Amorum Tr.* 3.3.73), *Her.* 7.59 *mater Amorum*, 16.203 *uolucrum ... mater Amorum.*

3 'quid tibi' ... 'mecum? certe maiora canebas: in the hierarchy of genres both epic and tragedy rated as *maiora* than elegy, but within elegy itself elevated subject matter also qualifies: see Introd. 2(v). As Barchiesi notes, Venus' question would recall to any reader familiar with Greek poetry Sappho's words to Aphrodite 1.15–18 L–P: 'Smiling you asked me what was my trouble, this time, and why I had called on you, this time.'

canebas: the imperfect denotes an unfinished or interrupted action; cf. *Am.* 1.1.1–2 *arma graui numero ... parabam | edere.*

4 num uetus ... uulnus habes?': the wound of love is an elegiac commonplace (with Hellenistic equivalent; cf. Gk ἕλκος in Callimachus, *Anth. Pal.* 12.134 = *HE* 13 'our guest has a wound and we knew it not'). Typical is Prop. 2.12.11–13 *ante ferit quoniam tuti quam cernimus hostem | nec quisquam ex illo uulnere sanus abit. | in me tela manent,* or 2.13.1–2 *non tot Achaemeniis armantur Etrusca sagittis | spicula, quot nostro pectore fixit Amor.* A more serious use is made by Virgil in the extended image of Dido's infatuation with Aeneas at *Aen.* 4.1–4 *saucia cura | uulnus alit uenis ... haerent infixi pectore uultus.* O. elaborates with related concepts at e.g. *Am.* 2.9.4–7 (*laedere, uulnerare, figere, percellere, confodere*), *AA* 1.23–4 *quo me fixit Amor, quo me uiolentius ussit | hoc melior facti uulneris ultor ero,* 1.165–6 *illa saepe puer Veneris pugnauit harena | et qui spectauit uulnera, uulnus habet.*

in molli pectore: cf. *Her.* 16.126 *molli pectore, AA* 1.535 *mollissima pectora* (poetic pl. for sing. cf. 143 below) and of O. himself, *Tr.* 4.10.65, 5.8.28 *molle cor.* Here the epithet signals a recall of the sentimental ethos of elegy, the *mollis uersus, mollis liber* of Propertius 1.7.19, 2.1.2. (Contrast the association of *mollis* with Cybele's eunuch priests in 185, 243, 342 below.) In general the *pectus* is the seat of the affections but also of the intelligence.

The whole exchange can be seen as a variation on the opening of Hor. *Odes* 4.1–2 *intermissa, Venus diu | rursus bella moues?* (cf. Barchiesi

(1994) 46–7), but O. differs from Horace both in situation: he is not suffering the pangs of love; and in his literary record: Horace was returning to lyric after professing to put it behind him for dispassionate philosophical epistles, whereas O. had indeed professed to leave love behind him in the *Amores*, but had since composed four books of amatory didactic elegy. Now, however, he has no amatory concern and is invoking a more mature and respectable aspect of Venus herself; it is she who will be taking on a new role.

5–6 risit, et aether | ... ex illa parte serenus erat: both the characteristic smile of Aphrodite μειδιόωσα and the impact of divine favour are conveyed. Compare the description of Jupiter's smile and its effect in Ennius 446–7 Skutsch: *Iuppiter hic risit, tempestatesque serenae | riserunt omnes risu Iouis omnipotentis* and Virg. *Aen.* 1.254–5 *olli subridens hominum sator ... | uultu quo caelum tempestatesque serenat,* and the epiphany of Venus at Lucr. 1.8–9 *tibi rident aequora ponti | placatumque nitet diffuso lumine caelum.*

ex illa parte recalls Roman concern with the location of celestial omens.

7 'saucius an sanus: for *saucius* cf. Enn. *Medea* fr. 1 Jocelyn *amore saeuo saucia,* Virg. *Aen.* 4.1 *at regina, graui iamdudum saucia cura.* In O. cf. *Am.* 2.1.7 *aliquis iuuenum, quo nunc ego saucius arcu, AA* 1.169 (continuing the imagery cited in line 4 above) *saucius ingemuit, telumque uolatile sensit.* O. exploits assonance with *sanus* (more often *non sanus* or *male sanus* in love elegy). Here positive *sanus,* like the language of 8 below, is designed to recall his repeated use of *sanus* to mark the cured lover in *Rem.* 493, 504, 546, 621 and 794. The physical force of both words is partly retained in the continuing military image. For the conjunction *an* outside an interrogative sentence, with the force of *siue,* cf. 487n. and H–S II 504 §273, *TLL* II 6.61ff.

numquid tua signa reliqui?: O. made the same claim to Amor in *Am.* 2.9.3 *qui miles numquam tua signa reliqui,* but resigned his loyal service in *Am.* 3.15.16 (cited above). Here too he echoes Hor. *Odes* 4.1.16 *late signa feret militiae tuae. numquid* is adverbial acc.: 'at all', 'in any respect'.

8 tu mihi propositum, tu ... opus: cf. *AA* 1.29–30 *usus opus mouet hoc ... | ... coeptis, mater Amoris, ades,* 3.769–70 *sed alma Dione | 'praecipue nostrum est quod pudet' inquit 'opus.'* For *propositum* (subst.) of the poetic enterprise, cf. *F.* 1.468 *propositoque faue, Rem.* 53. *Remedia* too opens with protestations of loyalty to Amor *nec noua praeteritum Musa retexit opus* (12) and Amor's authorization at 39–40 *mouit Amor gemmatas aureus alas | et mihi 'propositum perfice' dixit 'opus.'*

9 quae decuit ... sine crimine lusimus: for the internal object, cf. Virg. *Ecl.* 1.10 *ludere quae uellem, Georg.* 4.565 *carmina qui lusi.* There as here the reference is to the poetry of play (love) rather than to the play itself. Bömer cites *Aen.* 4.550–1 *non licuit thalami expertem sine crimine uitam | degere* as first instance of this idiom. *sine crimine* is part of O.'s self-commendation to the imaginary mistress of *Am.* 1.3.13 *sine crimine mores*; for the combination with *ludere* cf. *Her.* 17.19, *Tr.* 3.2.5. For the poetic deprecation of love poetry as *ludere* cf. Virgil's description of the *Eclogues* at *Georg.* 4.565 cited above, *F.* 2.6 *cum lusit numeris prima iuuenta suis.* O. uses his youth both to extenuate his interest in love and to classify his old genre of poetry as lightweight. The combination with the image of equestrian exercise in 10 *teritur ... area maior equis* is adapted from *Am.* 3.1.25–8. Aetiological elegy claims itself, like epic, as a more adult exercise ground, cf. *Am.* 3.1.25–8 *cane facta uirorum: | 'haec animo' dices 'area digna meo est.' | quod tenerae cantent lusit tua Musa puellae, | primaque per numeros acta iuuenta suos.* Allusion to horses evokes training for either cavalry combat or chariot racing: cf. Prop. 2.10.2 *campum Haemonio iam dare tempus equo*, and the mixed imagery of triumph and chariot racing in Prop. 3.1.10–14.

11–12 This couplet echoes the opening couplet (or *incipit* by which a poem was often known) of the *Fasti*, but replaces the specific calendar reference *Latium digesta per annum* with 1.7 *annalibus eruta priscis*, stressing the origin of the festivals. Miller (1991) 10 and n. 8 raises the question whether O. is implying his own research into the ancient texts (e.g. *Annales Pontificum*) or that of Verrius Flaccus and others (see Introd. 3(i)(*a*)), but the Latin leaves this open: what matters is the emphasis on antiquity: these *sacra* belong to the *prisci.* Cf. Prop. 4.1.69 *sacra diesque canam et cognomina prisca locorum.*

12 lapsaque sub terras ortaque signa cano: for poetic *-que ... -que* linking paired elements, an epic imitation of Homeric τε ... τε, cf. G–L 476 n. 5d. Coupling single words, the idiom neatly facilitates successive dactylic feet; coupling phrases, it provides symmetry in the two halves of the pentameter: cf. *Am.* 1.3.14 *nudaque simplicitas purpureusque pudor*, or the more elaborate arrangement of *Am.* 2.9.50 *gaudiaque ambigua dasque negasque fide.* O. is not speaking of the daily rising and setting of constellations, but of the first occasions on which they are seen to rise (and last occasions of setting) in their annual phases in the morning and evening skies. As in Homer their disappearance is interpreted as if they set into Ocean, below the level of earth. Both manuscripts and early editors are divided between *cano* (U), as in 2.7, and *canam* (A), as in 1.2, but Alton–Wormell–Courtney (henceforward A–W–C) rightly read the continuous present; the poem has now been under way for three books.

13 uenimus: cf. 38. One favoured etymology derived Venus' name from *uenire*, Cic. *ND* 2.69 *quae autem dea ad res omnes ueniret Venerem nostri nominauerunt.* (See *LALE* s.v. *Venus.*)

ad quartum ... mense: the case of *mensis* is attracted into that of the relative clause; A–W–C compare 146 *eo, ... qui locus umet aqua,* and 1.581 *constituitque sibi, quae maxima dicitur, aram,* 2.619 *a tumulis et qui periere propinquis.* Venus will be given public honour both by name of the month and the two festivals, held on the Kalends and 23 April respectively. O.'s last words to Venus assure her of his continued devotion. (There may be conscious play between line 14 and line 2 in which not the poet but the *uultus* receive the expected epithet *tuos.*) What was forestalled in 2 is now granted.

15–16 mota ... leuiter mea tempora myrto | contigit: Venus makes a gesture of benediction, which can be compared with Call. *Aetia* 7.13–14 Pfeiffer where the Muses anoint and inspire the poet. (There is soothing assonance on *m* and *t.*) Noting that the verse-ending *tempora myrto* echoes two passages in which Virgil assigns myrtle to Augustus (*Georg.* 1.28) and Aeneas (*Aen.* 5.72 *materna tempora myrto*), Barchiesi (1994) 48–9 suggests that O. is drawing attention to his appropriation of the trappings of Venus' privileged descendants. More convincing is his suggestion that since *tempora* are the theme and virtual title of O.'s poem both in 1.1 and 4.11 above, O.'s word-play fuses his newly blessed brow with the poem.

Cytheriaca ... myrto: cf. *Am.* 1.1.29 where O. appeals to his Muse to *cingere litorea flauentia tempora myrto.* This was Venus' plant, cf. Virg. *Ecl.* 7.62 *formosae myrtus Veneri* (sc. *gratissima*), and 139, 143, 869 below. In Hesiod's account of the origin of Aphrodite, Venus' Greek counterpart (*Theog.* 191–200, cf. 62, 130nn.) she was born from the sea near Cythera (the island to the immediate SE of the Peloponnese, cf. 286) and is called *Cytherea*; so also Homer, *Od.* 8.288, etc.

Similarly in *Aen.* 1.657 Venus, conceived not as mother, but as goddess of erotic love, is called *Cytherea*, and speaks of Cythera (1.680) as a beloved cult place. Of the two derivative forms, *Cytheriacus* (only here and in *Her.* 7.59–60 *mater Amorum | nuda Cytheriacis edita fertur aquis*) relates directly to Cythera, *Cythereïus* (see 195 below) is an epithet of Aeneas as son of Venus *Cytherea*.

16 'coeptum perfice' ... 'opus: cf. Cupid's order in *Rem.* 40 *'propositum perfice' dixit 'opus.'*

17 sensimus, et subito causae patuere dierum: *causae dierum* recalls *tempora cum causis* of *F.* 1.1, the *aitia*, or historical origins of the Roman celebrations. The order of *subito causae* varies in the MSS. This text prefers the rapid and alliterative *sensimus et subito* (Bömer) to *causae subito* (A) read by A–W–C.

18 dum licet et spirant flamina, nauis eat: O. uses the nautical image for his poetic progress in 2.3 *nunc primum uelis, elegi, maioribus itis*; cf. also 2.863–4 *uenimus in portum libro cum mense peracto. | nauiget hinc alia iam mihi linter aqua.* The image is particularly characteristic of didactic; cf. Virg. *Georg.* 2.39–41 (but the book ends with the alternative, chariot, metaphor), *Georg.* 4.116–17, Ov. *AA* 1.3–8 (both ship and chariot), 1.772, 2.9–10, 3.99–100, 747–8, *Rem.* 811–12. See Harries (1989) 170 and n. 30.

dum licet also accompanies the opening recommendations of *AA* 1.41, 3.61 and *Rem.* 79 (cf. 81). In all three passages the poet focuses on the legitimate time for the lover, not on himself as composer, but O. has already indicated that he is trading on indulgence to his advanced years. Venus has authorized him to continue writing in her honour. He must move ahead while the wind of her favour is behind him.

19–132 The address to Caesar Augustus: naming the month

19–60 In this first and longest part of O.'s discussion of the name *Aprilis* O. addresses *Caesar* (originally Augustus, but equally susceptible of being construed as Germanicus, the addressee of the partially remodelled second edition; cf. 81 below). Here the poet returns to the formal public *Fasti* (the *pictos ... fastos* of 1.11) and claims April as Caesar's because of his (rather than its) *magna imago* and *adoptiua nobilitas.* But the omission of a possessive is diplomatic: both *imago* and *nobilitas* can be associated as much with the glory bestowed on the month by the prince's ancestral descent from Venus as with his own glory. Because O. has attributed the Roman Calendar to Romulus, *pater Iliades* (23; cf. 1.37 *trabeati cura Quirini*) his adaptation of the Julian genealogy will begin before Aeneas and continue through him (37 and 78 below), making him a staging-post between Jupiter and Romulus.

19–20 Si qua . . . pars te . . . tangere debet, | . . . tenearis: two metaphors for affective impact: cf. *Met.* 4.639–40 *seu gloria tangit | te generis magni*. Bömer compares *Her.* 6.113 *si te nobilitas generosaque nomina tangunt*. A more explicit form is *Her.* 8.15 *cura mei si te pia tangit*, cf. *Aen.* 12.932–3 *miseri te si qua parentis | tangere cura potest*. Both use the pathetic indefinite *si qua*, most common in the Ovidian *si qua fides*, *Am.* 1.3.16, 1.8.11, 2.6.51, *Met.* 9.55, etc. Heinsius argued for *quo tenearis* (U) rather than *quod tuearis* (A, printed by A–W–C and Castiglioni–Landi) with the parallel of *Rem.* 150 *da uacuae menti, quo teneatur, opus*. *quod tuearis* is good Ovidian usage elsewhere (e.g. 1.32, 86, 529, 673, etc.), but would mean, not 'something to gaze upon' but 'something to protect', scarcely appropriate here. Note the characteristic insertion of the final relative clause before completion of both line and sentence.

Aprili: originally adjectival with *mensis*, cf. substantival *Quintilis*, 3.149 above, 5.73 *Maio*, 6.88 *Iunius*.

21 magna . . . imagine: reading *imagine* (AGM, with A–W–C and Castiglioni–Landi) rather than *origine* (U), O. is alluding to the wax mask of an honoured ancestor kept in noble Roman families for public display at funerals: but this *imago* must paradoxically be that of a female, and a god, rather than the standard male curule magistrate. Octavian's adoption by Julius Caesar entitled him to all of Julius' ancestry right up to Venus. However, given the poem's preoccupation with *origines* (*aitia*), *origo* would also be highly appropriate: for MS confusion of *origo/imago* Heinsius compares 1.65, where the sense requires *origo*.

22 adoptiua nobilitate: cf. 5.564 *Iuleae nobilitatis auos*. Whether *Caesar* above is understood as Augustus or Germanicus, both princes owed their *nobilitas* as members of the patrician *gens Iulia* to adoption, Octavian by his mother Atia's uncle Julius Caesar, Germanicus by Tiberius, who was himself simultaneously adopted by Augustus in

AD 4. O. uses *adoptiuus* metaphorically at *AA* 2.652 *firmaque adoptiuas arbor habebit opes*.

23 Iliades: Romulus is so called as son of Ilia, descendant (or daughter, according to Cato) of Aeneas, a unique matronymic, which incidentally evokes his Trojan origin. The name is original to O. *Am.* 3.4.39–40 *in qua Martigenae non sunt sine crimine nati | Romulus Iliades Iliadesque Remus* may well be the first usage, since it slips in the abnormal matronymic after an equally conspicuous patronymic: as here and at 3.62 *Iliadae fratres* the name occurs in a Mars-centred context; cf. also 5.565, *Tr.* 4.3.8, quoted at 837–44n., *Met.* 14.781 and 824.

For the impregnation of Ilia (also called Rhea Silvia), by Mars, cf. Enn. *Ann.* fr. 29 Skutsch (where she is unnamed), *F.* 2.598, 3.11–45 (where she is called Silvia), 3.233, and *Am.* 3.6.47–82. Both names are given by Dion. Halic. 1.76.3 and Plut. *Rom.* 3.3. O.'s use of both variants for Romulus' mother in this poem is an unobtrusive mark of his erudition.

longum ... annum: the actual solar year was too long for Romulus to comprehend. Cf. 1.26–38, 3.100–24, where O. notes that Romulus' ten-month year fell far short of the required number of days.

24 auctores rettulit ... suos: most editors prefer *tuos*, the reading of AU, as a continuation of the argument for his imperial reader's concern in 21–2. But O. nowhere calls Mars ancestor of the Julii, and he is moving on to the argument completed in 57 *suos ... parentes*. Thus 25–8 explain that Mars was given the first month, as Romulus' immediate parent (26 *proxima causa*), Venus the second, as his more remote ancestor (27 *gradibus multis*); cf. 1.39 *Martis erat primus mensis, Venerisque secundus*.

25 fero Marti: cf. 3.1 *bellice*, 3.5 *fera bella*, and 3.85–6 *Mars ... uenerandus erat, quia praesidet armis; | arma ferae genti remque decusque dabant*. *fera bella* / *arma* is common in O., cf. 5.556 *hinc fera Gradiuum bella mouere decet*, *Am.* 1.10.19, 2.6.25, etc. *Mars ferus* is found only in *Her.* 7.160. There is no matching epithet for Venus.

26 nascendi: the gerund (governed by *causa*) is more idiomatic than dat. participle *nascenti* (AUGM), retained by Bömer. In other Ovidian passages apparently constructing *causa* with a dative, the dative is ind. obj. of the main verb, e.g. 4.96 *satis causas ... dedit*, *Met.* 10.552, 11.683.

27 gradibus multis ... receptam 'retrieved from many steps back in the family'; *receptam* is read only by A. For *gradus* of degrees of descent, cf. *Met.* 13.143 *totidemque gradus distamus ab illo*, and *F.* 2.622 *generis dinumerare gradus*. But *repertam* (UZ), 'discovered', gives equally good sense. Either verb might seem to place unwanted emphasis on human agency in discovering or re-establishing divine ancestry. But any implication of recent manipulation by the Iulii Caesares is dispelled by the reference in 29 to Romulus' own search for a first ancestor, and the epithet *cognatos deos*. For the recurring MS confusion of these forms, cf. 3.728 *reperta / referta / recepta* and 846 *reperta / recepta*.

29 principiumque sui generis reuolutaque ... | saecula: *principium generis* echoes the genealogy of Aeneas given in *Aen.* 7.219 *ab Ioue principium generis*. For *reuoluere*, which parallels the unrolling of memory or time with the physical unrolling of a ball of yarn, or book-scrolls, cf. 667 below. Literal and metaphorical usages are merged in Statius' description of the Fates rewinding their threads at *Theb.* 7.774 *immites scis nulla reuoluere Parcas | stamina*.

30 cognatos ... deos: compare O.'s claim of *cognatio* between Augustus Caesar and Venus' son Amor, *Am.* 1.2.51 *aspice cognati felicia Caesaris arma*; 3.425–6, apparently relating Caesar as *ortus ab Aenea* to the *cognata numina* of Vesta, is more simply explained by taking *cognata* as 'related to Aeneas'. *adusque* (5 times in O., cf. 3.125) neatly marks both the thoroughness of the search and its goal; all heroic genealogy had to be traced back to the gods.

31–2 Dardanon Electra ... Atlantide natum | ... Electran concubuisse Ioui?: the whole sentence is ironized by *scilicet* (cf. 123 below, 1.29 and 131), since it prompts the reader to realize that no eighth-century Roman could have known the familiar Homeric and Virgilian account of Aeneas' ancestry (*Il.* 20.213–41, *Aen.* 8.134–5 *Dardanus ... | Electra ut Grai perhibent Atlantide cretus*), giving Dardanus as first human ancestor, father of Erichthonius, grandfather of Tros, and great-grandfather of Ilus, who founded the house of Priam, Ganymedes, and Assaracus. (So also Apollodorus, *Bibl.* 3.12.) Assaracus was founder of Aeneas' family through his son Capys and grandson

Anchises. O. returns to the Pleiad Electra in 173, 177 below. Her role as Trojan ancestress is not recorded in Homer, but first attested in Hellanicus. The Greek form *Dardanon* is required to avoid unwanted elision here but, like the other Greek accusatives, *Electran* and (34) *Assaracon*, *Capyn*, is attested in only a few MSS.

concubuisse Ioui?: the verb is regularly applied to the female in sexual union (e.g. 172 below, 5.86), most often in the perf. inf., found 10 times in this position.

34 The descendants of Assaracus (see 123 below): cf. Enn. *Ann.* 28–9 Skutsch *Assaraco natus Capys optimus isque pium ex se | Anchisen generat*, Virg. *Georg.* 3.35–6 *Assaraci proles demissaeque ab Ioue gentis | nomina, Trosque parens* and recurring allusions in the *Aeneid*, 1.284, 6.778 *Romulus, Assaraci quem sanguinis Ilia mater | educet*, 9.259, 9.642–3 (Iulus addressed as *dis genite et geniture deos ... | gente ... Assaraci*).

35 proximus Anchises: cf. *proxima causa* 26 above. O. uses *proximus* for both 'next before' (26 above) and 'next after' as here.

commune parentis | ... nomen: cf. *Aen.* 2.789 *nati ... communis.*

36 non dedignata est: the verb is usually found in litotes (with a negative), cf. *Met.* 13.586, *Ex P.* 2.2.77; it is positive only at *Am.* 1.10.63, *Ex P.* 3.5.31.

37–8 pietas spectata per ignes | sacra patremque ... altera sacra, tulit: *pietas s. p. i.* is also found at *Met.* 14.109, and the play on Anchises as *sacra altera* occurs at *Met.* 13.624 (which may, but need not, precede the composition of this passage). O.'s Dido recalls and rejects the story of Aeneas' shouldering of his father (cf. *Aen.* 2.717–23) in *Her.* 7.79–80 *nec, quae mihi ... iactas, | presserunt umeros sacra paterque tuos*, cf. 107 *pater, pia sarcina nati.*

39 felix aliquando nomen Iuli: *aliquando*, 'at last' (*OLD* s.v. 5, cf. *Met.* 2.391, *Am.* 2.19.43), marks the founder of the *gens Iulia* to which the genealogy had been leading. *Iuli* (from *Iulus*, whom Virgil and Ovid equate with Ascanius) is scanned with vocalic *i* as three syllables: cf. quadrisyllabic *Iuleos* at 124. Both etymology and phrasing are echoes of *Aen.* 1.288 *Iulius, a magno demissum nomen Iulo.* This distich introduces the phase of descent from Iulus to Romulus, O.'s starting-point. The list goes back at least to *Aen.* 6.763–70; cf. O.'s parallel treatment in *Met.* 14.609–21.

These Alban kings were probably absent from Ennius' prehistory (see O. Skutsch, *The Annals of Q. Ennius* (Oxford 1985) 190) but were created by early Roman historians to eke out the centuries between the fall of Troy (1187 BC) and 753, the Varronian dating of the foundation of Rome. Thus Dion. Halic. 1.70–1 credits the dynasty with 432 years of rule over Alba, and Virgil more approximately speaks of three hundred years of the Alban dynasty (*Aen.* 1.272). Augustan poets seem to have felt obliged to incorporate the newly reconstituted Alban king-line into their verse: cf. *Prop.* 3.3.1–4 *uisus eram ... | reges, Alba, tuos, et regum facta tuorum | hiscere.* O.'s list, coming late in the sequence, is enlivened by etymological allusions, many of them playing with Virgilian etymologies (see O'Hara (1996a) 95–102 and n. 354 listing and discussing 41–2, 51–2, 61–2, 85–7). On the Alban tradition see Frazer (1929) III 171–3 (with n. 4).

41–2 Postumus ... qui, quod siluis fuit ortus in altis | Siluius ... uocatus: O. etymologizes one of this mythical figure's two 'speaking' names, Virgil (*Aen.* 6.763–5) the other, alluding to the alternative name Postumus with the etymological phrase *tua postuma proles*. The relative clause is perhaps influenced by Livy 1.3.6 *casu quodam in siluis natum.* In the rival 'Italian' version of the Alban king-line used by Virgil, Postumus was Iulus' Italian half-brother, born to Lavinia after Aeneas' death.

43 Latine ... subit Alba Latinum: cf. *Met.* 14.611–12 *quo satus antiquo tenuit repetita Latinus | nomina cum sceptro. clarus subit Alba Latinum.*

44–6 proximus ... Epytus ... | ille dedit Capyi ... | et tuus est idem, Calpete, factus auus: so too *Met.* 14.613 *Epytus ex illo est, post hunc Capetusque Capysque.* In Anchises' review (*Aen.* 6.767–9) only Silvius, Capys, Numitor and Procas (52 below) are named.

titulis ... tuis: either O. implies the presence of these names in the Alban Fasti, or he is thinking of the *tituli* inscribed by Augustus under the representatives of the Julian line in the *Forum Augustum*. *tuis* ... *tuus* introduce the common device of varying the catalogue with (metrically convenient) apostrophes to Latinus and Calpetus.

45 Capyi repetita uocabula Troiae: *uocabula* is poetic pl. for sing. Besides Aeneas' grandfather (34 above) Virgil includes both a Capys and an Epytus among his Trojans: the Capys of *Aen.* 2.35, Aeneas' contemporary, was presumably the founder of Capua named at *Aen.* 10.145; cf. Coelius Antipater fr. 52 (Peter *HRR*). For *repetita* stressing the sentimental renewal of ancestral names cf. *Met.* 14.611 quoted at 43n.

47–8 Tiberinus ... | dicitur in Tuscae gurgite mersus aquae: according to Varro, *LL* 5.30 the death by drowning of this king gave the river Albula (see 68n.) its new and lasting Roman name. Cf. 2.389–90 *Albula, quem Tiberim mersus Tiberinus in unda | reddidit, Met.* 14.614–16 *Tiberinus ... in Tusci demersus fluminis unda | nomina fecit aquae.* According to Cicero, *ND* 3.52 Tiberinus was the river's correct augural name. Prose writers use the form *Tiberis,* but both Virgil (*Aen.* 8.64) and O. (5.635, 637) apply a third form, the archaizing *Thybris,* to the river god. When Virgil gives the same *aition* of the drowned king, naming both king and river as *Thybris,* the speaker is Evander, and the drowned king must therefore be a prehistoric, not an Alban, figure *a quo post Itali fluuium cognomine Thybrim | diximus* (*Aen.* 8.331–2). (See A. Momigliano, 'Thybris pater', *Terzo contributo* (Rome 1966) 609–37.)

Tuscae ... aquae: cf. *Met.* 14.615 quoted above and 294 below. The north bank of the Tiber was the southern limit of Etruria, hence Hor. *Odes* 1.2.14 *litore Etrusco.*

49–50 iam tamen ... | uiderat 'but not before he had seen'.

Agrippam natum Remulumque nepotem: so also Livy 1.3.9, Dion. Halic. 1.71.2 and the historical tradition. Omitted from Anchises' review in *Aeneid* VI, Agrippa is given as Acrota in *Met.* 14.617–18, and called (younger?) brother of Remulus.

fulmina missa ferunt: as in *Met.* 14.618 *fulmineo periit imitator fulminis ictu,* Remulus is struck by lightning. This seems to be a recurring legend; cf. Livy 1.31.8 on the death of King Tullus Hostilius *tradunt ... ira Iouis sollicitati praua religione fulmine ictum cum domo conflagrasse,* 1.3.9 on Aventinus (51n.) and Virg. *Aen.* 6.585–94 on the death of Salmoneus.

51 uenit Auentinus ... locus unde uocatur, | mons quoque: O. derives the place name (which he takes up again in 67) from the king's burial there, but also implies derivation of his name from (*ad*)*uenire*: these are two of Varro's four etymologies in *LL* 5.43 (see *LALE* 64–5). This reverses O.'s Virgilian model *Aen.* 7.656–60, where Aventinus is born – not buried – *collis Auentini silua.* In Livy 1.3.9 Aventinus dies struck by lightning.

52 tradita regna Procae: for Procas (Livy 1.3.9, Dion. Halic. 1.71.4) cf. *Aen.* 6.767 *Procas, Troianae gloria gentis*; according to Dionysius he reigned 23 years.

53–5 duri Numitor germanus Amuli; | Ilia cum Lauso de Numitore sati: | ense cadit patrui Lausus: Livy 1.3.10 has Amulius expel his elder brother the rightful king, slay his unnamed son, and turn his daughter into a Vestal (cf. 2.383 *Siluia Vestalis*, 3.11). Did O. have a source for the name Lausus? In Dion. Halic. 1.76.2 (who has already reported the death of Mezentius' son Lausus at 1.65.3) the name of Ilia's brother is Aegestus.

55 placet Ilia Marti: since O has already first alluded to, then narrated, Silvia's impregnation by Mars, following the Ennian story in which she was raped in her sleep (3.11–40), he can gloss over the circumstances here.

56 gemino iuncte Quirine Remo: Quirinus is properly only the name given after his death to the deified Romulus (cf. *Aen.* 1.292, *F.* 2.475–512) but partly because of the metrical awkwardness of *Romulus*, whose internal short syllable allows only the voc. (cf. 2.133.) or nom. in dactylic verse, *Quirinus* is often preferred. Cf. *Aen* 1.292 *Remo cum fratre Quirinus*, *F.* 3.41 *crescente Remo, crescente Quirino.*

57–60 These lines serve primarily to recall the starting-point of 23–9 by echoes of word and idea, creating 'ring composition', a typical Ovidian device to frame and articulate units of argument.

58 emeruit ... fidem stresses Romulus' own authority, confirmed by his deification, implying further support for the contemporary claims of the Julian house (59 *secuturi nepotes*).

59 neue ... possent nescire: cf. similar double negatives at 1.45 *ne tamen ignores*, 2.47 *antiqui ne nescius ordinis erres.*

60 tempora dis generis continuata: *tempora* is used of calendar units at 1.27, 3.155. *continuare* denotes juxtaposition in space (e.g. 2. 243, *Ex P.* 4.15.16) or time; cf. 2.53–4 *creduntur spatio distantia longo | tempora bis quini continuasse uiri*, 5.491–2 *haec tria sunt sub eodem tempore festa | inter se nulla continuata die.* O. plays on the same idea in naming the Kalends of April at *AA* 1.405–6 *siue Kalendae | quas Venerem Marti continuasse iuuat.*

With the reference to *dis generis* O. recalls 29 *principium ... generis*, as *suos ... parentes* (57) may recall *auctores ... suos*, if that is the correct reading in 24.

61–84 This new section takes its cue from an etymology deriving *Aprilis* from Greek *aphros* in Aphrodite (full references in Maltby,

LALE 44). This etymology is now accepted by E. Benveniste, *Origines de la formation des noms en indo-européen* (Paris 1935) and Schilling (1954) 178 as coming through the Etruscan by-form *Aphro* (see 62n.). This derivation is implied by the (admittedly lacunose) text of Verrius Flaccus' *Fasti Praenestini* cited here from Degrassi, *Inscr. It.* XIII 2.126–7: *[Aprilis a] V[e]n[ere], quod ea [cum Anchisa iuxta mater fuit Aene]ae, regis [Latinor]um, a quo p(opolus) R(omanus) ortus e[st. Alii ab Ape]ri[li] q[uod]am i[n m]ense, quia fruges flores animaliaque ac maria ac terrae aperiuntur.*

Macr. 1.12.8 shows that the rival derivations were disputed before Varro, who gives the derivation from Aphrodite at *LL* 6.33 *[mensis] secundus, ut Fuluius scribit et Iunius, a Venere, quod ea sit Aphrodite*, but rejects it for the alternative from *aperire*: ... *natam e spumis Venerem, cuius nomen ego antiquis litteris quod nusquam inueni magis puto dictum, quod uer aperit, Aprilem.* Horace too adopts this derivation in *Odes* 4.11.15–16 *mensem Veneris marinae* | ... *Aprilem.*

The next section (85–130) skilfully reconciles the conflicting etymologies by associating the fertilizing or generating function of Venus in spring with the opening of earth and sea: see especially 128–32.

61 Graio sermone notatum: similar Greek etymologies are offered at 1.330 (Agonia from ἀγών), 552 (*malum* as gloss on Cacus), 2.599–600 (Lala glossed as from λαλεῖν). For *Graius*, a poetic equivalent of *Graecus*, cf. Enn. *Ann.* 140 Skutsch *quem perhibent Graium genus aera lingua* 165, 357, Lucretius 1.66, 136, 640, etc., *Aen.* 3.163 *est locus, Hesperiam Grai cognomine dicunt.* Like *nomen* (over 120 instances in *Fasti*) *notare*, 'to mark', 'record' or 'write', is common in this poem because of its concern with naming and recording; cf. 1.8 *quo sit merito quaeque notata dies*, 328 *a pecoris lux est ipsa notata metu.*

62 auguror: elsewhere in O. the verb denotes actual prediction, e.g. *AA* 1.205 *auguror en, uinces.* This, the only instance in the *Fasti*, is hardly a prediction, and must stand for 'I guess'. Characteristically the account is followed by a simpler explanation in the pentameter.

a spumis ... maris: cf. Cic. *ND* 3.59 *Venus ... altera spuma procreata*, distinguishing this Venus from three other versions of her identity. This etymologizing account of Aphrodite's birth from *aphros*, 'sea foam', first appears in Hesiod, *Theog.* 190–200, where the goddess is born from the foam that forms around the severed genitals of Kronos cast into the sea near Cythera, or in other versions Cyprus. (See M. L. West, *Hesiod: Theogony* (Oxford 1966) 212–13.)

63 nec tibi sit mirum: the addressee is probably no longer the dedicatee Caesar of 20, but the generic addressee of didactic; this anticipation of doubt with *mirum, mirari* is common to rhetoric and didactic introducing new or controversial claims: it is most often found in prooemia (cf. Pl. *Aul.* 1 *ne quis miretur qui sim*, Ter. *HT* 1 *ne quoi sit uostrum mirum*, Cic. *Rosc. Am.* 1 *credo uos iudices mirari*, Cic. *Cael.* 1 *si quis ... miretur*, Lucr. 5.748, 799, etc. *quo minus est mirum si*); see 267, 326nn.

64 tellus Graecia maior: word play on the traditional name for Greek Italy, *Magna Graecia*, in favour of Italian pride.

The later books of the *Fasti*, like the last three books of *Metamorphoses*, are filled with westward migration, whether of gods (Aesculapius in *Met.*, Cybele, Ino in *Fasti*) or heroes. In fact O.'s colonizers (except Diomedes) are not associated with Magna Graecia, but with Latium (65–74), central and northern Italy. The tendency to attribute the founding of Italian communities to Homeric heroes, Greek or Trojan, can be traced back to Cato's *Origines* and is probably even older.

65 uenerat Euander: the anaphora of *uenerat* binds 65 to 66 and 73. The choice of pluperfect tense, like the imperfect *iam ... stabant* of 71–2, arouses anticipation. All these comings are subordinated to a still unmentioned event; it will emerge only in 77–8. For the exiled Argive prince Evander, whose story O. has already told in 1.471–542, O.'s readers would look first to *Aen.* 8.51–4, 100, 330–6, and Livy 1.7.8. In Livy as in the *Aeneid* it is the new settler Evander who receives Hercules (here as often called *Alcides* from an ancestor of his mortal foster-father Amphitryon) on his return from Spain with the cattle of Geryon and who helps him inaugurate the *Ara Maxima*. In Dion. Halic. 1.42–4, Evander comes to Italy as part of Hercules' army and Pallas is his grandchild by Hercules and a variously named daughter. (For Evander's role as a founding figure and counterweight to Aeneas in the *Fasti* see Fantham (1992a).)

66 Graius uterque genus: *genus* is acc. of respect, cf. G–L 338.

67–8 hospes ... | clauiger: *clauiger*, an Ovidian coinage, is used either for Gk κορυνήτης (e.g. as epithet of the club-wielding assassin

Periphetes at *Met.* 7.437), or perhaps for βαρυσκίπων as applied to Hercules/Heracles in Call. *Aitia* I, fr 23.19. Hercules' club (*claua*) was proverbial; cf. Varro, *LL* 8.26, and Virgil's saying *ap.* Suet. *Vit. Verg.* 66 *facilius esse Herculi clauam quam Homero uersum subripere* (see *TLL* III 1316.61–4); so 253 below, 1.544, *Met.* 15.284.

At 1.228 O. applies *clauiger* in a different connection, to Janus who carries a *clauis* (key), a usage later applied by Christian writers to St Peter.

68 tanto est Albula pota deo: for *Albula* = Tiber see 47n. The Tiber itself will recall Hercules' visit in 5.645–6 *uenit et Alcides turba comitatus Achiua | Albula, si memini, tunc mihi nomen erat.* The reference to Hercules' drinking the Tiber may be simply a poetic periphrase to affirm his presence, but in view of the legendary thirst motivating his intrusion on the forbidden shrine of Bona Dea in Propertius 4.9, it is quite possible that tradition had included some episode based on his drinking up the Tiber waters. At his coming to the site of Rome Hercules was not yet a god, as O. himself indicates in Carmenta's prophecy at 1.583–4. (These allusions to Evander and Hercules may represent the beginning of the remodelling in late exile evident in 79–84: perhaps all of 63–84 is a later insertion; see 81–2n.)

69–71 dux ... Neritius; testes Laestrygones ... quod adhuc Circes nomina litus habet; | et iam Telegoni: all these allusions relate places in Latium to the wanderings of Odysseus.

Neritius, a Greek epithet of Odysseus derived from Neriton, a mountain in Ithaca (*Od.* 9.21), was subsequently misunderstood by e.g. Virg. *Aen.* 3.271, as referring to an island near by. In *Met.* 13.712, 14.563, it is a synonym for 'Ithacan', or 'belonging to Odysseus'. Formiae in Latium was supposedly founded by his cannibal foes, the Laestrygones (cf. Hor. *Odes* 3.16.34 and the allusion to their king Lamus in 3.17.1) and Tusculum by Telegonus, Odysseus' son by Circe (cf. *F.* 3.92 *factaque Telegoni moenia celsa manu*, Dion. Halic. 4.45.1, Hor. *Odes* 3.29.8). Other legends made Telegonus founder of Praeneste or Caere. In *Aen.* 7.10–24, Aeneas sails past Circe's island (Monte Circeii, near modern Tarracina) on his way from Cumae to the Tiber mouth.

71–2 iam moenia Tiburis udi | stabant: according to Cato's *Origines* fr. 56 *HRR*, and the tradition used by Hor. *Odes* 1.18.2, 2.6.5 and *Aen.* 7.670–2, Tibur was founded by the Argive Catillus, whose three sons were Tiburtus, Catillus and Coras. O. infers the priority of Tibur from the role of its second generation in fighting for the Latins against Aeneas.

73–4 Atridae fatis agitatus Halaesus | ... terra Falisca putat: cf. *Am.* 3.13.32–3 *Agamemnone caeso | et scelus et patrias fugit Halaesus opes.* According to Servius on *Aen.* 7.695 Halaesus was either a bastard son or a follower of Agamemnon. The Falisci of Falerii are an Argive foundation in Cato, *Origines* fr. 47 *HRR*. However, in *Aen.* 7.695 they are commanded by Messapus, while *Agamemnonius ... Halaesus* leads the peoples from wine-producing Campania (7.723–4).

Falerii has family associations for O., whose wife came from there: in *Am.* 3.13 he describes attending one of its rites.

75–6 adice ... suasorem Antenora pacis, | et generum Oeniden, ... Daune, tuum: two more heroes. First, the Trojan Antenor, founder of Padua, mentioned with Aeneas by both Livy 1.1 and Virgil, *Aen.* 1.242–6. Livy groups him with Aeneas as spared by the Greeks *quia pacis reddendaeque Helenae semper auctores fuerant*, but it suited Virgil to omit this aspect of Aeneas' patriotism. The second, Diomedes (*Oenides* = grandson of Oeneus of Calydon), settled in Italy, founding Argyripae (Arpi) in Apulia. He claims Daunus, son of Iapyx, the legendary Apulian king (cf. Hor. *Odes* 3.30.11–12) as his father-in-law in *Met.* 14.458 and 510–11.

77 serus ab Iliacis ... flammis: the dating of Aeneas' coming after Antenor recalls Venus' protests in *Aen.* 1.242–6 that Antenor has already reached Illyria and colonized Italy while Aeneas is struggling in the storm off Carthage. For the flames cf. *Aen.* 2.431 *Iliaci cineres et flamma extrema meorum*, but contrast *F.* 3.29 *ignibus Iliacis* of the fires of Vesta (often called *Iliaca* in the *Fasti*).

78 attulit ... deos: this feature distinguishes Aeneas from the rest of the list: he alone brought his gods with him: thus 77–8 reaffirm the significant details of 37–8. Caesar adopted this image of Aeneas carrying Anchises and the gods from Troy on the reverse of the denarius which features Venus on the obverse (see frontispiece).

79–80 huius erat Solymus ... | a quo Sulmonis moenia nomen habent: the founder of O.'s birthplace Sulmo (81 *patriae ... nostrae*) may have been recorded locally as a companion of Aeneas. There is a tribe of this name, the *Solymoi*, at *Il.* 6.184. But it is perhaps too convenient that this founding figure of Sulmo should have been a loyal comrade of the ancestor of the imperial house. O. is the first surviving witness, and source of the allusion in Silius Italicus 9.70–6. For other allusions to Ovid's homeland cf. 685–6n. and 3.95 *miles Paeligne.*

81–2 This outcry to Germanicus is the only undisputedly late passage in book IV or subsequent books of the *Fasti.* Is it possible that more, perhaps the entire sequence of colonizers, is a later addition? They seem rather intrusive after the broader time-sweep of Romulean genealogy.

Scythico ... solo: cf. *Tr.* 3.12.51, *Ex P.* 1.2.108, for O.'s regular designation of his place of exile in Tomis (modern Romania) as Scythian, though actual Scyths seem to have centred on the Crimea at this period.

83 ergo ego tam longe: *ergo ego* typically introduces indignation at some supposed injustice; cf. *Am.* 1.4.3, 1.7.11, 3.11.9 and Medea's highly rhetorical protests in *Met.* 7.51.

83–4 sed supprime, Musa, querellas; | non tibi sunt maesta sacra canenda lyra: for the discreet political aposiopesis (trading on the supposed improvisation of lyric and elegiac poetry, and blaming the indiscretion on the Muse) cf. Hor. *Odes* 2.1.37–8 *sed ne relictis Musa procax iocis | Ceae retractes munera naeniae*, and 3.3.69–72 *non hoc iocosae conueniet lyrae: | quo Musa tendis? desine peruicax | ... | magna modis tenuare paruis.* But there is a significant change of emphasis: Horace pretends to scold his Muse for touching on sad or serious themes in what is supposedly the light or small-scale genre of lyric. O. argues that his purpose and theme of honouring *sacra* must not be spoiled by the sadness of his poetic voice. It is the voice (here *lyra* as if lyric, not elegiac, poetry) that is at fault.

85–132 Venus, spring, and the opening of the year. In six transitional lines (85–90) O. turns to Venus' claims on April *ab aperto tempore* and a hymn-like enumeration of her services to gods, men and civilization: this aretalogy can be compared with e.g. the hymn to Ceres (401–12), or Tibullus' hymnic praises of Osiris in 1.7. Whether in a hymn proper, addressed to the god, or a narrative hymn, it is typical to emphasize the God's name or pronoun with anaphoric repetition; cf. Enn. *Ann.* fr. 61 Skutsch *tu produxisti nos intra luminis oras*; Lucr. 1.6 *te dea, te fugiunt uenti, te nubila caeli*, an important model for this passage. Stories of civilization too had developed a traditional form, from the Epicurean version of Lucr. 5.900ff. to Hor. *Sat.* 1.3.99–111. Prose and verse authors alike competed to ascribe the formation of civilized communities to *Logos* (Reason or Language, personified Philosophy or Rhetoric), or to culture gods like Ceres and Bacchus (Tibullus' Osiris is an equivalent). But neither Lucretius' hymn to Venus, nor Virgil's adaptation in *Georgics* III go so far as to include among her powers and their praises responsibility for civilization itself: rather they imply a contrast between her role in Nature, and the world of culture. Thus O.'s only precedent for his praise of Venus' *blanda uoluptas* as a civilizing force here is his own condensed prehistory in *AA* 2.467–88, quoted below.

85 Quo non Liuor abit? 'To what extremes does envy not stray?' In support of *abit* (MG) against *adit* (AU) A–W–C cite *Met.* 15.111 *longius inde nefas abiit.* It would be natural for a scribe to change the less common *abit* to *adit* after *quo.*

This text follows A–W–C and other editors, in beginning a new paragraph after the intrusion at 81–4. But although the protest *quo non Liuor abit* obviously relates forward to its own distich, on the envy of Venus, the thematic importance of poetic or critical Livor is so established in O.'s poetry, and in Horace before him (cf. *Odes* 4.3.16 *iam dente minus mordeor inuido, Sat.* 1.4.93–101, *Ep.* 1.19.35–6) that it is natural to continue the association with O.'s personal complaint: this would indirectly ascribe O.'s exile to a new motive – not of course for the Emperor's own decision but for O.'s detractors at court.

For *Liuor* in O.'s earlier work cf. *Am.* 1.15.1 *quid mihi, Liuor edax, ignauos obicis annos?*, 39 *pascitur in uiuis Liuor, post fata quiescit*, and *Rem.* 389–90 *rumpere Liuor edax: magnum iam nomen habemus;* | *maior erit*, ending the personal apologia generally thought to be a late addition. *Liuor* and related words are more common in exile: cf. *Tr.* 4.10.123–4 *nec qui detractat praesentia, Liuor iniquo* | *ullum de nostris dente momordit opus, Ex P.* 3.1.65, 3.3.101, 3.4.73–4 *laedere uiuos* | *Liuor et iniusto carpere dente solet*, and the very late *Ex P.* 4.16, whose coda, starting at 47–8 *ergo summotum patria proscindere, Liuor,* | *desine* links envy with the poet's exile in the same fashion as these lines of *Fasti.*

86 eripuisse uelint: the periphrastic combination of *uelle* with perfect infinitive echoes the language of ancient laws; cf. D. Daube, 'No kissing or else', 222–31 in L. Wallach, ed., *The classical tradition:*

literary and historical studies in honor of Harry Caplan (Ithaca, NY 1966): the hint of legalism here will be realized four lines later, at 90.

87–8 quia uer aperit tunc omnia ... fetaque terra patet: O. recalls here his first (somewhat premature!) salute to spring in 1.151 *omnia tunc florent, tunc est noua temporis aetas*, cf. 159 *tum patitur cultus ager et renouatur aratro*. But in keeping with the stress on *aperire*, explained in 89, the language of growth is replaced by language of openness.

88 frigoris asperitas: an unusual combination; but cf. *Met.* 11.490 *aspera crescit hiems*: a storm, not winter chill. In general *asper* designates what is felt as harsh or rough; cf. 911 *aspera Robigo* (because it hurts the crops), 6.470 *aspera saxa*; cf. also *Met.* 6.76 of rough grindstones.

89 memorant: a typical indefinite 3rd pers. plur. of reported tales and explanations: from *Fasti* compare 2.114, 459, 3.729, 5.384, 6.184, 257, 285, and contrast the specific 2.669 *ut ueteres memorant*, *Met.* 15.325 *quod indigenae memorant*. The same function is performed by *dicitur* in 110.

90 quem Venus iniecta uindicat alma manu: a nicely ironic juxtaposition of 'motherly' Venus (her nurturing qualities are about to be enumerated) and the aggressive legal act of reclaiming stolen goods by seizure; for *manus inicere*, one of O.'s favourite gestures and metaphors, cf. *Am.* 1.4.6, 40, 2.5.30 *iniciam dominas in mea iura manus* (repeated *Her.* 8.16), 3.9.20 (of death, cf. *Tr.* 3.7.35 of old age), *AA* 1.116, *Met.* 13.170. For O.'s use of legal terminology see Kenney (1969) 242–63.

91–2 illa quidem totum dignissima temperat orbem, | illa tenet nullo regna minora deo: for *temperare*, normally used of male control, cf. Hor. *Odes* 1.12.13–16 *parentis* | ... *qui res hominum ac deorum* | *qui mare ac terras uariisque mundum* | *temperat horis*, *Epod.* 16.56, *Epist.* 1.12.13–16. So too O. *Met.* 15.859 of Jupiter, and 869 *quem temperat orbe relicto* of Augustus. (Compare other divine controllers at *Met.* 1.1770, 4.169, 12.94, 580 but not, probably, Maiestas at *F.* 5.25 where the variant *quae mundum temperat omnem* may be interpolated in recall of this passage.) *regna tenere*, while less striking, evokes the threefold partition of the universe between Jupiter, Neptune and Hades. Venus superimposes her claims to these at *Met.* 5.368–72. But Venus' rule is through animal life, and her embodiment of sexuality.

92 tenet nullo regna minora deo: a 'compendious comparison' for the logically correct *minora nullo ullius dei regno*; cf. Kenney on *Her.* 18.69 citing *Am.* 1.8.25, *AA* 3.106, etc., K–S II 566–7, H–S 826. Venus' dominion is compared with the threefold partition of the universe.

93–4 iuraque dat ... | perque suos initus continet omne genus: again *iura dare* is the role of a ruler, but *per ... suos initus* recalls Lucr. 1.12–13 *aeriae primum uolucres te diua, tuumque | significant initum* and 19–20 *omnibus incutiens blandum ... amorem | efficis ut cupide generatim saecla propagent* (cf. also Lucr. 1.159–64 on the reproduction of *omne genus*). Venus both propagates and controls, hence the negative-sounding *continet.*

natalibus undis: another reminder of Aphrodite's birth (see 15, 61–2, 131) from the sea.

95–6 illa deos omnes ... creauit, | illa satis causas arboribusque dedit: O. recalls Lucretius' argument that without the first law of reproduction (nothing can come from nothing) beasts and plants would reproduce at random: 1.165–6 *nec fructus idem arboribus constare solerent | sed mutarentur.* Thus Venus stands for more than sexual fertility; she represents natural heredity, and the reference to *sata* ('agricultural crops') like *pecudes* ('domestic animals') touches on human interest in ordered reproduction. This is also implied by the stress on correct partners in 98.

97–8 illa ... docuit iungi cum pare quemque sua: this variation on his earlier prehistory at *AA* 2.473–80, esp. 477, 479–80 *blanda truces animos fertur mollisse uoluptas | ... ipsi nullo didicere ministro; | arte Venus nulla dulce peregit opus*, imitates the argument but not the language of Lucr. 5.962–5.

The argument of 95–8 expands on O.'s representation of normal reproductivity at 3.193–4, cited to protest at the Sabine denial of marriage rights to the first Romans: *cum pare quaeque suo coeunt uolucresque feraeque | atque aliquam, de qua procreet, anguis habet.*

99 quid genus omne creat uolucrum nisi blanda uoluptas?: for the argument compare Lucr. 1.12–13 and *AA* 2.477 (cited 93–4, 97–8nn.). Is there an attempt at a new derivation of *uolucris*? O.'s *blanda uoluptas* goes back to Lucretius (2.966, 4.1263, 5.178) recalling the initial *uoluptas* and *blandus ... amor* of Lucr. 1.2 and 1.19.

100 nec coeant pecudes: not the *ferae pecudes* of Lucr. 1.14, but as in the expanded *armenta atque aliae pecudes* of 1.163, the focus is now on domesticated flocks whose reproduction sustains man with food. So Virgil's pastoral Georgic rephrases Lucretius to introduce the passion of animal reproductivity as a factor (or hazard?) in stock-breeding: 3.242–4 *omne adeo genus in terris hominumque ferarumque | et genus aequoreum, pecudes pictaeque uolucres, | in furias ignemque ruunt.*

leuis ... amor 'easy' as in *Am.* 1.2.10 *leue onus*, or *Met.* 10.698 *poena leuis*, not 'fickle' as *leuis* is used of love in *AA* 2.19 and *Her.* 3.42 *quo leuis a nobis tam cito fugit amor?*

101–6 Sexual desire as a civilizing force in animal life. The antithesis between *Mars ferus* (25 above) and Venus as a source of peaceful coexistence is brought out through the three instances of ram, bull, and by way of humorous surprise, fish. (Are they associated by their role as signs of the Zodiac?) The combative aspects of bulls and to a lesser extent rams were proverbial (cf. the much imitated description of the battle of the bulls for the *formosa iuuenca* in *Georg.* 3.219–36). O. likes to assimilate the sexuality of men and beasts: thus the praise of sex as conciliator of creatures and men in *AA* 2.467–86 culminates in *laeta salitur ouis, tauro quoque laeta iuuenca est; | sustinet immundum sima capella marem*: he appeals constantly (but inconsistently) to analogies from the sexual behaviour of animals: cf. *Met.* 9.732–4 (Myrrha), *Am.* 1.10.27–8, 2.12.25–6 *uidi ego pro niuea pugnantes coniuge tauros: | spectatrix animos ipsa iuuenca dabat.* Both *trux* (of *tauri* at *Met.* 8.297, 9.81, *Her.* 4.166, of boars and he-goats, *Met.* 10.715, *AA* 3.193) and *feritas* (e.g. of wolves, *Met.* 1.239, *Tr.* 5.7.46) are regularly applied to animals (especially males) to contrast them with human gentleness.

102 dilectae: the poet is transfusing into the tamed animal the quality he is recommending in humans; *diligere* properly denotes only human affection (even the bird of *Met.* 7.467 has just been transformed from a human gold-digger).

103 deposita ... feritate: both words recall the warfare associated with *Mars ferus*, invited at 3.1 to listen *depositis clipeo ... et hasta.*

106 innumeris piscibus implet aquas: O. turns away from sex as civilizer to sex as propagator, supplying the sea with fish. In *Met.* 1.74 this is attributed to the *deus* who creates the world.

107–14 Venus as first teacher of grooming: a reprise of the poet's stress in *AA* 3.101–28 on the link between courtship and cultural refinement.

107 prima: *primus* is characteristic of aretalogies, litanies that praise the gods by recording their inventions and cultural benefactions to mankind, e.g. Tib. 1.7.29, 31 *primus* ... *Osiris* | ... | *primus*, *Georg.* 1.147, Ov. *Met.* 5.341, see also 401n. O. then transfers this laudatory motif in 109 to the human inventor, inspired by the goddess.

feros habitus . . . detraxit 'stripped off their uncouth habits'. Is *habitus* here 'conditions', 'behaviour' (*OLD* 1.2) or more specifically 'clothing' (*OLD* 3), as elsewhere in O.? The Horatian precedent of *Odes.* 1.10.2 *feros cultus hominum* and O.'s own movement to *cultus* in 108 might suggest that he wants to evoke both the narrower and wider sense, gliding from the predictable allusion to culture into a more personal association with the *bella figura* and even erotic nakedness.

109–12 The lover is the inventor of poetry, and also of persuasive eloquence: the *carmen uigilatum*, a παρακλαυσίθυρον, the laborious artistic product of a night waiting at the beloved's door, for which cf. Propertius 1.16, Tib.1.6, Ov. *Am.* 1.6.

109 uigilatum: O. uses *uigilare* both with the night (cf. 167 below, *AA* 1.735 and *Her.* 12.169) as acc. of duration, and subject of the passive verb, and with the product of wakefulness as direct object, cf. *AA* 2.285 *uigilatum carmen in ipsas* (where the girls are the target of the vigil spent in composition), *Tr.* 2.11 *pretium curae uigilatorumque laborum.*

nocte negata: for *negare* of the inhospitable beloved cf. Prop. 2.14.20, Tib. 1.6.7, Ov. *Am.* 2.19.20; for *nox* as direct object, *Am.* 1.8.73 *saepe nega noctes.*

111 duram exorare puellam: so the first aim of the lover who has found a girl to pursue in *AA* 1.37 is *placitam exorare puellam.* For *durae* ... *puellae* cf. *AA* 2.527, and for *eloquium*, the necessary alternative to *eloquentia* in dactylic verse, cf. *Aen.* 11.383, *AA* 1.462 *tam dabit eloquio uicta puella manus*, Luc. 7.62–3 *Romani maximus auctor* | *Tullius eloquii.* Eloquence was an elite professional skill; hence the claim here that need will make the lover *disertus*, and conversely the mockery of the serious professional *disertus* rendered helpless by love and forced to plead his own case in *AA* 1.85–6.

113 mille per hanc artes motae: O. implicitly denies the Virgilian account in *Georg.* 1.133–45 of the evolution of *artes* as a result of Jupiter's creation of agricultural need.

114 latuere ... reperta correspond to *inuentum* in *Georg.* 1.140.

115–16 hanc quisquam titulo mensis spoliare secundi | audeat?: this reformulation of 85 leads to a transitional couplet 117–18 recapitulating the claims of Julian Venus (119–24) and her association with the fertility of spring (125–32).

115 mensis ... secundi: the Roman year originally began in March; cf. 1.39.

116 a nobis sit furor iste procul: *procul* is characteristic of apotropaic wishes, such as Cat. 63.92 *procul a mea tuus sit furor omnis, era, domo*, *Am.* 1.14.29 *uim procul hinc remoue*, and 41 *procul omen abesto*, *AA* 2.107 *sit procul omne nefas* (see 365–6, 763nn.).

117–18 ubique potens ... | urbe tamen nostra ius dea maius habet?: Venus, *potens* in the Greek οἰκουμένη as Aphrodite, power of love, has a different claim on Rome, through her role as ancestress, but in the amatory elegies O. combines this claim with her erotic patronage: cf. *Am.* 1.8.42 *Venus Aeneae regnat in urbe sui*, and the variation of *AA* 1.60 *mater in Aeneae constitit urbe sui.*

templisque frequentibus aucta: despite Aphrodite's many temples in the Greek cities of Sicily and Italy, Venus had no temple in Rome before that dedicated by Fabius Gurges to Venus Obsequens in 295 BC; this was followed by Fabius Maximus' dedication to Venus Erycina on the Capitol, 217 BC; another to Erycina *ad portam Collinam* of uncertain date (see 871n.); a temple to Venus Verticordia in 114 BC (see 159n.); Pompey's temple and theatre complex honouring Venus Victrix, 55 BC; and Caesar's temple of Venus Genetrix, completed by Octavian in the Forum Julium. (Cf. Koch s.v. *Venus*, *RE* XVIII 828–9; on the cult in general see 137n.)

urbe ... nostra: ablative of place where, without preposition. Cf. G–L 285 n. 1: even in prose the preposition can be omitted when the noun is qualified by an adjective. Poets in quest of compactness substitute case inflections for prepositions whenever possible.

119–24 Three links between Venus and Rome's mother city of Troy.

119–20 pro Troia ... arma ferebat, | cum gemuit: Homer depicts Venus' unheroic groans when she intervened in battle against the Greeks to save Aeneas and was lightly wounded in the lower arm (cf. *Met.* 14.477–8 *memores de uulnere poenas* | *exigit alma Venus*).

tua (abl.) reaffirms Rome's descent from Troy.

120 teneram ... laesa manum: acc. of the part affected, a subclass of the Greek acc. of respect (see 66n.): *tener* conveys male sentiment or condescension to the unwarlike goddess.

121–2 caelestesque duas ... uicit | (a ... deas!): the judgement of Paris rewarded by Venus with Helen was hardly a service to Troy; and O.'s expression of regret *nolim uictas ... meminisse deas* shows that he is aware of the harm her victory caused (cf. 6.99–100 *perierunt iudice formae* | *Pergama: plus laedunt, quam iuuat una, duae*). Nevertheless the role of this couplet must be to reinforce the notion of the old alliance between Venus and Rome's forebears.

123–4 Assaracique nurus dicta est, ut ... | magnus Iuleos Caesar haberet auos: the name of Assaracus recalls 34–6, and Anchises, son of Assaracus, with whom Venus conceived Aeneas. What is the point of *dicta est*? Simply to evoke the fame of the legend? Hardly to hint at the illegitimacy of the union (cf. *Tr.* 2.261–2, arguing that the inquiring *matrona* might be shocked by Venus' adulterous role as *Aeneadum genetrix*). Ostensibly O. implies that Venus sacrificed her dignity (cf. 36 *non dedignata est*) if not her honour, on behalf of Troy and in the service of Rome and her great leader. *Iuleos* (scanned as a quadrisyllable ⏑ – – –) is an Ovidian coinage; cf. 5.564 *Iuleae nobilitatis*, 6.797 *Iuleis ... Kalendis*, *Ex P.* 2.5.49.

magnus ... Caesar: uncommon in poetry, but quoted and then restricted in Prop. 2.7.5 *'at magnus Caesar': sed magnus Caesar in armis*. This is apparently the first instance in O., cf. 859 below and from his exile poetry e.g. *Tr.* 1.2.3, 2.230, *Ex P.* 1.8.24.

125–32 The praise of spring as Venus' season: O. reverts to the promise implicit in his Lucretian *alma ... Venus* and his preference for spring expressed at 1.149–50 *nouus ...* | *annus qui melius per uer incipiendus erat*. The triple anaphora of *uer* 125–6 (intensifying the anaphoras of successive distichs at 91, 95, 97 and 107, 109) is resumed in 131 after further anaphora of *nunc* at 127–8; cf. *Georg.* 2.323–4 *uer adeo frondi nemorum, uer utile siluis,* | *uere tument terrae et genitalia semina poscunt*.

126–8 uere nitent terrae, uere remissus ager; | nunc herbae rupta tellure cacumina tollunt, | nunc ... gemmas

cortice palmes agit: the paired anaphoras should not be subordinated by A–W–C's unnecessary parenthesis. This picture of spring bursting out all over, the thawed land sprouting grass and the vine shooting, rewrites *Georg.* 2.330–5 *parturit almus ager* ... | *laxant arua sinus* ... | *inque nouos soles audent se gramina tuto* | *credere, nec metuit* ... *pampinus Austros* | ... *sed trudit gemmas et frondes explicat omnes.* This is O.'s third variation on the theme of spring growth in *Fasti*; cf. 1.152 *et noua de grauido palmite gemma tumet,* 154 *prodit et in summum seminis herba solum* and 3.238 *uuidaque in tenero palmite gemma tumet.* For similar language of the spring release of growth cf. Hor. *Odes* 4.7.1–4, 4.12.3.

nitent: not usually found with *terrae,* but cf. 430 *flore nitebat humus,* and the variant reading at *Met.* 15.202–3 *herba nitens* ... | *turget* of Glaucus' magic grasses.

cacumina adapts the technical use of *cacumen* for the growing tip of plants, less common than e.g. *cacumina siluae* (2.439, 3.329); cf. 398, 912nn.

129 formosa Venus formoso tempore: the figured repetition (*polyptoton*) of *formosus* takes over from anaphora. In fact the application to *tempore* of *formosus* (derived from *forma* and so appropriate to finely formed animals, shapely boys, men and women, and naturally to Venus, *Ecl.* 7.62 *formosae myrtus Veneri*) is the novel element in the verse.

130 utque solet, Marti continuata suo est: with *tempore* (129) the pentameter recalls the opening of the section at 60 *tempora dis generis continuata,* varying the construction. There *continuare* had as object the time, here the goddess herself, and O.'s *ut solet* gives her proximity to Mars a hint of their adultery. Barchiesi (1994) 51 compares *Tr.* 2.295 *stat Venus Vltori iuncta, uir ante fores* in which O. points to the improper interpretation that could be given to the divine pair in the cella of the temple of Mars Ultor (noted but dismissed by Zanker (1988) 195–200).

131–2 uere monet curuas ... puppes | ire: for inf. instead of subjunctive of ind. command, cf. G–L 423 n. 2.

materna per aequora: 61–2, 93n.; as the medium in which the semen of Kronos gave birth to the goddess the sea is equated with her mother.

132 hibernas ... timuisse minas: cf. *minas frigoris* 700n. The perf. infin. here has no time value and is an extension of the common usage with *posse*, *uelle*: dactylic forms are favoured in this position in the pentameter (32, 110nn.).

133–64 1 April C KAL F The Veneralia

Following Merkel's practice this text inserts before each entry the calendar date: first the nundinal day (C), then the lunar holy day where applicable (KAL), and finally the status (F = Fastus).

To understand this unusually compressed and composite passage we need to consider first (briefly) the development of the cult of Venus at Rome up to Ovid's day, secondly the actual calendar entry for the Veneralia, which would have been a point of departure for Ovid, and finally O.'s artistic motives and procedures in adapting the rituals to his poem.

(1) It is clear that Venus had an ancient origin as one of the *numina* or natural powers, revered by Rome and Latium, but the earliest Greek-style cult associating Venus with the sexual powers of Aphrodite dates back only to 295 BC, when the Aedile Q. Fabius Gurges used fines for immorality exacted from some married women to dedicate a shrine to Venus Obsequens. Because books XI–XX of Livy covering 290–220 BC are lost, the first evidence of her worship at Rome comes in 217 when another Fabius, Fabius Maximus, imported the cult of Aphrodite from Eryx in Sicily and vowed the temple of Venus Erycina on the Capitol. By this time Venus had clearly taken on her character from the many Aphrodite cults of Magna Graecia and Campania. By 217, too, Venus is paired with Mars as 5th and 6th of the twelve gods honoured in Rome's first Greek-style *lectisternium*. It is not clear whether the first cult honour to Venus Verticordia (see 155–62n.) preceded or followed shortly after 217. For subsequent temples honouring various aspects of Venus see 117–18n., and on the full history of her cult in Rome up to O.'s time K. Koch s.v. 'Venus', *RE* XVIII 828–87, H. Wagenvoort, 'The origin of the goddess Venus', 166–96 in *Pietas: selected studies in Roman religion* (Leiden 1980), and (with reservations) Schilling (1954).

(2) In recording the Veneralia itself, the *Fasti Praenestini* of Verrius Flaccus, O.'s principal source for the calendar, reads: *frequenter mulieres supplicant Fortunae Virili; humiliores etiam in balineis quod in iis ea*

parte corporis utique uiri nudantur qua feminarum gratia desideratur (*CIL* I 2.235), but most scholars have been persuaded by Mommsen's arguments that reference to Venus Verticordia and the cult acts of elite women has dropped out; they have adopted his supplement and repunctuation as it is now read in Degrassi (1963) 126–7 *frequenter mulieres supplicant ⟨honestiores Veneri Verticordiae⟩, Fortunae Virili humiliores, etiam in balineis*. It is certainly difficult to imagine a calendar entry for the Veneralia without some reference to the cult of Venus, but the chiasmus produced seems too sophisticated for the style of a calendar notice, while the appendix *etiam in balineis* is less awkward qualifying the simple *humiliores* than an antithetical unit which is already subordinated.

(3) We come to O.'s own treatment, and his motives for selection and presentation. Scholars of Roman religion have been baffled by his blending in this passage of an otherwise unattested ceremony of washing the goddess's image in the running water of the river (135–8) with two, perhaps three, separate ritual practices: bathing garlanded in myrtle; offering incense to Fortuna Virilis in the baths (139–54); and supplicating to Venus Verticordia (155–62). These rituals honouring more than one deity may well have been observed in different places; from the evidence of the *Fasti Praenestini* quoted above it has usually been assumed that lower-class women, and/or those ineligible for marriage (*quis uittae longaque uestis abest*), were excluded from the cult of Verticordia, while married women (*matresque nurusque*) would not take part in the sexually directed cult of Fortuna Virilis.

Ovid mentions only one location, the baths, and after his comprehensive address to women of all classes, deliberately does not distinguish the separate groups in his combined instructions and description of the cult acts. He is apparently blurring the fine social distinctions of place and performer in order to include the working women and courtesans of Rome. The reason for this becomes apparent later, from reading O.'s account of the Vinalia of 23 April (4.863–76), for in this second cult of Venus it is the turn of the *uulgares puellae* to pray to Venus (Erycina) for sexual charm.

Within book IV, the Vinalia and its *aition* (863–900) symmetrically correspond to 133–60, the composite account of the Veneralia. (See also Fauth (1978) 153–6.)

133–4 Rite ... colitis makes two points. Within this section it confirms the legitimacy of both types of women (*matresque nurusque | et uos*, etc.) sharing in the ritual – an exception to most female cults. But it also creates another deliberate symmetry between the opening phases of March and April (cf. Braun (1981) 2347). In the entry for the matrons' cult of the *Matronalia* on 1 March Mars answers the poet's query 3.170 *matronae cur tua festa colunt?* with an *aition* ending *rite colunt matres sacra diemque meum* (3.234). For the formula cf. Val. Max. 1.8.11, where Minerva addresses the women who have dedicated her image: *rite me, matronae dedistis, riteque dedicastis.*

matresque nurusque: while the two groups can simply be construed as two generations, the older mothers of adult couples and the newer brides, the very recent allusion to Venus as *Assaraci nurus* (123) and the return in 161 to *Aeneadae* and their wives as *tuas ... nurus* suggest an assimilation of the Roman wives to the goddess. These women would wear the long, fringed *stola* and the headbands, *uittae*, as marks of their respectability (cf. *AA.* 1.31–2 *este procul, uittae tenues, insigne pudoris, | quaeque tegis medios instita longa pedes*, quoted in exculpation of O.'s guilty *Ars* at *Tr.* 2.247–8). The fact that women without respectable status are also included in the poet's opening address can either be construed as including both groups in each successive ritual, or more conventionally imply the role of elite wives in the main rituals, while subordinating the working women's offering to Fortuna Virilis (145–9).

135–8 The bathing of the image. There is no other evidence for this ritual at Rome, but public calendars would normally include only ceremonies supervised by magistrates; a purely female ritual of this kind, like the *lauatio* of Cybele described in 337–40 below, would not find a place in the official records. There are cult parallels for such ritual washing in the bathing of the statue of Hera at Argos (for which Frazer cites Pausanius 2.38.2), and the Roman ritual seems to have been provoked by O.'s desire to adapt Call. *H.* 5, the *Loutra Pallados.* Like O.'s narrative, the hymn is the sole and unsupported evidence for the bathing of this particular cult image (see Introd. 3(i) (*c*), *RE* VIIIA s.v. *lauatio* 857.28–9). Clearly only a few women could participate in undressing the goddess, bathing her and giving her new adornments of necklaces and flowers: but given the allusion to *matres* and *nurus* in 133, Floratos (*Hermes* 88 (1960) 197–216) cannot be right in arguing that this is a group of unwedded girls; it also seems unlikely that the same group is addressed throughout and conceived as participating in all three rituals at 139 and 144, at 145–6 *discite* ... *quare* ... | *detis*, and again in 155.

135 aurea marmoreo redimicula demite collo: there is play on colour, play on the contrasting but unrelated forms *demite* and *redimicula* (from *redimire*, not *redimere*; cf. *redimite* in 661 below) and play on the symmetrical form of the imperatives and the epithet *siccato* (itself compressing the whole action of drying the image). Finally the anaphora of *nunc alii, nunc noua* in 138 echoes the repetition of 135 in 137. Floratos (*Hermes* 88 (1960) 213–14) compares Callimachus' exhortation to the women tending Pallas in *H.* 5.1–4 and 13–32, but O. has improved on Callimachus, composing a far more compressed and patterned vignette. He repeats the common elements of the ritual action and its reversal, like a stage direction, at the beginning of successive couplets. (For the same device cf. the tying and untying of Cybele's boat in 331 and 333 below.) This may well imitate the repetition from one hexameter to the next in Call. *H.* 5.13 and 15 'Go, Achaean women, and do not bring myrrh or perfume flasks ... do not, ritual washers, bring Pallas myrrh or perfume flasks.' But the Greek verbal echo is a reiteration, not a reversal.

marmoreo: more likely to denote the pale (white?) colour of the statue, than its material. The most venerable statues were wooden ξόανα and marble was rare in Rome before the age of Augustus: for *marmoreus* = 'pale', cf. *Am.* 2.11.15 *litora marmoreis pedibus signate puellae*, and *Met.* 3.481 *nudaque marmoreis percussit pectora palmis*.

136 demite diuitias: anadiplosis and assonance intensify the tone of urgency. This is the only instance of *diuitiae* in *Fasti*: except in the exile poems, the word is usually metaphorical of natural abundance.

138 nunc alii flores, nunc noua danda rosa est: internal rhyme is created by *danda* with *lauanda* in 136. For the offering of flowers, see 869–70n. listing Venus' myrtle (omitted here, but prominent in 139), mint, and roses woven on a base of reeds.

139 sub uiridi myrto: if there are few parallels for this use of *sub* it may be because myrtle foliage offers little cover. Carna in 6.125 is caught *sub rupe latentem*, and O. has many women hiding (unsuccessfully) in woods and thickets: Echo, *Met.* 3.393–4 *spreta latet siluis, pudibundaque frondibus ora* | *protegit* (cf. 400), or Oenone, *Her.* 5.135 (see 142n.).

lauari: this single word is the link between the ritual bathing of the goddess, which would require a running stream, and the periphrastically described *frigidarium* of 147. Just as *myrto* here blurs the distinction between garlands or cut stems and the living shrubs of 143, so O. blurs the distinction between natural and artificial waters.

140–4 The *aition*: both *causa* ... *certa* and *discite* in 140 (cf. 145) announce the approach of an *aition*; cf. 17, 26, 96, 368 *an sua causa subest?*, 681–708n.; *causa* ... *subest* again at 5.350, 6.266. O. varies between direct and indirect use of *discere*: the imperative is addressed to the poet by divine informants at 1.101, 133, 2.584, 3.177 and 436, but like the women here other figures are instructed in direct speech or indirect forms.

141 litore siccabat rorantes nuda capillos: cf. *Met.* 2.12 *pars in mole sedens uirides siccare capillos. siccare* forms another link with the preceding vignette. Bömer suggests that O.'s anecdote is designed to explain the famous pose of Apelles' Venus *anadyomene* in the painting which Augustus put on display in the temple of divine Julius (Pliny, *NH* 35.91). She was shown covering herself as she emerges from the water. *rorare*, to be wet with *ros*, 'dew' (1.375 *ora* ... *rorantia*, *Met.* 1.267 *rorent pennaeque sinusque*, 5.488 *rorantesque comas*), is transitive (= 'to bedew') at 5.679 *spargit et ipse suos lauro rorante capillos.*

142 turba proterua: compare the very similar episode reported by Oenone, in *Her.* 5.135–6 *me satyri celeres (siluis ego tecta latebam) | quaesierunt rapido, turba proterua, pede.* Helen in *Her.* 17.27 and 77 calls Paris and his eyes *proteruus.*

143 opposita texit sua corpora myrto: for *opponere* of covering one's eyes, cf. 3.46, 596, 4.178 below, 6.614. Of covering one's body, *AA* 2.583–4 *non uultus texisse suos, non denique possunt | partibus obscenis opposuisse manus*, 3.731–2 *surgit et oppositas agitato corpore frondes | mouit.*

corpora: poetic plural (cf. 159n.) as often in O.; cf. *Am.* 2.10.24 *pondere, non neruis corpora nostra carent*, or *Met.* 2.663 *in equam cognataque corpora uertor*, 8.256 *non tamen haec alte uolucris sua corpora tollit*, 416, 871, 10.128 *fessus in herbosa mouit sua corpora terra.*

144 uosque referre iubet: the worshippers are invited to reenact (*referre*) the experience of the deity. With *iubet* O. rounds off the tale that began *cur iubeat, discite.* For another tale of Venus in flight and attempting concealment, see 2.459–72.

145–6 discite nunc quare Fortunae tura Virili | detis eo,

gelida qui locus umet aqua: the antecedent *locus* has been attracted into the case of the relative clause. The next explanation (not a mythological *aition*) concerns a new deity, and an offering that, according to Verrius' *Fasti Praenestini*, was made in the baths only by the *humiliores*. Some commentators refer to the baths as the men's baths, thus increasing the atmosphere of impropriety, but a recent article (R. B. Ward, 'Women in Roman baths', *Harvard Theological Review* 85 (1992) 125–47) shows that women usually had separate bath-suites in O.'s time (cf. Vitr. 5.10.1, Varro, *LL* 9.68 *unum ubi uiri, alterum ubi mulieres lauarentur*). This is supported by the archaeological remains of separate women's suites in two second-century BC Pompeian baths and the contemporary baths at Stabiae. In the first century of our era, when baths began to be designed with only one, elaborate, suite, there is literary evidence for simultaneous bathing by both sexes. There may also have been regular times of day when women who wished to bathe apart were admitted.

Given the motive and secular setting of the offering, it does seem more likely that O. is describing an optional ritual by those whose livelihood depended on appealing to men: such women were never far from O.'s thoughts. Line 146 combines a tasteful avoidance of the prosaic word *balneae* and a hint at the paradox of kindling incense or anything in a damp place.

147 posito uelamine: *uelamen* is both an Ovidian coinage and a favourite, especially in this ablative absolute (2.379, *Met.* 3.192, 10.578, *Am.* 1.5.17). Cf. also 2.169 *uelamina ponunt* and *AA* 2.613–14 *ipsa Venus pubem, quotiens uelamina ponit, | protegitur laeua semireducta manu.* The logic of the offering appears to be that Fortuna Virilis can only help women conceal blemishes which are shown to the deity (*uitium ... omne uidet*), therefore the offerings must be made in the baths. The explanation offered by the *Fasti Praenestini* ('because there the part of the man's body is bared which desires the charm of women') seems absurd.

149–50 ut tegat ... celetque uiros ... | praestat: *praestare* typically refers to providing a service in some sense owed; cf. *Met.* 7.336–7 *si pietas ulla ... | officium praestate patri*, *Met.* 14.170–1 *nec umquam | esse satis potero, praestem licet omnia, gratus*, 631 *sucos alieno praestat alumno* (a paradox). Construction with dependent clause is rare in O., cf. *Her.* 18.90, *Ex P.* 3.1.65, both with *ne*-clauses. *celare* with acc. of the person kept in the dark is common at all times in Latin. Note the verbal rounding-off of the episode with *Fortuna Virilis* and *ture* echoing the introductory *Fortunae tura uirili* of 145.

151–2 nec pigeat ... | sumere: a standard didactic substitute for the simple imperative *sumite*; cf. *AA* 1.621. O. returns to a mythological *aition*, from Venus' marriage (to Vulcan). Again the worshippers re-enact the behaviour of the deity, this time by consuming poppy seed pounded in milk and honey (*tritum ... cum lacte papauer*). Poppy seed is more commonly associated with Demeter (cf. 547n., Call. *H.* 6.42, Theocr. 7.157, Virg. *Georg.* 1.212). Bömer cites Eitrem (1915) 102 and 480 for the Greek offering, without Roman parallel and suggests the soporific may be assigned to Verticordia because of her equivalence with Aphrodite *Apostrophia*, in turn associated with Demeter *Erinys*. Schilling (1995) II 111 comparing the Roman *cocetum* of poppy and honey (Paul. *Fest.* 35 Lindsay) thinks a new bride might need a sedative rather than a stimulant.

152 expressis mella liquata fauis: *exprimere* can take as object either the liquid squeezed out (as here and e.g. *AA* 1.82, *Met.* 12.438) or the substance containing the liquid (Venus' hair at *AA* 3.224). *liquata* is found only here in O.

153–4 cum primum cupido ... est deducta marito, | hoc bibit: the language is epithalamial; cf. Cat. 64.374 *dedatur cupido iamdudum nupta marito*) or 61.55–6 *cupida ... aure maritus*, Ov. fr. 8.7 = *Priapeum* 3 *quod uirgo prima cupido dat nocte marito*, and [Tib.] 3.4.31 *ut iuueni primum uirgo deducta marito*. Hence Bömer's suggestion that O. has in mind Venus' union with Mars, not her less happy marriage to Vulcan. But Vulcan too is naturally *cupidus* of such a bride, cf. *Aen.* 8.388–90. For *deducere* of escorting the bride to the groom's house or bed, cf. 3.689.

154 ex illo tempore nupta fuit: *ex illo tempore* marks the *aition* as at 5.44. It is implied that the ritual drink ensured consummation and the married state.

155–62 The cult of Venus Verticordia. With 155 *supplicibus uerbis illam placate* as with each new imperative, O. moves on to another ritual. This certainly, if not also 151–4, concerns Verticordia, who can preserve beauty and also virtue and reputation, the natural concerns of the *matronae* with whom the section opened. More is known about Verticordia than O. tells us. Her cult was inaugurated in the period of or just before the Hannibalic wars, with an image dedicated by Sulpicia, daughter of Ser. Paterculus and wife of the consul Fulvius Flaccus, chosen for her purity from a hundred selected ladies (cf. Val. Max. 8.15.12); but Verticordia had no temple until the crisis caused by the incest alleged to have been committed by three Vestals in 114 BC. According to Plut. *Qu. Rom.* 83, this occasioned the last human sacrifices at Rome, but was also remedied on the advice of the Sibylline books (cf. 158n.) by the dedication of a temple to Venus 'changer of hearts' on the Capitol. Without actually using the name *Verticordia* (the isolated inner short syllable excludes it from dactylic poetry) O. supplies it through its etymology: *inde Venus uerso nomina corde tenet.* The cult statue is depicted on a denarius of Cordius Rufus from 46 BC (Crawford, *RRC* 463a; see frontispiece). She holds a pair of scales and a sceptre and is attended by Cupid.

157 Roma pudicitia proauorum tempore lapsa est 'Rome fell from chastity in the time of our great-grandfathers.' Here the lapse is set four generations back: usually chastity and purity are seen as qualities of the remote past. Even elegists bewail the loss of *pudicitia*; cf. Prop. 1.2.24, or 16.2 for the *pudicitia* of past heroines. In his exile O. looks to Livia to remedy the moral decline: *Ex P.* 3.1.115–18 *quae praestat uirtute sua, ne prisca uetustas | laude pudicitiae saecula nostra premat: | quae Veneris formam, mores Iunonis habendo | sola est caelesti digna reperta toro* (cf. *Ex P.* 4.13.29).

proauorum: here fairly accurate for a lapse of 110–20 years, but usually simply denoting remote ancestry; cf. O.'s own boast to be *usque a proauis uetus ordinis heres* at *Am.* 3.15.5, *Tr.* 4.10.7.

158 Cumaeam ... anum: not the Sibyl herself, but the collection of prophesies ascribed to her; cf. Livy, *Per.* 63, Obsequens 37, and 259 below.

160 uerso... corde: this abl. abs. surely relates to Venus' own heart. Thus the poet derives the title of Verticordia, not from Venus' power to turn wanton hearts back to chastity, but from her own renewed favour towards the Romans.

nomina: a poetic extension of licence from the semantically justified plurals *corpora*, *pectora* etc., on which see 143n.

161–2 semper ... placido ... uultu | respice ... tuere: a typical Ovidian invocation or farewell, whether to imperial future gods (Germanicus, 1.3 *excipe pacato ... uultu*; Augustus, 2.17–18 *placido* *paulum mea munera uultu | respice*) or Olympians like Bacchus; cf. 3.789 *mite caput, pater, huc placataque cornua uertas*. Venus is to look with favour upon the descendants of Aeneas, and watch or guard (word-play on *tuas/tuere*) the new brides – if only against their own weakness.

diua: despite the careful distinction by which deified mortals were called *diui* rather than *di*, *diuus*, *diua* are used for Olympians; e.g. Prop. 2.2.13 (Juno, Pallas, Venus), 2.14.27 (Venus), Hor. *Odes* 1.35.1 (Fortuna), *CS* 17 (Eileithuia).

163–4 Dum loquor ... | Scorpios ... praecipitatur: the rising of Scorpio was noted at 3.712 (16 March) and the constellation will be noted as again visible in the sky on 6 May (5.417, introducing O.'s tale of the catasterism of Orion when he saved Hera from the Scorpion sent by Earth).

dum loquor is a common Ovidian device for closing a theme, cf. *Am.* 1.11.15, 3.2.41, 3.6.85, *Tr.* 1.4.3 and the extreme case *Tr.* 1.2.34 *dumque loquor uultus obruit unda meos*.

elatae metuendus acumine caudae: the scorpion raises its tail to sting; cf. Lucilius 1022–3 Marx *scorpios cauda | sublata*, *F.* 5.541–2 *fuit impetus illi | curua ... spicula ferre deae*.

uirides ... aquas: the waters of Ocean into which the stars were supposed to set, except for the Great Bear; cf. *Georg.* 1.246 *Arctos Oceani metuentes aequore tingi* and *Met.* 2.530. For the epithet cf. *AA* 2.92 *clauserunt uirides ora loquentis aquae*.

165–78 2 April D F

The fourth nundinal day, *fastus* for courts. A vivid description of the early dawn introduces an astronomical notice on the rising of the Pleiades, the stars named after the seven daughters of Atlas. 'Seven are they in the songs of men, albeit only six are visible to the eyes,... small and dim are they all alike, but widely famed they wheel in heaven at morn and eventide, by the will of Zeus who bade them tell of the beginning of summer and of winter and of the coming of the ploughing time' (Aratus, *Phaen.* 257–8, 264–7). O. exploits the mythological relationships of the seven sisters (as reported by e.g. Apollodorus, *Bibl.* 3.10) to explain why one cannot be seen.

165 Nox ubi transierit: cf. 2.639. But O. constantly varies his time indicators: contrast 3.399 *tertia nox de mense suos ubi mouerit ortus*.

Variation on recurring markers like dusk and dawn was common to poetry and rhetoric, cf. Quint. 8.6.60 *ornatum ... qui est apud poetas frequentissimus*, Sen. *Ep.* 122.11 on Julius Montanus' addiction to them, and the parody in Sen. *Apocol.* 2.

165–6 caelumque rubescere primo | coeperit: for the verb cf. *Met.* 3.600–1 *aurora rubescere primo | coeperat.* Since *rubescere* is inceptive the use of *coepisse* here is an unnecessary intensifier.

tactae rore querentur aues: here too a standard line-ending (*Am.* 3.1.4 *queruntur aues*, *Her.* 10.8, 15.152) is varied with a unique detail, *tactae rore*; for dew as symbol of the new day cf. 1.312, 3.880.

167–8 semustamque facem uigilata nocte uiator | ponet: travellers used torches by night unless there was moonlight; cf. 2.500 *lunaque fulgebat, nec facis usus erat*, Prop. 3.16.15–16 *luna ministrat iter, demonstrant astra salebras, | ipse Amor accensas percutit ante faces.* For discarding the torch, cf. the simile of *Met.* 1.493–4 *ut facibus saepes ardent, quas forte uiator | ... iam sub luce relinquit.* On *uigilata nocte* see 109n.

ad solitum rusticus ibit opus: *Am.* 1.13, the poet-lover's reproach to the dawn goddess, lists the same signs – birdsong (8), the traveller (13) and the farmer's hoes and plough oxen (15–16).

169 Pliades incipient umeros releuare paternos: according to Hesiod, *Theog.* 517, Atlas the father of the Pleiades (*caelifero Atlante* 5.83) bore the sky on his head and arms (for other versions see M. West ad loc.). The constellation, one of the first to be identified, was used by farmers as an indicator of the seasons, cf. Hesiod, *Erga* 383 and 619, Virg. *Georg.* 1.138, 221 (Atlantides) and *F.* 3.105 *Pliadas Atlanteas.*

171 seu quod in amplexum ... hinc uenere: *hinc* (cf. 37n.) takes the place of the phrase *ex his. amplexus* is more often plural in this idiom; cf. *Rem.* 668 *uenit in amplexus*, and *AA* 1.770 *ire in amplexus*, 3.732, *Her.* 17.96, *Met.* 11.228 and 459. Six lines, 171–6, offer O.'s first explanation for the hidden sister. O. groups the sisters' unions with the gods, giving priority to the partner of Romulus' ancestor Mars (cf. 55n), then the two with whom Neptune slept, and Jupiter's three partners. Maia is honoured at 5.85–6 *quarum Maia suas forma superasse sorores | traditur et summo concubuisse Ioui*, as mother of Mercury and a contender for explaining the name of the month. Taygete is unimportant, but Electra has already been twice named (cf. 31–2) as ancestress of Aeneas and the Trojan dynasty.

175–6 septima mortali . . . nupsit; | . . . facti sola pudore latet: Merope, wife of King Sisyphus of Corinth, is here named as the sole Atlantid to marry a mortal, but according to Apollodorus, *Bibl.* 3.10 Sterope married King Oenomaus. *paenitet* itself suggests only regret at a missed opportunity, and colours what might otherwise seem genuine shame. Since she alone has conformed to traditional (and Augustan) morality, this *pudor* at correct behaviour is revealed as snobbery, rating an important lover over a lesser husband. It may indirectly cast a shadow over Venus' union with a mortal, Anchises, and out of wedlock at that (see 35–6).

177–8 siue quod Electra: *siue* returns the exegesis to *seu* in 171.

non tulit 'she could not bear it', a favourite phrase especially in this *sedes*, introducing a new step in the action; cf. *Met.* 1.753, 2.628, 3.487, 6.134, 8.437, etc.

opposuitque manum: the postponed enclitic follows a quadrisyllable in the second half of the pentameter at 200, 254, 354, etc. It is the most common type of postponement: see *LEV* 91. A less common pattern puts the enclitic after a monosyllable as in 610 *longa uixque refecta mora est.* The *aition* of Electra's mourning is also found in a Scholiast on Homer, *Il.* 18.486, who explains the streaming tail of a comet as Electra's hair pulled over her face to cover her grief for Troy. The motif enables O. to bring his theme neatly back to Troy.

179–372 (3 April E C) 4 April F C The Megalensia

This is the sixth day, F, of the nundinal sequence, and *C(omitialis)*, available for meetings of the *comitia.*

Ludi M(atri) D(eum) M(agnae) I(daeae). Megalesia uocantur, quod ea dea Megale appellatur. Nobilium mutitationes cenarum solitae sunt frequenter fieri, quod Mater Magna ex libris Sibullinis arcessita locum mutauit ex Phrygia Romam (*Fasti Praenestini*, Degrassi (1963) 126–7). O.'s account of the Megalensia opens with a description of the Great Mother's exotic procession and offers aetiological myths, before narrating her coming to Rome. The elite dinner parties (*mutitationes*) are postponed to 353–4.

179–80 Ter sine . . . uersetur in axe, | ter iungat . . . terque resoluat equos: O. marks the passing of three (in our reckoning two) days, from 2 to 4 April. The triple anaphora and magical associations of 'three times saying three' (see Clausen on *Ecl.* 8.72, Gow on Theocr. 2.43) add solemnity.

Syntactically O. could have conveyed the same meaning with the simple jussive *uersetur*, but the imperative *sine* (here only in *Fasti*, but cf. *AA* 2.555 *sine ... tegantur*, also addressed to the reader) involves the reader in observing the rotation of the heaven (179) and the voyage of the sun-chariot. With *uersari* here cf. Virg. *Aen.* 2.250 *uertitur interea caelum et ruit Oceano nox*; in Greek and Roman poetry the sky is usually equated with its axis, and both treated as static, but O. himself combines the notion of the sun-chariot's journey with that of the revolving firmament, and plays upon their contrary motion at *Met.* 2.70–5 *adde, quod adsidua rapitur uertigine caelum | sideraque alta trahit celerique uolumine torquet. | nitor in aduersum, ... | ... et rapido contrarius euehor orbi | ... poterisne rotatis | obuius ire polis, ne te citus auferat axis?*

180 Titan: a common Ovidian antonym for the Sun, as son of the Titan Hyperion, cf. *Met.* 1.10 *nullus adhuc mundo praebebat lumina Titan*, and for the yoking of his horses at dawn and their unyoking when they reach the Ocean and end of their journey at dusk, *Met.* 2.118 *iungere equos Titan uelocibus imperat horis*, *F.* 2.73–4 *Hesperias Titan abiturus in undas | ... cum iuga demet equis.*

181–6 The approach of Cybele's procession. O.'s introduction selects four elements from the *pompa*, the procession of the goddess through Rome: the music of the curved Phrygian double pipes (182); the castrated Galli beating their drums and brass cymbals (183–4); the image of the goddess born on a bier on their shoulders (185); and the wailing or howling (of the Galli). O.'s closest model was Lucretius' famous description of the Great Mother's procession (2.600ff.), especially 618–21 *tympana tenta tonant palmis et cymbala circum | concaua, raucisonoque minantur cornua cantu, | et Phrygio stimulat numero caua tibia mentis | telaque praeportant uiolenti signa furoris.* Most recently Summers (1996) 342–51, writing on the Lucretian account, argues that the *pompa* was a Roman feature without Greek precedent. Other elements in this passage influenced by Lucretius are the *aition* for the Curetes (Lucr. 2.629–39, see 210n.) and the collecting of alms (350–1n.) described in Lucr. 2.626–8 *aere atque argento sternunt iter omne uiarum | largifica stipe ditantes ninguntque rosarum | floribus umbrantes Matrem comitumque cateruas.*

Passing over Cybele's imposing and bountiful appearance as described in Lucr. 2.624–5 and Virg. *Aen.* 6.784–7 *qualis Berecyntia mater | inuehitur curru Phrygias turrita per urbes | laeta deum partu, centum complexa nepotes*, O. stresses the alien aspects of her cult, opening with the barbaric music as a signal or fanfare for her festival (*protinus inflexo ... tibia cornu flabit et ... festa ... erunt*). Far from offering a silent benediction (Lucr. 2.625 *munificat tacita ... salute*), the goddess is *exululata*, and the stage resounds invitingly.

For the importation of Cybele's cult to Rome, see 255–349n. On O.'s presentation see Littlewood (1981) 381–95, Miller (1991) 82–90, and Summers (1996) 337–66.

181 inflexo Berecyntia tibia cornu 'the Berecyntian pipe with its curving horn': cf. also O.'s references to the pipe in Dionysiac revels at *Met.* 11.16 *infracto Berecyntia tibia cornu*, 3.533–4, 537 *aerane tantum | aere repulsa ... adunco tibia cornu | ... obscenique greges et inania tympana uincant?*, and 4.391–3 *tympana cum subito non apparentia raucis | obstrepuere sonis et adunco tibia cornu | tinnulaque aera sonant.* The habitual distinction made by Roman poets between *cornu* and *tibia* is misleading (cf. C. Daremberg and E. Saglio, *Dictionnaire des antiquités grecques et romaines* (Paris 1874). I 312 s.v. *tibia*). The Phrygian pipes were a double instrument with a small straight recorder-like treble (*tibia*), and an elongated bass (*cornu*) curved at the bottom like a bass clarinet or saxophone. The bass had a hollow or hoarse sound, its function was accompaniment rather than melody. The Romans describe the music of Dionysus and Cybele in the same terms, apparently unable or unwilling to distinguish one kind of oriental music from another: cf. with Lucr. 2.618–19 (cited above 181–6n.) the similar descriptions of the music of Cybele at Cat. 63.21–4 (cited below on 183–4) and of Bacchus in Cat. 64.261–4. (O. differs from Lucretius in omitting the Etruscan semicircular *cornua*. On the difference between Greek and Roman instruments associated with Cybele see now Summers (1996) 358–60.)

Berecyntia is also an epithet of the goddess; cf. *Aen.* 6.789, *Aen.* 9.619–20 *buxus ... Berecyntia matris | Idaeae*, and 355 below.

182 Idaeae ... parentis: cf. Aeneas' prayer at *Aen.* 10.252 *alma parens Idaea deum*, and *Aen.* 9.619–20 *matris | Idaeae.* Cybele is known in the public *Fasti* as *Magna Deum Mater Idaea*, from her association with Mt Ida in Phrygia, an aspect developed in Virgil's association of Aeneas with the goddess and her sacred mountain (on Cybele in Virgil see Wiseman (1985) 117–28).

183 semimares: the castrated Galli. This cult practice associated with Phrygia gave rise to many abusive terms like *Aen.* 4.215 *semiuiro comitatu.* O. uses both *semimas* and *semiuir* for those rendered effeminate (cf. *Met.* 4.381 *semimas*, followed by 386 *semiuir* in the same sense). The eunuch Bagoas in *Am.* 2.3 is *nec uir nec femina* (1). But both terms have other references. *semimas* denotes a castrated sheep at *F.* 1.588, a cowardly warrior at *Met.* 12.506. In contrast *semiuir* is applied to half-human hybrids like centaurs (5.380, *Her.* 9.141), and the Minotaur (*AA* 2.24 *semiuirumque bouem semibouemque uirum*). In general O. prefers the more sensual *mollis* for these eunuchs, cf. 185, 243, 342 below.

183–4 inania tympana tundent, | aeraque tinnitus aere repulsa dabunt: alliterative variations on *Met.* 3.533 and 537 quoted at 181–6n. above. For the metallic clash of *tinnitus* cf. Cat. 64.262 *aut tereti tenues tinnitus aere ciebant.*

185 ipsa sedens: the goddess is imagined seated in her throne carried on the shoulders of the Galli, like the *pompa frequens caelestibus ... eburnis* (the parade of gods in the Circus) of *AA* 1.147, or a saint in a modern procession. As Scullard (1981) 99–100 and Summers (1996) 343 note, the Goddess seated in her chariot drawn by lions was probably a composite representation conveyed on a bier or litter. (For illustrations see Vermaseren (1977) pl. 46, a Pompeian fresco; L. Budde and R. Nicholls, *Catalogue of Greek and Roman sculpture in the Fitzwilliam Museum* (Cambridge 1964) 77 (no. 125) and pl. 41, the Fitzwilliam altar.)

186 exululata: while *ululare* and *ululatus* are used of lament (*Met.* 3.725, 4.404), animal and ghostly howls (*Met.* 1.233, *F.* 2.553), and Bacchic revelling (*Met.* 3.528, 11.17), *exululare* seems to be the *vox propria* for the cries of the Galli: cf. 341 *exululant*, *AA.* 1.507–8 *quorum Cybeleia mater | concinitur Phrygiis exululata modis.* (*Tr.* 4.1.42 *stupet Idaeis exululata modis*, in spite of its parallel form, must be deponent, not passive.) Here there is stress on the incongruity of such sounds in the ordered city of Rome.

187 scaena sonat, ludique uocant: spectate, Quirites: the three brisk cola of the announcement dramatize the activities of the holiday. For 4 April was not just the Megalensia, it was the first of six days of *Ludi Megalenses*, in the form of *ludi scaenici*, comedy and tragedy. O.'s proclamation to his fellow-citizens (on the supposed origin of the name *Quirites* see 805 below) will be repeated for the games in honour of Mars (5.597) and offerings to Fortuna (6.775). At *Am.* 3.2.73 *reuocate, Quirites*, the address to the Circus crowd is a poetic fantasy.

188 fora . . . litigiosa uacent: the day was *comitialis* (see Introd. 3(i)(*a*)), available for public meetings and assemblies, but closed to legal actions in the Praetor's courts; for similar language on the opening day of the civil year, cf. 1.73–4 *lite uacent aures, insanaque protinus absint | iurgia.* Only the court *de ui*, because of its role in handling emergencies, continued to function during the Megalensia (cf. Cic. *Cael.* 1–2) and other *feriae.* April was a month of holidays; not only were there no regular *dies fasti* for the lawcourts, but the 4th is the last *dies comitialis* until the 24th. So Romulus' people were free to be spectators.

litigiosa: cf. *Rem.* 670; O.'s epithets for the *fora* are usually negative, because parental pressure to become an advocate had made him hostile to the courts: cf. *Am.* 1.15.6 *ingrato uocem prostituisse foro. Tr.* 3.12.17–18 echoes this passage in celebrating the conflicts of the courts abandoned for the Games of this spring season: *otia nunc istic, iunctisque ex ordine ludis | cedunt uerbosi garrula bella fori.*

189–91 quaerere multa libet . . . 'da dea, quem sciter: the vocabulary of research (*quaerere*, *scitari*, *docta*, even *adesse*, often used of jurisconsults) establishes O.'s serious credentials as antiquarian and didactic poet. This scene reverses the expectations of readers who have followed his prolonged interview with Janus in 1.89–288, or the briefer dialogue with Mars at 3.167–258. Instead of interviewing the goddess, O. makes a pretext of the noise around her to seek a private consultation.

189–90 sonus aeris acuti | . . . et . . . lotos adunca: cymbals and pipes are denoted by their materials, a standard metonymy. With *aeris acuti* cf. *Met.* 6.589 *sonat Rhodope tinnitibus aeris acuti. lotos* is also found at *Rem.* 753 *eneruant animos citharae lotosque lyraeque*, where Henderson explains it as a kind of pipe made from the Libyan nettle-tree (*Celtis australis*, cf. Theophr. *HP* 4.3.4). The metonymy occurs in Eur. *El.* 716, *Hel.* 170, etc. but O. is first to adopt it into

Latin, as he uses *buxum* ('boxwood') for pipes at 6.697, etc. See Pliny, *NH* 16.172 *nunc sacrificae* [sc. *tibiae*] *Tuscorum e buxo, ludicrae uero e loto ossibusque asininis et argento fiunt*, and R. Meiggs, *Trees and timber in the ancient world* (Oxford 1982) 282 n. 5 and 426. *adunca* = 'curved around': see 181n. on *inflexo.*

terret et horrendo ... sono: Summers (1996) 340 notes Lucretius' similar stress on the fear generated by the clashing weapons at 2.623–4 *pectora uulgi* | *conterrere metu quae possint*, and strange dress, 2.632 *terrificas ... cristas.* The repetition of *sonus* with each instrument is emphatic. For *horrendus* of sound, cf. *M.* 3.38 *horrenda ... sibila*, and *F.* 6.140 *horrenda stridere.*

191 quem sciter: O. has no other instance of *scitari* with acc. of the person interrogated but cf. *Aen.* 2.114–15 *scitatum oracula Phoebi* | *mittimus.* Elsewhere in O. the verb is used either intransitively (*Met.* 2.548, expressing the person with *ab* + abl. in 1.775, 10.357) or with the information sought as direct object (*Met.* 2.511 and 741, 4.793); that is, it is usually constructed by analogy with *quaerere*, but here with *rogare.*

Cybeleïa: the adjectival form (cf. *AA* 1.507 *Cybeleia mater*, *Ibis* 451) associates Cybele with the mountain *Cybelus*/*Cybele* (mentioned as a cult site at 249 below); cf. Diod. 3.58.1–2, Strabo 12.5.3, Festus p. 45 Lindsay s.v. *Cybele.*

doctas ... neptes: the Muses, as daughters of Cybele's son Zeus and Mnemosyne. Here as in the *aition* of 197–214 and e.g. *Aen.* 6.784–7, *F.* 6.321, Cybele is equated with Rhea, mother of the gods.

192 curae ... adesse meae: *adesse* (here 'attend to' rather than the usual sense of 'favour', 'support') is more common with a personal indirect object, but cf. 3.834 *studiis adsit amica meis*, 6.652 *ades o coeptis ... meis*, *Met.* 3.613 *nostrisque laboribus adsis.*

193–4 pandite ... Heliconis alumnae, | gaudeat ... cur dea Magna: since he is addressing the Muses O. adopts the traditional formal diction of epic poets appealing to the Muses for special knowledge, e.g. Virg. *Aen.* 7.641, 10.163 *pandite nunc Helicona, deae, cantusque mouete.* In contrast with Virgil, O. uses *pandere* both here and in *Met.* 15.622–3 *pandite nunc Musae, praesentia numina uatum* | *(scitis enim) ... unde ...* not transitively, but to introduce an indirect question. Helicon is identified at *Met.* 5.254 *uirgineumque Helicona*, by its connection with the Muses (5.268 *Mnemonidas*) as daughters of

Mnemosyne (Memory). Thus *mandati memores* plays on their mother's name. Here *mandatum* is indefinite, 'whatever has been entrusted to you', rather than the usual legalistic substantive 'commission', or 'errand'.

cur introduces the *aition* of 197–214, an epic narrative more suited to the solemn phrasing than the inquiry might suggest. Cf. 2.303 *cur praecipue fugiat uelamina Faunus* and other requests introducing *aitia* at 219, 353, 342.

195–6 Erato ... quod teneri nomen Amoris habet: *nomen amoris* recalls Apollonius' reference to Erato's 'lovely (ἐπήρατον) name' when he invokes her to introduce the second half of the *Argonautica*, concerned with Medea's love for Jason (*Arg.* 3.5). The allusion is more obviously appropriate in *AA* 2.15–16 *nunc mihi ... puer et Cytherea, fauete, | nunc Erato, nam tu nomen Amoris habes*. The use of *tener* here implies the personified *Eros*/Cupid (cf. *Am.* 3.15.1 *tenerorum ... Amorum*). Although Virgil appeals to Erato for aid in *Aen.* 7.37, Erato is otherwise rare in Augustan poetry.

mensis Cythereïus illi | cessit 'Venus' month passed into her care' (for *Cythereius*, 'pertaining to Venus of Cythera', see 15n.): *cessit* (cf. *OLD* s.v. 15) alludes to the transfer of property or control to another party. Like the three Muses who will speak at 5.9–106, Erato answers only the specific questions put to her.

197–214 The *aition* for Cybele's enjoyment of noisy music. O. has already twice (1.236, 3.796) introduced into the *Fasti* a later stage in the power struggle between Saturn (Kronos) and Jupiter, that is the expulsion of Saturn; he will return to the rearing of Jupiter (Zeus) in 5.111–28 to celebrate the rising of the Goat-star Olenia, and her broken horn (the original horn of plenty). There he describes how the infant Jupiter was suckled by the she-goat when he was hidden by the nymph Amalthea (sometimes equated with the she-goat) on Mt Ida in Crete. This *aition* goes back to the original Hesiodic account (*Theog.* 459–91), in which Kronos resolved to kill his male children in order not to be dethroned by his son, but his wife Rhea's deception ensured the infant Zeus's survival. The story is retold in detail in Call. *Hymn to Zeus*, and more briefly in Aratus and Apollonius. Among Roman poets it was Lucretius who explicitly associated the presence of Curetes in the procession of the Magna Mater with their role in concealing the infant Jupiter from Saturn: 2.633–4,

638–9 *Dictaeos referunt Curetas qui Iouis illum | uagitum in Creta quondam occultasse feruntur, | . . . ne Saturnus eum malis mandaret adeptus | aeternumque daret matri sub pectore uulnus.* In this and the succeeding *aition*, however, O. jars the reader with a series of stylistic and moral dissonances designed to make the cruelty of the old myths disturbing. (I owe this observation to Edward Gutting.)

197 reddita . . . sors haec erat: O. turns the indefinite verb πεύθετο, 'he discovered', in Hesiod, *Theog.* 463 into an oracular reply. Nothing is told of Kronos in myth to justify the compliment *optime regum* (for which cf. *Aen.* 11.353, addressed to Latinus). But his Italian counterpart, Saturnus, was the original 'good king', cf. 1.193–4, 235–7 based on the tradition in Tib. 1.3.35 *quam bene uiuebant Saturno rege* (with Murgatroyd ad loc.), Virg. *Aen.* 8.319–25, Ov. *Am.* 3.8.35–42. Here the address conflicts with Kronos' subsequent behaviour.

198 sceptris excutiere: cf. *Aen.* 7.299 *patria excussos.* Both there and here *excuti* is a more drastic synonym for *expelli*; cf. 1.238, 3.796 *Saturnus regnis ab Ioue pulsus erat.* The verb is standard for being thrown from a chariot (so *AA* 3.468, *Med. fac.* 42, *Ibis* 576) or ship (*Met.* 3.627). A father's futile attempt to avert the prophecy that his son (grandson) will supplant him is common to many hero-myths, such as that of Pelias and Jason, Acrisius and Perseus, or even Laius and Oedipus, Astyages and Cyrus; there are also variants like the warning to Zeus that any son of Thetis would be stronger than his father.

199–200 suam metuens, ut quaeque erat edita, prolem | deuorat: cf. Hesiod, *Theog.* 459–60. *suam . . . prolem* is object of both *metuens* and *deuorat.* (*quaeque* reflects the gender of the noun *proles*, not the sex of the children. In the early myth only male children were devoured, and a female, Hera, even assisted Rhea in deceiving her father.)

immersam uisceribusque tenet: Bömer mistakenly claims this as the first such use of *immergere* = 'devour'. But cf. *Met.* 14.203–4 *iam nunc mea uiscera rebar | in sua mersurum*, and *Met.* 6.664 *egerere inde dapes immersaque uiscera gestit*, of Tereus who has unknowingly swallowed the son Itys served to him by his vengeful wife as a meal. Like 664, 651 *uescitur inque suam sua uiscera congerit aluum* exploits the double sense of *uiscera* as 'flesh' and 'child' (as in 'killing his own flesh and blood'). For shock effect O. also uses *uiscera* in contexts of child murder (*Met.* 8.478, *Rem.* 59) and incest (*Met.* 10.465).

tenet: a necessary part of the myth, for in due course Kronos was forced to regurgitate the children he had swallowed and they returned to life.

201–2 Rhea . . . totiens fecunda nec umquam | mater: the name Rhea (as used repeatedly in Callimachus' *Hymn to Zeus*) occurs only here in O. As mother of the gods, *Magna Mater* is equated with the wife of Kronos (elsewhere Ge, Gaia). The enjambment emphasizes the paradox of childlessness, in spite of fertility.

indoluit fertilitate: although *fertilitas* is not found elsewhere in O. of human or anthropomorphic beings, the theme of human infertility is important in the *Fasti.* (Cf. 2.421–52, 3.243–58.) Rhea–Cybele's grief and resentment imitate Hesiod, *Theog.* 467 Ῥέην δ' ἔχε πένθος ἄλαστον. For *indolescere* (a medical term brought into poetry by O.) cf. 509n. *Met.* 4.173, *Tr.* 2.570, *Ex P.* 2.5.8. O. often marks a new narrative phase with an emotional reaction expressed by the perfect of an inceptive verb; cf. 2.377 *risit et indoluit,* 3.197 *indolui,* 3.201 *intumuere Cures.*

203–4 pro magno teste uetustas | creditur; acceptam parce mouere fidem: for the claim of *uetustas* as witness cf. *Met.* 1.400 *quis hoc credat nisi sit pro teste uetustas?* Like Virgil's *prisca fides facto, sed fama perennis* (*Aen.* 9.79) the appeal to antiquity as witness precedes a miraculous tale. It was all the more necessary as O. himself elsewhere appeals to the practice of disbelieving poets: *Am.* 3.12.19 *nec tamen ut testes mos est audire poetas.* But it is a generic feature of *Fasti,* imitating Callimachean aetiological didactic (ἀμάρτυρον οὐδὲν ἀείδω, fr. 442 Pfeiffer) to cite even places as witness to the events narrated, cf. 69, 344, *F.* 2.273 *testis erit Pholoe, testis Stymphalidos undae,* 3.707 *testes estote Philippi!,* 6.765.

parce mouere: for *parcere* with inf. in strong prohibitions cf. 6.621 *parcite, matronae, uetitas attingere uestes, Met.* 10.545 *parce meo, iuuenis, temerarius esse periclo,* 15.75 and 174, etc. Horace has similar prohibitions with *fuge, parce,* etc. *mouere* is often used of provoking reactions (e.g. Cic. *Brut.* 144 *suspicionem*), but here exceptionally it is used for negative *amouere*; *TLL* VI 683.69 explains this phrase by glossing *acceptam fidem* as *famam cui fides habenda est.*

205 ueste latens saxum caelesti gutture sedit: cf. Hesiod,

Theog. 485–8. O. incorporates plot and fulfilment in one sentence, abandoning Kronos in his well earned plight: readers must assume Kronos realized that he had only swallowed a stone wrapped in swaddling clothes and began searching for the new infant. If the reading *sedit* in the MSS is correct it must mean 'stuck', 'settled' (*OLD* s.v. *sedeo* 9), but there is good cause (cf. A–W–C in ap. crit.) to read *sidit*, 'sank' (*OLD* s.v. *sido* 3). See also 297–304n.

206 fatis decipiendus: probably dat. of agent. The syntax allows us to construe the Fates as either conscious agents or impersonal instruments; necessity overrode the will of the gods concerned.

207 ardua . . . resonat tinnitibus Ide: with assonance on *r*, *d* and *t*, *a* and *i*. Picking up *tinnitus* from 184, O. reverses narrative order, from the clashing back to the weapons used as noise-makers, then back to the agents. This Ida is the Cretan mountain, associated with Rhea and the concealment of Zeus (cf. Call. *H.* 1.50, Aratus, *Phaen.* 33, *F.* 5.115–16, etc.) just as Phrygian Ida was with Cybele. The confusion of names recurs in the treatment of the Curetes and Corybantes (210n.). Hesiod takes Rhea to Lyktos in Crete to give birth, but does not include the role of the Kouretes, though a disconnected fragment (123, cited by Strabo) refers to them in the same context.

208 infanti . . . ore: literally 'unable to speak', 'with a baby's inarticulate noise'. *uagire* is the *vox propria* for a crying child, cf. 2.405, 6.146 *at puer infelix uagit opemque petit*, Lucr. 2.634 (cited 197–214n.). Denis Feeney suggests (*per litteras*) that *puer* is an interlingual pun evoking the *kouros* who produces the baby-cries (κουρίζοντος, Call. *H.* 1.4).

209 pars clipeos sudibus, galeas pars tundit inanes: the cymbals of the contemporary ritual echoed noise created by the warriors striking their weapons (*sudes*, 'wooden stakes', as attested by Lact. *ID* 1.21.40, cf. Prop. 4.1.28, rather than *rudes*, 'practice blades', a correction in G and M) and beating on their convex shields or helmets as they danced a war-dance (the Pyrrhic, called *Prulis* in Call. *H.* 1.52.

210 hoc Curetes habent, hoc Corybantes opus: O.'s wording evades the question which body, the Cretan *Curetes*, or Asiatic

Corybantes, performed this service for Jupiter. Callimachus too has both (*H.* 1.45, 51). Aratus (*Phaen.* 35), Lucretius (2.629, 633) and Virg. (*Georg.* 4.151) choose the Curetes. The Augustan geographer Strabo (10.3.11, pp. 468–77) tried to distinguish the two groups, claiming that in the Cretan account the *Kouretes*, rearers of the κοῦρος ('boy') Zeus, were summoned to Crete by Rhea, whereas Demetrius of Scepsis on the slopes of Phrygian Ida claimed the rite for Phrygia. He saw the name *Corybantes* as derived from the verb describing their head-butting dance. (See Immisch, *RE* XI 2141–2 s.v. *Kouretes*.)

211–12 res latuit patrem, priscique imitamina facti | aera ... mouent: J. B. Hall (*Proc. Afr. Class. Assoc.* 17 (1982) 72) argues convincingly for *patrem priscique*, the reading of A, as opposed to *priscique manent* (UMG and Lact. *ID* 1.21). O.'s regular practice of citing evidence with *manere* (see below), and an assumption that *imitamina* would be nominative, has led to the early corruption *manent* ousting *patrem* before the time of Lactantius. *latuit* picks up the concealment motif from 205 and confirms its success; it also creates an oxymoron between the successful concealment and the deed's commemoration. *priscique* (*-que* is adversative, 'and yet', see *OLD* s.v. 8, Bömer on *Met.* 3.524) rounds off the *aition*, as regularly in O. with a reference to contemporary practice, whether as *nomen* (1.237), *fama* [*forma* A–W–C] ... *facti* (2.379, cf. 6.265 *forma ... templi*), *mos* (352 below), *monumenta* (709 below), or in ritual (5.44 *Maiestas ... culta manet*). Compare the gently parodic *AA* 1.133–4 *theatra* | *nunc quoque formosis insidiosa manent.*

imitamina: a typical Ovidian verb-based formation, found only here and *Met.* 4.445, 11.626, 15.200. The word does not recur in classical authors, but a parallel prose formation *imitamentum* is used freely by Tacitus.

213 cymbala pro galeis, pro scutis tympana neatly picks up not only *aera* (= *cymbala*) and *raucaque terga* (= *tympana*) of 212, but (in reversed order) the *clipei* and *galei* of the Curetes in 209. From 212 almost every word, including *deae comites* (cf. 185) echoes or provides a synonym for elements in O.'s introduction.

214 tibia dat Phrygios, ut dedit ante, modos: *ut dedit ante* seems unjustified, for although this line neatly returns to the contemporary procession (adding the detail of the Phrygian melodies) and to 181–2, it has no equivalent within the *aition*. The Phrygian *modi* probably allude to the Phrygian *nomos* or mode, a melancholy minor key as opposed to the martial Dorian mode.

215–21 An interlude between *aitia*, and two brief questions.

215 desierat; coepi: the formulaic half-line (also found in O.'s interview with Tragedy at *Am.* 3.1.61) is mirrored and gently parodied by *desieram; coepit* (217). The deliberate symmetry with 217 marks off question and answer in successive couplets as in 135, 137 above and 331, 333.

215–18 Both lions and chariot are to be imagined as represented (in wood and plaster, like a modern portable saint?), not real; cf. 185n.

215 genus acre leonum is Lucretian (5.862), but its position at the line-end echoes Virgil's variant on Lucretius at *Georg.* 3.264 *genus acre luporum.*

216 insolitas ad iuga curua iubas: virtual enallage; it is the lions, not their manes, which are unaccustomed to the yoke. For animal response to the yoke cf. *Her.* 12.39–40 *ut* ... | *insolito premeres uomere colla boum* of Aeetes' wild bulls, and *Met.* 2.162 (where Phaethon's team miss their usual driver) *solitaque iugum grauitate carebat.* The lions are explained at *Met.* 10.698ff. as Atalanta and Hippomenes, transformed by Cybele to serve her: *Met.* 10.698–9 *modo leuia fuluae* | *colla iubae uelant* ..., 703–4 *aliisque timendi* | *dente premunt domito Cybeleïa frena leones.* With the formulaic *iuga curua* cf. *AA* 1.318, *Ex P.* 1.8.54, and *Am.* 1.13.16 *iuga panda, Her.* 6.10.

217–18 feritas mollita per illam | creditur: the language recalls Lucretius' explanation of the lion team (2.604–5 *adiunxere feras, quia quamuis effera proles* | *officiis debet molliri uicta parentum*) without adopting Lucretius' allegory of human morality.

testificata renews O.'s concern with evidence to prove his *aition*; the verb is deponent here, passive at 326.

219 cur turrifera caput est onerata corona?: *turrifera* is used here as a 'naive' literal description, to contrast with the regular epithet *turrigera* found in Virgil (*Aen.* 10.253), the elegists (Tib. 1.4.68, Prop. 3.17.35) and *F.* 6.321 *turrigera frontem Cybele redimita corona, Tr.* 2.24 *turrigerae* ... *Opi.* O. reserves the familiar epithet for Erato's reply in 224; elsewhere he uses *turrita*, e.g. *Met.* 10.696, as in *Aen.* 6.785. While alternation of *-ger* and *-fer* forms in one author is not uncommon, this is the only instance where they are confronted (see J. Perret, 'La forme des composés poétiques du latin', *REL* 30 (1952) 157–67). *onerata* evokes not only the size of this crown as shown on coins and reliefs, but the weight of the masonry it represents.

220 an primis turres urbibus illa dedit?: the question had been answered in similar terms by Lucretius 2.606–7 *muralique caput summum cinxere corona | eximiis munita locis quia sustinet urbis*. Even before O. the turreted crown had become a symbol not only of Cybele, protector of cities but of cities themselves and their Tyche: thus she merges with Dea Roma, the city *par excellence*. Cf. the veiled and turreted Cybele on the denarius of 102 BC (Crawford, *RRC* 322/1b) in the frontispiece; other coinage illustrating Cybele is cited by Summers (1996) 341, 344. Coinage precedes literature: cf. *Aen.* 6.785 (cited 191n.), and Lucan's Patria *turrigero* ... *uertice* (1.188). O.'s Cybele is a creator of urban civilization, not just its sustainer.

221–2 'unde uenit' ... 'sua membra secandi | impetus?': O.'s question, springing from Roman revulsion at the self-castration of Cybele's foreign eunuch priests, introduces his second *aition*, a variant on the tale of Attis known to O. and his contemporaries from Catullus 63.

membra: always plural in O.; normally, like *artus*, a synonym for *corpus*, but applied specifically to the *membrum uirile* at *Am.* 2.3.3 *qui primus pueris genitalia membra recidit*, and used euphemistically at *Am.* 3.7.13, *Met.* 6.616–17 *quae tibi membra pudorem | abstulerunt, ferro rapiam* (see 240 below on *partes*).

O. uses *membra secare* of castration again in *Ibis*, recalling both the legend of Saturn and that of Attis and the Galli: 271–2 *sic aliquis tua membra secet, Saturnus ut illas | subsecuit partes unde creatus erat* and 451–4 (adapted from Catullus) *attonitusque seces, ut quos Cybeleia mater | incitat, ad Phrygios uilia membra modos. | deque uiro fias nec femina nec uir, ut Attis, | et quatias molli tympana rauca manu.*

Pieris orsa loqui: the Muses were often called *Pierides* (e.g. Lucr. 1.926, Virg. *Ecl.* 6.13) from their association with Helicon in Pieria. O. himself exceptionally contrasts the Muses as *Mnemonides* (*Met.* 5.268, 280), *Thespiades* (5.310) and *Aonides* (5.333) with the daughters of Pieros, but avoids the confusion of calling them Pierides.

orsa loqui is a variant of the epic formula: cf. *Aen.* 1.325 *sic filius* *orsus*, 2.2 *toro sic orsus ab alto*, 6.562 *sic orsa loqui*, 7.435, 9.656, 12.806, *Met.* 5.300, *sic orsa*; with *loqui*, cf. *Met.* 4.320 and 6.28 *sic orsa loqui*, and *Her.* 12.72 *orsus es infido sic prior ore loqui. ordiri*, 'to set up a loom', is an established metaphor for the careful setting-up of a narrative or persuasive speech (hence *exordium*).

223–44 The story of Attis, Cybele and Sagaritis.

224 turrigeram ... deam: the goddess is now no longer Rhea, the long-suffering consort of Kronos, but the Phrygian Great Goddess. Borgeaud (1996) 56–88 distinguishes between the Lydian and Phrygian versions of the myth of the Great Mother and her lover Attis, showing that the Romans knew only the Phrygian tradition from Pessinus. Pausanias 7.17.9–12 (garbled by Christian writers, Lact. *ID* 1.17.6–7 and Arnobius 5.5) cites a similar local story (ἐπιχώριος λόγος) of Attis, the *Phryx puer*, and Agdistis (the cult name of the Mother Goddess of Pessinus in Phrygia). Agdistis originally had the organs of both sexes, but the gods cut off the male organs, which fell on the ground; an almond tree sprouted from them, and the daughter of the river Sangarius conceived Attis from its fruit. The boy Attis grew up and was about to marry a princess when the jealous Agdistis destroyed the palace, killed his bride and drove him mad so that he castrated himself. O.'s (?) version, or that of his source, substitutes a nymph for the princess, but shares with this tale the boy's chaste devotion and the goddess's later jealous vengeance: Borgeaud (1996) 70 compares Attis' role in O. with that of Phaethon as consort of Aphrodite in Hesiod, *Theog.* 988–91.

In adopting the Near Eastern cult of Cybele the Romans marginalized its mythical associations and ecstatic practices: cf. Dion. Halic. 2.19 'Even though [Rome] has, in obedience to oracles, introduced some rites from abroad, she celebrates them according to her own traditions, throwing out all mythical nonsense. The rites of the Idaean goddess are an example; for the Praetors perform sacrifices and celebrate games in her honour every year according to the Roman customs, but the Priest and Priestess of the god are Phrygians and it is they who carry her image through the city in procession ... by a law and decree of the Senate no native Roman walks in procession ... or participates in the Phrygian orgiastic rites.' The earliest Roman account of Attis' devotion and self-castration is the rather different account of Catullus 63, perhaps adapted from

Callimachus (cf. *Iamb.* 3. fr. 93). (See 365n., Vermaseren (1977) cited at 185n., R. Turcan, *Les cultes orientaux dans le monde romain* (Paris 1989) 42–75.)

223 Phryx puer ... facie spectabilis: the epithet is most common in O. in connection with glittering ornaments; but in *Met.* 7.496 Cephalus is *spectabilis heros,* | *et ueteris retinens etiam nunc pignora formae*; cf. *Ex P.* 2.2.79 where Germanicus is *placido spectabilis ore.* The wilderness setting *in siluis* evokes a shepherd like Endymion or hunter like Adonis (cf. *Met.* 10.535, 711).

225 hunc sibi seruari uoluit, sua templa tueri: Attis' role, passive in the first phrase, must be active, 'to watch over her temple', in the second. Burman compares *Met.* 8.707–8 *esse sacerdotes delubraque uestra tueri* | *poscimus.* It would be normal to appoint young and sexually pure males (like Ion in Euripides' play) as temple keepers (*aeditui*/νεωκόροι).

226 puer esse here implies abstinence from intercourse (Latin, like English, had no regular male equivalent for 'virgin'): this is also implied by *esse* | *quod fuit* in 229–30 below.

227–8 In this dialogue Attis' actual oath is only reported as *fidem iussis dedit*; if it took the form *semper puer esse uolam*, the imprecation by which he binds himself *si mentiar* can only make sense with a present reference, 'if I shall prove myself then to be lying now'. With *qua fallam* and *fallit* (229) compare the typical Roman oath *si sciens fallo.* Should we read *mentior*?

ultima ... sit Venus illa mihi: *Venus* points to sexual union, not mere sentiment. By wishing that any deceitful love for another may be his last, he justifies Cybele's reaction.

229 in nympha Sagaritide: *in* + abl. 'in the case of', 'in relation to', cf. *OLD* s.v., B42; cf. 6.576 *in hoc uno non fuit illa uiro.* The euphemism *desinit esse quod fuit* applies equally to his loss of virginity and the ensuing loss of virility.

230 poenas exigit ira deae: with *poenas exigere* cf. *Met.* 4.190, 14.478 (both of Venus demanding punishment), 8.125 and 532, *Her.* 7.58 and *Tr.* 5.8.9.

231–44 In Cat. 63.75–89 Cybele's anger is vented by driving the already castrated Attis in madness away from civilization to the mountain heights. O. makes the self-mutilation the climax, not the beginning, of his narrative, following the single couplet in which she causes the death of the beloved Sagaritis with ten lines (233–42) describing first his hallucinations, then his act of violence expiating his oath and her anger against himself.

231–2 Naida . . . succidit . . . fatum Naidos arbor erat: the poet combines nymph and tree in making her the object of *succidere*, normally used of felling trees (so Erysichthon at *Met.* 8.752), but subordinating the tree in a participial phrase. For *fatum* = 'doom', 'cause of death', there are no parallels before Justin on the *fata Troiae* (20.1.16); even the singular *fatum* = 'death' is rare in Augustan poetry, but cf. *Met.* 9.359 *spectatrix . . . fati crudelis*. If she can be killed by destroying her tree, Sagaritis, O.'s own creation, should be a Hamadryad (or Dryad), cf. Hom. *h. Aphr.* 257ff., but O. often uses the terms interchangeably; cf. *Met.* 1.690–1 *inter Hamadryadas celeberrima Nonacrinas | Naïas una fuit*. As Herter (*RE* XVII 1542) shows, O. develops further the bond between nymph and tree under the influence of Hellenistic metamorphoses of women like Dryope (*Met.* 9.336ff.). At *Met.* 8.757–64 the tree cultivated by Dryads and felled by Erysichthon bleeds like a living creature.

233–4 hic furit, et . . . | effugit: *hic furit*, following *illa perit*, suggests his madness was caused by shock at her death rather than directly sent by Cybele. We do not know O.'s source, if any, for details such as Attis' delusion of the collapsing bedchamber.

cursu Dindyma summa petit: *Dindyma* (cf. Greek singular *Dindymon* avoiding elision at 249) is near Cybele's cult place Pessinus. At this point O.'s account converges with the beginning of Catullus' poem: 63.2–4 *citato cupide pede . . . | stimulatus ibi furenti rabie*, but although Catullus calls Cybele *Dindymi* or *Dindymena domina* (35.14, 63.13) he sets Attis' self-mutilation away from Dindyma on Phrygian Ida (63.30 and 52).

235 et modo "tolle faces", "remoue" modo "uerbera" clamat: O. simulates Attis' panic with the entirely dactylic line, and multiple disruption between his cries and the narrative. Madmen like Orestes or Alcmaeon regularly saw Furies with torches and whips: cf. Enn. *Alcmaeon* XIV–XV Jocelyn, *Aen.* 4.472–3 *armatamque facibus matrem . . . cum fugit*.

236 saepe Palaestinas iurat adesse deas: Attis should be imagining some kind of avenging Fury, hence Roeper's ingenious suggestion *palam Stygias* (*Philol.* 4 (1849) 352. However, the form *Palaestinus* is Ovidian (cf. 2.464 *Palaestinae* ... *aquae*), even if these goddesses cannot be identified. Schilling (1995) II 113 ad loc. suggests that they are a collective version of Derceto / Dea Syria / Atargatis, since Pliny, *NH* 5.81 cites a Palestinian cult site of Atargatis. Despite the difficulty of identification the word is surely not corrupt, but O.'s original text.

237 saxo corpus laniauit acuto: cf. Cat. 63.5 *deuolsit ili acuto sibi pondera silice* and Pliny, *NH* 35.165, Mart. 3.81.3, Juv. 6.514. Stones (or even potsherds) seem to have been preferred to steel, which was excluded from ritual use.

238 longaque ... tracta coma est: Attis' long hair is a mark of his youth, whereas in his followers it will be associated with effeminacy. Bömer points to the original model for this sign of degradation in Achilles' treatment of Hector's corpse, *Il.* 22.398ff., adapted by Virgil for Turnus' threats against the 'effeminate' Aeneas: *Aen.* 12.99–100 *semiuiri Phrygis et foedare in puluere crines* | *uibratos*. For the long hair of youth compare Troilus dragged in the dust at *Aen.* 1.477–8 *comaeque trahuntur* | *per terram*, and for *immundo puluere* cf. *Aen.* 12.611. The adjective is felt as undignified and avoided by O. in *Met.*, *Tr.*, *Ex P.* and *Fasti*, except here; cf. *Tr.* 1.3.93–4 *foedatis puluere turpi* | *crinibus* and *Met.* 8.529 without epithet. There will be added point to *immundus* if the dust is mixed with blood.

239 uoxque fuit: Attis' words have status as a *uox*, because they are quasi-oracular with significance for his followers, cf. 3.77 *uox rata fit*, 6.699 *uox placuit*, *Met.* 3.349.

merui: meritas do sanguine poenas: with the *polyptoton*, *merui/meritas*, cf. 184 *aeraque* ... *aera* and 324n. For *merui* absolute, cf. *Met.* 8.127, 10.484, *Her.* 5 155, 7.71, *Tr.* 1.2.95, etc. *meritas* ... *poenas* is a natural combination; cf. *Met.* 8.689 *meritasque luet uicinia poenas*, *Her.* 12.197 and variants, *Met.* 5.200 *ex merito poenas*. The combination *sanguine poenas* is traditional at the verse-end from Enn. *Ann.* 100 Skutsch, cf. *Aen.* 7.595, 9.422, 10.616, 11.592, Luc. 4.805; but there is point in the special application of *sanguis*, not to life but to sexuality.

240, 241 a, pereant!: for elegiac *a*(*h*), first attested in the Gallus citation of *Ecl.* 10.48–9, cf. Prop. 1.20.32, Tib.1.10.59, Ov. *Am.* 1.3.3, 2.19.11 and 13, 3.7.19, 3.9.4 (10 times even in *Met.*: 2.489

and 491, 6.386 (*bis*) etc.). It is highly affective, often associated with repetitions and/or the curse *pereat/pereant*; cf. Prop. 1.11.30 *a pereant Baiae crimen amoris aquae*, Ov. *AA* 2.272, 3.494.

240 partes quae nocuere mihi: J. N. Adams, *The Latin sexual vocabulary* (London 1982) 45 notes that 'as a euphemism *pars* (sing. and pl.) usually has some form of specification'. It is preferred in scientific and moral works (Cic. *ND* 2.64, 128, *Off.* 1.126, Lucr. 4.1044, 6.1209, Pliny, *NH* 2.93, 26.96), usually defined by epithets or relative clauses. O.'s euphemisms conform to this: cf. *Am.* 3.7.6 *inguinis effeti pars*, 69 *pars pessuma nostri* and *AA* 2.584 *partibus ... obscenis*, 618 *pars ... pudenda*, 707 *partibus illis*. So too Petr. *Sat.* 112.2, 129.1, 132.12, writes *ea pars corporis* but leaves it to be understood at 138.7 *dum rediret hoc corpus et resipiscerent partes*.

241 onus inguinis: O. uses *inguen* for *membrum uirile* at 1.400, 2.346, *Met.* 14. 640 (cf. *Am.* 3.7.6 cited 240n.), but *nulla ... signa ... uiri* suggests removal of both testicles and penis. The phrase is a synonym of Catullus' *ili ... pondera* at 63.5.

242 signa ... uiri: cf. Cat. 63.6 *sine uiro. signa* may be legal usage (*signa* = Gk σημεῖα were incontrovertible legal evidence): there is no parallel in any of O.'s narratives of sex-change or sex-loss. Contrast e.g. 586 *signa dolentis*, 6.66 *signa uigoris*.

243 uenit in exemplum furor hic 'this frenzy became a model': for purposive *in exemplum* cf. *Am.* 1.10.25 *sumite in exemplum pecudes. exemplum* is anything copied, whether desirable or not: thus O. classifies the infectious *furor* of Actaeon's hounds and the Theban Bacchae with *exemplo* at *Met.* 3.122, 4.431.

243–4 mollesque ministri | caedunt ... membra: *-que* is epexegetic, 'and so now', 'that is why', *OLD.* s.v. 6a. O. is recalling *molles comites* (185) and his question at 221–2 *unde uenit ... sua membra secandi | impetus?* But *secare* is replaced by *caedere* ('hack', 'slash', = Gk κόπτειν), elsewhere in O. used only of killing, or felling trees. For *ministri* of religious attendants, cf. 2.287, 317, 4.413, 637, and *ministra* of vestals, 3.47, 6.283, etc.

244 iactatis uilia membra comis: cf. *crinem/crines iactare* of Bacchic frenzy at *Met.* 3.726, 11.6; of a sober dancer *AA* 3.141 *alterius crines umero iactentur utroque. uilia* as often in O. does not represent his own valuation but the warped point of view of the Galli. (On the origin of the name Galli see 361, 363nn.)

245 Aoniae ... Camenae: O. stresses the blend of Greek and Roman elements in his poetry, but nowhere else is Italian *Camena(e)* (a nymph or nymphs with the gift of *carmen*, 'song' or 'prophecy', 3.275, *Met.* 15.482) applied to a Greek Muse. For *Aonius* ('Boeotian') of the Muses cf. *Tr.* 4.10.39–40 *et petere Aoniae suadebant tuta sorores | otia* and the similar *Aonides*, *Met.* 5.333, 6.2.

facunda uoce: cf. Hor. *Odes* 3.1.35 *facunda ... lingua*, *Ex P.* 4.4.37 *facundo tua uox hilarauerit ore.* The word *facundus*, like *facundia*, first appears in comedy, but is absent from prose and verse, apart from Horace (*Odes* 1.10.1, 4.1.35), before O. (*TLL* VI 160.32–6).

246 reddita quaesiti causa furoris erat: either 'this was the explanation of the frenzy I had asked about', with *quaesitus* transferred from *causa*, its proper referent, or 'of their sought frenzy', describing the *secandi impetus* of the Galli. O. rounds off the *aition* by recalling his question of 221–2.

247 dux operis treats the temporary interlocutor Erato as real Muse and generator of this section of the poem.

247–8 unde petita | uenerit ... ?: O. asks not about the cause, but the geographical origin of the Goddess (really her sacred stone, see 255–349n.) as is shown by the alternative (introduced by *an*) that Cybele's cult was autochthonous at Rome. The foreign, imported, nature of the cult was notorious, but the question enables O. to open with a surprise remodelling of official history; the goddess all but came at the fall of Troy, with Aeneas and the city's ancestors.

249–54 Introduction to the coming of the Great Mother to Rome. Rome developed several religious links with Greece during the third century. She sent historically attested embassies and votive offerings to Delphi in 222 and 205. The Senate also imported the cult of Greek Asclepius from Epidaurus (297 BC) and that of Aphrodite from Eryx in Sicily (Venus Erycina, see 871–2n.) in 217, some years before deciding on consultation of the Sibylline books, and probably also of Delphi to bring the Goddess's cult to Rome from the kingdom of Rome's ally Attalus of Pergamum, invoking Rome's claims to descent from Troy. For a detailed historical analysis see Gruen (1990) 5–34. Julian family ideology greatly increased the importance attached to the Goddess, evident in her role in the *Aeneid.* (Cf. Bömer (1964), Wiseman (1984).)

Before the long narrative answer to O.'s first question *unde petita* Erato deals with the alternative in Virgilian terms.

249 Dindymon et Cybelen: cf. *Aen.* 10.252 *alma parens Idaea deum cui Dindyma cordi*, and on Mt Cybele see 191n.

amoenam fontibus translates the Homeric πολυπίδακος used of Ida in *Il.* 14.157, 307, 20.59, etc.

250 Iliacas ... opes: cf. *Her.* 17.223. Virgil speaks of *Troianas ... opes* at *Aen.* 2.4 and 10.609.

251–2 cum Troiam Aeneas Italos portaret in agros, | est dea ... paene secuta: Aeneas brought Troy's gods to Rome (cf. 78 above); so also Prop. 4.1.39 *huc melius profugos misisti, Troia, Penatis*, and Tib. 2.5.40 *Troica qui profugis sacra uehes ratibus*; but along with the coined epithet *sacriferas ... rates* O. has adopted the identification of Troy with her gods made by Virgil at *Aen.* 1.68 *Ilium in Italiam portans uictosque Penates.* Neither Cybele's words to Jupiter in *Aen.* 9.83–92, describing her protective concern for the fleet, nor her manifestation at the transformation of the ships off Ostia quite justify the imaginative leap of *paene secuta* in 252.

253–4 nondum fatis Latio sua numina posci | senserat: contrast *Aen.* 4.612–14 *si ... sic fata Iouis poscunt*, 7.272–3 *hunc illum poscere fata | ... reor*, or Aeneas' own confident *ego poscor Olympo* (8.533). At *Aen.* 1.666 *tua numina posco*, 'I call on your divine aid/presence', *numina* is direct object of *poscere*, as in the passive form here. With the poetic plural *sua numina* here and at *Aen.* 1.666 compare 865 *numina ... Veneris*, 2.506 *numina nostra* of Quirinus, 3.426 *cognata numina* of Vesta, 3.776 *numinibusque tuis* of Bacchus.

254 adsuetis substiteratque locis: *adsuetis*, normally of the person or creature accustomed, is transferred to the familiar object; this is unique in O., but cf. *insolitas*, 216n. The verb *subsistere*, normally of brief hesitation, is here extended to Cybele's staying put, to emphasize that the pause was temporary in her eyes – a mere 500 years.

255–349 The bringing of the Great Mother from Pergamum. What O. treats throughout as the coming of the goddess herself to Rome was in fact something more primitive than the importation of an ancient cult statue. Cybele was represented in her native Phrygia by a meteoric stone, or βαίτυλος, but it would spoil O.'s sacred narrative to introduce this embarrassing material detail. Many aspects of Rome's adoption of the Great Mother are undisputed – the dating, the action in response to consultation of the Sibylline books and further consultation of Delphic Apollo, the mediation of Rome's political ally King Attalus of Pergamum (241–197). Two problems remain.

(1) Did the sacred stone come from Pessinus itself, the major shrine of Cybele, as Livy (29.11.7) claims? Although the Galati, in whose territory Pessinus lay, were hostile to Attalus, the Temple authorities themselves were on good terms with him, but even so they would not have given away their actual primary cult object – the meteoric stone identified with the goddess. (Nor would the priesthood of Asclepius at Epidaurus have bestowed a unique serpent upon the Romans, as O. seems to imply in *Met.* 15.645–50.) Varro, *LL* 6.15 claims the stone came from Pergamum itself, O. (264n.) that it came from Ida, an idea endorsed by Gruen (1990) 15. But there were other βαίτυλοι and it seems reasonable to assume that the priests of Pessinus who continued to favour Rome (cf. Plb. 21.37.5), provided Rome with a βαίτυλος (wherever it came from) that they had sanctified by dedication to Cybele.

(2) Livy's account of the reception of the stone (29.14.10–14) has 'the goddess' disembarked at Ostia into the pure hands of Scipio Nasica, the young man (29.14.7–9) previously nominated by the Senate as the best (*uir optimus*) in Rome. After he carried it to land *matronae primores ciuitatis ... per manus succedentes deinceps aliae aliis, omni effusa ciuitate ... in aedem Victoriae quae est in Palatio pertulere deam pridie Idus Apriles: isque dies festus fuit.* Leading *matronae*, including the famous Claudia Quinta (see 293–326, 305nn.) passed it from hand to hand until it reached its first home in the Palatine temple of Victory. The problem is that this story is incompatible with the journey upstream after Claudia Quinta (according to O. and Propertius) had relaunched the grounded barge with the miraculous aid of the goddess. Wiseman (1979) 94–9 treats the story of Claudia Quinta in O.'s narrative as a popular myth enhanced by O.'s imaginative reconstruction, as is his account of the voyage by ship from Pergamum to Ostia. There is at least one topographical conflict in his account of the supposed river journey between details of the image's reception

in Rome, the washing in the Almo and the entry by the Porta Capena (see 337–40, 345–6nn.).

Finally Livy (29.14.13) dates the original coming of the Great Mother to 12 April: *pridie Idus Apriles*, but after the inauguration of the Games of Ceres on that date in 203 BC, Cybele's Games were advanced to start on the 4th as celebrated by the *Fasti Praenestini* and all other calendars. (See 395 below.)

255–6 post, ut Roma potens opibus ... sustulit ... caput: at *Ecl.* 1.24 Virgil speaks of Rome *haec tantum alias inter caput extulit urbes*. (He does not otherwise use *tollere* in this way.)

256 edomito ... orbe: *edomare*, a rare intensive of *domare* (see *TLL* v 2.111.62–3), not found in Virgil or the elegists, and only here in O., may derive from Hor. *Odes* 4.5.22 *edomuit nefas*. But cf. *o. domitus*, at *AA* 1.177 *ecce Caesar parat domito quod defuit orbi*, 3.113–14 *Roma ... domiti magnas possidet orbis opes*; conceptually closest is the triumphalism of *Met.* 15.878 *quaque patet domitis Romana potentia terris*.

257 carminis Euboici fatalia uerba: cf. 6.210 (of Apollo) *deus Euboico carmine munus habet. Euboicus* is applied by Virgil to the Euboean colony of Cumae at *Aen.* 6.2 and 42, 9.710; so too *Met.* 14.155 *Euboicam ... urbem*. As at 158 these *carmina* from the Sibylline books consulted by the *decemuiri* are treated as genuine prophecies of a Sibyl. The same equation is exploited by Cic. *Har. resp.* 26–7 *in mentem ueniebat tibi, Sibyllino sacerdoti, haec sacra maiores nostros ex uestris libris expetisse? ... hac igitur uate suadente*. Hence O.'s stress on *fatalia uerba* not in the sense of a fated event or fateful object (as in 6.445) but like *fatales libri* (Livy 5.11.4 and 15.11 or Cic. *Div.* 1.100), 'containing or uttered by the fates' (*TLL* vi 332.78–80). Livy 29.10.4–5 reports *ciuitatem repens religio inuaserat inuento carmine in libris Sibyllinis ... quandoque hostis alienigena terra Italiae bellum intulisset, eum pelli Italia uincique posse, si Mater Idaea a Pessinunte Romam aduecta foret.*

259–60 "Mater abest: Matrem iubeo, Romane, requiras: O.'s account is more compact than Livy's (known to O. but not to his source?). In Livy 29.10.6 the first envoys to Delphi return with the god's promise of victory, but only with the second consultation of Delphi by the envoys to Attalus is there any reference to the Great Mother (29.11.6). It is then that the Romans are told to delegate the best man at Rome to receive her.

For similar oracular play on *Mater* compare Livy's account

(1.56.11) of the oracle given by Delphi to L. Iunius Brutus and the sons of Tarquin that power would come to whichever of them first embraced their mother. Brutus interpreted this correctly and embraced the earth of Italy on landing. O. himself uses the same conception of Earth as Mother in the oracle of *Met.* 1.383 *ossaque post tergum magnae iactate parentis!* The quest for the Mother/Motherland features in a different way in *Aen.* 3.96 where Anchises is misled by an oracle of Apollo *antiquam exquirite matrem*, to advise settling on Crete, as home of the Great Mother, instead of Italy, motherland of Dardanus (cf. 3.111–15 and 163–5). O.'s oracle copies these ambiguities, confirming his readers' expectations and allowing them a feeling of superiority to the baffled senators.

260 casta est accipienda manu: O.'s words allow reference both to Scipio Nasica, the young man chosen as *uir optimus* by the Senate in Livy 29.14.8–9 (and ignored by O.'s narrative), and to the eventual story of Claudia Quinta. Both Scipio and Claudia (*femina autem quae matronarum castissima putabatur*) are mentioned by Cic. *Har. resp.* 27.

261 obscurae sortis ... ambagibus errant: cf. Deucalion's and Pyrrha's confusion at *Met.* 1.388–9 *repetunt caecis obscura latebris* | *uerba datae sortis secum*; *ambages* similarly denotes the Sibyl's mysterious prophecy at *Aen.* 6.99 *horrendas canit ambages*. Elsewhere in Virgil it describes an extended tale (*Georg.* 2.46, *Aen.* 1.342) or the physical meandering of the labyrinth (6.29).

262 quaeue parens ... quoue petenda loco: Ovidian aetiology delights in such puzzles. Livy offers no equivalent of this senatorial uncertainty over the identity or location of the 'mother'.

263 consulitur Paean: Bömer cites Cic. *Verr.* 2.4.127 *signum Paeanis ex aede Aesculapi praeclare factum* as first independent Latin use of Apollo's title *Paean* ('the Healer' as in e.g. Hom. *h. Ap.* 272, 500, 517) to identify the god; cf. *Met.* 1.566 *finierat Paean*, a pointed usage, since Apollo has just admitted that his art of healing cannot heal his own lovesickness (521–4). Otherwise *Paean* is rare in O., occurring only at *Met.* 14.720 and in the double invocation *Io Paean* at *AA* 2.1.

"diuum"que "arcessite matrem": for the attachment of *-que* from the narrative to a word quoted in direct speech, an Ovidian logical trick first noted by M. Haupt, *Opuscula* II 510–12, see Introd. 4(i), and McKeown on *Am.* 1.1.3–4.

264 "in Idaeo est inuenienda iugo": for *iugum/iuga Idaea* cf. *Her.* 16.204, and 5.138 *in immensis qua tumet Ida iugis*; also *AA* 1.684, *Her.* 4.48. *iugum* can denote as small a hill as the Aventine, Quirinal or Esquiline (3.884, 6.218 and 794), but may be vague enough (cf. e.g. *Met.* 1.62 *radiis iuga subdita matutinis* of the Bactrian or Himalayan ranges) to cover even Pessinus, somewhat removed from the Trojan Mt Ida.

265 mittuntur proceres: *proceres*, 'leading men', 'princes' (equivalent to Homeric βασιλῆες?), occurs 9 times in the *Aeneid*, once (3.103) addressing the Trojans consulting Delphi. Livy supplies the five names of this enlarged delegation (the norm was three): M. Valerius Laevinus (Cos. 211), M. Caecilius Metellus, (Praetor 206), Ser. Sulpicius Cotta (Aedile 209) and two ex-quaestors.

265–6 Phrygiae tum sceptra tenebat | Attalus: for *sceptra tenere* cf. *F.* 2.432 *Romulus, hoc illo sceptra tenente fuit, Met.* 1.596, 3.265, 14.611–12 *tenuit repetita Latinus | nomina cum sceptro.* Attalus I of Pergamum (241–197 BC) became Rome's ally against Philip V of Macedon and the alliance with his dynasty continued until the death of its last member, Attalus III, in 133.

266 Ausoniis negat ille uiris: *Ausonius* (cf. *Aen.* 3.171) seems to be O.'s choice when he speaks of Romans from a Greek or external point of view; cf. 1.55 *Ausonias ... Kalendas*, 541–2 *neque alter | montibus Ausoniis Arcade maior erat, Met.* 14.7, etc., and in the Aesculapius narrative 15.647, 693.

267 mira canam: for this kind of foreshadowing, either to forestall disbelief (*praemunitio*) or to solicit belief (*captatio*) before a miraculous event, cf. *Met.* 4.394 *resque fide maior*, 7.549 *mira loquar*, 11.731 *mirumque fuit potuisse, uolabat*, and in *Fasti* 3.370, 6.612 *mira sed acta loquor* and 326 below *mira, sed et scaena testificata loquar.* Elsewhere O. uses parenthetic *mirum*; cf. 2.413, *Met.* 7.790, 11.51.

longo ... murmure: otherwise only of Medea's incantations, *Met.* 7.251, but compare earth tremors as a supernatural manifestation at *Met.* 5.356 *tremit tellus*, and the tremors of buildings and altars at 3.47, *Met.* 4.486, 9.783; and of forests in 2.439, 501, 3.329. For the pattern of incipient resistance resolved by divine action compare the hesitation of the Epidaurian council in *Met.* 15.648–52, resolved by the Roman's vision of Aesculapius (653 *cum deus in somnis*

... *uisus*), the apparition of the snake (669–70 *cum* ... *aureus* ... | *in serpente deus* ... *sibila misit*) and confirming nod (683–4).

269 "ipsa peti uolui; ne sit mora; mitte uolentem": the stress on Cybele's wish (*uolui* ... *uolentem*) to go to Rome gives new justification to the traditional account of her coming. Compare 250–2: since Cybele had always loved Troy, she really belonged to the new Troy and to its re-founder Aeneas. Ritually the goddess's statement of her wish to leave also compensates for the omission of the Roman ritual of *euocatio* (cf. Livy 5.21) used to ensure a god's willing transfer to Rome. *ne sit mora* is emphatic: even the positive form is unparalleled in O.

270 dignus Roma locus quo deus omnis eat: a more hyperbolic version of Venus' preference for Rome; cf. 876 below *inque suae stirpis maluit urbe coli*, and the earlier version of *Am.* 1.8.42 *Venus Aeneae regnat in urbe sui*, modified in *AA* 1.60 *Mater in Aeneae constitit urbe sui.*

271–2 ille soni terrore pauens "proficiscere!" dixit: | "nostra eris: in Phrygios Roma refertur auos": *soni terrore*, a natural reaction to the speech of a god, may also be intended to recall O.'s own fear at the goddess's approach in 189–90 (*me sonus* ... | *terret*). Attalus' speech 'Go, then: you will still be ours, for Rome has always been traced back to Phrygian ancestry' is a blend of many Augustan allusions to the Trojan legend. *nostra eris* rewrites Priam's offer of Trojan protection to Sinon, *Aen.* 2.149 (in the same position), while *in Phrygios* ... *refertur auos* (echoing Prop. 2.1.42 *Caesaris in Phrygios condere nomen auos*) plays between the literal 'Rome goes back to' and the other sense of *referre* for the report of tradition, *fama*: compare 305nn., and Livy, *Praef.* 7 *origines suas* ... *ad deos referre auctores.* This supposedly third-century recognition of Rome's Trojan ancestry both anticipates the poetic claims of Augustans like Propertius, and returns O. to the theme of his opening section on Venus and Iulus, ancestor of the Caesares: thus O. confirms the Caesarian claim of Trojan ancestry through one goddess, by the authority of an even more senior goddess – the mother of them all.

273 protinus innumerae caedunt pineta secures: for *protinus innumer-* opening the Ovidian hexameter cf. *Met.* 7.312, *Med. fac.* 62, *Ex P.* 1.8.18. O. favours *innumerus* in connection with tree-felling; cf. *Met.* 8.774–6 *labefactaque tandem* | *ictibus innumeris* ... *arbor* |

corruit, and the shipbuilding of Paris, *Her.* 16.107, 110 *Troica caeduntur Phrygia pineta securi* | ... *innumerasque mihi longa dat Ida trabes.*

274 Phryx pius: more than a gloss for *pius Aeneas*, the epithet recalls Cybele's claims in *Aen.* 9.88–9 that she had volunteered this sacred grove for Aeneas' fleet. The scene of eager shipbuilding at Pergamum (implied by *pineta*: *pinus* is a standard metonymy for ships) draws on the same stands of timber used by Aeneas: *Aen.* 3.5–6 *classemque sub ipsa* | *Antandro et Phrygiae molimur montibus Idae*, 9.80–1 *tempore quo primum Phrygia formabat in Ida* | *Aeneas classem.*

But the busy image of countless axes and *mille manus* (275 below) goes back to the felling of timber for the pyre of Patroclus (*Il.* 23.114ff.), imitated by Ennius (*Ann.* 75–9 Skutsch) and Virgil (*Aen.* 6.176–82). The three passages are compared by Macr. *Sat.* 6.2.27; see Skutsch 340–2, and G. Williams, *Tradition and originality in Roman poetry* (Oxford 1968) 264–7.

275–6 picta coloribus ustis | caelestum Matrem ... puppis habet: another paradox, the mother of all gods on board ship! cf. *Met.* 15.693–4 *numinis illa* | *sensit onus pressa estque dei grauitate carina.* Aesculapius' ship is also presented pictorially, its *puppis* ... *recurua* garlanded (696, 698, cf. *Tr.* 1.4.7). Neither Virgil's nor O.'s ship descriptions are usually so visual. For painted boats cf. *Aen.* 5.663 *pictas abiete puppes*, *Met.* 3.639, 6.511, *Ex P.* 2.10.33, *Her.* 21.72 *picta* ... *texta ratis*; other ships have *pictos deos* at the stern: *Her.* 16.114, 116, *Tr.* 1.4.8. The paint was burnt in (*ustis*) with wax: Pliny, *NH* 35.11 notes that such paint *in nauibus nec sole nec sale nec uentis corrumpitur* (Rossbach, *RE* v 2571). See also 430n.

276 concaua puppis: (*con*)*cauus* = Gk κοῖλος; cf. *AA* 1.402, *Am.* 3.6.4 *concaua* ... *cumba*, so also *F.* 2.407 *cauus alueus*, *Her.* 18.8 *cauae* ... *rates.*

277–90 The route taken is through the Propontis, along the shore of Troy to Tenedos, Lesbos and the Cyclades, passing from the north coast of Crete to Cythera, south of Cape Malea in the Peloponnese: thence along the E and S coast of Sicily to Drepanum (see *aequora* ... *Afra* 289n.), and through the Tyrrhenian sea to Ostia.

277 sui per aquas ... tutissima nati: rather than refer particularly to the waters of the Hellespont (*Phrixeae stagna sororis*) this treats the whole sea-voyage as Poseidon's realm. (At 93 above the seas were associated with Venus.)

278 longaque . . . stagna: an oxymoron, since *stagnum* is usually a small pool, but cf. *Met.* 1.38 *stagna immensa.* The Hellespont (cf. 567 below) is regularly glossed by allusion to the fall of Helle, sister of Phrixus, from the golden ram which gave the strait its name, just as the constellation Aries is identified by the story. O. has already told the full story at 3.852–76 (cf. 870 *femina cum de se nomina fecit aquae*), and will add retrospective allusions when Aries sets (715, 903nn.); so also *AA* 3.336 *uellera germanae, Phrixe, querenda tuae,* and *Her.* 18.141–4 *et satis amissa locus hic infamis ab Helle est* | . . . | *inuideo Phrixo, quem per freta tristia tutum* | *aurea lanigero uellere uexit ouis,* combining the myth and the safety motif of 277.

279 Rhoeteumque rapax: *rapax* (for which A–W–C print *capax*) is common of rivers and could apply to the strong current of the straits; cf. 566 below, and *Met.* 8.551, *Ex P.* 4.10.49.

279–80 Sigeaque litora . . . | et Tenedum et ueteres Eëtionis opes: Homer mentions in *Il.* 1.366–7 the wealth of Andromache's father Eëtion, whose city of Hypoplakian Thebes was sacked by Achilles (*Il.* 6.395–7, 415–19, *Met.* 12.109–10, 13.173–5). To this Virgil adds the notion of the former wealth of Tenedos: *Aen.* 2.21–2 *Tenedos, notissima fama* | *insula, diues opum Priami dum regna manebant.* All these names recall both Homer's and Virgil's Troy: cf. *Met.* 11.197–8 *dextera Sigei, Rhoetei laeua profundi* | *ara,* and *Am.* 1.15.9 *uiuet Maeonides, Tenedos dum stabit et Ide.* O. loves to cite heroic names in polysyndeton: cf. with *-que* . . . *-que* . . . *et* . . . *et* here *Met.* 1.516 *et Claros et Tenedos Patareaque regia seruit,* the seven Greek place-names of *AA* 2.79–82, or the ninefold polysyndeton of *Met.* 15.705–8.

281 Cyclades excipiunt, Lesbo post terga relicta: for the Cyclades on the part of Demeter's aerial journey that reverses Cybele's voyage see 565n. O. also mentions them at *Met.* 2.264 and *Tr.* 1.11.8. Lesbos, south of Tenedos, is listed among Achilles' successful raids in *Met.* 13.173, but there is no Ovidian parallel for the *Carysteis* . . . *uadis,* the waters south of Carystos in Euboea.

282 frangitur unda: for *frangere* of waves broken by the shoreline cf. *Met.* 11.569, *Her.* 19.207 and the similar motif in Hor. *Odes* 1.11.5 *quae nunc oppositis debilitat pumicibus mare.*

283–4 Icarium, lapsas ubi perdidit alas | Icarus: the Icarian Sea lay to the west of Crete. This time O. spells out the etymology of the sea in the fall of Daedalus' son Icarus, when his wings were melted by the heat of the sun – a story which he has already narrated twice (*AA.* 2.21–96, *Met.* 8.183–230, cf. 230 *aqua quae nomen traxit ab illo*).

nomina fecit aquae: cf. Virg. *Georg.* 1.137 *stellis ... nomina fecit.* O'Hara (1996a) 272 notes that O. always uses *nomen/nomina facere* to mark an etymology: cf. 3.869–70, 5.149, 182, *Met.* 14.616.

285–6 laeua Creten ... | deserit: the ship had already left Crete in 283–4; this couplet marks a change of course, NNW to Cythera.

Pelopeïdas: with the Gk fem. form *Pelopeïs* here cf. *Pelopeïas* in *Met.* 6.414 *Pelopeïadesque Mycenae* and *Pelopeïus* at *Met.* 8.622, *Tr.* 4.4.67. For other instances of O.'s morphological variations of Greek names see Kenney (1973).

Pelops threw Myrtilus, the treacherous charioteer of Oenomaus, into this sea, which received the name *Myrtoum* from his drowning. O.'s inclusion of Cythera *Veneri sacra* (rather than gen. *Veneris* as read by most MSS) in this sketchy itinerary recalls the importance of Venus throughout this month/book.

287 hinc mare Trinacrium: O. passes rapidly over what would have required several landings: only the hint of *candens ubi tinguere ferrum ... solent* suggests that Cybele's ship (like that of Aeneas, *Aen.* 3.684–708) followed the coastline SW from Aetna, and along the S shore of Sicily, avoiding the passage through the straits. The Cyclopes' forge is situated under Aetna, (e.g. *Georg.* 4.173, *Aen.* 8.416–17) but also on the Aeolian island of Lipare (*Aen.* 8.416) NW of Messina. *mare Trinacrium* points ahead to the introduction of Sicily, *terra ... Trinacris* in the Ceres narrative (419–20n.)

288 Brontes et Steropes Acmonidesque: an adaptation to the pentameter of *Aen.* 8.425 *Brontesque Steropesque et nudus membra Pyracmon*, itself a remodelling of Hesiod, *Theog.* 140. While *Brontes* and *Steropes*, named for thunder and lightning, are constant, the name of the other smith (in Hesiod *Arges*, 'the shiner') varies.

289 aequoraque Afra legit: the 'African seas' are not a standard geographical term, but O.'s readers might think of the waters in which Aeneas was shipwrecked when blown off course towards Carthage, on the voyage north from Drepanum. For *legere* of stages followed in a sea voyage cf. 566, *Aen.* 3.127, 292, 706, *Met.* 14.89,

15.705 and 709, but this use is not confined to verse; cf. Livy 21.51.7 *oram Italiae legens Ariminum peruenit.*

Sardoaque regna: *regna* is odd, since in 204 BC Sardinia was already a Roman province. The course too is studiously vague: any landfall in central Italy could be described as looking back to Sardinia on the left. Contrast the loving detail of Aesculapius' course up the Italian coastline in *Met.* 15.701–18.

291 Ostia contigerat: both *tenere* (290) and *contingere* denote reaching land, but at Ostia the ship would leave the sea. The Tiber (for *Tiberinus* see 47–8n.) is stressed both for its sentimental importance and its role in the coming miracle narrative: for the force of its flow, cf. *Aen.* 7.31–2, *uerticibus rapidis et multa fuluus harena | in mare prorumpit* and contrast 8.87–9.

292 campo liberiore: cf. *Met* 1.41–2 *campo ... | liberioris aquae.*

293–326 The story of Claudia Quinta. There was undoubtedly a historical Claudia Quinta, who according to Cic. *Har. resp.* 27 was chosen by the Senate for her chastity, to be the female representative welcoming the goddess alongside Scipio Nasica. Gruen (1990) 26 notes that one of the censors for this year 204 BC was C. Claudius Nero, which would favour the choice of a kinswoman. All the evidence until the first century AD or later makes this woman a *matrona* (not a Vestal as in later sources), and no republican sources say anything of her reputation being suspect or her having miraculously dislodged the goddess's grounded barge. That story is first attested in Prop. 4.11.51–2 *tu quae tardam mouisti fune Cybeben | Claudia, turritae rara ministra deae.*

Wiseman (1979) 94–99, reconsidering Bömer (1964) 146–51, argues that Ovid's story has developed after several shifts from history into legend. First the original respectable matron was impugned by writers hostile to the Claudii. Some alleged that her reputation was poor, giving rise to a popular legend and drama of her vindication by the miracle; at least one historian, probably Valerius Antias, claimed that the Senate chose a Valeria for the honour (Diod. 34/35.32–3). Claudia's low profile in Livy is the result of his attempt to reconcile conflicting traditions. According to Val. Max. 1.8.11 and Tac. *Ann.* 4.64 a statue of Claudia Quinta survived the burning of the temple of Magna Mater in AD 3, as it had survived a previous fire. It may have been the earliest statue of a historical laywoman at Rome. As noted (255–349n.), O. diverges here from Livy, whom he so often follows. In Livy 29.14.11 the 'goddess' is lifted by Cornelius (Scipio Nasica) from her ship at Ostia and brought to land, where the women successively pass it overland to its destination in Rome. There is no mention of any group of male Romans meeting the ship at Ostia.

293–6 O. opens with a comprehensive assembly of Romans: *omnis eques mixtaque grauis cum plebe senatus* (cf. 2.127–8 *tibi plebs, tibi curia nomen* | ... *hoc dedimus tibi nomen eques*, *Tr.* 4.2.15–16 *plebs pia cumque pia laetetur plebe senatus* | *paruaque cuius eram pars ego nuper eques*); but one might make the criticism that this stratification was more appropriate to O.'s own time than that of Scipio Africanus, when *equites* were not a recognized civilian *ordo*. The corresponding subdivisions of the women in 295–6, *matres nataeque nurusque*, are of course private, based on the family relationships of secular women as mothers, daughters and daughters-in-law – probably all should be considered adult *matronae*. Contrasted with them are the public Vestals, marked off from either sex by their ritual virginity. O. makes similar divisions within the category of *matronae* at 133 *matresque nurusque*, and *Met.* 3.529 *mixtaeque uiris matresque nurusque*, *Tr.* 4.2.11–14 (influenced by Hor. *Odes* 3.14.1–9) *cumque bonis nuribus pro sospite Liuia nato* | ... | *et pariter matres et quae sine crimine castos* | *perpetua seruant uirginitate focos.*

nataeque nurusque: read by only a minority of MSS, and first adopted by Heinsius; most MSS read *natique uirique*, superfluously reiterating the men already listed in 293 (cf. 297 and 304). But the continuation with the Vestals guarantees that 295 includes only females.

296 quaeque colunt: cf. *Tr.* 4.2.13–14 quoted above: the virgin status of the Vestals is instrumental in keeping pure (*sanctos*/*castos*) Vesta's public hearth.

297–304 These lines sketch a kind of comedy, as a couplet describing sturdy masculine effort meets no response from the grounded ship, then renewed effort in 301–2 is answered by a paradox – its fixture like an island. It is a *monstrum* (portent), because the unnatural phenomenon indicates (*monstrat*) divine purpose. In each couplet the strain and its failure are juxtaposed in asyndeton, and the focus shifts from men to ship and back again. Yet O. offers natural causes for the problem: 298 *aduersas* ... *aquas*, 299–300 *sicca* ... *tellus* ... *limoso* ... *uado*; even the weight of the ship's sacred cargo (300 *pressa*). All the forces applied *fune* ... *contento*, *sedula* ... *bracchia*, *fortes* ... *manus*, even the synchronized call *uoce* ... *sonante* ('yo heave ho!'), as in a tug-of-war, have no effect. Once settled in the mud of the estuary (aor. *sedit*) the boat sits (*sedet*) firm (*stabilis*) like an island: in turn the men stand (*stantque*) in helpless awe. (Other vocabulary is discussed below.)

297–8 Compare the same image as analogy in *Tr.* 4.1.7–8 *cantat et innitens limosae pronus harenae, | aduerso tardam qui trahit amne ratem*, which combines the notion of dragging a barge upstream and singing, as in 302, to add strength.

298 subit ... aquas 'enters the river's stream': for the phrase cf. *Tr.* 4.3.4 *maris* ... *non subeatis aquas*.

299–300 There is assonance approaching anaphora in *sicca* ... *sitis* ... | *sedit limoso*. For the applications of *siccus* and *sitis* to land cf. *Met.* 15.268–9. For *limosus* besides *Tr.* 4.1.7 cited above, cf. Virg. *Ecl.* 1.48, *Aen.* 2.135 *limosoque lacu*, Ov. *Am.* 3.6.1, *Met.* 1.634, 7.6. The Tiber mouth silted up easily; cf. 1.242 *harenosi Thybridis* and Strabo 5.3.5.

301 plus quam pro parte 'more than his share': cf. *pro sua parte*, *pro uirili parte*, *OLD* s.v. *pars* 8c and d. The line continues from 275 the idea of unanimous co-operation to ensure the goddess's transfer to Rome.

303 O.'s wit lies in the unusually negative application of *stabilis* not as 'steady', or 'stationary', the regular positive sense of the word (*OLD* 2 and 2b), but 'stopped', 'immobilized'. For the comparison implied by *uelut medio* ... *insula ponto*, cf. *Aen.* 8.691–2 *pelago credas innare reuulsas | Cycladas* (where both ships and islands are conceived as mobile).

305–12 This vivid character sketch of Claudia Quinta is in the tradition of elegy, but may be based on O.'s contemporary, Augustus' daughter Julia, exiled as a result of her alleged adulteries, and known for her sophisticated *cultus* (including hairstyling) and ready wit: cf. Macr. *Sat.* 2.5.1–8 and A. Richlin, 'Julia's jokes ... and the Roman use of women as political icons', in B. Garlick, S. Dixon and P. Allen, eds., *Stereotypes of women in power* (New York 1992) 65–91. If the portrait was meant to be recognizable, the political implications of *falsi criminis acta rea est* are so controversial that O. could hardly have written it while living at Rome. Composition or remodelling in exile, ultimately unprovable, is rendered more likely by the coincidence of 297–8 with *Tr.* 4.1.7–8.

305 genus Clauso referebat ab alto 'traced her ancestry back to lofty Clausus': cf. *Aen.* 7.707–8 *Clausus* ... | *Claudia nunc a quo diffunditur et tribus et gens.* (On this use of *referre* see 271n.) According to Livy 2.16.4 Attius Clausus, the Sabine ancestor of the patrician Claudii, was welcomed to Rome in 504 BC (cf. Dion. Halic. 5.50, Plut. *Publ.* 21, Servius on *Aen.* 7.706). Suet. *Tib.* 1 mentions and rejects a tradition dating the coming of the Claudii to the time of Romulus.

306 nec facies impar nobilitate: an elegant litotes. For the conception and phrasing cf. *Elogia Scipionum, CIL* I 2 *cui forma uirtutei parissuma fuit.* The abl. with *impar* (*TLL* VII 520.45) is here guaranteed by the metre. Burman compares 6.804 *in qua par facies nobilitate sua.* The abl. *aetate* at *Met.* 7.514 cited by Bömer is surely abl. of respect, 'equal in age'.

307 casta quidem: *casta* recurs in 315, 321, and 324 *bis.*

sed non et credita: cf. *Met.* 15.74, where *credita* refers not to the person, but his teaching. *rumor iniquus* | *laeserat*, with 310 *obfuit ad rigidos ... senes*, recalls Cat. 5.2–3 *rumoresque senum seueriorum* | *omnes unius aestimemus assis.*

308 falsi criminis acta rea est: cf. 2.497 *falsaeque patres in crimine caedis*, *Rem.* 388; an informal accusation, not a legal charge. Under the influence of *iniquus* the passive *falsus* suggests that the charge was not only untrue but lying.

309 ornatis uarie prodisse capillis: cf. Prop. 1.2.1 *quid iuuat ornatis procedere, uita, capillis?* Her habit of appearing in public and her attention to grooming both suggest a regrettable interest in attracting admirers.

310 obfuit ad rigidos ... senes: for this sense of *rigidus* cf. Hor. *Ep.* 1.1.17, Ov. *Am.* 3.4.44 and *AA* 2.664, used specifically of judge or censor. Parallels appear to be lacking for *ad* = *apud*, 'in the judgement of'; *obesse* + *ad* normally denotes the purpose obstructed (*TLL* IX 266.15–19).

311 conscia mens recti: the only use of *rectum* in *Fasti*, this echoes Virg. *Aen.* 1.604 *mens sibi conscia recti*; so also *F.* 1.485 *conscia mens.*

famae mendacia: cf. *Met.* 9.137–9 *fama loquax ... quae ueris addere falsa | gaudet et e minimo sua per mendacia crescit* and Prop. 4.2.19 *mendax fama, Aetna* 370.

312 sed nos in uitium credula turba sumus: while *credulus* (see *TLL* IV 1152.13ff.) is found in Tib. 1.9.38 (*credula turba* at [Tib.] 3.10.18) and Prop. 2.25.22 before O.'s many instances, only here is *credulus* combined with *in* + acc.

313–24 Two groups of six lines report Claudia's ritual actions (313–18) and the terms on which she asks the goddess to judge her (319–24). At 313 she steps out from her group, lets fall her hair (cf. 3.257) sprinkles her head three times (cf. 551n.) with ritually pure running water taken from the river, then kneels in supplication (317, cf. 319 *supplicis*, 2.438 *suppliciter posito ... genu*) before raising her hands three times in prayer as she gazes on the goddess's image. Only 316 *quicumque aspiciunt ... putant* alerts the reader to the public reaction to this unauthorized behaviour. It is Claudia's initiative, not her gestures or language, that shocks the onlookers.

315 inrorat: for *inrorare* cf. Virg. *Georg.* 1.288, 3.304, and its regular use by the technical writers Celsus and Columella. For its ritual context cf. *Met.* 1.371 (purification) and the parallel sequence of Medea's magic ritual at 7.188–91 *ad quae sua bracchia tendens | ter se conuertit, ter sumptis flumine crinem | inrorauit aquis, ternisque ululatibus ora | soluit et ... submisso poplite.* (O. has reported Medea's loosened hair at 7.183.)

317–18 uultus in imagine diuae | figit: an echo of *Aen.* 12.70 *figitque in uirgine uultus.*

318 hos edit ... sonos: grandiose epic diction, cf. *Met.* 3.237–8 *sonumque ... quem non tamen edere possit | ceruus, Her.* 11.94 *edidit ... sonos* and *edere uocem* at *Am.* 3.6.72 (an elegy with epic colouring foreshadowing *Fasti*), etc. With *crine iacente* cf. 2.772 *sic iacuere comae, Met.* 2.673 *uagi crines per colla iacebant.*

319 alma ... genetrix fecunda deorum: Claudia addresses Cybele with words Romans would associate with Venus Genetrix, ancestress of the *gens Iulia* (see 1n.).

320 sub certa condicione echoes the language of laws and contracts: besides historians and jurists cf. *Tr.* 1.2.109 where O. asks the gods *sub condicione uocati*, to spare him if innocent, but drown him if guilty.

321 casta negor: Claudia is as firm in her request as she is brief in explaining her problem. If Cybele finds Claudia guilty (*si . . . damnas*) she accepts death, but if – O. shifts syntactical subjects – there is no charge against her, the goddess is to give a *pignus*, 'guarantee', of her right to live, by moving in answer to her pressure.

322–3 morte luam . . . pignora uitae: since in Republican law adultery was a private, not a public offence, Claudia can only have in mind either suicide or execution by private decision of her Paterfamilias in consultation with the family council. Although Augustan law and earlier custom permitted a father (or husband, if the wife was *in manu*) to avenge his honour by killing an unfaithful daughter/wife if caught in the offence, a decision in cold blood would require the approval of a family council; see Treggiari (1992) 264–5.

324 re dabis et castas casta sequere: *re* denotes 'action', 'event'. With the *polyptoton*, *castas casta*, cf. 184 *aeraque . . . aere* and 239n. The futures *dabis*, *sequere* have the force of polite imperatives.

325 exiguo . . . conamine traxit: *conamen*, a Lucretian coinage, is common in O.; cf. *Met.* 3.60 *magnum magno conamine misit*, 8.366, 10.390, 15.224. Claudia's effortless pull is contrasted with the previous struggle.

326 scaena testificata: O. cites the theatre as his witness. But given the normal fictionality of ancient theatre, performance of a Miracle play on this theme was no guarantee of historical fact.

327 mota dea est, sequiturque: a delightful pun on the two senses, emotional and physical, in which the goddess is moved. (Contrast the more conventional *mota* of 15 above and *mota dea est* at 729, *Met.* 7.711.) *laudatque sequendo* construes the goddess's movement as her positive verdict (as 328 *sonus* testifies to human approval and rejoicing that the portent is resolved).

328 index laetitiae: cf. *clamor* as *index* of enthusiasm in Livy 3.62.4, 7.37.3, 23.46.2, and e.g. Cic. *Agr.* 2.4 *uocem uiuam indicem uestrarum erga me uoluntatum.* (See A. D. Nock, *Essays on religion and the ancient world* II (Oxford 1972) 252–70 on the pattern of these divine tests, and this narrative in particular.)

329–30 fluminis ad flexum . . . Tiberina . . . | Atria: cf. Virg. *Georg.* 3.14–15 *tardis ingens ubi flexibus errat | Mincius*, and of the journey up the Tiber *Aen.* 8.95 *longos superant flexus.* The *atria Tiberina* at this bend northwards are otherwise unknown: there were clearly no 'halls' in O.'s own time but the name may refer to a natural feature. The stress on naming is typical of this aetiological poetry; cf. 338n.

331–6 A little set-piece, balancing symmetrical accounts of the mooring and relaunching of the boat overnight against concern for the needs of men and gods: cf. Hor. *Sat.* 1.5.19–20 *nauta piger saxo religat* ... | *iamque dies aderat*; both are gentle parodies of the formulaic diction of epic for recurring actions. The metrical and grammatical symmetry of the procedure and its reversal in 331/333 with its curiously specific stump of oak is a *jeu d'esprit* like the undressing and dressing of 135/137.

331 querno ... in stipite: for *religare in* cf. *Met.* 14.248; elsewhere it is found with bare abl., or with *a* or *e*; but cf. *OLD* s.v. 3b citing Hor. *Odes* 1.32.7–8, Virg. *Aen* 7.106 *gramineo ripae religauit ab aggere classem.* The reading *a stipite* of IM may be right.

332 dantque leui somno corpora functa cibo: cf. 2.327 *sic epulis functi sic dant sua corpora somno*, 2.791 *functus erat dapibus*; but the recurring Homeric formula of satiety in e.g. *Il.* 1.469, *Od.* 1.150 is followed by conversation or drinking, not sleep! Bömer claims this use of *fungor* with food words as an innovation of *Fasti*, and *TLL* VII 1589.58ff. offers no later instances.

334–6 ante ... dedere ... coronarunt ... mactarunt: the three pious acts, subordinated and retrospective, are listed in crescendo; the simple portable or improvised altar and incense (cf. Hor. *Odes* 3.23.3), the garlands for the ship (cf. 6.779, Liv. 23.11.5, Prop. 3.24.15, *Met.* 15.696 (another parallel from the voyage of Aesculapius' serpent to Rome)) and finally a costly sacrifice of an unblemished heifer, unmated and *operum* ... *rudem* (cf. 1.83) unused for draught work.

335 sine labe iuuencam: with the adnominal or adjectival use of the prepositional phrase cf. *Met.* 2.537 *totas sine labe columbas*, Am. 1.3.13 *sine crimine mores*, 1.7.51 *sine sanguine uultu* and McKeown ad loc., citing parallels with other prepositions.

337–40 est locus (cf. 2.491) introduces a diversion, a change of place (ἔκβασις τόπου) framed by the name *Almo* (337, 340) and probably corresponding as Bömer suggests to a ritual performed apart from the main procession into Rome. O. incorporates the *lauatio* into his reconstruction of Claudia's day of triumph, in which she accompanies the goddess on the ox-drawn wagon along the Via Appia to enter by the Porta Capena.

Although a *lauatio* is recorded in response to prodigies in 38 BC (Cassius Dio 48.43.5) there is no evidence for regular washing of the goddess's image at Rome before the time of Claudius (cf. Bömer, *RE* XXI 1949–1952) when it was part of the March rituals more than eight days before the Megalensia. But given the Roman attitude to the Cybele cult, of which only one part, the Megalensia, was official, rituals that were conducted by the Phrygian priests would not be mentioned in public calendars. Although the significance of this and similar rituals is disputed by Bömer, its association with the approach of spring brings it into line with other Roman ritual cleansings (e.g. of Vesta) whether the purpose was purificatory or to foster fertility.

With *lubricus ... Almo* cf. 6.238 *lubrice Thybri.*

338 nomen magno perdit ab amne minor: sc. *minor amnis.* For *perdit* 'loses', 'is robbed of', cf. *Ex P.* 4.10.46 *uimque ... multo perdit ab amne suam. ab* is causal, 'as a result of'. See K. Guttmann, *Sogenanntes instrumentales ab bei Ovid* (Dortmund 1890) 15–20. (I owe this reference to Professor Kenney.) For the motif of tributaries losing their identity cf. e.g. Luc. 6.375–6 *solus in alterius nomen cum uenerit undae | defendit Titaressus aquas.*

339–40 purpurea canus cum ueste sacerdos | ... dominam sacraque lauit: for the juxtaposition of contrasted colours cf. 135 *aurea marmoreo,* 5.28 *aurea purpureo.* The Phrygian priest (not a Gallus) washes both the image and the vessels used in her service. Here Cybele is called *domina* for the first time in the poem (but cf. Cat. 35.14, 63.13 and 91, Virg. *Aen.* 3.113) because she has now accepted patronage over Rome.

341–2 exululant comites ... | et feriunt molles taurea terga manus: the procession resumes with echoes of 185–6 (*molli comitum ceruice ... exululata*) and 183 (*inania tympana*). *taurea terga* is adapted from Cat. 63.10.

344 credita uix tandem acts as an inner ring-composition, recalling Claudia's introduction in 307, as her chastity is vindicated (but barely – O. knows human malice) *teste ... dea.*

345–6 ipsa sedens plaustro ... inuecta ... | sparguntur ... boues: the last stage of the journey. The reference to the Porta

Capena implies that she was travelling the Via Appia, built by Claudia's ancestor Appius Claudius. With *sedens* O. evokes the familiar enthroned image of Cybele, as crowds throw fresh flowers over her ox team.

347 Nasica accepit: with a sudden change of narrative pace the Senate's hero Scipio Nasica (a sort of Roman Albert Herring designated to meet the Mother; see 249–346n.) is dismissed in a half-line, and the temple foundation likewise. In fact Cybele was housed in the temple of Victory until her own could be completed near by: both temples stood on the Palatine close to the site of Augustus' house. Livy does not record the vow or senatorial decree to erect it, but it was dedicated by M. Iunius Brutus in 191 (Livy 36.36.3).

348 Augustus nunc est, ante Metellus erat: Augustus himself records his restoration (*Res gestae* 19) in AD 3, one of the last datable events in the main body of the *Fasti* (Val. Max. 1.8.11). The temple of 191 had burnt down in 111 BC. Any one of four senior Metelli could have been the rebuilder: M. Caecilius, or C. Caecilius Caprarius, after their triumph in 111 BC, Q. Caecilius Numidicus, Cos. 109, or the Pontifex Maximus Delmaticus.

349 O. returns to Erato (195–6n.) and marks a pause before four supplementary questions.

350 'parua cur stipe quaerit opes?': *stips* (with short *i*, contrast *stipes* with long first syllable in 331, 333) was alms gathered by the priests, cf. Lucr. 2.626–7 (cited 181–6n.), Cic. *Leg.* 2.22 *praeter Idaeae matris famulos eosque iustis diebus, ne quis stipem cogito*, and Pliny, *NH* 18.15, where a statue is erected, like Metellus' temple *a populo stipe conlata.*

351 delubra: the pl. is common (cf. e.g. 2.56 *Sospita delubris dicitur aucta nouis*) in prose and verse of Roman temples enclosed by a portico (so Probus, *GLK* IV 202.23–4).

352 mos ... inde manet: the mark of an *aition*, see 211n.

353–4 'I asked why, more than at other times, people take turns going to parties and attending formally invited dinners in throngs.' For *dapes* of religious feasts cf. 424, 745 below, 2.633, 6.172 and 671. With *concelebrare* cf. [Cic.] *Comm. pet.* 44 *in conuiuiis quae fac abs te et ab amicis tuis concelebrentur.*

355–6 'quod bene mutarit ... | 'captant mutatis sedibus omen idem: *mutarit* = *muta(ue)rit*, pf. subjunctive, because this explanation is attributed to those who cite it as their motive for copying (*captare*) the omen. The best omens were *oblata*, not sought out (*impetrata*) or angled for. Cf. Quint. 9.3.73 on word-play, contrasting a *uox* ... *non captata sed uelut oblata*). The changing of *sedes* for dinner imitates the goddess's immigration. The inadmissibility of *mutitationes* (the term used in *Fasti Praenestini*) in dactylic verse ensures that they go unnamed here, but they are recalled by the marked use of *mutare* in both the *aition* (355) and its current manifestation.

In Cic. *Cato* 45 Cato (a plebeian) reports that the dining clubs (*sodalitates*) were established this year, and he dined with his *sodales*. But Gellius 18.2.11–12 reports this as patrician practice, whereas plebeians exchanged dinners at the (much older) Cerialia. However, the custom may not have been so exclusive. At 2.24.2 Gellius speaks only of *principes ciuitatis qui ludis Megalensibus antiquo ritu mutitarent, id est mutua inter se dominia agitarent.*

357–60 institeram ... cum dea ... inquit: here *insistere* implies a verb of asking. O. varies the syntax of his frame with an inverse *cum*-clause (in which the main event is grammatically subordinated to its context) and an unvoiced question which the goddess, being divine, anticipates.

primi ... ludi | urbe ... nostra: first not in foundation but in the calendar of each year.

principiumque dati ... honoris habet: for *ludi* as a human honour to the gods cf. 3.783–4. But Cybele's privilege is accorded to her by the gods themselves out of respect for her seniority and role as Ur-Mutter. For other places where O. in Roman fashion stresses priority, cf. 25–30 above (where *principium* denotes origin), 1.178 *omina principiis* ... *inesse solent*, and 3.75–6 and 135.

361 'cur igitur Gallos qui se excidere uocamus?: *excidere* is 3rd pl. perf. ind. of *excido*, 'to cut out'. The usual word is *secare* (221–2n.). In his last recall of the self-castrating Galli to add one more *aition*, O. pretends ignorance, associating *Gallus* only with the western Gauls and Roman Gaul (*Gallica* ... *humus*). For the Gauls of Asia and Roman identification of the Galatae in Phrygia with Galli see Plb. 21.33–9, Livy 38.12.27, Pliny, *NH* 5.146–7 and 363n.

362 cum tanto ... distet 'although it is so far away': *tanto* is abl. of measure of difference, as in *tanto maior* (G–L §403).

363 'inter' ... 'uiridem Cybelen altasque Celaenas |

amnis it insana . . . aqua: for Mt Cybele, see 191n.; Celaenae, source of the Marsyas, was the first capital of Phrygia (Livy 38.13.5). O. may have derived this notice on the river Gallus from Verrius Flaccus (cf. Paul. *Fest.* 84.25 Lindsay) or from a mythical narrative of Callimachus. Pliny records the rivers Sangarius and Gallus at *NH* 5.147 *a quo nomen traxere Matris deum sacerdotes.* At 31.9 he cites Callimachus for the properties of this river, whose waters could heal gall-stones: *sed in potando necessarius modus, ne lymphatos agat.* O.'s list of psychotropic waters at *Met.* 15.317–18 *sunt qui . . . animos etiam ualeant mutare liquores* includes rivers that produce madness or coma (320–1).

365–6 qui bibit inde furit . . . qui bibit inde furit: reiteration of the first hemistich of the hexameter to end the pentameter is closural and emphatic; cf. Platnauer, *LEV* 34, citing *Am.* 3.6.61–2, *Her.* 5.117–18, 15.213–14, *Rem.* 385–6 and *F.* 2.235–6 (where the pentameter splits the opening hemistich: *ad bellum . . . una dies*).

procul hinc discedite, quis est | cura bonae mentis: *quis* (possessive dat.) = *quibus*. The warning recalls Catullus' envoi in 63.92 *procul a mea tuos sit furor omnis, era, domo.* But here it is diverted to others, and the stress on *Bona Mens* – a respected deity at Rome – would recall the association of *Bona Mens* with recovery from the *furor* of love in Prop. 3.24.19 *Mens Bona, si qua dea es, tua me in sacraria dono!*

367–8 'non pudet herbosum' . . . 'posuisse moretum': O.'s last question touches on the offering to the goddess. Since sacrifice is measured by its cost to the giver the simple vegetarian offering appears 'cheap'. The ritual meal was a poor shepherd's diet: the ingredients in [Virg.] *Moretum* 95–116 are shavings of hard, smoked pecorino cheese, pounded into a blend of four garlic bulbs, parsley, rue and cilantro and seasoned with salt and moistened with olive oil and a little vinegar to form a ball. E. J. Kenney on 116 *effecti species nomenque moreti* notes that the recipes given by Col. 12.59 and Apicius 1.21 list other herbs instead of garlic.

369–70 'lacte mero ueteres usi narrantur et herbis' | sponte sua siquas terra ferebat': the Muse's answer goes back to a pastoral stage in society before the introduction of agriculture, when peasants without grain to make porridge or (later) bread had only the milk products of their sheep and wild plants to season them. Compare 395 *panis erat primis uirides mortalibus herbae,* in the sequence designed to mark Ceres' benefaction by stressing the limited foodstuffs available: there 396 *quas tellus nullo sollicitante dabat* rewords 370. See also 743n. on the shepherd's offering of millet cakes and *lac tepidum*.

371 elisae miscetur caseus herbae: the rather drastic *elidere* (not found elsewhere in *Fasti* or the erotic elegies) here is a substitute for e.g. *contundere* (*Ecl.* 2.11 *herbas contundit olentis*) of pounding grain or seeds. Although *miscere* is often found with abl. with or without *cum*, dat. is quite common. In many cases such as 3.561 *mixta … lacrimis unguenta*, 5.343 *mixtus nullis … racemis*, the inflections do not permit us to decide; but cf. 6.440 *mixtaque erat flammae flamma*, *Her.* 4.9 *pudor est miscendus amori*.

372 priscos … cibos: Burman cites Athen. 4 137e for the Athenian offering of cheese, barley bread and olives to the Dioscuri as a reminder of the old diet (ὑπόμνησις … τῆς ἀρχαίας ἀγωγῆς).

373–92 (5 April G NON N, 6–8 April H N, A N, B N, 9 April C N, 10 April D N)

Four short entries (for 5, 6, 9 and 10 April) alternate the astronomical notices of 373–6 and 387–8 with scenes set at the theatrical and circus games of the *Ludi Megalenses*.

373–6 On the Nones (5 April), the *Fasti Praenestini* read *non(ae) n(efastus). Ludi. Fortunae Publicae Citerio(ri) in Colle.* For lack of colourful historical details O. enriches this brief notice with a mythologizing periphrasis for the coming of dawn.

373 Postera cum caelo … Pallantias: for *Pallantias* identifying dawn as child of the Titan Pallas (the son of Megamedes in Hom. *h. Herm.* 100), cf. *Met.* 9.421, and the periphrasis of 15.190–1 *cum praeuia lucis | tradendum Phoebo Pallantias inficit orbem*; for inflected cases O. uses the by-form *Pallantis* at 6.567, *Met.* 15.700.

motis … astris: compare the variation of 389–90, where dawn, *proxima Eos*, having put the morning star to flight (*stella fugata*) makes way for the sun (*dederit Phoebo … locum*, cf. *Met.* 15.191 cited above).

374 niueos Luna leuarit equos: *leuare* here of lightening the horses' burden, as the moon unharnesses them; *niuei* reflects the silvery colour of moonlight.

375–6 qui dicet … uerus erit: O.'s odd formulation comments ironically on the vagueness of the entry: no date, no dedicator, and no clear indication which of the three shrines of Fortuna Publica on the Esquiline (cf. Vitr. 3.2.2 *exemplar erit ad tres Fortunas, ex tribus quod est proxime portam Collinam*) is in question.

377–86 In this anecdote one couplet introduces and one follows the wise words of the old veteran.

377 Tertia lux . . . ludis erat: 6 April was the anniversary of the battle of Thapsus in 46, where Julius Caesar defeated the remaining Pompeians under Metellus Scipio and the African King Juba. The battle was represented at Caesar's triumph and in Augustan texts as a victory only over the barbarian enemy.

377–8 mihi . . . | spectanti senior continuusque loco: they would be watching the stage entertainments, wherever they had been transferred from the open space in front of the temple of Cybele; *continuusque loco* suggests formal seating. (Cf. *AA* 1.135–6, on seating ibid. 142 *lege . . . loci.*) The veteran, as a military tribune under Caesar, must have been well over 65. This encounter is modelled on Callimachus' reports in the *Aitia* of conversations with strangers or fellow guests (cf. 937–42, O. and the priest of Robigo, 6.397–416, O. and the matron).

379–80 Libycis . . . in oris | perfida magnanimi contudit arma Iubae: poets regularly use *Libycus* for African; cf. *Tr.* 1.3.19 *Libycis aberat diuersa sub oris*, *Ex P.* 4.16.23 *quique acies Libycas Romanaque proelia dixit.* Stranger is the juxtaposition of *perfida*, denoting Juba's rebellion from Rome, and modelled on the proverbial *perfidia . . . Punica* (Livy 21.4.9, W. Otto, *Die Sprichwörter . . . der Römer* 291) with the admiring *magnanimi*, perhaps a tribute to Juba's suicide.

381 dux mihi Caesar . . . sub quo meruisse . . . | glorior: Latin regularly uses *stipendium merere* (or deponent *mereri*) for doing one's military service (382 merely repeats the same idea in inverted form *officio* = *meruisse*).

glorior: only the first pers. sing. of this verb is admissible in dactylic verse, cf. 6.28, *Met.* 6.176 *Iuppiter alter auus; socero quoque glorior illo*, *Ex P.* 1.5.63.

383 hanc ego militia sedem, tu pace parasti: they are probably sitting in the first two rows of the fourteen assigned to the Equites by the Lex Roscia of 67 BC: compare Horace's protest against the upstart *tribunus militum* who sits in the *sedibus . . . primis* at

Epodes 4.15–16. E. Rawson, '*Discrimina ordinum*: the *lex Iulia theatralis*', *Studies in Roman culture and society* (Oxford 1993) 533–5 argues from the scholia of Ps.-Acron and Porphyrio ad loc. that Augustus' *lex Iulia theatralis* privileged those who served or had served in equestrian army posts and in the junior magistracies of the Vigintivirate with seats in front of the mass of Equites.

384 inter bis quinos usus honore uiros would make O. one of the board of ten *stlitibus iudicandis*, presiding over lawsuits. But in *Tr.* 4.10.34 he claims that he was one of the *tresuiri capitales*. Such positions were usually alternatives, since they were all included in the Vigintivirate through which aspirants to the Senate passed. But shortage of candidates may have enabled O. to hold successive offices (cf. Kenney (1969) 245–8).

385–6 plura locuturi ... seducimur ... Libra mouebat aquas: cf. *Met.* 7.348 *plura locuturo*. The sudden shower is blamed on the setting of Libra, perhaps because it is imagined with tipping scales (*pendula*) pouring out their content of rain. Pliny, *NH* 18.247 reports *Caesari VI Idus significatur imber librae occasu*, which dates the setting to 8 April, but its true setting did not begin until 10 April.

387 Ante tamen ... sistat 'but before the last day can end the shows': the subjunctive is anticipatory, cf. G–L 577. This is 9 April, the last day of the Ludi Scaenici. (*spectacula* would not be used for the circus races of 10 April.)

388 ensifer Orion: O. marks the apparent setting of Orion. MSS and editors disagree whether O. wrote *ensifer* (G) or *ensiger* (UIM), as in the only other instance of the form: *AA* 2.55–6 *tibi ... ensiger/-fer Orion aspiciendus erit*. Here the corruption *ensiferro* in A suggests miscopying of *-fer* (cf. 58n on *clauiger*). The name *Orion* is usually a molossus (– – –), as here, cf. 5.543; 6.788; but elsewhere (e.g. *Met.* 8.207, 13.294, 692, *AA* 1.731, *Aen.* 1.535) either the initial *O* or the subsequent *o* is treated as short to admit inflected forms.

389–90 Proxima uictricem cum Romam inspexerit Eos | ... locum: 10 April. O varies the time indication from 373–4, but *uictricem ... Romam* is new (otherwise found in O. only at *Tr.* 3.7.51, and *Ex P.* 4.3.46) and demands comment. Does it reflect Caesar's victory of 6 April as the victory of Rome herself? The notion of emerging greatness is reflected in the pentameter where Lucifer (*stella fugata*) makes way for the Sun.

391 pompa celeber numeroque deorum 'thronged with the parade with its number of gods': the last day of this as of other festivals was reserved for the chariot races, held in the Circus Maximus. O. describes both the setting and the *pompa deorum* at the unidentified festival in *Am.* 3.2. There seems to have been a *pompa* on race-days at most festivals.

392 primaque uentosis palma petetur equis: cf. *Am.* 3.2.82 *ille tenet palmam, palma petenda mea est*, and for the *palma* in stage contests, 5.189 *circus in hunc exit, clamataque palma theatris*. *equis* is dat. of agent. The marked words in this reference are *prima*, the first racing of the year, and *uentosis*, an innovative application of an adjective common in Virgil (*Georg.* 1.206, *Aen.* 6.335, etc.) and in O., of windy skies and seas. Applied to horses it surely recalls the Homeric tradition that horses were sired by the wind (*Il.* 20.221–9, Virg. *Georg.* 3.275).

393–620 (11 April E N) 12 April F N The Cerialia

Only the extreme left-hand side of the entry in *Fasti Praenestini* survives, containing F, the sixth day of the nundinal sequence, and Pr. (sc. *Idus*) the day before the Ides.

393 Hinc Cereris ludi: O. is not bound by the requirements of the official calendar: thus he passes over without indication the day intervening between the final *Ludi Circenses* of the Megalensia and the opening of the *Ludi Cereris*. His celebration of the games does not try to represent the cult of Ceres at Rome either in its origin or its current rituals.

The cult was brought to Rome in 493 BC when Sp. Postumius vowed a temple to Ceres with Libera (Proserpina) and Liber (Bacchus/Iacchus). Erected outside the Pomerium at the foot of the Aventine near the Circus Maximus, the temple was dedicated by Sp. Cassius in 486. It was burned down in 31 BC, restored (like the adjacent temple of Flora) by Augustus and Tiberius, and rededicated in AD 17 (Tac. *Ann.* 2.49). At some time before 202 BC *Ludi Cereris* began to be offered in the Circus by the Plebeian Aediles on 19 April, the Cerialia proper. In the next quarter century these were expanded with *ludi scaenici* to fill 12–18 April.

But earlier in the third century before it is first attested after the battle of Cannae in 216 BC (Livy. 22.56.4–5, Plut. *Fabius* 18), Rome had imported a second form of her worship from Greek Italy. This women's cult was public and official, and conducted by priestesses, *sacerdotes publicae Cereris populi Romani*, but these were brought from Magna Graecia, and the ritual itself was Greek (*sacra Graeca*, Cic. *Verr.* 2.4.114–15, *Balb.* 55). Each year at an unknown date in high summer the *sacrum anniuersarium Cereris* was observed by the *matronae* with nine days' fasting to mark the recovery of Proserpina, *inuentio Proserpinae* (Paul. *Fest.* 86 Lindsay). It is this women's festival which O. seems to recall in *Met.* 10.431–3 *festa piae Cereris celebrabant annua matres | illa quibus niuea uelatae corpora ueste | primitias frugum dant spicea serta suarum.* In *Am.* 3.10, an elegy whose praise of Ceres otherwise closely resembles *F.* 4.399–416, he regrets the cult's requirement of chastity. (See Le Bonniec (1958) chs. 8, 10 and 12.)

Here, then, O. chooses the first day of the games, not the actual holy day, 19 April, to offer as homage the religious narrative that really belongs to the later, summmer, festival (Le Bonniec (1958) 331): to blend the two occasions, he addresses the farmers in the opening hymn (407 *orate, coloni*, 410–11 *detis*, *accendite*) and returns to them at 619–20.

non est opus indice causae: for the phrase cf. *Her.* 16.3 *eloquar, an flammae non est opus indice notae?* The word *index* (cf. 328n.) here alludes to O.'s practice in the *Fasti* of consulting divine interlocutors, Muses (like Erato), priests, and informed fellow citizens (see 195, 379, 689, 938). Compare his citation of witnesses in *Ex P.* 2.1.21 *indice te didici*, 3.9.49–50 *Musa mea est index nimium quoque uera malorum | atque incorrupti pondera testis habet*, 4.13.3, and 4.14.36. Kenney (1969) 253 notes *index* (26 times in O.: not found in Lucr., Cat., Virg., Hor., once in Prop.) as one of the legal terms brought into poetry by O. under the influence of his experience as a *iudex priuatus*.

394 sponte deae munus promeritumque patet: given the Roman sense of reciprocity a service (*munus*) also deserves recompense (*promeritum*). Man's obligation to Ceres for his basic food is apparent: despite the *praeteritio*, *patet* leads into the account of Ceres' *munus*.

395–416 O.'s account of Ceres' benefactions opens with a summary of human life before Ceres' gift of agriculture, expands into hymn-like celebration of her gifts (401–4), touches briefly on the moral decline brought by further technical progress (405–6) and invokes Ceres as a moral force against war and the sacrifice of working domestic animals. Each of these themes has a long history before and within O.'s poetry, but the immediate poetic model for much of the language and thought is Virgil's *Georgics*, both for its praise of Ceres and its general perspective on human civilization. (See Fantham (1992b) 39–56.)

395 panis erat ... herbae: the first word, *panis* (AU), would shock O.'s readers as it seems to have shocked the scribe who originated the variant *messis* (Z): it occurs nowhere in Virgil, or indeed in O. before this passage, and returns only in the anecdote of the loaves thrown from the besieged Capitol at 6.311, 315. For 'bread', elevated poetry used the periphrase *dona ... Cereris* (*Met.* 5.655), or the metonymy *Ceres* (Naevius s.v. *cocus* ap. Festus 51 Lindsay, Lucr. 2.655, *Aen.* 1.177, 701, 7.113, *Met.* 3.437), but *Ceres* is more often used to denote wheat itself, as seed-corn (*AA* 1.401), as the growing plant, *Am.* 3.7.31 *carmine laesa Ceres sterilem uanescit in herbam*, or as grain (645n.). For *herba(e)* as the food of primitive men cf. 2.291–3 *uita feris similis ... | pro domibus frondes norant, pro frugibus herbas*, *Am.* 3.10.9–10 *sed glandem quercus ... ferebant; | haec erat et teneri caespitis herba cibus*, *AA* 2.475 *silua domus fuerat, cibus herba, cubilia frondes*. For grass as fodder see 767.

396 nullo sollicitante: the verb implies harassment (e.g. 1.304, 418, *Tr.* 4.8.6 *me nullo sollicitante metu*). The pre-agricultural golden age is described in similar terms at *Met.* 1.103 *cibis nullo cogente creatis*.

397 et modo carpebant uiuax e caespite gramen: *carpere gramen* is common of grazing animals, cf. *Aen.* 9.353, *Met.* 1.299, *Tr.* 4.8.20, but also denotes picking, e.g. *Met.* 7.232 *carpsit et Euboica uiuax Anthedone gramen*. In this passage, as in 7.418 (*aconita*) *nascuntur dura uiuacia caute*, *uiuax* denotes the freshness and potency of magic herbs.

398 nunc epulae tenera fronde cacumen erant: *modo ... nunc* varies the regular pairing *modo ... modo* or *nunc ... nunc*. As in 395 and 398 the verb takes the number of the predicate (see Kenney on *Her.* 16.52). Most MSS read *erant*, but Burman notes that several offer *erat*, which may be right. For *cacumen* of the growing tips of plants cf. 127, and with the mock grandeur of *epulae* cf. 545, Luc. 2.384 *huic epulae uicisse famem*.

399–400 postmodo glans nota est: bene erat . . . magnificas . . . opes: *postmodo*, 'in due course,' is a prosaic adverb not found in Virgil or *Met.* apart from 12.5, but common in Ovidian elegy (1.636, 2.53, 749, 3.272, etc., *AA* 2.322 *tum sere quod plena postmodo falce metas*. There is equal MS support for *nota* (A) and *nata* (UZ), but *nota* with its stress on human discovery of the acorn's food value (for which A–W–C compare 2.293) maintains the concern with human experience, whereas *nata* would divert attention to plant evolution. From Hesiod onwards tradition had it that acorns were men's first food: cf. *Met.* 1.106. Here his ironic praise of acorns as an improvement on grass gently reacts against Virg. *Georg.* 1.7–8 *Alma Ceres, uestro si munere tellus | Chaoniam pingui glandem mutauit arista*, and 1.147–9 cited at 401–2n.

magnificas . . . opes 'sumptuous wealth': the adjective (not found in Virgil or *Met.*) evokes luxury, cf. 6.637 *magnifica . . . aede*.

401–2 prima Ceres . . . | mutauit glandes utiliore cibo: cf. Virg. *Georg.* 1.147–9 *prima Ceres ferro mortales uertere terram | instituit, cum iam glandes atque arbuta . . . | deficerent*, also imitated by O. in the Muses' Hymn to Ceres, *Met.* 5.341, also at *Am.* 3.10.11, *F.* 1.349 (a late, seemingly negative treatment: see Fantham (1992b)). O.'s *mutauit* here echoes *Georg.* 1.8. With *meliora alimenta* compare *Met.* 5.342, 656 thanking Ceres for *mitia alimenta* (but contrast *mitiora alimenta* of vegetarian diet at *Met.* 15.478).

403–4 illa iugo tauros collum praebere coegit; | tum primum soles eruta uidit humus: the art of ploughing attributed variously by Greek thought to Ceres or her Eleusinian protégé Triptolemus (see 559–60n.) is divided between the skill of breaking animals (normally neutered oxen, not bulls) to the yoke, and the new ability to open the earth (*eruta . . . humus*) to a good depth. But there were differences in ancient thought over the relationship of ploughing to metallurgy and (more sinister) mining. Ploughing is possible but inefficient without metal ploughshares, but with metal-working come weapons of war and mining for ore, first for useful iron, then luxurious gold and silver. All these ideas were sufficiently commonplace for O. to leap in one line (404) from the good uncovering of earth to the sunshine by ploughing (cf. *Georg.* 1.45–8 *depresso incipiat iam tum mihi taurus aratro | ingemere . . . | illa seges demum uotis respondet auari | . . . bis quae solem, bis frigora sensit*) to the bad discovery of metal ores. For *eruere* of uprooted crops cf. 1.352, 3.340 *hortis eruta cepa meis*, *Met.* 15.113; the construction (*humus* as object of *eruere*) is without parallel.

405 aes erat in pretio: O.'s development of this theme of human greed in 1.217 *in pretio pretium nunc est* and 221 *aera dabant olim; melius nunc omen in auro est* allows bronze (whether as weapon or bullion) relative innocence; the age of bronze was either equated with the Heroic Age (as in *Met.* 1.125–7) or seen as immediately following it.

405–6 Chalybeïa massa latebat: | eheu, perpetuo debuit illa tegi: the wish that iron might have remained hidden recalls Callimachus' curse on the inventors of forging at *Aitia* fr. 110.13 Pfeiffer translated by Cat. 66.48 *Iuppiter, ut Chalybon omne genus pereat.* Pentasyllabic *Chalybeïa* (⏑⏑ –⏑⏑) is formed from *Chalybes*, the mythical forgers of iron believed to dwell East of the Black Sea (Ap. Rhod. 2.374–7 'the Chalybes, most wretched of men, ... sons of toil, they busy themselves with working iron'): cf. Virg. *Georg.* 1.58 *at Chalybes nudi ferrum*, and in the forging scene of *Aen.* 8. 421 *stricturae Chalybum*, 446 *uulnificusque chalybs ... liquescit*, 453 *uersantque tenaci forcipe massam.*

407 et uos ... coloni: the apostrophe to (tenant) farmers assumes a rustic setting like the celebration of the *Sementiuae* in 1.695 *haec uos optate, coloni*, which also ends by invoking Peace at 1.704 *Pax Cererem nutrit: Pacis alumna Ceres.* The linking of Ceres and agriculture with Peace echoes Tib. 1.10.45–6 *interea Pax arua colat. Pax candida primum | ducit araturos sub iuga curua boues*; cf. also Hor. *Odes* 4.5.17–18 *tutus bos etenim rura perambulat | nutrit rura Ceres, almaque Faustitas.* Both Peace and Ceres are among the suggested identities of the suckling mother goddess surrounded by fertility symbols on the Ara Pacis, and Zanker (1988) 175 supports the identification, commenting 'in a different context the goddess ... can indeed represent Tellus, Italia or Ceres ... the mother goddess of Augustan art, whatever we call her, always embodies the same ideas'.

408 pacificumque ducem: *pacificus* (also found in Cic. *Att.* 8.12.4, where it is contrasted with poetic *bellator*) is probably recoined to honour the *dux* who is O.'s addressee. When O. first wrote *Fasti* this was Augustus himself, but another late reference to Germanicus cannot be excluded, in view of the emphatic association of Peace with his triumph in 1.281–2.

For the Romans Peace (originally the treaty ending a war) implied victory. This victorious Peace is a recurring theme of *Fasti* book 1: close to 408 is 285–7 *Iane fac aeternos Pacem Pacisque ministros*, and the appeal to Pax (1.709–12) in connection with the dedication of the Ara Pacis on 30 Jan.

409–10 farra deae ... licet ... | detis: permission to make these simple offerings is virtually a command, as 411 *accendite* shows. Twice already in *Fasti* (1.672 and 2.520 *primitias Cereri farra resecta dabant*) O. has associated *far* ('spelt', or more precisely 'emmer'), one of the oldest Italian grain crops, with Ceres. According to Pliny, *NH* 18.7–8 Numa invented the sacrificial seasoning of *mola salsa* made from ground *far* mixed with salt: see also 1.128 *farraque mixta sale*, 337–8 *ante, deos homini quod conciliare ualeret, | far erat et puri lucida mica salis*.

micaeque ... salientis honorem: adapted from Hor. *Odes* 3.23.20 *farre pio et saliente mica*. In both poets *mica saliens*, 'dancing spark', puns on *sal*. On modes of sacrifice see Introd. 3(i)(*c*).

411 et si tura aberunt, unctas accendite taedas: as O. argues in 1.337ff., men offered *far* before incense and myrrh and saffron were imported. In 2.28 he cites the use of pine branches in ritual; here pine brands are dipped in oil to form torches (a symbol of Ceres' search, held by her worshippers, see 493–4n.).

412 parua ... sint modo casta 'little ... if ritually pure': while *parua* looks back to the *mola salsa* and incense, *sint modo casta* warns of the next prohibition.

413 a boue ... cultros remouete: to sacrifice the labouring ox is unjust, hence the prohibition in Ceres' name. In fact the normal sacrifice to her in Greece and Rome was a pig. In 414 *ignauam sacrificate suem* the pig is blamed for its idleness: contrast 1.349 *prima Ceres auidae gauisa est sanguine porcae*, where the more usual reason is given that greedy pigs root up the grain.

succincti ... ministri: the *popae* who butchered the victim hitched up (*succingere*) their skirts to reduce the mess from spilt blood.

414 sacrificate: usually intransitive, and prosaic, but cf. Ennius, *Ann.* 214 Skutsch *Poeni soliti suos sacrificare puellos*.

415–16 non est ferienda securi; | uiuat et ... laboret: this couplet recapitulates 413–14. *uiuat et ... laboret* recalls *aret*, as *securi* is a variation on *cultros* (for which cf. 1.327). The victim was killed instantly by a knife-thrust to slit its throat, but an axe (chopper) would be needed to sever the neckbones.

417–618 Pluto's rape of Proserpina, Ceres' search, and the final compromise that restored fertility to earth.

This is O.'s longest elegiac narrative, just as the alternative version composed as a competition piece by the Muse Calliope and reported to Pallas/Minerva in *Met.* 5.346–661 is the longest secondary narrative in the *Metamorphoses*. Their differences in content, tone and form were first discussed in generic terms by Richard Heinze (1915); Herter (1941) 236–68 reopened the old problem of O.'s sources, arguing that *Fasti* depended on a lost account in Callimachus' *Aitia* (of which some fragments survive: 43–6 Pfeiffer) but he rejected *a priori* the possibility of O.'s dependence on the Homeric Hymn to Demeter. The relationship of the *Fasti* account to that hymn has now been definitively established by Hinds (1987a). For the hymn itself see Richardson (1974) and Foley (1993).

We cannot know what mythical events were re-enacted in the secret ritual of the Eleusinian mysteries, but for non-initiates at least the Homeric Hymn established a canonical Greek version of Demeter's visit to Eleusis after the Rape: and its narrative contents are largely reproduced in *Fasti* IV (whereas the version of *Metamorphoses* reduces Demeter's stay in Eleusis to a mere notice, substituting extensive subsidiary Sicilian episodes).

For the location of the rape at Enna there was a Sicilian historical tradition (derived from Timaeus of Tauromenium, cf. Diod. Sic. 5.3–6), and an influential Roman text: Diodorus describes Enna (Ovid's *Henna*) as 'sacred groves surrounded by marshland and a huge grotto which contains a chasm leading down to the earth and opens to the north: through it as the myth tells us Pluto came with his chariot and ravished the Maiden; violets bloom the whole year long and the whole aspect of the place is one of flowers and delight'. On Cicero's digression on Enna and the rape of Proserpina in *Verr.* 2.4.106–7 see Hinds (1987a) 38–42 and (1982) 476–8.

O.'s narrative moves in three main sections. (A) 417–98: the rape and Ceres' futile search in Sicily; (B) 499–562 (499–502 are transitional): her arrival in despair at Eleusis and her stay with Celeus; the interruption of her attempt to immortalize young Triptolemus and her prophecy of his future as a cult-hero, founder of agriculture; (C) 563–618 (the wanderings of 563–74 are transitional): Ceres' discovery of Proserpina's whereabouts from the Sun, her protest and negotiation with Jupiter, the final compromise and the restoration of Ceres' happiness and blessings to man on earth.

417–98 (A) The rape and Sicilian search

417 Exigit ipse locus raptus ut uirginis edam: the poet presents his theme in self-conscious metaliterary form, like a formal religious narrative (The Passion, The Annunciation) or a modern title; O.'s 'Rape of the Maiden' modernizes the introduction of the Homeric Hymn, 'Demeter and her daughter, whom Hades snatched away' (*h. Dem.* 2–3), but omits the Hymn's reassuring allusion to the resolution of the act of violence by Zeus's decision. Instead O. represents the impending tale as a task required by the occasion, but *locus* (the point in the calendar/poem) can also perhaps be taken (Hinds (1987a) 39–40) as the traditional site, the *locus* of Enna, demanding the celebration of its most famous episode. Even O.'s language, with the unprecedented pl. *raptus* (the sing. is found at *Met.* 3.722, and a variant reading at *Tr.* 5.10.16) and solemn *edam* (see 318n. for the tone of *edere*) carries a hint of ironic (self-mocking) inflation.

418 recognosces: the verb occurs once in Virgil (of Augustus reviewing the offerings of his triumph, *Aen.* 8.721); in O. only at 1.8 *sacra recognosces*, also addressed to his dedicatee, and *Met.* 11.62. Hinds (1987a) 39–40, 71, takes the verb as a pointer alerting the reader to recall and compare the well known Homeric Hymn. Combined with *docendus eris* this introduction promises O.'s imperial reader a narrative both familiar and novel.

419–20 terra tribus scopulis ... | Trinacris, a positu nomen adepta loci: O. is first to adopt in Latin (cf. *Met.* 5.348) the Greek formation *Trinacris* of the more common *Trinacria* (based on τρι- and ἄκρος: *a triangula specie* (Pliny, *NH* 3.86)). The name Trinacria (*Aen.* 3.440, 582, 5.393; O. *Met.* 5.476, *Ex P.* 4.15.15) is itself simply the feminine form (sc. *terra* as here) of *Trinacrius*, found in Latin from Cat. 68.53 *Trinacria Rupes* = Aetna, so *Aen.* 3.384, 429, 554 etc. It was understood by O. (*Met.* 5.350–1), and Pliny to refer to the island's three promontories, Pelorus, facing Italy, Pachynus on the SE towards Greece and Lilybaeum facing Carthage (see *LALE* 621).

419 uastum procurrit in aequor: adapted by Luc. 2.427 *procurrit in aequora* to a river.

421–2 Grata domus Cereri: multas ibi possidet urbes, | in quibus est culto fertilis Henna solo: *ibi* (G) should be preferred to *ea* (AUM), since the goddess does not need the stress of the repetitive pronoun. Cic. *Verr.* 2.4.107 and 114, reports that all Sicily was thought to be under Ceres' protection because of its fertility. In this context *culto ... solo* itself suggests Ceres' gift of ploughing, but could be a contemporary reference (see 487, 617–18nn.)

422–3 frigida caelestum matres Arethusa uocarat: Arethusa, Muse of Theocritean bucolic (and Virg. *Ecl.* 10.1), was nymph of the fresh-water spring that can still be seen near the shore of Ortygia, island site of ancient Syracuse. Hence *frigida*, appropriate to cool springs and places, cf. *Ecl.* 5.25, *Georg.* 2.469, 3.324 etc., O. *Am.* 1.13.7, 2.16.36. In *Met.* 5.572–640 Arethusa tells the questing Ceres how she came to Sicily. Here she offers a sacred feast to other goddesses (*caelestum matres*), itself the prototype of the future women's rites for Ceres. *matres*, normally a periphrase for *matronae* ('wives') anticipates Ceres' absence when her only child is taken from her. Other divine gatherings in *Fasti* are hosted by Cybele (6.321) or held in honour of Bacchus (1.393–6).

424 dea flaua denotes Ceres, because her hair is the colour of ripe corn (cf. Virg. *Georg.* 1.96 *flaua Ceres*, *Am.* 3.10.43, also *Met.* 6.118 *et te flaua comas, frugum mitissima mater*); but O. also regularly alludes to Minerva and once to Apollo as *flauus/a.*

425 filia: in this version Ceres' child is not named until 483, where Ceres calls her Persephone (cf. 485, 579, 591); she calls her daughter Proserpina only once, at 587.

consuetis ... puellis: according to *Met.* 5.554–60 Persephone's attendants were turned into the Sirens. Europa is similarly *uirginibus Tyriis comitata* at *Met.* 2.845.

426 nudo per sua prata pede: Proserpina has the right to be at ease in her own land; cf. 3.604 (Aeneas walking *nudo pede* on his dotal beach), *Am.* 3.6.50 (*Ilia*) *errabat nudo per loca sola pede.*

The flower-gathering scene which in *Met.* v occupies only four lines, 391–4 *quo dum Proserpina luco | ludit et aut uiolas aut candida lilia carpit, | dumque puellari studio calathosque sinumque | implet et aequales certat superare legendo*, is teasingly extended over 20 lines here.

427–30 O. paints a generalized *locus amoenus* in the best tradition, with shade and running water (cf. Herter (1941) 246). With *ualle sub umbrosa locus est*, cf. 3.17–18 *umbrosae salices uolucresque canorae | fecerunt somnos et leue murmur aquae*; for shady valleys *Georg.* 3.331 *aestibus at mediis umbrosam exquirere uallem, AA* 1.289 *sub umbrosis nemorosae uallibus Idae.*

427 aspergine multa | uuidus ex alto desilientis aquae: for the waterfall, cf. *Met.* 1.572–3 (*Peneus*) *summis . . . aspergine siluis | impluit.* The word had an agricultural use, but is brought into poetry by Virgil, *Aen.* 3.534, and is common in *Met.* This is the only Ovidian instance of *aspergo* outside *Met.* With *desilientis* cf. Hor. *Odes* 3.13.15–16 *unde loquaces | lymphae desiliunt tuae.* Either *uuidus* (AU), or *umidus* (Z = IGM) as in *Met.* 5.390, could stand here; *uuidus* is to be preferred as the less familiar form, and appropriate to things/persons soaked (by rain etc.), cf. Varro, *LL* 5.109, Virg. *Ecl.* 10.20, *Georg.* 1.418 *Iuppiter uuidus Austris*, and 685n.

429–30 tot fuerant illic . . . colores | pictaque dissimili flore nitebat humus: cf. *Met.* 5.390 *dat . . . uarios* (*Tyrios* Anderson) *humus umida flores*, 10.261 *flores mille colorum*, 15.202–5 *tunc herba nitens* (*recens* Anderson) *et roboris expers | turget . . . florumque coloribus almus | ludit ager*, *Tr.* 3.12.7 *prataque pubescunt uariorum flore colorum.* O. plays with conventional diction: *pingere* can be used of variegated animals (*Met.* 3.669, 4.24) and for the colour contrast of golden marigold and purple *uaccinia* in Virg. *Ecl.* 2.50. *nitebat* evokes brightness or glistening rather than colour, cf. 126 *uere nitent terrae* and *Met.* 15.202 cited above.

431 'comites, accedite' dixit: O.'s elegiac narrative uses more direct speech than that of *Met.*, cf. 447–8, 452, 456.

433 praeda puellares animos prolectat inanis: *praeda* foreshadows Proserpine's own immediate future as plunder (for *praeda* of ravished women cf. *Met.* 13.200 (Helen), *AA* 1.114, 125 (Sabines), *Her.* 12.111 *uirginitas facta est peregrini praeda latronis*). *puellaris* (cf. *Met.* 5.393 (cited 426n.), 463, and 5.611), like *puerilis* (540), offers an elevated alternative to the genitive case, and its possessive function helps to mitigate the double epithet, felt as a solecism by O.'s time: see Kenney on *Her.* 16.45–6.

prolectat is unique in O. or high poetry. The verb is used of seduction and bribery: Plaut. *Ba.* 567, Cic. *Flacc.* 18.

434 sedulitate: the girls' childish innocence is shown by their serious attention to this playful task. Prosaic and conversational (Varro, Cic., a letter of Caelius, Hor. *Sat.*), *sedulitas* is common in Ovidian elegy (3.668, 6.534) but limited in *Met.* to 10.409, the speech of Myrrha's nurse.

435–42 In this flower catalogue the impression of abundance is created by *distributio* (breakdown of a group into individual variants) first of the girls' choice of containers (*haec – haec – illa*), then their choice of flowers, in the third person (437–8 *illa – huic – illa*) with variation of case, then by apostrophe to the flowers which take over as subjects, and then are replaced by the girls (*pars – pars*) before 441 moves from the preferred rose to the nameless wild flowers and finally to Proserpina as subject.

435 haec inplet lento calathos e uimine nexos: with *lento*... *uimine* cf. Virg. *Georg.* 4.34, *Aen.* 6.137. O. expands Met. 5.393–4 *calathosque sinumque | implet* to a distich, its first line enriched by assonance on each letter of *lento*: *l*, *e*, *n*, *t*, and *o*.

436 haec gremium, laxos ... illa sinus: *laxus* should be understood with both nouns, the *gremium* of the extra fold above the girdle at the hips, *sinus* of the loose material above the waist girdle.

437–42 O. begins and ends his parade of flowers with varieties (*calthas*, *papauera*, etc.) not mentioned in the Homeric list of 'roses, crocuses, violets, iris and hyacinth and narcissus' (*h. Dem.* 6–7).

437 uiolaria: clumps or beds of violets; cf. Hor. *Odes* 2.15.5. Diodorus 5.4 claims these bloomed at Enna all year long.

438 papauereas subsecat ungue comas: for the language cf. Cat. 62.43 *cum tenui carptus defloruit ungui*, Ov. *Am.* 3.10.12 *falce coloratas subsecuitque comas*, *AA* 1.299–300 *nouas frondes et prata tenerrima* ... | *fertur* ... *subsecuisse manu. papauereus*, here only, is O.'s coinage.

439 has, hyacinthe, tenes; illas, amaranthe, moraris: apostrophe and symmetry of form and syntax; change of pronoun and verb converts the first hemistich (–∪∪ –∪∪ –) to the second (– –∪∪ –∪∪ –×) The familiar *hyacinth*, with its exotic Gk sounds of *y* and *th*, provokes O. to add the rarer *amaranth*. According to Pliny, *NH* 21.64–5, *uiola* (437) *hyacinthus* (439), *rosa* (441) and *lilia* (442) were the regular spring flowers of Italy.

440 pars thyma, pars rhoean et meliloton amat: three fragrant and useful flowers: *thyma* (n.pl.), popular for honeymaking *rhoea*, the field-poppy, a medicinal plant so called from the fall (ῥεῖν) of its petals (Pliny, *NH* 19.168–9, 21.165), *meliloton* (Pliny, *NH* 21.53, 63, 151), with medicinal uses, and a favourite filler in garlands. But it is surely a pointed coincidence that O. has introduced with *rhoea* a flower whose name coincides with the fatal pomegranate of *h. Dem.* 372, 412.

441–2 The pickers are forgotten, the flowers become so rare as to be yet unnamed, in contrast to Proserpina's own choice of *croci* and *lilia alba*: contrast *Met.* 5.392 cited at 426n.

443 carpendi studio ... longius itur: cf. 434 *sedulitate*, and *Met.* 5.393–4 *dumque puellari studio ... aequales certat superare legendo*. For *longius ire*, 'going too far', cf. 5.650, *Met.* 3.89, 8.349. For impersonal *itur*, leaving agent unspecified, cf. 3.791, *Aen.* 6.179, 12.529.

445 hanc uidet et uisam patruus uelociter aufert: *polyptoton* (*uidet/uisam*, cf. 324n.) and alliteration of initial *u* replace the *polysyndeton* of *Met.* 5.395 *paene simul uisa est dilectaque raptaque Diti*. No motive is given here for Dis's passion, which is caused by Cupid's arrow at *Met.* 5.384. In contrast the version of *Fasti* IV puts more stress on Proserpina's family connections with Jupiter as father and Dis as uncle (see 587, 598nn.).

446 caeruleis ... equis: only the colour of their harness is given in *Met.* 5.404. For this darker infernal shade (Gk κυάνεος) cf. *caeruleus imber* of storm cloud, *Aen.* 3.194, 5.10, Charon's boat at *Aen.* 6.410, Tisiphone's snakes at *Georg.* 4.482.

447–8 illa quidem clamabat 'io, carissima mater, | auferor!': *quidem* with its note of limitation anticipates failure. *Met.* 5.396–8 spells out her fear, *territa maesto | et matrem et comites sed matrem saepius ore | clamat*, and marks the torn garment, *summa uestem laniarat ab ora. clamare* becomes a reiterated motif; cf. 452 *clamant*, 453 *clamata*.

io: not always a cry of triumph, as at Hor. *Odes* 4.2.49–50 *io triumphe*; here it is a summons to help as in *Aen.* 7.400 *io, matres, audite*, *Met.* 3.729 *io comites, opus hoc uictoria nostra est.* With *auferor* cf. *AA* 2.91 (Icarus).

448 absciderateque: for postponed *-que* in the second half of the pentameter see *LEV* 92.

449–50 panditur interea Diti uia: cf. *Aen.* 10.1 *panditur interea* *domus omnipotentis Olympi*, but also 6.573–4 *horrisono stridentes cardine sacrae | panduntur portae*. The half-line, the idiom *uiam pandere* (*Aen.* 6.97, 12.626) and the allusion to the underworld are Virgilian; cf. with *Aen.* 6.573–4, 8.262 *panditur extemplo ... domus* of Cacus' hellish cave. The rapid re-entrance of Dis into the underworld in *Fasti* contrasts with his extended travels across the Sicilian plain to Cyane's pool and final entry in *Met.* 5.401–24.

inadsueti: a variant, also occurring at *AA* 1.300, *Ibis* 10, for the more common *insueti*, found only twice in O. Like Cerberus brought out of Hades in Sen. *HF* 821–7 these hell horses cannot bear the daylight.

451 at chorus aequalis: i.e. *aequalium*; cf. *Met.* 5.394 *aequales.*

452 clamant: plural for the collective subject; a necessary correction of MS *clamat* to provide length by position before *ad.*

453 ut clamata silet: compare Actaeon, *Met.* 3.244 (*comites*) *uelut absentem certatim Actaeona clamant*; Picus, *Met.* 14.397–8 *comites clamato saepe per agros | nequiquam Pico* (with the same passive use of *clamare*); and Hylas, Theocr. 13.56–8, Ap. Rhod. 1.1272, Prop. 1.20.49–50; all called by their companions without reply.

453–4 montes ululatibus implent | et feriunt ... pectora nuda manu: the cries, the bared breasts and the reiterated blows alike are marks of mourning, cf. 3.863–4 *mater | ... ferit attonita pectora nuda manu* (see also *plangor* 455). Hinds (1987a) 61 notes that O. has transferred the pathetic motif of the echoing mountains from the cries of Persephone (*h. Dem.* 38–9) to her attendants.

455–66 Ceres discovers her loss. The first six lines evoke her emotions by explicit comparison with a Bacchante and a grieving heifer, similes that recall famous passages: Dido's frenzy of grief when she hears of Aeneas' desertion, *Aen.* 4.300–2 *saeuit inops animi totamque incensa per urbem | bacchatur qualis commotis excita sacris | Thyias*, and the cow in Lucretius whose calf has been taken for sacrifice, Lucr. 2.355–9 *saltus orbata peragrans | quaerit humi pedibus uestigia pressa bisulcis | omnia conuisens oculis loca ... completque querellis | frondiferum nemus adsistens.*

But the Maenad simile had already been applied to the goddess in *h. Dem.* 386 at a much later narrative stage, when Demeter learned that Hades had taken Persephone and feared that she would never be reunited with her daughter (Hinds (1987a) 74).

455 attonita est plangore Ceres: cf. *Met.* 5.509–10 *mater* ... | *attonitaeque diu similis fuit*, and for *attonitus* 304, 3.864 *et ferit attonita pectora nuda manu.*

456 nec mora: sc. *fuit*, a common narrative marker (cf. 2.471, 709, 831, etc.), usually followed by a (coordinate) verb of action in aor. or historic present.

457–86 For stylistic analysis of this passage see Introd. 4(i).

457 mentis inops rapitur: Ceres too is carried away, but metaphorically, demented with shock. With *mentis inops* cf. *Aen.* 4.300 *inops animi*, Ov. *Met.* 6.37, and synonymous phrases 316 above *mente carere*, 2.753 *mens abit*, 797–8 *neque* ... *aliquid toto pectore mentis habet*, *AA* 1.122 *sine mente.*

457–8 quales audire solemus | ... fusis maenadas ire comis: O. is laughing at the convention he repeats; besides *Aen.* 4.300 cited above cf. *AA* 1.312 *ut Aonio concita Baccha deo*, *AA* 3.710, *Her.* 10.48. *quales* should be preferred to *ut quas* (A) which would require an artificial lengthening of the last syllable of *rapitur.*

459–60 Cf. *Rem.* 183–4 *sonant* ... *siluae mugitibus altae* | *et queritur uitulum mater abesse suum*; simple language relying on the pathetic *sua mater* (*uitulo* is psychological subject) and *fetus*... *suos* to recall the extended and famous Lucretian model.

461–2 nec ... et ... et: *polysyndeton* contributes to the tone of panic excitement.

concita cursu | fertur: *concita* indeed, for she will criss-cross Sicily before evening without a conveyance (cf. 497–8n.); for the phrase cf. *Aen.* 12.902 *cursu concitus heros*, *Met.* 3.711–13 *insano concita cursu* ... *mater* and other *concitae*, e.g. Ino 4.519, Procne 6.594.

463–4 puellaris nacta est uestigia plantae | et pressam ... pondere ... humum: Ceres finds tracks, raising the reader's hopes. For the language of tracking cf. *Met.* 8.333–4 *pars pressa sequuntur* | *signa pedum*, 13.548 *signaque nacta pedum sequitur* (another analogy of a bereaved mother animal). The preceding evocation of the Lucretian heifer who searches by sniffing the calf's tracks adds a touch of comedy to Ceres' search (we know the relatively happy outcome), but it also introduces the *aition* of 465–6. Although O. has taken pains to let readers know Proserpina was barefoot (426), readers might recall Euripides' scepticism in *Electra* 534–7 about recognition by footprint. On *puellaris* see 433n.

465 forsitan illa dies erroris summa fuisset: *errores* are a major narrative type in *Fasti* as in *Met.*, and the word signals a promise of exotic itineraries (467–80 and 563–74) to come, *nacta est* and *reperta* tease with false hope. So too in *Met.* 5.465–6 *ea ni mutata fuisset, | omnia narrasset*, and 468 *signa tamen manifesta dedit*, the reader is teased with Cyane's inability to inform Ceres.

466 si non turbassent signa reperta sues: pigs had blurred the footprints, a possible reason for their regular sacrifice to Ceres. But the link is not explicit here, and at 1.349–53 and *Met.* 15.112–13 the pig is simply punished for uprooting grain crops. *turbare* is used for the confusion of the Sibyl's prophetic leaves at *Aen.* 6.75 and of battle order at *Aen.* 11.618, 12.269, etc.

467–80 Ceres' detailed journeys across Sicily have no counterpart in *Met.* v, where she is constantly distracted by local nymphs and figures from SE Sicily. O. draws imaginatively on Aeneas' circumnavigation of Sicily from Aetna to Drepanum in *Aen.* 3.689–707. Both O. and Virgil very probably draw on Callimachus' *catalogue raisonné* of the cities of Sicily in *Aitia* book II, fr. 43 Pfeiffer (see Geymonat, *HSCP* 97 (1993) 323–31), but the only recognizable echo of Callimachus, the treatment of Zancle/Drepanon in 474, could derive from other sources such as Nicander, *Fr. Gr. Hist.* 15.

O. carefully regroups Virgil's geographically consecutive ports and rivers (cf. 471–2, 475, 477 and 479–80nn.), interweaving other sites, many virtually unknown.

467–70 Starting with inland Enna Ceres covers the east coast, Leontini, the rivers Amenanus (cf. *Met.* 15.279) and Acis, Cyane's pool, and the rivers Anapus (husband of the nymph Cyane, *Met.* 5.417) and Gelas.

468 herbifer Aci: with the Ovidian *herbifer* (also *Met.* 14.9 *herbiferos colles*) compare alternatives *herbosus* (Virg. *Georg.* 2.199), *herbidus* (*Met.* 8.282). The transformation of Acis, son of the local nymph Symaetha, into this river is told at *Met.* 13.885–97.

469–70 lenis Anapi | . . . uerticibus non adeunde Gela: cf. *Aen.* 3.702 *immanisque Gela fluuii cognomine dicta*. The abl. *uerticibus* is instrumental, as if *non adeunde* were a passive participle. The slow and swift currents are contrasted (for *uertices*, 'river currents', cf. 6.502, *Met.* 9.106, Virg. *Georg.* 3.241).

471 liquerat Ortygien Megareaque Pantagienque: Ceres

is now putting the east coast behind her. For the island Ortygia, ancient city centre of Syracuse, cf. *Aen.* 3.692–4 *iacet insula contra | Plemyrium undosum: nomen dixere priores | Ortygiam*; for coastal Megara and Pantagia, cf. *Aen.* 3.688–9 *uiuo praeteruehor ostia saxo | Pantagiae Megarosque sinus Thapsumque iacentem* (O. postpones Thapsus to 477). Unlike Virgil, O. prefers Greek inflections, especially the accusative in *-n* even when it was not needed to avoid elision. (See Quintilian 10.12.31 for the appeal of Gk terminal *-n* to Roman ears.)

472 Symaetheas: metrically ∪ – – –; an alternative adjectival form from Symaethus. Virgil has *Symaethius* (∪ – ∪×) at *Aen.* 9.584.

473 antraque Cyclopum positis exusta caminis: the subterranean forges of the Cyclopes are most commonly set under Mt Etna, but also under the volcanic Aeolian isles as in *Aen.* 8.416–19 *insula Sicanium iuxta latus Aeoliamque | erigitur Liparen ... | quam subter specus et Cyclopum exesa caminis | antra Aetnaea tonant.* In both allusions of this distich (see next n.) O. plays with mythical or geographical variants to tease his readers into uncertainty between Etna/Messina, or Aeolian Isles / Trapani, before disabusing them with references to Didyme and western Sicily in 475 and the explicit naming of Etna at 491. His substitution of *exusta*, 'scorched' (cf. Virg. *Georg.* 1.107 *exustus ager*, 3.432 *exusta palus*), for *exesa* in his Virgilian model is another literary challenge to his readers. O. reserves *exesus* for the crater of Etna (495).

474 quique locus = *et locus qui*: the relative precedes its grammatical antecedent.

curuae nomina falcis habet: the epithet is standard, cf. *Am.* 1.15.12 *incurua falce.* A famous but ambiguous aetiology, this 'place of the curved Sickle' could be either Drepanon (Trapani) in the far west or Zancle (present-day Messina). In fact both Etna and Zancle/ Messina are postponed (see 491, 499). Ceres is beginning to rush farther afield, and the Aeolian Isles (including Didyme, 475) Drepanon and Himera represent a visit to the NW before she crosses to the S coast.

475 Himeraque et Didymen Acragantaque Tauromenumque: for the pentasyllabic ending cf. 471. Of these polysyndetic Greek names only Acragas occurs in *Aen.* 3 (at 703). The Aeolian island of Didyme, N of Sicily, is far from Acragas on the S coast, and so is Acragas from Tauromenium (Taormina) on the E coast. *Taur-omenum* is a by-form to adjust the name to dactylic verse.

476 sacrarumque Mylas pascua laeta boum: because of its name Trinacria, Sicily was identified with *Thrinacie*, the island grazed by the cattle of the sun in *Odyssey* XII; hence both Pliny (*NH* 2.220) and Seneca (*NQ* 3.26.7), identify the rich alluvial promontory of *Mylai* as their pastures.

477 hinc Camerinan adit Thapsonque et Heloria Tempe: Camerina is on the S coast; Thapsus is on the E, near Syracuse, and not far from the Helorus. The three places appear in a different order in *Aen.* 3.689–707, at 701, 689 and 698 *solum stagnantis Helori*, and the intrusion of Tempe (the Thessalian valley, used as a generic term for pastoral landscape since Virg. *Georg.* 2.468, Hor. *Odes* 3.1.24) adds to the geographical confusion.

478 quaque iacet Zephyro semper apertus Eryx: assonance on *e*, *per* and *r*; Mt Eryx, exposed on the N coast of western Sicily (*Aen.* 12.701), was the cult centre of Aphrodite from which Rome imported Venus Erycina (874n.).

479–80 iamque Peloriaden Lilybaeaque, iamque Pachynon | lustrarat ... cornua trina: *trina*, the proposal of Heinsius' friend Jan Ulitius for *prima* in MSS, restores the Ovidian play on Sicily's name *Trinacria*; cf. 419 *terra tribus scopulis* ... and *Met.* 13.724–7 *tribus haec excurrit in aequora pinnis | ... uersa Pachynos ad Austros, | mollibus oppositum Zephyris Lilybaeon, ad Arctos | ... Peloros*. The distributive *trin-* is uncommon in O. (only 5.146, where A–W–C read the variant *terna*) and would be easily confused. The three capes of the island are seen as defences (*cornua*, the wings of an army arrayed for battle; *pinnae* of battlements).

Peloriaden (AUZ) is a fictitious patronymic, 'son of the giant', hence Gk 1st decl. acc. like *Iliaden* at 5.565. A–W–C print *Peloriadem* as if 3rd decl. Latin acc. of Gk *Pelorias*, but their own index shows that O. uses only the Gk acc. form in *-ada* of *-as* words.

Lilybaeaque: pl., for the sing. *Lilybaeum* in *Met.* 5.351, 13.726. Virg. *Aen.* 3.706 has adjectival *Lilybeïus*.

481–2 miseris loca cuncta querellis | implet: the Lucretian cow *omnia conuisens oculis loca, ... complet ... querellis | frondiferum nemus* (2.357–9), but the pentameter glides into a new parallel, Philomela, lamenting her murdered son Itys.

amissum cum gemit ales Ityn assimilates the child Itys, murdered by his mother, to the lost daughter. Besides Virg. *Georg.* 4.511–15 (cited Introd. 4(i)) cf. Hor. *Odes* 4.12.5–6 *Ityn flebiliter gemens | infelix auis.* Transformed as a nightingale Philomela is the prime example of maternal grief in Gk lyric and elegy, used for a similar comparison in Call. *H.* 5.93–5. O. tells the myth at *Met.* 6.438ff., cites it at *Am.* 2.6.10, 2.14.30, *Tr.* 2.390, and ends the pentameter with *ales Ityn* at *Am.* 3.12.32.

483–4 modo 'Persephone!' modo 'filia!' clamat, | clamat et alternis nomen utrumque ciet is answered (as if echoed) in 485–6 with formal and metrical correspondence of *Persephone, filia* (485), and *alternis nomen utrumque* (486). This patterned play outdoes earlier instances at 135/137 and 331/333 (see 135, 331–6nn.; cf. Introd. 4(i) p. 47). In the pentameters both framing disyllabic verbs *clamat/ciet, audit/perit* correspond. For the echoing of searchers' calls in place of a reply cf. Virg. *Ecl.* 6.43–4, Prop. 1.20.49–50.

484/486 alternis draws attention to O.'s poetic form as well as to Ceres' experience. For the adv. *alternis* of amoebean response, cf. Virg. *Ecl.* 3.59, 7.18. The adjective *alternus* is used by O. for statement/question and reply: cf. 1.176 *damus alternas accipimusque preces, Met.* 3.385 *alternae deceptus imagine uocis* (Echo, as implied also here), and for the alternating hexameter and pentameter of elegiac verses, cf. 2.121 *alterno carmine, Tr.* 3.1.11 and 56, 3.7.10.

nomen ... ciet: a heroic verb, cf. *Aen.* 3.68 of calling on the dead. The corresponding *perit* implies both 'is wasted', and 'dies away'.

487 pastorem uidisset an ... colentem 'whether she saw a shepherd or ploughman'; as in 17 *an* introduces an alternative. The subj. *uidisset* is iterative: see G–L 567, L–H 751, 774, 780

arua colentem: has agriculture been invented yet? There is some inconsistency in this narrative. Celeus' family certainly live on pre-agricultural foods, and (in contrast with *Met.* 5.475ff.) Ceres is not reported as killing grain crops in her anger: but see 422 above. The arable tilling of 487 seems confirmed by 617 *cessatis ... in aruis,* implying previous cultivation.

Ploughmen, shepherds and fishermen are the usual witnesses of outdoor incidents; cf. *Met.* 8.217–19.

488 gressus ... tulit is ironically misleading, like the search for footsteps: Proserpina was carried off (445–6 *aufert | ... portat*).

489–90 color unus ... tenebrisque teguntur | omnia: an original formulation of sunset, designed to contrast with the joyous brilliance of 429 *tot fuerant illic, quot habet natura, colores*. For the loss of colour with darkness cf. *Aen.* 6.271–2 *ubi caelum condidit umbra* | ... *et rebus nox abstulit atra colorem*: nothing in O. quite resembles this; 5.222 *unius tellus ante coloris erat* speaks only of the earth without flowers.

490 iam uigiles conticuere canes: the Romans called this time of night *conticinium*; for *uigiles* ... *canes* cf. 764n., 5.142 *peruigilantque canes*, 430 *et canis et uariae conticuistis aues*.

491 alta iacet uasti super ora Typhoëos Aetne: cf. *Met.* 5.346–8 *insula* ... | *Trinacris* ... *urget* | *aetherias ausum sperare Typhoëa sedes*, 352–3 *degrauat Aetna caput* ... | ... *flammamque ferox uomit ore Typhoeus*. Here and in *Met.* 5.321, 325, 348, Typhoëos is a quadrisyllable (∪ – ∪∪). It is trisyllabic in *Met.* 5.353 as in Virgil (*Georg.* 1.279, *Aen.* 9.716); at *Aen* 1.665 quadrisyllabic *Typhoëus* is the derivative adjective. The volcanic activities of Aetna were attributed to Zeus's crushing a defeated giant under the land mass of Sicily, cf. *Met.* 14.1 *iamque Giganteis iniectam faucibus Aetnen*. He is named as Typhoeus in Pindar, *Pyth.* 1.15–24 as in O.; in *Aen.* 3.578 Virgil names Enceladus.

492 anhelatis ignibus: fire is usually the subject of intransitive *anhelare* but is here made passive as the breath of Typhoeus. O. also attributes *anhelati ignes* to the fire-breathing bulls of Aeetes (*Met.* 7.116 = *Her.* 12.15).

493–4 illic accendit geminas ... pinus: | hinc Cereris sacris nunc quoque taeda datur: as in *Met.* 5.442–4 *illa duabus* | *flammiferas pinus manibus succendit ab Aetna* | *perque pruinosas tulit inrequieta tenebras*, Ceres uproots two pine trees as torches to continue her search. Hence she is called *taedifera* ... *dea* at 3.786. (For republican denarii depicting Ceres searching with these torches and in the serpent-drawn chariot (described in 497) see Frontispiece.) As an aetiological poem *Fasti* reports this as the origin (*hinc*) of the distribution (*datur*) of torches in contemporary cult (cf. 411n.). With *nunc quoque* cf. 504, 710, 806, and see Kenney on *Her.* 20.106, S. Myers, *Ovid's causes* (Ann Arbor 1994) 66 and n.22.

495–8 Only now does Ceres harness her chariot, in order to cross the sea: in the *Metamorphoses* narrative Ceres is depicted as travelling over all land and sea (*Met.* 5.462–4: the Eleusis episode is delayed and reduced to a notice at 645–7) before returning to Sicily; but there is no reference to her chariot until she learns that Proserpina has been taken by Dis, and ascends to Olympus to tackle Jupiter (*Met.* 5.511–12).

495 est specus exesi structura pumicis asper: the brief ἔκβασις τόπου ('change of location') exploits uncommon words (*exesus* only here and 3.747 in O., but see 473n.; prosaic *structura* only here and *Ex P.* 4.13.4) to provide harsh combinations of *s* with consonants, *sp*, *x*, *str*, *sp*, suggesting the rough volcanic surface of the crater/cave in which Ceres keeps her serpents and chariot.

496 non homini ... non adeunda ferae: Ovidian *non adeundus/a* (usually with dat. of agent, but cf. 470) covers forbidden places which it is not *fas* to approach; cf. 6.450 *non adeunda uiro*, *Met.* 8.785; Rome, from which O. was banned, *Tr.* 1.4.18, 1.8.38, 3.1.70; but also physically inaccessible places, *Ex P.* 1.8.12 *positu uix adeunda loci.*

497–8 frenatos curribus angues | iungit: a more detailed account in *Met.* 5.642–4 *geminos dea fertilis angues | curribus admouit frenisque coercuit ora | et medium caeli terraeque per aëra uecta est.* Are Ceres' serpents distinct in type from Medea's *dracones*? See 561–2n., and for Medea's *dracones*, *Met.* 7.220 *frenataque colla draconum*, *F.* 2.41 *frenatis ... draconibus*, *Tr.* 3.8.3 *frenare dracones.*

498 aequoreas ... aquas: a recurring internal pentameter rhyme; cf. 1.340, 2.68 and 116 and passim, but the epithet–noun combination is also found in other *sedes* (cf. 578 and *Met.* 11.520).

sicca pererrat is perhaps a pun: Ceres is not only dry-shod as she flies, but also hungry and thirsty. Contrast Circe walking dry-shod on water at *Met.* 14.48–50 *undas | in quibus ut solida ponit uestigia terra, | summaque decurrit pedibus super aequora siccis.* The verb *pererrare* (cf. 568 *pererrat iter*) is regularly transitive in Augustan poetry and prose; see *OLD* s.v. But transitive *errare* is limited to the past participle passive: besides 573, *TLL* v 2.812.77–83 cites only *Aen.* 3.690–1 *errata ... | litora* and *F.* 3.655 *erratis ... | in agris.*

499–502 Transition from A, the Sicilian narrative, to B, the Eleusinian narrative.

499–562 (transition 499–502) (B) The Eleusinian narrative

499–500 effugit et Syrtes, et te, Zanclaea Charybdi, | et ... uos, Nisei ... canes: the apostrophe of *te* serves metrical convenience, of *uos* conceptual symmetry. Ceres is able to escape the proverbial sea hazards, the pair of monsters besetting the Straits of Messina and the North African shifting sands: cf. *Am.* 2.16.21–6, *Tr.* 5.2.73–4 *hinc ego dum muter, uel me Zanclaea Charybdis | deuoret, Ex P.* 4.14.9–10 *in medias Syrtes, mediam mea uela Charybdin | mittite.* On Zancle (Messina) see 474. The original Greek colony was called Zancle either from the shape of its harbour (Thuc. 6.4.5) or more notoriously from the discarding by Kronos of the sickle with which he castrated his father Uranus, as reported by Call. *Aitia* 2 fr. 43.68–72 and Nicander, *Fr. Gr. Hist.* 15.

Nisei, naufraga monstra, canes: the only instance in O. of *naufragus* with the active sense of 'causing shipwreck', not the regular passive 'shipwrecked'. The dogs, not Scylla, are the *monstra*: cf. *Met.* 14.60, *Ex P.* 4.10.25. But they should not be *Nisei*, since Scylla, the marine hazard on the Calabrian shore of the straits of Messina, was not the daughter of Nisus of Megara, but the nymph victimized by Circe, as O. well knew (see *Met.* 14.60–7). The conflation of the two Scyllas may have been made by a Greek poet before Virg. *Ecl.* 6.74–5 *Scyllam Nisi, quam fama secuta est | candida succinctam latrantibus inguina monstris*, O.'s model for this passage as for *Am.* 3.12.21–2 *per nos Scylla patri caros furata capillos | pube premit rabidos inguinibusque canes, AA* 1.331–2.

Granted normal weather conditions Ceres' route from Aetna to Corinth would not bring her near any of these three hazards.

501 Hadriacumque patens late bimaremque Corinthum: sc. *effugit.* For the adjectival *Hadriacum* cf. Prop. 3.21.16 *Hadriaci ... aequoris*, [Ov.] *Hal.* 125.

The Adriatic was notorious for storms: cf. Hor. *Odes* 1.3.15, 33.15–16 *fretis acrior Hadriae | curuantis Calabros sinus.* In reporting his own parallel journey at *Tr.* 1.11.4–5 *mediis Hadria uidit aquis, | aut postquam bimarem cursu superauimus Isthmon* O. uses *Hadria* and the Horatian *bimaris* (*Odes* 1.7.2–3 *bimarisue Corinthi | moenia*); cf. *Met.* 5.407 *bimari gens orta Corintho*, 6.419–20 *bimari ... ab isthmo* (*bis*), 7.405, *Her.* 12.27. Corinth's position on the isthmus gave it access to both Saronic and Corinthian gulfs.

502 Attica terra, tuos: repeated in the same *sedes* at *Ex P.* 1.3.68 *legit enim sedes, Attica terra, tuas.* Elsewhere O. speaks of *Athenae*, but here Eleusis, not Athens, is the setting for Ceres' experiences. At this point the serpent-drawn chariot disappears, to materialize again only in 561: it cannot have been part of the Eleusis narrative as O. read it.

503–62 The visit to Eleusis. Despite the essential similarities between O.'s account of Ceres' visit to Eleusis and the narrative of the Homeric Hymn, O. has made major changes in both the timing of this episode and its detailed action. Thus where Demeter in the hymn came to Eleusis only in angry despair after Zeus had denied her request for Persephone's return (92–5), O.'s Ceres goes to the site of Eleusis as part of her quest for her daughter. He offers no particular reason for her arrival: it is simply the place where she comes to land and sits down to rest. Where the disguised Demeter had sat by the village well, and been invited by the daughters and wife of King Celeus to work as a nurse for the late-born child Demophoon (*h. Dem.* 96–168, named at 234) Ceres is found in open country by the poor peasant Celeus, who invites her home; the child Triptolemus (named by O. at 550) is sick and it is in preparing a sleeping-draught for him that she breaks her fast by tasting poppy seeds. Taken into her arms the child recovers health, and they rejoice. The story line converges at 549 (= *h. Dem.* 239), where the goddess is disturbed by Metaneira while trying to make the child immortal in the fire, and tells her that now the child will only be a mortal (further details, 549–55n.); in the hymn she also appears in her divine form and promises glory to the child, demands a temple and altar, and undertakes to instruct the Eleusinians in her cult. O.'s goddess takes no time to identify herself, but names the child as future inventor of ploughing and agriculture.

503 gelido . . . saxo: cf. *Met.* 1.376 *gelidoque pauens dedit oscula saxo. sedit* and 505 *durauit* are the first aorist forms after the predominantly historic present of the narrative.

504 Cecropidae nunc quoque triste uocant: with *Cecropidae* = Athenians, descendants of the legendary king Cecrops, cf. 3.81 *Pallada Cecropidae* (sc. *colunt*), *Met.* 7.486, 502 and 671. In *h. Dem.* 98ff. Demeter sits by the Maidens' well near the palace of King Celeus. Eleusinian tradition honoured in her memory a stone near the precinct, called ἀγέλαστος πέτρα (Apollod. 1.30, Pausanias 1.39.1). Together *maestissima* and *triste* relate the contemporary name (*nunc quoque* marks the *aition* as in 494) to Ceres' grief.

505 sub Ioue durauit: cf. 2.299 *sub Ioue durabant.*

multis ... diebus: ablative expressing duration; the earliest instance in Cat. 109.5 *tota ... uita.* Fordyce ad loc. cites only examples with *totus* but the pattern spreads widely: cf. 614 *tribus ... mensibus* and see G–L 393, K–S I 360–1.

506 et lunae patiens et pluuialis aquae: for *patiens* with gen., cf. 1.247 *patiens ... terra deorum, Met.* 2.653 *patientem ... mortis, Met.* 5.611 *longi patiens ... laboris.* Night and rain (with *pluuialis aquae* cf. *Met.* 8.333) are the hazards of the homeless, or of excluded lovers (cf. Prop. 1.16.23–4, Hor. *Odes* 3.10.19–20 *non hoc semper erit liminis aut aquae | caelestis patiens latus.*

O. has set Ceres down away from habitation so that she seems to endure the open not as an act of mourning, but for lack of human contact (see 503–62, 514nn.).

507 sors sua cuique loco est: O. emphasizes the changing destiny of Eleusis from early poverty to the fame of its association with the goddess. For the contrast of present glory and humble past, often applied to Rome's beginnings (the 'einst und jetzt' motif) cf. *Aen.* 8.99–100 *quae nunc Romana potentia caelo | aequauit, tunc res inopes Euandrus habebat.*

Cerialis Eleusin: for the verse-ending cf. *Met.* 7.439, *Her.* 4.67. Latin poetry represents the nominative of names like *Trachis, Eleusis* with a final *-n*, taken from the inflected stem ('Ελευσῖνος gen.).

508 Celei rura ... senis: the prosperous king of a small city in the hymn has been reduced to the Hellenistic cliché of a humble farmer, whose hospitality to the disguised god is a hardship that brings him reward. The welcome given to Theseus by the poor old woman in Callimachus' epyllion *Hecale* set the tone (and fashion) for episodes like the hospitality of Celeus to Ceres, or Hyrieus to Jupiter and Mercury (5.499–534) or that of Baucis and Philemon (*Met.* 8.629–720). See esp. App. 3 'The hospitality theme' in A. S. Hollis, ed., *Callimachus: Hecale* (Oxford 1990).

509 glandes excussaque mora rubetis: the diet of men in the pre-agricultural golden age of *Met.* 1.105–6 *in duris haerentia mora rubetis | et ... glandes* (cf. 402). Celeus is represented as a 'gatherer' of acorns and berries (but also like Aristaeus, as a shepherd and apiarist: cf. 545–6).

510 ligna focis: Celeus uses fire not for cooking but for warmth.

511–12 filia parua duas ... redigebat capellas, | ... filius aeger erat: the descriptive imperfects contrast with the prevailing historic present forms (cf. 503n.). O. has made three changes towards pathos: the tiny flock, the reduction of Celeus' four (named and articulate) daughters to one, and the conversion of the late-born Demophoon into a sick baby.

tener in cunis: cf. 6.135–6 *puerosque ... nutricis egentes | ... cunis corpora rapta suis*, *Met.* 3.310–11 *infans ... tener* (Bacchus), Met. 3.313–14 *furtim illum primis Ino matertera cunis | educat*, *Am.* 3.10.22 *exiguus tenero lac bibit ore puer.* In the later version of the myth cited by Apollod. 1.5.1–2 Demophoon burned to death when Demeter was interrupted as she was trying to make him immortal by fire: so the goddess bestowed the role of inventor of ploughing upon his elder brother Triptolemus. O. avoids the painful detail of the burnt child by making Triptolemus both the inventor (as he had always been in Attic cult) and the child set in the ashes of the hearth.

513 'mater' ... (mota est dea nomine matris): literal at 327, *mota dea est* simply denotes emotion here, but at 729 will imply granting an answer to prayer. O. has already made much of *nomen matris* in the Cybele episode at 259–64.

514 'quid facis in solis incomitata locis?': for the pathetic combination of *sol-* and *incomitata* cf. *Aen.* 4.466–8 *semperque relinqui | sola sibi, semper longam incomitata uidetur | ire uiam.* The negative participle (with which cf. 450 *inadsueti*) occurs also at *Aen.* 2.456, and 5 times in O.: cf. *Met.* 7.185, *Rem* 592, *Tr.* 2.480, and *Ex P.* 2.3.36. O. has not, like the Homeric hymn, set Ceres down at a public gathering-place, but on a rock in rough private land from which this shepherd gets his sustenance.

515 perstitit et senior, quamuis onus urget, et orat: for *perstare*, little different from *instare* in 518, cf. *Met.* 3.701–2 *perstat Echionides nec iam iubet ire sed ipse | uadit*, 4.368, 6.50–1 *perstat in incepto, stolidaeque cupidine palmae | ...ruit*, etc. The invitation depends on the father. In this again O. has rewritten and simplified the hymn, in which the daughters of Celeus meet the disguised Ceres without their parents, and go to ask their mother to invite her into their household as a nurse.

516 tecta suae subeat quantulacumque casae: for *subeat* in this context, cf. *Aen.* 8.362–3 *haec ... limina uictor | Alcides subiit*, perhaps with a notion of literal stooping to enter, as in the parallel situations of 5.505 *tecta senis subeunt*, *Met.* 8.638 *submissoque humiles intrarunt uertice postes*. With the modest *quantulacunque* here cf. 3.572 *haec . . . tellus quantulacumque tua est*, and O. speaking of his own 'modest efforts' at *Am.* 3.15.14, *Ex P.* 4.15.14.

517–18 illa negat (simularat anum, mitraque capillos | presserat): for a similar disguise as old lady cf. Met. 14.654–6 *ille etiam picta redimitus tempora mitra | innitens baculo, positis ad tempora canis | assimulauit anum*, and other grandmother disguises (they may be taken over from mime) at Aen. 7.416ff. *in uultus sese transformat aniles* etc., *Met.* 6.26 *Pallas anum simulat.*

instanti 'when he pressed her' (*OLD* s.v. 7b): such dat. forms are often used by O. to associate the questioner with the reply, cf. 3.687, *Met.* 4.685 *saepius instanti.*

talia dicta refert: an epic formula to introduce a new speech, variant of *Aen.* 1.94, 208 *talia uoce refert*, or 580 (below) *talia uerba refert*, *Met.* 1.700, 14.28, cf. 13.908 *uerba refert.*

519 'sospes eas semperque parens: *sospes*, glossed by Festus (300 Lindsay) as *saluus*, and of uncertain derivation, chiefly occurs in good wishes for the preservation of family or of the city's essential leader, Augustus and his dynasty. With 519, 525 cf. 6.220 *filia qua felix sospite semper ero* (of his own daughter), *Met.* 7.425 *sospite nato*, 11.580 *utque foret sospes coniunx suus utque rediret* and, in a personal *uotum* to Augustus, *Tr.* 2.165 *sospite sit tecum natus quoque sospes*. There are clear affinities with Gk σωθείς of 'survival' or 'safe arrival' at journey's end: contrast the near-synonym *superstes*, 'outliving' (derived by *OLD* from *superstare*, 'to stand over the fallen enemy'), which can be comically ambiguous (Plaut. *Cas.* 817–18 *sospes iter incipe hoc, uti uiro tuo | semper sis superstes*).

520 melior quanto sors tua sorte mea est!': dramatic irony. Ceres' wish and envious comment touch a sorrow of Celeus, known to O.'s readers, of which she is still unaware.

521 dixit, et: for this formulaic use of *dixit* absol. (like *sic haec locutus* etc.) cf. *Met.* 1.466, 762, 2.76, 3.474, 4.162, etc.

(neque enim lacrimare deorum est): the infin. serves as a verbal noun, cf. 889 *uestrum est dare, uincere nostrum*. Gods can weep, at least the goddesses Artemis (*Il.* 21.493ff.) and Demeter (Call. *H.* 6.17), but at Eur. *Hipp* 1396 Artemis calls weeping οὐ θέμις for the gods; so

O. in *Met.* 2.621–2 *neque enim caelestia tingi* | *ora licet lacrimis*. Here he plays with the motif, seeming to imply that the *lucida gutta* of 522 is a divine equivalent. *gutta*, most often in O. denoting a drop of blood, but also rain, seawater, sap, etc., is defined by *lucidus*, associated with sparkling purity (cf. 1.338 *lucida mica salis*, *Met.* 2.365 *lucidus amnis*, 13.795 *lucidior glacie* (Galatea).

523 molles animis: 'soft-hearted' (abl. of respect): young women and old men were seen as physically and emotionally weak.

525–6 'sic tibi . . . sit filia sospes: | surge, nec . . . despice: reiterating his invitation of 515 and answering her good wish with a corresponding one, Celeus represents her acceptance of their hospitality as a favour she will do them, in return for which he wishes for her the reward she urgently desires. On the parallel formulation in *h. Dem.* 135–7 Richardson notes that a prayer or wish accompanied by a request is expressed in Gk by a μὲν . . . δέ sentence and that Latin also uses parataxis, as at Hor. *Odes* 1.3.1–7 *sic te diua . . . regat . . .* | *reddas*.

quereris (preserved in the Z family) with *raptam esse* as acc. and inf. is more colourful than the literal *quaeris* of (A)U.

526 exiguae . . . tecta casae: cf. 5.500 *exiguam stabat ut ante casam*, or the home of Baucis and Philemon at *Met.* 8.630–3 *parua quidem stipulis et canna tecta palustri* | . . . *casa* (where, however, *tecta* is participle, not substantive).

527 'duc' . . . 'scisti qua cogere posses' 'You knew the way to compel me'. Celeus' imprecation is binding: Ceres takes it as a precondition for recovering her daughter, and so obeys (528 *subsequitur*, given added emphasis by 529 *dux comiti*).

528 seque leuat saxo: the real marker of her entry into human society, but she rises in order to lower herself. Twenty-five lines have elapsed since Ceres first sat on this rock (503). The equivalent concession occurs much later in the Homeric Hymn, within Celeus' palace, after her prolonged and veiled silence on the seat which she is offered (*h. Dem.* 196–200). O.'s next marker will be the breaking of her fast at 534.

529 dux comiti 'guiding her as she accompanies him': a neat way of indicating that Celeus conducted her to his home.

530 nec capiat somnos: only here and at 3.185 *placidi capiebat munera somni*, but here sleep is elusive.

inuigiletque malis: cf. *Tr.* 1.5.43 *inuigiles igitur nostris pro casibus* and *Ex P.* 1.5.58 *Pieriis inuigilate choris*; both constructions denote the object of vigil, rather than its cause, as here.

531–2 soporiferum ... papauer adapts (with new *sedes*) *Aen.* 4.486 *spargens umida mella soporiferumque papauer*; so also *Tr.* 5.2.24 *quotue soporiferum grana papauer habet*; for *soporifer* cf. *Met.* 11.586, *Tr.* 4.1.47. Virgil calls the poppy *Lethaeo perfusa papauera somno* at *Georg.* 1.78 and *Cereale papauer* at 1.212, probably from its role in the Eleusinian ritual (but see Servius ad loc.).

paruos initura penates: cf. *Met.* 8.637 *ergo ubi caelicolae paruos tetigere penates.*

533 dum legit: poetry often prefers the simple verb where prose has chosen the compound form. O. rings the changes between simple and compound forms: see 534–5 *exsoluisse, posuit*; but *legit* here also illustrates another stylistic feature, the resumption of compound by simple verb. Cf. C. Watkins, *HSCP* 71 (1966) 115–19, C. Murgia, *CQ* 41 (1991) 210 n. 69.

oblito fertur gustasse palato: *oblitus* with active force is usually limited to a personal subject: cf. however *Tr.* 5.5.5 *lingua ... nostrorum oblita malorum.* The notion is repeated by 534.

534 imprudens exsoluisse: *imprudens* = 'unwittingly'; with *exsoluisse* (*u* is vocalized to make five syllables – ⏑⏑ – ⏑) cf. the simple verb at 607 *soluit ieiunia granis* = *Met.* 5.534–5 *quoniam ieiunia uirgo | soluerat* of Persephone's unwitting end of fasting in Hades.

The impersonal *fertur* reminds O.'s readers that he is reporting a traditional myth and at the same time disowning responsibility for the narrative, although he has himself initiated so many changes. The breaking of Ceres' fast is one particularly significant change. In the Homeric Hymn Demeter refuses the wine offered by Metaneira, as 'unlawful' (207 οὐ θεμιτόν) but accepts a drink of groats and water, the κυκεών with which the initiates at Eleusis traditionally broke their fast. In Call. *H.* 6.8–16 Demeter at first refuses the κυκεών, but her resolve yields to Baubo's comic obscenity and she drinks. Like the scholiast on Nicander, *Alexipharmaka* 130, O. implies that her fasting is self-imposed in grief for her daughter: see Arbesmann (1929) 77–80.

O.'s Ceres breaks her fast with a taste of the poppy seeds she is gathering as a sleeping-potion for the sick child, after which she will still abstain from the meal she is offered at 545–6. Roman women seem to have practised fasting at the *sacrum anniuersarium* also called *castum Cereris* (Arbesmann (1929) 11–12, 95, Le Bonniec (1958) 416–20). O. himself protests at their ritual chastity and abstention from wine: *Am.* 3.10.47 *festa dies Veneremque uocat cantusque merumque*, cf. Dion. Halic. 1.33.1.

535 quia principio posuit ieiunia noctis: synonymous with *soluere famem*, this phrase is varied with the compound verb at 6.530 *longam deposuisse famem*. O. gives the version invented by religious tradition to explain its own ritual. Persephone's fasting too may have been part of the ritual *aition* (see 603–4, 607–8nn.). But other religions, such as Islam, postpone breaking fast until nightfall (Ramadan).

536 tempus habent mystae sidera uisa cibi 'initiates treat the sighting of the stars as the time for food': another *aition*, but also an allusion to Call. *H.* 6, which honours Hesperus, the evening star for making Demeter break her fast (7–8) and twice (12 and 16) reports that Demeter went without food, drink and washing out of grief for her daughter.

mystae: the first literary example in *TLL* VIII 2.1758.50ff. (the next, also of the Eleusinian *mystae*, is at Sen. *HF* 847) may well have been anticipated by epigraphic use (largely undatable), since *mysticus* (*Georg.* 1.188) is found in both Virgil and O. (*Her.* 2.42 *taediferae mystica sacra deae*, *AA* 2.640, *mysteria* at *AA* 2.609).

537–8 luctus uidit omnia plena; | ... spes ... nulla salutis erat: a return to the mood of elegiac lament. Cf. *Her.* 8.75–6 *omnia luctus | omnia solliciti plena timoris erant*, *Tr.* 3.11.10 *omnia solliciti sunt loca plena metus* and 5.12.56. *spes ... salutis* also finds parallels in the exile poems: *Tr.* 1.2.33 *nec spes est ulla salutis*, *Met.* 7.564–5 *utque salutis | spes abiit.*

539 mater Metanira uocatur: in this odd parenthesis O. de-emphasizes a figure who is named repeatedly in the Homeric Hymn, in which Metaneira is responsible for Demeter's welcome into the home. By mentioning Metaneira here just before Ceres' immediate act to save the baby in 540, O. foreshadows the coming catastrophe when Ceres' attempt to immortalize him will be aborted by Metaneira's panic in 555–8.

540 iungere dignata est os puerile suo: *puerili*, like *puellaris* 433n., 463, offers an alternative in elevated style to the gen. *pueri.*

Bömer takes this as a kiss (cf. O.'s regular phrase *oscula iungere* at *Met.* 2.430 etc.): one is tempted rather to imagine a sort of divine artificial respiration. (Did O. conceive the child as asthmatic?)

542 **tantus caelesti uenit ab ore uigor:** *uigor* often seems a divine gift; cf. Virg. *Georg.* 4.415–18 *defundit odorem | quo totum nati corpus perduxit; at illi | ... habilis membris uenit uigor* and *Aen.* 6.730 *igneus est ollis uigor et caelestis origo.* This half-divine strength is a token of the greater divinity which Ceres will later try to bestow.

543–4 **tota domus ... materque paterque | nataque: tres illi tota fuere domus:** cf. Met. 8.636 *tota domus duo sunt, idem parentque iubentque,* where the small servantless household is emphasized by the *polysyndeton,* a device normally used to generate fuller lists. The partial repetition (*epanalepsis*) from the hexameter opening at the end of the pentameter is an Ovidian mannerism; see 365–6n.

545–6 **mox epulas ponunt, liquefacta coagula lacte | pomaque:** the use of *epulae* is ironic. Compare Polyphemus' diet of apples, *Met.* 13.812, and cheese curds, *Met.* 13.830 *partem liquefacta coagula durant.* The verb *liquefacere* is also applied, like *liquata* at 152, to honey, cf. Virg. *Georg.* 4.35–6 *frigore mella | cogit hiems, eadem calor liquefacta remittit.*

546 **in ceris aurea mella suis:** the honey served in the comb may recall the *cerae* of *Georg.* 4.38, 57, 162.

547 **abstinet alma Ceres:** Ceres continues fasting, perhaps as a precondition of the quasi-magic ritual she will attempt.

somnique papauera causas: a variation on 531 *soporiferum p.*; cf. *Am.* 2.6.31 *causaeque papauera somni.*

549–55 The break in continuity marked by the new point of time introduces Ceres' attempt to immortalize the baby by fire. In the Homeric Hymn the goddess-nurse fed the child on ambrosia and set him in the ashes for many nights, creating in him the quasi-divine appearance of health which O. ascribes to the single action of 540 (*h. Dem.* 237–8, 239–50). But O. compresses Ceres' three services to the child (the kiss, the sleeping-draught of poppy and the attempt to immortalize by fire) into one night, in which Ceres is surprised by the unknowing mother. He also combines the supernatural ritual of 553–4 with a more routine magic by touch and spell quite absent from the Homeric model.

549 **noctis erat medium placidique silentia somni:** so

5.429 *nox ubi iam media est somnoque silentia praebet*, 6.384 *mediae tempora noctis erant*, *Met.* 10.368–9 *noctis erat medium, curasque et corpora somnus | soluerat.* Descriptions of times of day and night were a regular feature of Roman poetry: cf. Quint. 8.6.59ff. *ornatum ... solum qui est apud poetas frequentissimus*, Sen. *Ep.* 122.11 on Julius Montanus' favourite sunrises and sunsets, and Seneca Rhetor, *Contr.* 7.1.27 on O.'s criticism of evocations of night in both Varro of Atax and Virgil (*Aen.* 8.26–7).

As in *Aen.* 4.522–6, 8.26–7 the imperfect verb of the main clause is designed to provoke expectation, contrasting the universal sleep of man and beast with the stealthy actions of the wakeful protagonist. In this and other details, Ceres, practising beneficent magic, is assimilated to Medea and her spells.

550 Triptolemum gremio sustulit: so Myrrha's nurse takes her protégée into her arms, *Met.* 10.406 *et gremio lacrimantem tollit anili.*

551 terque manu permulsit eum, tria carmina dixit: like Virgil O. avoids the oblique cases of *is/ea/id* as unpoetic (except when used adjectivally as in 146); cf. Axelson (1945) 70–3. With *ter ... tria* compare the triple ritual acts of Circe at *Met.* 14.387 *ter iuuenem baculo tetigit, tria carmina dixit*, or Medea in *Met.* 7.153 *uerbaque ter dixit*, and 189–91 *ter se conuertit, ter sumptis flumine crinem | inrorauit aquis ternisque ululatibus ora | soluit.* The word *permulcere* describes Mercury's bewitching of Argus at *Met.* 1.716, and Medea's control over her dragon team at 7.221; cf. Circe *conantem uirga mulcere capillos* at *Met.* 14.295.

552 carmina mortali non referenda sono: anadiplosis (typically of a dactylic form from 5th foot to 1st) stresses the divine aspect of her spell. O. teases his readers, claiming that the spell is not just beyond his power, but literally *nefanda* for him to repeat.

553–4 inque foco corpus pueri ... | obruit: J. G. Frazer, *Apollodorus* II, App. 3 cites the parallel of Thetis, who tried to immortalize Achilles, putting him in the hearth by night and smearing him with ambrosia by day, and compares the post-natal practices of carrying babies around the hearth in Greek, Scottish and other cultures. Romans were more familiar with the myths of Servius Tullius and Caeculus of Praeneste, begotten in the hearth from a magic flame.

humanum purget ut ignis onus: at 785 O. claims *omnia purgat* *edax ignis*; compare also 6.301 on the etymology and generative power of *focus*. O.'s language is completely original, but for the concept of *humanum* ... *onus* compare Anchises' account of humanity's original fiery purity, weighed down by the body and by sin (*Aen.* 6.730–1 *igneus est ollis uigor* ... *quantum non noxia corpora tardant*) and the purification of souls by wind, water and fire, ibid. 742 *infectum eluitur scelus aut exuritur igni*. For (*re*)*purgare* in apotheoses, cf. *Met.* 13.951–3 *ego lustror ab illis* | *et purgante nefas nouiens mihi carmine dicto* | *pectora fluminibus iubeor supponere centum*, and Aeneas at *Met.* 14.600–3 *quaecumque obnoxia morti* | *abluere* ... | *quicquid in Aenea fuerat mortale repurgat*, 605–7 *diuino corpus odore* | *unxit et ambrosia* ... | *contigit os fecitque deum*.

The *Fasti* are much concerned with purification (e.g. 2.35–46, 4.731–79, 6.227–34). See Introd. 3(i)(*c*).

555 excutitur somno: cf. 1.547 *excussus somno*. The model may be *Aen.* 2.302 *excutior somno*. For variations cf. *Met.* 11.621 where Sleep *excussit tandem sibi se*, 677–8 *soporem* | *excutit*.

stulte pia mater: for the oxymoron here and in 557, compare the daughters of Pelias in *Met.* 7.339–40 *his ut quaeque pia est, hortatibus impia prima est* | *et ne sit scelerata, facit scelus*. Metaneira is blamed at *h. Dem.* 243 for her uncomprehending folly, Gk ἀφραδίῃσιν.

555–6 amens | 'quid facis?' exclamat: *amens* acts adverbially, 'shocked out of her wits', cf. 2.185–6 *adstitit amens*, | *et gemuit*. *membra* (cf. *OLD* s.v. 2) often denotes the whole body, here the child.

557 'dum non es' ... 'scelerata fuisti: *dum* is used causally (cf. *OLD* s.v. 4), 'by acting in innocence, you have behaved criminally'. O. makes the same distinction between *sceleratus* determined by criminal intent and by the outcome of *scelus* in *Met.* 7.340 (555n.).

558 inrita materno sunt mea dona metu: cf. *Met.* 10.52 *inrita dona futura*. The adj. *inritus* (neg. *in* + *ratus*) is frequently used by O. of frustrated vows, prayers, rituals where there is a religious sanction. So 4.642 below *inrita decepti uota colentis erant* (= *Am.* 3.10.34). *metu* is instrumental as if *inrita* were a true passive.

559 iste quidem mortalis erit; sed: the limiting *quidem* (like Gk μέν, with *sed* corresponding to δέ), promises some compensation for the loss of hope for immortality.

559–60 primus arabit | et seret et culta praemia tollet humo: Triptolemus (Iacchus in *Georg.* 1.166) is praised as inventor of the plough, as of sowing and reaping (cf. *Georg.* 1.161–2). The narrative of *Met.* v postpones Ceres' visit to Eleusis: she first goes to Attica after Proserpina has been found, and orders Triptolemus to sow seed from her sky-chariot on both wild and retilled land and proclaim, 655–6 *dona fero Cereris ... quae ... | frugiferas messes alimentaque mitia reddant.*

But neither in *Fasti* (see 421–2, 487, 617–18nn.) nor in *Met.* does O. maintain consistently the conception of human society as pre-agricultural before Triptolemus. Previous cultivation is required by *Met.* 5.474–86; hence the reference to tilled land at 5.646 and the implication of restored harvests in 5.656.

praemia: for harvest as reward cf. 1.677–8 *satiate colonos | ut capiant cultus praemia digna sui*; so also honey at 3.744 *inuenti praemia mellis habet.*

561 dixit, et: cf. 521n.

561–2 nubem trahit, inque dracones | transit: does Ceres need the cloud to reach the *dracones*? Are they still air-borne or have they landed? There is some discontinuity with 497–502: there her team were *angues*, there was no indication of how or where she left them, and there was no cloud. Or does the cloud make her invisible, as Venus or Diana cover favoured mortals with a cloud (*Aen.* 1.412, 586–7, *Met.* 5.621, 12.32 *nubemque oculis obiecit*)?

aligero: see on *clauiger* 67–8n., *turriger* 219n.; for the MS variants *aliger/alifer* there are no Ovidian parallels to serve as control. Virgil seems to prefer *aliger* (*Aen.* 1.663, 12.249).

563–618 (C) Jupiter's settlement and the reunion

563–78 Ceres' third journey zigzags as in 467–80, but this time to both ends of the earth (contrast the brief generic references at *Met.* 5.439 *omnibus ... terris*, 462).

563–4 Sunion expositum Piraeaque tuta recessu | ... in dextrum quae iacet ora latus: within Attica O. contrasts the high exposed promontory of Sunium with Piraeus' safe harbour (cf. Prop. 3.21.23 *Piraei ... litora portus*, *Met.* 6.446 *Piraeaque litora tangit.* The noun *recessus* (cf. Virg. *Aen.* 8.193, and *F.* 1.555 of Cacus' cave) here replaces *secessus*, the *vox propria* for a safe harbour as in *Aen.* 1.158. The 'shore along her right side' would seem to be the NE coast of the Peloponnese.

565–6 init Aegaeum ... | Ioniumque rapax Icariumque

legit: although each of these substantival names is listed by the concordance separately from other adjectival forms used by O., they are simply the neuter adj. presupposing *mare/aequor*; with *Aegaeum* cf. *Her.* 20.22 *Aegaeo ... mari*; with *Ionium* (also Prop. 3.21.19) compare *aequor* | ... *Ionium* at *Met.* 15.49–50 and *aequor* | *Ionium* at 699–700, *Tr.* 1.4.3 *Ionium ... aequor*; *Ionium mare* at *Aen.* 5.193, Ov. *Tr.* 2.298, *Ex P.* 4.5.6.

quo Cycladas aspicit 'from which she gazes on ... the Cyclades': *quo* is abl., but the variant *quod* (UGM) making the sea the subject of *aspicit*, may be right. The *a* in the last syllable of Gk 3rd decl. acc. pl. *Cycladas* is short: but the parallel form *Arabas* is lengthened by position at 569.

Ceres' zigzag wanderings include part of the voyage made by Cybele, cf. *Cyclades* and *Icarium* (sc. *mare*) 281, 283–4nn.

567 perque urbes Asiae: the glorious Greek coastal cities of the Eastern Aegaean and Propontis; a Roman would think of Cat. 46.6 *ad claras Asiae uolemus urbes*, echoed at *Ex P.* 2.10.21 (cf. *Tr.* 1.2.78 *oppida ... Asiae*).

longum petit Hellespontum: cf. 278 above *longaque Phrixeae stagna sororis*; here the spondaic epithet adds to the weight of the spondaic line-ending (also found at 6.341, *Met.* 13.407, and Luc. 2.675).

For other dispondaic endings in *Fasti* cf. 2.275 *Nonacrini*, 3.105 *Atlanteas*, 5.7 *Hippocrenes*, 5.535 *Vriona*, 5.731 *Amphitrite* and see Introd. 4(ii). *Fasti* is more conservative than *Metamorphoses*, which allows dispondaic Latin words as well as names to end hexameters at e.g. 6.6, 128, 247, 7.114, 581.

568 diuersumque ... pererrat iter: *diuersum* is borne out by her flights to east and south in 569–70, to north and west in 571–2.

569 modo turilegos Arabas, modo ... Indos: Ceres flies east. *Arabes* are known at Rome from the 50s BC; cf. Cat. 11.5, Cic. *Fam.* 3.8.10, Tib. 2.2.4, Prop. 2.29.17. O. seems to have regarded the Arabs (cf. *Met.* 10.478 *palmiferos Arabas*) and Indians (cf. 3.720 *turifer Inde* addressed to the river as producer of the incense gathered by the local *Indi*) as more or less interchangeable. *turilegos* is unique, but behind *tus*- compounds (such as *turifer* at *Georg.* 2.139 and *turicrem*- at Lucr. 2.353, *Aen.* 4.453) lie Greek compound adjectives based on θύειν ('to sacrifice').

570 hinc Libys, hinc Meroë ... subest: Ceres flies south. *Libys*, collective singular, also occurs at *Met.* 5.75, cf. the adj. *Libys* ... *Ammon* at *Met.* 5.328; but *Libycus* (379–80n.) is more common in both Virgil and O. Meroe, an island at the first cataract of the Nile, only recently discovered by Roman military exploration (cf. Augustus, *Res gestae* 2.65 *In Aethiopiam usque ad oppidum Nabata peruentum est, cui proxima est Meroe* and Vitr. 8.2.6) was the southern limit of empire. Conceived as equatorial, it became a byword in later geographers and poets for its alleged lack of shadow at the summer solstice (Luc. 4.333, 10.237, 251, 303, Pliny, *NH* 2.184, 6.189).

siccaque terra: the Sahara stretching between Libya and the Nile.

In typical catalogue fashion patterns are created within the *distributio* of items by symmetry with variation (*hinc* ... *hinc* answers *modo* ... *modo*, singular *Libys* and *Meroe* answer plural *Arabas* and *Indos*); and by inversion of syntax (the geographical object in 569 is subject in 570) and point of view (*subest* looking upwards from below answers *despicit* looking downwards).

571–2 nunc adit Hesperios, Rhenum Rhodanumque Padumque | ... parens, Thybri, potentis aquae: cf. *Met.* 2.258–9 *Hesperiosque amnes Rhenum Rhodanumque Padumque, | cuique fuit rerum promissa potentia Thybrim.* In general *Hesperia*, the land of the evening star, meant for the Greeks Italy, and for the Romans anything from Italy westwards including Spain. But the concept of *Hesperii* ('westerners') develops later: first found in Prop. 2.3.43–44 (opposed to *Eoi*) it is imitated by O. at *Am.* 1.15.29. This passage is directly remodelled from *Met.* 2.258–9.

Thybris is rather the river god (see 47–8n.) than the river scorched dry by Phaethon's ride in *Met.* 2.259. River and god are as important in *Fasti* (see 47–8, 68, 291nn. and e.g. 5.635–60) as in O.'s model *Aen.* 8.31–100, whose association of the Tiber with *potentia* (8.99) these passages recall.

573 quo feror? inmensum est erratas dicere terras: the poet breaks the illusion to remind us of his (lack of) control of the text. So too *Met.* 5.462–3 *quas dea per terras et quas errauerit undas | dicere longa mora est*; but the exceptional transitive use of *erratas* gives O. the compression he is seeking (see 568n.).

574 praeteritus ... nullus in orbe locus 'no place in the world is unvisited' (*OLD* s.v. 2c), as opposed to 468–9 where *praeterit* is used for 'go past' (*OLD* s.v. 1) in a positive sense. Rhetorically, too, O. comments on his own *praeteritio* in 573. This line corresponds to *Met.* 5.439 *omnibus est terris . . . quaesita* expanded in 440–3.

Cereri: cf. *Ex P.* 3.4.43–4 *si quid | erratum . . . praeteritumque mihi*; the dat. of the agent is common with the passive in O.

575 errat et in caelo: this is still undirected wandering, in contrast with Ceres' purposeful flight to Jupiter at *Met.* 5.511–12.

575–6 immunia ponti | . . . gelido proximo signa polo: cf. *Met.* 13.293 *immunemque aequoris Arcton.* Arctos or Cynosura, the Great Bear, and Helice, the Lesser Bear (cf. 580 and 3.107), were always visible in the northern night sky, and so were conceived as excluded from the waters of Ocean, a concession made to Juno's anger at Jupiter's catasterism of Callisto as *Arctos* (cf. *Met.* 2.528–30, where O. teasingly uses their alias of *Septemtriones*, the plough-team). As 577–8 explain, because they never set they could see every deed committed by night.

577 'Parrhasides stellae: Parrhasia is a district of Arcadia, where Callisto's father Lycaon was King: hence she is *Parrhasis* at *Met.* 2.460; cf. *Tr.* 1.3.48 *Parrhasis Arctos* and *Her.* 18.152.

578 aequoreas . . . aquas: cf. 498n.

579 Persephonen natam miserae monstrate parenti: *Persephonen* (Gk first decl. accus.) adds assonance (on *-n*, *-m*, then *-n* and *-t*).

580 dixerat . . . talia uerba refert: epic formulae to mark a change of speaker. For *dixerat* (a variant of *dixit*, 521n., 561), cf. *Met.* 1.367, 2.40, 4.271, etc., and for *talia . . . refert*, 517–18n.

581 'crimine nox uacua est 'night is innocent of this charge'; while *crimen* here is the first of increasingly dense legal terms applied to the rape, *uacuus* (treating night as spatial, the night sky?) is unparalleled: Virgil, who has no instance of *uacuus* with the abl., actually supplements *uacuus* with *sine* at *Aen.* 4.588 *uacuos sine remige portus.* O. expresses human innocence by *sine crimine* (9n.), *crimen abest* (323), or *nullo crimine.*

581–2 Solem de uirgine rapta | consule: the language verges on the legal rubric (with *de uirgine rapta* cf. 417 *raptus . . . uirginis*). *consule* too may hint that Ceres' problem goes beyond finding her daughter (*Met.* 5.520 *scire ubi sit*) to obtaining legal redress. In *h. Dem.*

75–87 the Sun revealed Persephone's location but offered no prospect of redress. But O. not only postpones their encounter after her visit to Eleusis; he delays it by this false start. Katz in Foley (1993) 221 n. 15 notes that different versions of the myth have Ceres informed by mortals: Euboulos and Triptolemus (Orphic), citizens of Eleusis or of Hermione (Apollodorus 1.5.1) or an Argive woman (Paus 1.14.2).

582 qui late facta diurna uidet: cf. *Met.* 1.768 *per iubar hoc … quod nos auditque uidetque*, 4.195 *quique omnia cernere debes*, 226–7 *ille ego sum … | omnia qui uideo, per quem uidet omnia tellus.*

583 Sol aditus … ait: while *adire* is regularly transitive and gerundive *adeundus* is common, neither Virgil nor O. offers any parallel for passive participle *aditus.*

583–4 'quam quaeris' … | nupta Iouis fratri … tenet: the relative clause represents its suppressed antecedent as subject. *tertia regna*: not third, but one of the three divisions of the cosmos; cf. *Met.* 5.368 *triplicis cessit fortuna nouissima regni*, 15.859 *mundi regna triformis*, *Am.* 3.8.50 *caelum, tertia regna.* The division of heaven, earth–sea, and underworld between Kronos' three sons goes back to *Il.* 15.187–92.

'ne uana labores 'so that you may not toil mistakenly': cf. *Met.* 14.131 *neu nescius erres* etc. For the use of n. pl. adj. here as 'inner object' cf. G–L 33.2, n. 6.

585 questa diu secum: Ceres' long, private lamentation is all that remains of Demeter's withdrawal from Olympus to live disguised among men in the Homeric Hymn. Similarly when she learns that Persephone has been taken to the underworld in *Met.* 5.509–13 *stupuit ceu saxea … | attonitaeque diu similis fuit, utque dolore | pulsa graui … | ante Iouem passis stetit inuidiosa capillis.*

Tonantem: cf. 2.69 *Capitolinumque Tonantem*, and 6.33, 349, referring to Jupiter Tonans, whose shrine near the Capitoline temple of Jupiter Optimus Maximus was dedicated by Augustus after he had escaped a lightning bolt in 22 BC (*Res gestae* 19, Suet. *Aug.* 29). But here as in e.g. *Met.* 1.170 the epithet is a poetic variation.

586 in uultu signa dolentis erant: cf. 6.66 *in uultu signa uigoris erant.* Here *dolere* implies anger as much as grief, as her speech (and the parallel *dolore graui … inuidiosa* above) shows. Ceres believes she has been wronged by her daughter's abduction, and Jupiter is doubly at fault, as indulgent brother and neglectful father.

587–618 O.'s treatment of Ceres' approach to Jupiter, his response, and its outcome, proceeds in parallel to *Met.* 5.514–71 though with significant variations. Thus:

(i) Ceres' complaint 587–96 is a fuller version of *Met.* 5.514–22.
(ii) Jupiter's reply 597–604 is shorter but essentially the same as *Met.* 5.523–32.
(iii) Mercury's journey to Hades, the fatal pomegranate seeds (605–8), and Ceres' desperate threat of withdrawal (609–12), correspond to the events of *Met.* 5. 533–8, before the two inserted transformations of 5.539–64.
(iv) 613–15, Jupiter's arbitration and Ceres' recovery of spirits, is a briefer version of *Met.* 5.564–71 , but in *Fasti* Ceres' restoration of agricultural fertility (616–18) is immediate, whereas *Met.*
(v) substitutes the long Arethusa narrative 572–641, and mediates the renewal of agriculture through Triptolemus (5.642–61).

587–96 Ceres' complaint here is more complex than in *Met.* 5.519–27, adding to its three elements (1) Jupiter's responsibility as father for his daughter's safety, (2) her search and its outcome in knowledge of her daughter's whereabouts without power to recover her, and (3) (treating the abduction as marriage) a complaint that the husband is unworthy and his method an insult to Ceres as parent, a fourth, incompatible, complaint (4) treating the abduction as rape (*stuprum*, a form of civil *iniuria*); on this assumption she agrees to renounce compensation, provided that Dis restore her daughter to her. Jupiter's reply is entirely in terms of (3), treating the union of Persephone and Dis as a consummated marriage.

587 'si memor es de quo ... sit Proserpina nata: cf. *Met.* 5.514–17 *'pro'que 'meo ueni supplex tibi ... | sanguine proque tuo. si nulla est gratia matris, | nata patrem moueat, neu sit tibi cura precamur | uilior illius, quod nostro est edita partu.'* Ceres conflates two versions of her grievance: Jupiter should remember that Persephone is his daughter and should give her his protective care. The ironic *si* raises the possibility that he is forgetful because he has fathered so many children.

588 dimidium curae debet habere tuae: like Horace (*Odes* 1.3.8) O. exceptionally brings *dimidium* (a prosaic word common in comedy and satire) into high poetry. It is found in the context of fatherhood at Plaut. *Amph.* 1125; cf. 5.459 *dimidium uestri parsque altera* *uoti* (Remus' ghost to his foster-parents). Even so Ceres distorts the logic of the traditional conception of parental rights underlying e.g. Cat. 62.65 *qui genero sua iura simul cum dote dederunt*. Half the responsibility for Persephone's well-being belongs to Jupiter and half to Ceres, but this does not entitle her to half of his concern.

589 orbe pererrato: Ceres stresses her own efforts to recover her daughter; cf. *Met.* 5.518 *quaesita diu tandem mihi nata reperta est.*

589–90 sola est iniuria facti | cognita: commissi praemia raptor habet: the contrast between knowledge and repossession is formulated differently at *Met.* 5.519–20 *si reperire uocas amittere certius, aut si | scire ubi sit reperire uocas*. But *Fasti* adds the twists of *iniuria*, civil grievance, and here implicitly rape (cf. *TLL* VII 1.1670.67ff. for precedents, but this passage is too indefinite to be cited) to be developed in 585–6. For *commissum* (substantival), 'offence', cf. 6.451 *si scelus est, in me commissi poena redundet*, *Am.* 3.14.12. *raptor* is used of Dis at *Met.* 5.402.

591–2 neque ... digna est praedone marito, | nec gener hoc nobis more parandus erat 'she did not deserve a brigand for a husband, nor was this the way for us to obtain a son-in-law' (cf. *Met.* 5.521–2 *neque enim praedone marito | filia digna tua est, si iam mea filia non est*). Ceres presents the abduction first as a wrong done to the unwilling bride, then to her parents (*nobis* is a true plural).

593 quid grauius uictore Gyge ... tulissem 'What worse could I have suffered as captive if Gyges had conquered?'. This new element in the rebuke draws on the attack of the Titans on the Olympians (cf. 3.797). O. here makes Gyges (or Gyas as in Hor. *Odes* 3.4.69 *centimanus Gyas*) an enemy of the Olympians, but according to Hesiod, *Theog.* 617–23, 713–21 the hundred-handed Gyges and his brothers fought for Zeus.

captiua: separation from family, rape and concubinage were the expected fate of captive women.

594 te caeli sceptra tenente: a scornful re-use of Jupiter's traditional symbol of kingship, with added point for readers aware of his abuse of this power symbol at *Met.* 1.595–6 *nec de plebe deo, sed qui caelestia magna | sceptra manu teneo.*

595–6 uerum impune ferat, nos haec patiemur inultae; | reddat et emendet facta priora nouis: the first jussive *ferat* has concessive force, 'though he may get away with it unpunished'.

reddat, *emendet* are real jussives. With *impune ferre*, 'to go unpunished', cf. *Met.* 2.474, 8.494, 11.207, 12.265, 14.383; but at *Met.* 8.279–80 *at non impune feremus* | ... *non et dicemur inultae* the verb *ferre* must mean 'endure'. For *emendare* (cf. 5.205 cited below) in the general sense of compensating for an *iniuria* cf. *TLL* v 2.464.56ff., citing Sen. *Dial.* 11.18.3, Quint. 4.1.45.

Unfortunately the parallel use of *emendare* in 5.205 *uim tamen emendat dando mihi nomina nuptae* argues against Ceres. Flora sees marriage as fair if not desirable compensation for rape. This was the first model of Roman marriage, achieved through the rape of the Sabines, and contemporary Romans would recognize that since return to her mother would not restore Persephone's virginity, marriage to her rapist was the only way to restore her place in society.

597–604 O. paraphrases Jupiter's exoneration of the rape, but turns to more authoritative direct speech for justification of the assumed marriage in 598–604: this closely matches the fuller reply given in *Met.* 5.523–32.

597 hanc lenit, factumque excusat amore: Ceres is treated as a woman, to be soothed by a sentimental answer; cf. *Met.* 5.524–6 *sed si modo nomina rebus* | *addere uera placet, non hoc iniuria factum,* | *uerum amor est.* Compare the conventional excuses for rape cited at Ter. *Ad.* 470–1 *persuasit nox amor uinum adolescentia:* | *humanum est.*

598 'nec gener est nobis ille pudendus': cf. the Sun's reply in *Hom. h. Dem.* 82–4 'among the gods Aidoneus is not an unsuitable bridegroom, commander-to-many and Zeus's own brother of the same stock' (tr. Foley) and 363n. In the gliding transition to direct speech *nec* conflates the connecting *et* of narrative with Jupiter's spoken negative, a uniquely Ovidian trick, which here permits an echo of Ceres' complaint in 592. see Introd. 4(i) and A. E. Housman, *Collected classical papers* (Cambridge 1972) I 413 (not 412 as in A–W–C).

600 possidet alter aquas, alter inane chaos: of the *tria regna* Jupiter's language, subordinating Poseidon/Neptune and Dis as an equal pair (*alter* ... *alter*) in the pentameter, preserves his own priority. *inane Chaos* is not here the unformed raw material of the universe called Chaos by Hesiod and O. (1.103, 5.11, *Met.* 1.1.7), but the gaping underworld chasms combined with Erebus in *Aen.* 4.510 (cf. 6.265), *Met.* 14.404 *Noctem Noctisque deos Ereboque Chaoque*, 10.29–30 *per ego haec loca plena timoris,* | *per Chaos hoc ingens uastique silentia regni.* The

Homeric motif of the honour awarded Dis by lot is more literally translated in *Met.* 5.528–9 *nec cetera desunt* | *nec cedit nisi sorte mihi.*

601 si . . . tibi non est mutabile pectus: O. uses *mutabilis* only of human resolve; so Sol to Phaethon, *Met.* 2.145–6 *si mutabile pectus* | *est tibi, consiliis . . . utere nostris, Tr.* 5.13.19–20 *mutabile robur* | *. . . pectoris esse tui* and Dido's riposte to *semper uarium et mutabile femina, Her.* 7.51 *tu quoque cum uentis utinam mutabilis esses.*

602 statque . . . rumpere uincla: for *stare* of being resolved, cf. *Met.* 10.709 *sed stat monitis contraria uirtus*; with inf., *Her.* 2.143 *stat nece matura tenerum pensare pudorem.* Although *rumpere uincla* can be used of release from undesirable bonds (e.g. *Rem.* 293–4 *laedentia pectus* | *uincula qui rupit*), the phrase *semel iuncti . . . tori* denotes a real marriage (cf. 3.511 *iuncta toro, Met.* 1.353 *deinde torus iunxit*), thus representing Ceres' request as a divorce that would destroy a valid bond. (So too *Met.* 5.530 *discidium.*)

603–4 siquidem ieiuna remansit; | si minus, . . . uxor erit: with the rather prosaic ellipse *si minus* = 'if not', here only in *Fasti*, cf. *Am.* 1.4.68 *si minus, at certe te iuuet inde nihil,* 2.10.22, *AA* 1.228, *Her.* 7.181, *Rem.* 478. According to *Met.* 5.532 this condition was imposed by the *foedus* or agreement of the Parcae. Scholars debate whether Persephone bound herself by eating food in her would-be husband's home (a bond of marriage; cf. Foley (1993) 108) or in the land of the dead as such, and whether the actual pomegranate (608 *Punica . . . poma*; cf. *Met.* 5.536) is to be associated with love and fertility or with death. On ritual prohibitions against the pomegranate see Arbesmann (1929) 60, and 608 below.

605 Tartara iussus adit sumptis Caducifer alis: Mercury (*caducifer* at 5.449, *Met.* 2.708, 8.627) is first choice as both divine messenger and psychopomp familiar with the underworld; Tartara here stands for the whole underworld (cf. *Met.* 5.371, 423), not just the place of punishment. Mercury is dropped from the *Metamorphoses* narrative, where Ascalaphus informs on Persephone (5.534–42).

606 speque . . . citius: not 'faster than hope travels' but 'faster than hoped for'; cf. *Rem.* 804 *spe breuius, Met.* 7.648 *speque fideque. . . maiora.*

607–8 'rapta tribus' . . . 'soluit ieiunia granis | Punica quae lento cortice poma tegunt: cf. *Ex P.* 4.15.7 *Punica sub lento* *cortice grana*. The Homeric hymn specifies the pomegranate seeds, but not their number; seven in *Met.* 5.537, three here. Yet the Greek tradition of *h. Dem.* 398ff., 445ff. and Apollodorus 1.5.3 kept Persephone underground for one-third of the year, and the Alexandrian–Roman tradition, for six months; no match to the number of seeds eaten. (See Richardson (1974) 276–7, 285.) The pomegranate was forbidden to Mystae at Eleusis and taboos restricted eating it at the Thesmophoria (Arbesmann (1929) 60).

609–10 non secus indoluit ... | maesta parens: cf. Ceres' first shock at 455–61, and renewed grief at 585–6 above.

rapta fuisset: the pleonastic plupf. form combining past participle with plupf., instead of impf. forms; cf. 6.359 *fuerat promissa*, 6.582 *confusam ... fuisse*.

longa uixque: for the postponed *-que* see 448n.

611 'nec nobis caelum est habitabile': *caelum* must stand for life both on Olympus and above ground among men. *habitabilis* (*Met.* 1.49, 8.624, 15.830 and *Tr.* 3.4B.51) normally denotes a climate fit for mankind).

'Taenaria ... ualle: *Taenarius* like *Taenaris* normally means Spartan (*Met.* 2.247, *Her.* 13.45, 16.276) but Taenarus in Laconia, like Avernus in Campania, was a supposed access to the underworld; cf. Virg. *Georg.* 4.467 *Taenarias etiam fauces, alta ostia Ditis*, echoed by *Met.* 10.13 *Taenaria ... porta* of Orpheus' descent to Hell.

613 et factura fuit, pactus nisi ... esset 'she was about to do it, and would have if Jupiter had not made the agreement': not only modal verbs denoting potential and obligation but future participles of intention stand in the logical indicative in main clauses of Latin counterfactual conditional sentences. (See G–L 597 R3.)

614 bis tribus ... mensibus: for duration expressed by abl. instead of acc. see 505n.

615 tum demum uultumque ... animumque recepit: *tum demum* (common in prose) marks the end of a narrative at *Met.* 9.413, 11.263, 13.391, *Her.* 11.91. With the zeugma compare *Met.* 5.568 *uertitur extemplo facies et mentis et oris*, representing Ceres' recovery of spirit as a metamorphosis. *animum recipere* is without parallel in O. but cf. 1.147 *sumpsi animum*, and the phrase *rediit animus* at 3.333 etc.

616 spicea serta: the typical attribute of Ceres, as in *Am.* 3.10.3

tenues spicis redimita capillos and 36 *deciderant longae spicea serta comae.* There too the absence of the garland is associated with distraction from her role as protectress of the harvest.

617–18 largaque prouenit ... messis ... | et uix congestas area cepit opes: Ceres brings abundant harvests to Crete to reward her lover in *Am.* 3.10.38 *omnia qua tulerat se dea messis erat.* For the combination of *messis* with *area* ('threshing-floor'), cf. 3.557 *tertia nudandas acceperat area messes, Met.* 8.292–3 *area frustra | et frustra exspectant promissas horrea messes.* For *prouenire* of crops cf. 672 and 773 and the noun *prouentus* in Pliny, *Ep.* 1.13.1.

cessatis ... in aruis: O. returns from his pre-agricultural portrait of life in Eleusis to the version of the myth found in *Met.* 5.474–86, in which agriculture was already practised when Persephone was abducted, and Ceres in her anger made the crops fail. *cessare* can mean 'to be left fallow', 'to be left untilled' (cf. Virg. *Georg.* 1.71) but here must refer to the cessation of growth in standing crops.

619–20 uestes Cerialibus albas | sumite: as at the Megalensia (367–72) O. returns at the close from myth to ritual detail. The placing of this notice advances the Cerialia beyond the 19th, the Cerialia proper, to cover the whole period of the *Ludi.* The apparently abrupt change of topic is helped by the association of Ceres' *spicea serta* (616) with the festival offerings of the white-clad *matronae* (*Met.* 10.432) and *spicea corona* tied with *albae uittae* of the Fratres Arvales (Pliny, *NH* 18.2).

Whom is O. addressing? Not his regular upper-class readers, who would automatically don their togas, but the *coloni* of 407, 409ff., to whom O. has directed the last words of the myth describing the abundant harvest brought by Ceres. Such peasants would normally work in *pulla uestis.* White garments were worn by laymen at public and private feasts like birthdays (*Tr.* 3.13.14, 5.5.7–8), and by Vestals (*Am.* 3.13.27) at all times. This means a bleached white toga (not the chalked *toga candida* reserved for electoral candidates), or if *uestis* also includes women's dress, the white *stola* worn by *matronae.*

In 5.355–6 when O. consults Flora about the colours worn for her festival she confirms his suggestion that the white clothes worn for Ceres symbolize the white of the ripe harvest: 357 *quia maturis albescit messis aristis.*

620 pulli uelleris usus abest: on the impropriety of wearing *pulla uestis* at festivals see Cic. *Vat.* 30 *ut in epulo cum toga pulla accumberes* and 31 *cum ipse epuli dominus albatus esset, tu in templum Castoris te cum C. Fibulo atrato ... intulisti.* Unbleached cloth, usually worn by slaves (*AA* 3.189–90) and peasants (Calp. Sic. 7.81), was sometimes put on as a gesture of mourning by the elite. *uelleris*, 'fleece', 'wool', is no idle synonym of *uestis* but foreshadows (as also 654–9, 663) concern with Rome's pastoral origins and the shepherd's wool crop at the Parilia (766, 773–4).

621–4 13 April G Eidus NP

On the designation NP for the Ides and most *feriae*, see Introd. 3(i)(*a*) n.52. (The *Fasti Praenestini* are again damaged; only the day of the nundinal sequence and EID (Eidus) survive.) O. marks two anniversaries of temple dedications.

621–2 cognomine Victor | Iuppiter: by *cognomine* O. distinguishes Jupiter Victor from e.g. Stator, Feretrius, or Tonans.

hac illi sunt data templa die: Livy 10.29.14 and 18 reports that Fabius Rullianus vowed a temple to Jupiter Victor at the battle of Sentinum. This seems to have stood on the Quirinal hill (cf. *CIL* I 2.802). L. S. Richardson, *A new topographical dictionary* (Baltimore 1992) 227 warns against assuming the identity of *Victor* with the deity called *Jupiter Inuictus* at 6.650.

623–4 ni fallor, populo dignissima nostro | atria Libertas coepit habere sua: why does O. add the cautious *ni fallor*? It could be a mark of genuine uncertainty: cf. *fallor, an ...?, fallimur, an ...?* etc. at 1.515, 2.397 and 853, 5.549. But O. has actually made a strange error in this entry. Bömer and Richardson 221 note that he has mistakenly referred an anniversary notice for C. Sempronius Gracchus' temple of Jupiter Libertas on the Aventine (vowed in 238, and dedicated on 13 April according to the republican *Fasti Antiates)*, to the secular *Atrium Libertatis* by the Forum, which would not find a space in a religious calendar.

The *Atrium Libertatis*, the office and archive of the censors from at least the third century, was rebuilt by Asinius Pollio in 39 BC (Richardson (1974) 41). While O. may have been misled by the changed date of the Augustan restoration of Gracchus' temple into finding an alternative building, Barchiesi (1994) 76–9 suggests that O. seized the pretext to mention Pollio's building, the first public library in Rome (cf. *Tr.* 3.1.71–72) and almost the last secular structure in the republican tradition. (Since Pollio was a self-conscious ideologue, he may even have chosen the date of Jupiter Libertas to dedicate his building.)

populo dignissima nostro: *dignissima* is certainly fem. sing. qualifying Libertas, rather than neut. pl. with *Atria.* Roman ideology gave a large place to the (somewhat restricted) *libertas* of the *Populus Romanus.*

625–8 14 April H N

Again the *Fasti Praenestini* are fragmentary, showing only the day of the nundinal sequence (H) XIIX (i.e. XVIII, the eighteenth day before the Kalends of May) and N(efastus). The *Ludi Ceriales* continued, but O. adapts the day to a weather notice (625–6) and recall of Octavianus Caesar's first victory at Mutina (627–8), recorded by the *Fasti Praenestini* for 15 April. This combination balances the notice of Julius Caesar's victory at Thapsus and the rainstorm of the circus games (10 April: 377–86).

625 tutos pete, nauita, portus: O. uses both prose *nauta* and the dactylic variant *nauita* in all types of verse; compare the formal twin of this passage, 2.101 *dubiam rege, nauita, puppem*; and the parallel content of 6.715 *si qua fides uentis, Zephyro date carbasa nautae.* Both the allusion to navigation and the direct warning hark back to the didactic mode of Hesiod; cf. Virg. *Georg.* 1.456–7 *non illa me quisquam nocte per altum | ire neque a terra moneat conuellere funem.* But this is a precept for the date (cf. Colum. 11.2.36), not a response to a weather-sign.

627 sit licet ut fuerit: *sit licet* is the reading of Z, 'Be that as it may'. The alternative reading *scilicet* (AU) adopted by A–W–C is difficult to parallel and awkward in sense.

627–8 Mutinensia Caesar | ... militia perculit arma sua 'Caesar shattered the arms/conflict at Mutina with his military action': *militia* nicely echoes the tribune's *militia* at 383. The stormy weather is used to enhance Octavianus Caesar's success while veiling the ambiguous military and political context of April 43 BC. In fact the war of Mutina was an embarrassment to all parties. The Senate had sent Octavian with a praetorian command to assist the consuls Hirtius and Pansa, who were trying to relieve Decimus Brutus by forcing the outlawed M. Antonius to lift his siege of Mutina. Antonius was driven off but Pansa died in battle, Hirtius of a wound within the same day, leaving the survivor Octavian to claim the *salutatio* for the victory. For the text of the *Fasti Praenestini* on this supplication see the entry for 15 April below.

629–76 15 April A FORD NP

More of the *Fasti Praenestini* survives for this holiday: besides the nundinal letter and date before the Kalends, the Fordicidia (so called *a fordis caedendis* by Varro, *LL* 6.15) is marked with FOR(D), and three incomplete lines show first a probable etymology of *fordus* (*Oscum et Sa*[*binum*]), then an imperial anniversary: Augustus Caesar's first *supplicatio* on the victory of his colleague the consul Hirtius.

[ ] *A. Hirtius, C. Caes*[*are conlega imperi, ad Mutinam uicit*] [*unde usque a*]*t nostros d*[*ies Victoriae Augustae supplicare solent*]

(Square brackets denote probable supplements: Degrassi 1963 128–9.)

629 Tertia post Veneris cum lux surrexerit Idus: by Roman inclusive reckoning 15 April was the third day after the Ides (13), here loosely called Ides of Venus because O. has presented April as her month.

630 pontifices, forda sacra litate boue: the ritual term *litare* occurs only here and in the Roman books of *Met.*, with the priestly agent (Aeneas) assumed at 14.156 *sacrisque ex more litatis*; but at 15.794, where the Pontifex Caesar has been murdered (cf. 763), the subject is not the priest but the offering: *uictima nulla litat.*

631 forda ferens ... fecundaque dicta ferendo: the etymology from *ferre* echoes Varro, *LL* 6.15 *bos forda quae fert in uentre; quod eo die publice immolantur boues praegnantes in curiis compluris; a fordis caedendis Fordicidia dicta* and Festus 74 Lindsay *Fordicidis: boues fordae, id est grauidae, immolabantur, dictae a fetu.* O. also incorporates etymologies of *fecundus* and *fetus*, which he will recall in ring composition at 671–2.

633 grauidum pecus est, grauidae quoque semine terrae is echoed with chiastic variation in 634 *Telluri plenae uictima plena*;

but *Tellus/terra* has two roles, both as deity and beneficiary. The offering is explained by the simultaneous gestation of cattle and earth, equated through O.'s application to both of *semine* (more common of plant life, though it applies equally to *pecus*, cf. *Met.* 9.280, 10.470, 15.216), and his unusual transference of *plenus* (proper to animal fertility: *Met.* 3.268, 344, etc.) to the earth. Despite such imagery as *uiscera terrae, terra parens* at *Met.* 1.138, 393, *tellus/terra plena* is not found elsewhere in O. This sympathetic ritual seems to subordinate stockbreeding to the field crops, as does the sacrifice of a pregnant sow at the January *Sementiua* (1.671–2 *placentur frugum matres, Tellusque Ceresque* | ... *grauidae uisceribusque suis*). Sabbatucci (1988) notes that man sacrifices at the time when the process of growth has passed out of his hands, between sowing and reaping. Because the embryo calf is equivalent to the buried grain, its sacrifice is exchanged for the successful germination of the seed corn (but see 639–40n.).

635–6 ter denas curia uaccas | accipit: a poetic distortion of *ter denas curiae* ... *accipiunt*, one cow to each *curia*. For religious purposes Rome still preserved the thirty Romulean *curiae*, each headed by a *curio* (cf. 2.527–32 on the *Fornacalia*); they seem to have been loose kinship groups, rather than locally based (Dion. Halic. translates as φρατρίαι), but resembled Attic demes in having their own hearths and sacrifices. They must have been obsolete or obscure if some Romans did not know to which *curia* they belonged (2.531). Presumably only one victim was killed (by the Pontifex Maximus?) on the Capitoline, and the *flamines* associated with the *curiae* slaughtered the others at curial hearths.

636 largo ... cruore: the epithet (cf. 617) marks the bloodshed as beneficent, even fertilizing; cf. *Met.* 1.157 *perfusam multo* ... *sanguine terram* | *immaduisse ferunt calidumque animasse cruorem.*

637–40 The delayed use of the calf embryos, carried forward from this festival and its celebrants and transferred to a new ritual celebrant at the Parilia, is imitated by a rare extension of the sentence over two couplets (*LEV* 27–33, type 2).

637 ast ubi: O. uses the archaic *ast* (= *at*) only here in *Fasti*, six times in *Met.* (*ast ubi* opens 6.685, 8.871), but it is absent from the erotic elegies.

637–8 uisceribus . . . exta: normally the sacrificial animal was divided between *exta* for the god and *uiscera* for the human participants. Here the *ministri* (cf. 243–4, 413nn.) pull out the embryos at the same time as they cut out the cow's *exta* to cook on the spit (cf. 2.364, 374).

fumosis . . . focis: cf. *Her.* 7.24 and 21.94, *Am.* 2.13.23 *fumosis. . . aris*; proleptic. The raw flesh would create the smoke.

639–40 igne cremat . . . purget ut ille cinis: the embryos would need to be burned separately so that the ashes could be reserved and then mixed with the other ingredients for distribution to the people at the Parilia (see 72–6, 733–4nn.).

quae natu maxima Virgo est: the chief Vestal, whether seniority came from birth date (Wissowa) or years of service (Mommsen). Bömer suggests O. has been influenced by a Virgilian reminiscence, *Aen.* 5.644–5 *quae maxima natu, | Pyrgo.*

luce Palis: synecdochic for *dies*, cf. 1.318 *agonali luce.* For the possessive cf. 878 *Iouis . . . dies*, 3.229 *diem quae prima meas . . . Kalendas*, 234 *diemque meum*, 5.725 *proxima Volcani lux est.*

populos: for the plural used of the Roman people, a surprising extension of the common poetic pl., see Bömer on *Met.* 6.179, Kenney on Apuleius, *Met.* 4.29.4. Here it may perhaps recall the Romulean *curiae*, cf. 1.38 *cum rudibus populis annua iura daret*, 2.510 *conuocat hic populos.* Line 731 refers back to this ritual purging with the singular *populus.*

641–72 Numa and Faunus. The *aition* of the Fordicidia in a nocturnal consultation and riddling oracular reply is partly based on Latinus' consultation of Faunus in *Aen.* 7.85–95 (see 651–60n.). Archaeological evidence for a shrine of Faunus at Tor Tignosa in the territory of ancient Lavinium has established the historicity of the kings' incubation practice (see Palmer (1974) 79–89). Within *Fasti* this scene repeats the pattern of Romulus' appeal to Lucina, when the Sabine wives were proving infertile (2.429–52), and of Numa's more elaborate encounter with Faunus and Picus, and decoding of Jupiter's ambiguous demands for sacrifice in 3.285–346. On O.'s treatment of Faunus, see H. C. Parker, 'Faunus in Ovid's *Fasti*', *TAPA* 123 (1993) 199–216.

641 rege Numa: Numa Pompilius, the second king of Rome, named without comment at 1.43, 2.69, *Pompilius* in 3.152. His first religious exploit is introduced in 3.262.

641–2 fructu non respondente labori, | inrita ... uota colentis erant: the language recalls *Georg.* 1.47–8 *illa seges demum uotis respondet auari | agricolae* (similar is 225–6 *sed illos | expectata seges uanis elusit auenis*) and O.'s evocation of wasted *labor* and *uota* at *Met.* 1.273–4 *sternuntur segetes et deplorata colonis | uota iacent longique perit labor inritus anni.* O. presents the disasters in three pairs: extremes of wet and dry weather or soil, failing corn displaced by weeds, and miscarriages and deaths of the ewes.

643 siccus erat gelidis Aquilonibus annus: for the cold and dry north wind cf. *Georg.* 2.404 *frigidus ... Aquilo*, 3.196–8 *Aquilo cum densus ... | incubuit, Scythiaeque hiemes atque arida differt | nubila*, *Met.* 1.262–3 *Aquilonem ... | et quaecumque fugant inductas flamina nubes* and 328.

644 adsidua ... aqua 'incessant rain' (cf. 686 and *Met.* 1.66 *nubibus adsiduis*).

luxuriabat: cf. *AA* 1.360 *ut seges in pingui luxuriabat humo*, and *Met.* 14.628–9 *falce, | qua modo luxuriem premit*; Virgil warns of harm done to the crop by *luxuria* of the stalks (*Georg.* 1.112) or foliage (*Georg.* 1.191).

645 saepe Ceres primis dominum fallebat in herbis: Virgil reserves 'Ceres' for the goddess throughout *Georgics* I and II, but O. here dismisses his previous reverent treatment of the goddess and her sufferings for a flippant metonymy, where *dominum* converts the goddess/grain into a cheating servant (for Ceres = 'grain', see 395n.). For the relationship *dominus/ager* cf. 2.516 *neglectus domino pauca ferebat ager*, *AA* 1.450 *sic dominum sterilis saepe fefellit ager.* Both Greek and Latin writers speak of land as repaying or cheating the farmer: cf. *Georg.* 1.225, Tib. 2.1.19, Ov. *AA* 1.401 *fallacibus aruis.*

646 et leuis obsesso stabat auena solo 'and the light wild-oat reared up occupying the ground': for the empty ears of the wild oat cf. Virg. *Ecl.* 5.37, *Georg.* 1.154 *steriles dominantur auenae.* O. extends *obsidere* to wild growth on uncultivated or wet-land at *Met.* 11.363 *iuncta palus huic est densis obsessa salictis*, 15.717 *Trachasque obsessa palude.*

647 ante diem partus ... acerbos 'tragic miscarriages': aborted or stillborn lambs; for *partus edere* cf. 5.26 and 35–6, *Met.*

5.517 *edita partu*, 13.486, Cic. *ND* 2.129 (*crocodili*) *cum in terram partus ediderint.*

648 necabat ouem: both lamb and ewe would probably perish; cf. the tragic labour of Virg. *Ecl.* 1.14–15 *modo namque gemellos | spem gregis, a! silice in nuda conixa reliquit.*

649 silua uetus, nullaque diu uiolata securi: cf. *Met.* 3.28 *silua uetus stabat nulla uiolata securi.* It was sacrilege for men to touch the trees of a sacred grove with axe or pruning-hook (see 753n. and Thomas (1988) 261–73): this grove (cf. Livy 1.21.3) is the model for Lucan's famous ecphrasis 3.399–425, beginning *lucus erat longo numquam uiolatus ab aeuo | obscurum cingens ... aera ... | et gelidas ... umbras.* Such unpruned groves are dark with overgrowth; cf. 2.165 *densa niger ilice lucus*, 3.295 *lucus Auentino suberat niger ilicis umbra*, 6.411 *lucus ... iuncis et harundine densus.*

650 Maenalio ... deo: Roman Faunus, a woodland spirit normally heard, not seen, associated with prophetic speech (from *fari*, cf. Varro, *LL* 7.36, Cic. *ND* 2.6, 3.15). Virgil makes him an ancestor of King Latinus, Livy (1.5.2) and O. (2.271–2) equate his Roman cult with that of Pan imported by King Evander from Arcadia. Hence Faunus is *Lycaeus* at 2.423, and worshipped on Mt Maenalus: 3.82–4 *colit | ... | pinigerum Fauni Maenalis ora caput.*

651–60 This account is based on Virgil's description of Latinus' incubation in the grove of Faunus at Albunea (*Aen.* 7.85–95).

651–2 dabat tacitis animo responsa quieto | noctibus: with *tacitis noctibus* cf. *Aen.* 7.87 *sub nocte silenti*; with *dabat ... responsa*, *Aen.* 7.85 *hinc ... responsa petunt.* However, incubation was a Greek, not an Italian practice, as Bömer notes, and the sacrifice to Somnus (not a Roman deity) is modelled on offerings to *Hypnos* in incubation to Asclepius at Epidaurus.

652–3 geminas ... mactat oues. | prima cadit Fauno, leni cadit altera Somno: *mactare* of ritual slaughter as in 336 above; cf. 3.300 (Numa again) and Aristaeus at 1.377, itself an echo of *Georg.* 4.546. Aristaeus' offering of victims to different deities may well be O.'s model for the allocation of these victims to the deities Faunus and Somnus. O. likes to elaborate ritual; so Medea in *Met.* 7.241 sets up two altars, one to Hecate and one to Iuventa.

654–60 sternitur in duro uellus utrumque solo ... supra

noua uellera corpus | ponit: the double reference echoes double elements in Virgil, the priest *caesarum ouium ... | pellibus incubuit stratis* (*Aen.* 7.87–8) and Latinus himself after sacrificing a hundred more *harum effultus tergo stratisque iacebat | uelleribus* (94–5). O. typically notices discomfort: with *duro ... solo*, cf. *Am.* 1.2.1 *dura ... strata*, 1.6.68 *limina*, 3.11.10 *dura ... humo*.

655 bis caput intonsum fontana spargitur unda: 6.264 *intonsi regia magna Numae* (cf. 2.30 *intonsos ... auos*) shows that Numa's beard is a permanent feature, not an immediate ritual choice. Ritual purity did require worshippers to sprinkle the head and/or body with running water, but the number of times varies: 5.435 *cumque manus puras fontana perluit unda*, *Met.* 12.413 *bis flumine corpora tingat*, 7.189–90 *ter sumptis flumine crinem | inrorauit aquis* (see 777–8n., and Introd. 3(i)(*c*), with von Eitrem (1915) 81, 127 for other ritual features in this scene).

656 bis sua faginea tempora fronde premit: cf. 2.25–6 *ramo qui caesus ab arbore pura | casta sacerdotum tempora fronde tegit*. Many types of foliage were worn in worship or carried in purification: laurel (for poetry, Hor. *Odes* 3.30.16), ivy (poetic 5.79, 6.483, etc.), poplar (for Hercules, *Aen.* 8.286) or myrtle (for Venus, 15n., *Am.* 1.1.29, *AA* 2.734, etc.). Schilling on this passage (n. 215) suggests the beech was chosen for its association with Jupiter (Paul. *Fest.* 77.13 Lindsay) but this seems irrelevant. Poets associated beeches with the pastoral world, and *faginea* enhances the assonance with *fontana* and *fronde*.

657 usus abest Veneris: with *Veneris usus* as a periphrase for *Venus* = 'sexual intercourse', cf. *Rem.* 357 *medio Veneris ... in usu*, Luc. 2.384 *Venerisque huic maximus usus*. For ritual abstinence from sex before sacrifice to Bacchus cf. 2.328–9, to Ceres, *Am.* 3.10.2 *secubat in uacuo sola puella toro* (cf. 4 *cur inhibes sacris commoda nostra tuis?*), to Isis, Prop. 2.33a.17.

657–8 nec fas animalia mensis | ponere: this probably prohibits all meat for the occasion, as *Met.* 15.72 (with the same ending *animalia mensis*) bans meat altogether. However, 657–8 may simply exclude consumption of the sacrificial victims.

nec digitis anulus ullus inest: unattested in Roman worship but not in magic. *in sacris nihil solet esse religatum* says Servius auctus on *Aen.* 4.518 *unum exuta pedem uinclis, in ueste recincta*; like sandals, girdles or hairbands (all cast off by Medea, *Met.* 7.182–3), a ring was seen as binding the body and so impeding ritual action.

659–60 ueste rudi tectus ... corpus | ponit, adorato per sua uerba deo: *sua uerba* (cf. *OLD* s.v. *suus* 12) indicates the use of correct ritual language. This use of *uerba* is prominent in *Fasti*; cf. 1.72 and 175, 510, 527, etc. Usually the prayer is given briefly before the divine reaction, not suppressed, as here: cf. 3.333–6 followed by 348 *adorantem destituitque Numam*, 5. 447–8 answered at 449 *uenit adoratus Caducifer.*

rudi: not a ritual requirement but a further index, like *intonsus* and *fagineus*, of Numa's primitive culture (cf. 1.36 and 131 *rudis ... uetustas*, 2.292, 97n.).

661 redimita papauere frontem: with *redimita frontem* cf. 3.269 *frontem redimita coronis*, 6.321 *turrigera frontem Cybele redimita corona*; *frontem* is acc. of respect defining the past part. pass. (G–L 338 n. 2). Garlands like Ceres' corn-ears were a device for identifying or characterizing different personifications: compare the benevolent Concordia at 6.91–2 *uenit Apollinea longas Concordia lauro | nexa comas, placidi numen ... ducis.* On poppies as sleeping-draughts see 531–2, 547nn.

662 Nox uenit, et secum somnia nigra trahit: homage to Tibullus' lovely *iam nox iungit equos ... post uenit ... | somnus et incerto somnia nigra pede* (2.1.87, 89–90).

663 Faunus adest: this is Latinus' divinely inspired dream.

pede ... duro: cf. 2.361 *cornipes*; like Pan, Faunus would have goat-hooves.

664 a dextro ... toro: in Roman tradition the left was the favourable side (cf. Cic. *Div.* 2.82). O. follows other Augustans in adopting the Greek code. Add to Bömer's citation of *Aen.* 8.302 *dexter adi pede sacra secundo* (uttered by Greeks), Prop. 4.1.68 *inceptis dextera cantet auis*, and *Fasti* 1.6 *dexter ades*, elaborated at 67, 69 *dexter ades ducibus, ... dexter ades patribusque tuis populoque Quirini.* On *edere uerba* see 318, 417nn.

665 'morte boum ... duarum: for *placare* with abl. *morte* here cf. *Met.* 12.28 and 151 *sanguine*, 13.468 *caede.* The ambiguity of the response comes only in the pentameter, where reference to *una iuuenca*, already puzzling after *boum ... duarum* (what is the other one for?), creates a paradox with *animas* ... *duas*. Cf. O.'s comment on Aristaeus' *bougonia* at 1.380 *mille animas una necata dedit.*

667 excutitur terrore quies: the construction is varied from 555 where the sleeper, not the sleep, is shaken.

uisa reuoluit 'reconsiders his dream': either from the unwinding of a scroll, or the rewinding of a ball of thread to retrace one's path through a maze, as in *Aen.* 9.391 *perplexum iter omne reuoluens*. Similar are *repetere* and *uolutare* of reviewing an oracle in *Met.* 1.388–9 *repetunt caecis obscura latebris* | *uerba* ... *inter seque uolutant.*

668 ambages caecaque iussa: cf. *Met.* 1.388 (cited in preceding note) *caecis* ... *latebris*, *Ibis* 55 *historiis inuoluam carmina caecis*. Here, as in *patres ambagibus errant* (261n.), the psychological sense of both *ambages* and 669 *errantem* plays on the spatial image of the maze.

669 expedit ... nemori gratissima coniunx 'his spouse, most dear to the grove, resolves his confusion': this is Egeria, the nymph of the *uallis Egeriae*; cf. 3.154, 261–2 and 275–6 *Egeria est quae praebet aquas, dea grata Camenis* | *illa Numae coniunx consiliumque fuit*, *Met.* 15.481–3 *Numam* ... | *coniuge qui felix nympha* ... *docuit ritus*, Livy 1.19.5 *simulat sibi cum dea Egeria congressus nocturnos esse; eius se monitu, quae acceptissima diis essent, sacra instituere* (Plut. *Numa* 4.2 is more credulous). O. has reoriented *Aen.* 10.607 *gratissima coniunx*, 'most pleasing to her husband', by relating *gratissima* to *nemori*, so as to evoke Egeria's association with wild nature.

670 'grauidae posceris exta bouis: cf. the sacrifice to Tellus and Ceres at 1.671–2 *placentur* ... | *farre suo grauidae uisceribusque suis.*

671 exta bouis grauidae dantur: with the rearrangement of words from 670, the narrative takes on a perfunctory tone, as if success barely needs mention. O's language echoes 631, 633 to round off the tale in ring-composition. Is the numerical coincidence between the sacrifices of the pregnant victim at 1.671 and 4.671 another correspondence between the two books?

673–4 Hanc quondam Cytherea diem ... | iussit: on Venus of Cythera see 15n. The goddess's intervention is O.'s own creation, a courtly compliment recalling the opening concern of this book with Venus as ancestress of the Julii Caesares.

properantius: the comparative form only here; for the positive, usually denoting premature or hasty action, O. uses both *properans* (1.507, *Met.* 3.657) and *properatus* (2.715, *Met.* 5.396, 9.587, 15.748. For other Ovidian comparatives formed from participles see Kenney on *Her.* 19.83.

admissos praecipitauit equos: as in 673 accelerated haste is implied; the horses were already galloping (cf. *admissus* at *Am.* 1.8.50, 2.11.56, 3.2.78, *AA* 2.732, 3.468, etc.). Given phrases like *Ex P.* 3.1.140 *spem festinando praecipitare meam,* Barchiesi (1994) 120–2 is justified in seeing implicit misgivings at the success of this young man in a hurry.

675 cum primum luce sequenti 'when the dawn followed as soon as possible': *cum primum* is adverbial; usually it is a conjunction, 'as soon as', with perf. indic. (*Met.* 4.292, 13.641, 14.70, etc.).

676 Augusto iuueni: or *augusto iuueni*? Neither Latin orthography nor the practice of recitation would distinguish between adjective and title, a nice ambiguity, since Octavian was not yet Augustus when he received his first *salutatio* and title of *imperator* on the day after the battle of Mutina. In recording this honour (listed in Verrius' *Fasti Praenestini* (see headnote 629–76), O. is true to his promise of 2.16 *per titulos ingredimurque tuos.*

677–8 16 April B N

Or perhaps 17 as in A–W–C: the 16th is the second nundinal day, and *nefastus* for court business.

677 Sed iam . . . quartus tibi Lucifer: the fourth morning star should herald 16 April (the same day anticipated as *luce sequenti* in 675), and mark the setting of the Hyades as occurring on the 16th. But the circus races of the Cerialia, celebrated on 19 April, are marked as two days later (679 *tertia post Hyadas . . . remotas*), suggesting that O. has lost a day in 677, and should have written *quintus* (17 April). Such forward dating from the Ides is not simply a poetic device to avoid cumbersome ordinals; it obviated the discrepancy in retrospective dating between the Republican and the Julian calendars caused by Caesar's addition of a day to the month.

For the morning star in poetic dating cf. 2.567–8 *tot de mense supersint | Luciferi,* 3.877 *tres ubi Luciferos ueniens praemiserit Eos.*

678 respicit: traditionally the morning star turned back in flight before the rising sun.

hac Hyades Dorida nocte tenent 'this night the Hyades occupy the ocean': *Dorida* is the 3rd decl. acc. form of Gk Δωρίς, wife of Nereus, equated with the ocean in Virg. *Ecl.* 10.5. Elsewhere O. identifies Ocean as Amphitrite (5.731), Nereus (*Met.* 1.187, 12.24), or Tethys (*Met.* 2.69). O.'s report of the evening setting of the Hyades is only three days early, but he mistakenly gives them an evening rising on 2 May (5.164) and reports their reappearance on the morning of 2 June (6.197–8). See L. Ideler, *Über den astronomischen Teil der Fasti des Ovid* (Abhandlungen der Akad. Berlin, Philos.-hist. Klasse 1822/3 (Berlin 1825) s.v. *Hyades*.

679–712 (17, 18 April, C N, D N) 19 April E CER NP

679–80 This is the true Cerialia (cf. 711) marked by the Calendar at the end of the festival sequence that began on 12 April. The place, Rome's Circus Maximus, stands for the activity. These games may also have been officially dedicated to Liber (Bacchus) and Libera (Proserpina): at 3.785–6 O. notes that Liber used to have his own games on the Liberalia (17 March) but now shares in the games of Ceres *taedifera ... dea.*

carcere partitos ... equos: each team would be assigned its individual *carcer*, 'starting-gate' (the singular is distributive; for plur. *carceres*, common in prose, cf. *Tr.* 5.12.26). *partior* is deponent in classical authors, but the past participle is used with passive force, especially in the abl. abs. as in Caes. *BG* 6.33.1 and examples listed in *TLL* x 1.526.81–2; deponent and passive coexist in e.g. Silius 7.520 *partitus socias uires* but 7.736 *partitis ... maniplis.*

681–708 A new *aition* (cf. 682 *causa docenda mihi est*), of the supposed ritual of releasing foxes set on fire into the Roman circus as an offering to Ceres before the chariot-racing. This entails the same cruel act as Samson's use of burning foxes to destroy the Philistine crops (Judges 15.4–6: see the discussions of von Eitrem (1915) 171, Frazer, *Fasti* III 332–3, Le Bonniec (1989) 27–33). F. Bömer, *Wiener Studien* 69 (1956) 372–84 argues from O.'s imprecision (where and when does this happen?) and from practicality that there can have been no such ritual, whether at Rome or at Carseoli; but his arguments do not eliminate Frazer's evidence for European peasant practices of tying up and burning foxes on their land to drive away other foxes. O. may have actual country practices in mind.

Despite the autobiographical guarantee, O.'s *aition* of the burning fox is clearly a Hellenistic moral tale, which the poet has adapted as a rustic vignette without the original Greek moral. For in Babrius' fable 11 the peasant set the fox on fire to injure his neighbour's crops, but it burned his own ripe crops instead, and Demeter took no pity on him. So O. has transformed the deserved human loss in the Greek fable into a loss brought on by a child's thoughtless revenge, and made this the *aition* of a contemporary practice. Perhaps he witnessed the firing of the foxes in the circus on one occasion and has generalized it.

As a work of fiction O.'s rite and its reported origins are vividly authenticated, by several personalizing devices. O. first introduces the autobiographical setting (681–90) as in the briefer anecdote of 377–86, with circumstantial detail of his visit to the country host at Carseoli (in the highlands of the Aequi on the Via Valeria between Rome and Sulmona's neighbour Corfinium).

681–2 missae ... | terga ferant uolpes: *missae* is designed to mislead. Since *mittere* is the *vox propria* for releasing the teams from the cage of 680 (*Am.* 3.2.9 and 66), the reader assumes this is a race, and the chariots are off. Instead, the subject and its torture are described before the identification as foxes, and the scene may not be set in the circus after all. On *taedae* see 407n.

683–4 frigida Carseolis nec oliuis apta ferendis | terra: for *frigida* of hill country cf. *Aen.* 7.715–16 *quos frigida misit | Nursia.* with *oliuis apta ferendis* contrast 3.151 *oliuiferis Romam deductus ab aruis* (also *Ibis* 317). Is the soil too cold or badly drained for olives? Cf. *Georg.* 2.109–14 on terrain, 420–5 on olives.

ad segetes ingeniosus ager: for *ingeniosus* of land cf. *Her.* 6.117 *Lemnos ... terra ingeniosa colenti.*

685–6 Paelignos, natalia rura ... | parua, sed adsiduis obuia semper aquis: *obuia* (A) should be preferred to *umida* (UZ), easily substituted for the less expected epithet. O. is diverted briefly from his theme to linger affectionately over his own well-watered family farm (cf. *Am.* 2.1.1 *Paelignis natus aquosis*, and descriptions of *rus Paelignum* at *Am.* 2.16.1–7, 3.15.3, *Ex P.* 1.8.42).

687 hospitis antiqui solitas intrauimus aedes: both epithets suggest intimacy, as the sunset of 688 brings leisure for conversation.

688 dempserat ... iam iuga Phoebus equis: another variation on sunset, cf. *Met.* 7.324 *ter iuga Phoebus equis ... dempserat, Her.* 21.86 *demere purpureis Sol iuga uellet equis.*

emeritis: used both of the soldier/worker who has finished a term of service and the time or duty served: cf. 1.665 *emeritum ... aratrum, Met.* 15.226 *emeritis ... annis.*

689–90 narrare solebat | unde meum praesens instrueretur opus: *solebat* refers to *multa* rather than this particular tale (*et haec*); yet the verb is a favourite for citation of supposedly oral sources in Ciceronian dialogues, perhaps to authenticate details as heard more than once, cf. *Rep.* 2.1.2. Like the sentimental recall of O.'s homeland in 685 *praesens* overtly breaks the context to draw the reader's attention to the author and his process of composition. This is the first such use of *praesens* listed in *TLL* x 2.849.63ff., followed by Colum. 2.21.6 *finem praesentis disputationis faciam.*

691 'hoc' ... 'in campo' (campumque ostendit): cf. Ulysses' storytelling in *AA* 2.133, 135 *'campus erat' (campumque facit).* The demonstrative and parenthetic stage-direction add authenticity and vividness; but the extra-textual reference of 690 highlights the artifice of the second-order dialogue. This kind of parenthesis, first found at *Aen.* 12.206 '*... ut sceptrum hoc' (dextra sceptrum nam forte gerebat)*, is common in O. (cf. M. von Albrecht, *Die Parenthese in Ovids Metamorphosen und ihre dichterische Funktion* (1959, repr. Hildesheim 1964) 103–7), often with pointed repetition of a key word, as in *Met.* 1.590–1 *'pete' ... 'umbras | altorum nemorum' (et nemorum monstrauerat umbras)*, or 7.218–19 '*draconum | currus adest.' aderat demissus ab aethere currus.*

691–2 'habebat | rus breue ... parca colona: with this use of *breue* cf. 2.137 *tu breue nescioquid uictae telluris habebas.* This note of poverty is maintained by *parcus*; cf. *Met.* 7.656; or the humble offering of *parca ... mica salis* at 2.538.

colona first occurs in O.; elsewhere only 2.646, 3.445 (U reading). But why does O. make the farmer's wife his focus (not only subject of this sentence, cf. 695–700)? Because the child's mischief makes his mother the central figure? (Neither parent is shown dealing with the crisis!)

693–4 ille suam peragebat humum, siue usus aratri, | seu curuae falcis, siue bidentis erat: the construction of *peragere* ('to carry through', 'to complete a task') with *humum* may be formed by analogy with *Georg.* 1.125 *subigere.* It is the only instance cited in *OLD*, and seems without precedent. The αὐτουργός tills his small plot unaided: plough, pruning-knife (*Georg.* 2.416, 421) and hoe (*bidens*, masc., cf. 927 below, and *Georg.* 2.355, 400) imply grain crops, vines, etc., and perhaps *olus.*

695–700 Having set up his Georgic figure O. dismisses him to give six lines to the wife's tasks in and outside the house, articulated by *modo ... nunc* (see 398n.), *aut ... aut ... aut, et tamen ... -que.*

695 uerrebat stantem tibicine uillam: usually metaphorical in verse, *uerrere* is used of domestic sweeping at 2.523 and 4.736 below. A dwelling in need of a prop (*tibicen*, cf. Juv. 3.193 *urbem ... tenui tibicine fultam*) can only be called a *uilla* with mock grandeur, perhaps the same tone audible in calling the brood hen of 695 *mater.*

696 plumis oua fouenda dabat: cf. 1.443 *plumis oua fouetis.*

697 uirides maluas ... fungos ... albos: salad greens and mushrooms (not *tartufi bianchi*) are still gathered by Italian peasants for food.

698 humilem grato calfacit igne focum: unlike Virgil (*calefacta* at *Aen.* 12.66 and 269), O. uses only contracted forms of *calfacere*; cf. *AA* 2.214, *Ibis* 46. Building (or reviving) a fire is part of such genre descriptions; cf. *Moretum* 8–12 with Kenney's note, Ov. *Met.* 8.640–5.

699–700 adsiduis exercet bracchia telis, | ... arma parat: the woman's weaving is couched in deliberately strenuous, almost masculine terms, echoing Virgil's militarization of the farmer's tools (*Georg.* 1.160 *arma*) and labours. For *telae*, 'loom' (missed here by R. J. Deferrari, M. I. Barry and M. R. P. McGuire, *A concordance of Ovid* (Washington 1939), cf. 3.819, *Met.* 4.275, *Georg.* 1.294 *arguto coniunx percurrit pectine telas.* Yet the periphrastic description of the cloaks she is weaving as *arma* ('defensive armour against the threats of cold' suggests that O. was seeking at least a passing pun on *tela.*

aduersusque: this is the only instance of prepositonal *aduersus* in O. It is avoided in high poetry except Lucr. 4.445, 5.310. See Axelson (1945) 77.

701 primo lasciuus in aeuo: cf. *lasciue puer* of Amor, *Met.* 1.456. The mischief is explained by his youth.

702 addideratque annos ad duo lustra duos: *-que* is explanatory, 'being in fact only twelve'. Like *quindecim* (*tria lustra* in 2.183), *duodecim* is inadmissible in hexameter poetry; a more common substitute is *bis seni* at e.g. *Aen.* 5.561, *Met.* 8.243.

703 capit extremi uolpem conualle salicti: the reader is to imagine a willow grove (cf. *Georg.* 2.13 and 415, *Met.* 5.590, 11.363) in the low land (the Virgilian *conuallis* occurs only here in O.) at the water's edge bounding the plot.

704 cohortis: the farmyard term (found in O. only here and *Met.* 11.89; cf. Varro, *RR* 3.3.6 *cohors in qua pascebantur gallinae*), like *mater* in 696, seems mock-solemn.

705 captiuam: resumptive from 703.

706 urentes . . . manus: a bold turn of phrase for the boy's hands as they ignite the inflammable materials wrapped round the fox.

707 incendit uestitos messibus agros: the parallel image of the fields clothed by the harvest as is the fox by burning straw (cf. 1.402 *gramine uestitis . . . toris*) brings home the reversal of the boy's revenge; fanned by the wind (unlike the controlled fires of *Aen.* 10.405–8), the fires destroy the crops.

709 factum abiit: a bold extension of O.'s normal use of *abire* for the disappearance of material things, like *somnus* (3.23, *Met.* 15.664) or *nox* (721, *Am.* 1.5.6).

709–10 monimenta manent . . . | nunc quoque: two characteristic signals of the *aition*. The present state of affairs, which the *aition* is designed to explain, is seen as a reminder or record (for the jingle of *monimenta* with *manere* cf. *Met.* 1.159, 5.227, 10.725); on *nunc quoque* see 504n.

nam †dicere certam†: *captam* UC, *certam* A; an insoluble crux. Bömer (*Wiener Studien.* 69 (1956) 375) prints *dicere* and *certa* qualifying *lex*: 'a fixed law of Carseoli forbids men to *name* a fox'. But even *dicere* must be uncertain: why should a local law forbid men to name a fox, still less to call it *captam* or *curtam*, 'mutilated', 'docked'? Better to change the verb: Heinsius proposed *uiuere captam*; others have suggested *ducere captam/curtam*, Courtney (*nisi*) *adurere curtam*. Nothing convinces.

711 utque luat poenas, . . . ardet: O. returns to his starting-point *ardentia* in 681. It is now explained as retaliation on the arsonist fox, killed to atone for its damage to the crops of its tormenter.

712 quoque modo segetes perdidit ... perit: the ancient lawcode of the Twelve Tables imposed the death penalty on men who bewitched or stole others' crops, and condemned those who burnt their stacks (*aceruum* ... *frumenti*) to death by fire (Table 8, frs. 8a, 9 and 10, S. Riccoboni, *Fontes iuris Romani anteiustiniani* vol. 1: *Leges* (Florence 1941)). The burning of standing crops was probably punished in the same way, so O.'s account of this vindictive treatment of foxes conforms to Roman retaliatory law.

713–20 20 April F N

713–14 The last four days were introduced fairly simply (625 *luce secutura*, 629 *tertia ... cum lux surrexerit*, 677 *quartus ... Lucifer*, 679 *tertia ... cum lux erit orta*. But as O. approaches the national birthday he raises the tone: a learned allusion to the dawn goddess (cf. 373 *Pallantias*, 389 *Eos*) is combined with a colourful expansion of Homeric dawn formulae. O. had told the story at *Met.* 13.576–99 of Aurora's mourning for her son Memnon, prince of the Ethiopians and ally of Troy killed by Achilles (cf. *Od.* 4.188, 11.522, *Aen.* 1.489); he also invokes her as Memnon's mother in *Am.* 1.8.4 (cited next note), 1.13.3–4 and 3.9.1.

714 Memnonis in roseis lutea mater equis: cf. *Am.* 1.8.3–4 *parentem* | *Memnonis in roseis ... equis*. The colour combination (also found at *Met.* 7.703) seems to derive from *Aen.* 7.26 *Aurora in roseis fulgebat lutea bigis*. More often O. associates her or the sky around her with *purpureus*: *Met.* 2.113, 3.184, 6.48. In Homer dawn had been ῥοδοδάκτυλος ('rosy-fingered': *Il.* 1.477 etc., *Od.* 2.1 etc.) or κροκόπεπλος ('saffron-robed'), but there is no mention of her horses: like Memnon, her team is post-Homeric.

715 de duce lanigeri pecoris, qui prodidit Hellen: the 'leader of the wool-bearing flock' is the constellation *Aries*, identified with the golden ram who carried Phrixus and Helle (see 278). *laniger* (cf. 1.334, 384 and 2.681, 4 times in *Met.*) is adopted from Virg. *Georg.* 3.287 *lanigeros ... greges*. The coincidence with Germanicus, *Aratea* 532–3 *nobilis hic aurato uellere quondam* | *qui tulit in tauros Phrixum, qui prodidit Hellen*, noted by Heinsius, suggests imitation, but by which poet? (Heinsius also notes *proditor Helles* in Luc. 4.56, Martial 9.71, surely influenced by O.)

This is the night of transition as the sun leaves this section of the zodiac for *Taurus*: by 25 April Aries will have passed out of sight (see 903–4). The 20th, the eve of Rome's birthday, was also seen as the beginning of the natural year: cf. Virg. *Georg.* 1.217–18 *candidus auratis aperit cum cornibus annum | taurus*, and Mynors ad loc.

716 uictima maior: the bull was the most important victim in the Roman sacrificial code, as contrasted with the ram (hence *maior* here) and boar of the *Suouetaurilia*. A bull and a ram, probably as signs of the zodiac, are shown on coins and reliefs mounted on free-standing columns in front of a shrine believed by Guarducci (*MDAIR* 78 (1971) 203–4) to be the shrine of Vesta on the Palatine (see 949–54).

717 non est cognoscere promptum: cf. *Met.* 3.96 *neque erat cognoscere promptum*, 13.10–11 *nec mihi dicere promptum, | nec facere est isti*, 14.481. The evasiveness of the phrase ('I am not in a position to say') suggests an official origin.

718 pars prior apparet: the traditional icon of the constellation showed only the forequarters. O.'s neatly antithetical pentameter turns the divergent astronomical identification of the constellation attested in C. Robert, *Eratosthenes: Catasterismoi* §14 p. 106 into a sly joke. (There was a similar debate over the gender of the constellation *Hippos/Hippe*.)

719 hoc ... signum is the common subject of both predicates, *taurus* and *femina*. O. explains the competing mythological identities as Europa's bull or Io in bovine form at the rising of Taurus (5.603–20), where he exploits the chance to tell the story of Europa's seduction by Jupiter.

720 Iunone inuita: the catasterism, whether of bull or cow, would be a lover's gift (*munus amoris*) from Jupiter, like the catasterisms of Callisto or of Ariadne's crown honoured by Bacchus. Traditionally only Io was actually persecuted by Juno (cf. *inuita* in *Met.* 1.612–13 *speciem Saturnia uaccae | quanquam inuita, probat*).

721–862 21 April G PAR NP The Parilia

Though damaged, the *Fasti Praenestini* entry for 21 April preserves the opening of PARILIA, and in the fourth line *ignes tran*[*siliunt* ... while line 5 begins: *principio an[ni pastorici*. This was the city's birthday. But the day celebrated as anniversary of Romulus' successful auspices (from Ennius, *Annales* 1 onwards) was also the holy day of Pales, a pastoral deity so ancient its gender was disputed. (On this problem, and the two Pales whose festivals celebrate the spring and late summer breeding-season of small or large cattle, see G. Dumézil, *Idées romaines* (Paris 1969) 273–87.)

Propertius had singled out the double role of the Parilia as beginning of both the city's and the shepherds' year when he made this festival the setting for Tarpeia's betrayal of the citadel in 4.4.73–5: *urbi festus erat (dixere Parilia patres), | hic primus coepit moenibus esse dies, | annua pastorum conuiuia*; there (75–8) and in the opening poem (4.1.19–20 *annuaque accenso celebrante Parilia faeno, | qualia nunc curto lustra nouantur equo*) he alludes to the other rituals which are described by O. at 723–34 below.

O. divides his celebration into a religious account of the shepherds' purification festival (721–82, cf. 723 *pastoria sacra*), an aetiological transition on the *moris origo* of the fire-leaping (783–806), and an idiosyncratic commemoration of the legendary *urbis origo* ending in the death of Remus (807–56); this is rounded off by a patriotic prayer (857–62).

For an interpretation of this sequence as reflecting the displacement of pastoral Rome by Augustan ideology see Mary Beard, 'A complex of times: no more sheep on Romulus' birthday', *PCPS* 33 (1987) 1–15.

721–82 *Pastoria sacra* The tradition connecting the foundation of Rome on the feast of Pales with its pastoral origins is reported by Varro, *RR* 2.1.9 *Romanorum uero populum a pastoribus ortum quis non dicit? quis Faustulum nescit pastorem fuisse nutricium, qui Romulum et Remum educauit? non ipsos quoque fuisse pastores obtinebit, quod Parilibus potissimum condidere urbem?*

Virgil (*Georg.* 3.1 and 294) invokes Pales as patron for his advice to stockbreeders and shepherds, and Tib. 2.5.25–30 links Pales etymologically with *Palatia*, *Pan*, and *pastor*. Tibullus' description 2.5.87–90 *madidus Baccho sua festa Palilia pastor | concinet; a stabulis tunc procul este lupi! | ille leuis stipulae sollemnes potus aceruos | accendet, flammas transilietque sacras* is echoed and varied at Prop. 4.4.75–8 *annua pastorum conuiuia, lusus in urbe, | cum pagana madent fercula diuitiis, | cumque super raros faeni flammantis aceruos | traicit immundos ebria turba pedes.*

Modern etymologists divide on the relationship between Parilia and Pales: was it a transformation of Palilia, or did the word come from *parere*, 'to give birth' (basically the same root as *aperire* in *Aprilis*)? Compare the derivation given by Festus 248 Lindsay, *uel ut alii uolunt dicta Parilia quod pro partu pecoris eidem sacra fiebant.*

721 Parilia poscor 'I am asked for the Parilia': cf. 253–4 *nondum ... sua numina posci | senserat*, 670, *Met.* 5.333 *poscimur Aonides*, and (if the passive is correct) Hor. *Odes* 1.32.1–4 *poscimur ... age dic Latinum, | barbite, carmen.* As in *Met.* 5.333 or 4.274 (or 2.144, of the sun's required daily round), there is a formal performance by one or more artists, but in this case the turn belongs not to the speaker but to the theme celebrated. *TLL* x 2.82.19–30 lists many active uses of the double acc., illustrated by the ruling of Servius on *Aen.* 1.414: *dicimus posco magistrum lectionem, non a magistro*; but O. provides five of the seven classical uses of personal pass. with object acc. (x 2.82.30–7). The only earlier instance is Plaut. *As.* 181.

722 non poscor frustra, si fauet alma Pales: her favour will ensure the quality of his performance.

723 alma Pales, faueas ... canenti: a neat resumption (with variation and chiasmus) of 722. (See 671n. and *LEV* p. 34). Lines 723–30 constitute a miniature proem, echoing the book's opening appeal to Venus (1 *Alma, faue*). Like Venus and Cybele (but not Ceres, despite Virg. *Georg.* 1.7), Pales is addressed by O. as *alma*, surely because of her association with milk and nurturing. In contrast, the poet does not ask Cybele or Ceres to favour him. (See Appel (1909) 99–100.)

pastoria sacra: see 721–82n.

724 prosequor officio si tua facta meo 'if I honour your benefactions with my service'. Since Pales has no mythical biography (no *facta*), *facta* here must be understood as *benefacta* (cf. *tua facta* of Egeria at 3.262), and O.'s *officium* as including both his poetic services and his actions (described in 725–8) as a citizen in her worship.

725–8 O. proclaims his personal participation in carrying the ashes (725–6), leaping the bonfires and sprinkling purificatory waters. But if he witnessed the ritual at all he is unlikely to have taken part in anything so down to earth: this is purely an authenticating device (cf. North (1989) 141).

726 saepe tuli plena, februa tosta, manu: *tuli* presumably stands for *abstuli*, since 731 makes it clear that the people received the material to take home. The *februa* for this festival have all been ritually burned and mixed by the Vestals, so that *tosta*, the reading of AUD, should be preferred to the predictable *casta* of Z. All the *februa* listed in 2.19–36 are issued by priests, like the Vestals here; a further distinction is made between their function of *piare* in cleansing and purifying human bodies and property, and its corollary of *purgare*, relating to the expulsion of *omne nefas omnemque mali* ... *causam* (2.35–6). See Introd. 3(i)(*c*).

727 transilui positas ter ... flammas 'I have leapt three times over the flames': *transilire* is also used by Tibullus (2.5.90 cited 721–82n.), Probus, and the *Fasti Praenestini* (cf. 781–2 *traicere*).

in ordine: probably 'set in a row', taken with *positas*, rather than temporal. Prop. 4.4.77 *raros* ... *aceruos* suggests heaps spaced at intervals for citizens to jump like a hurdle race: each man would then run the course three times. Frazer (1929) III 342–3 notes that such bonfires used to be lit at the old Celtic spring festival of Beltane in Scotland and Wales on 1 May, with various prescriptions of crossing or circling them three times. The fires were presumably made of waste material: old straw from the pens, winter deadwood, leaves, and perhaps pruned twigs.

728 udaque roratas laurea misit aquas: purification is by both fire and water shaken from laurel branches (other branches are used to adorn the pens in 737–8, and laurel is burned in 742); cf. Juv. 2.157–8 *cuperent lustrari si qua darentur* | *sulpura cum taedis et si foret umida laurus*. The carrying of laurel by soldiers marching in triumph is explained as a purification by Festus 104 Lindsay *ut quasi purgati a caede humana intrarent urbem, itaque eandem laurum omnibus suffitionibus adhiberi solitum erat*, cf. Pliny, *NH* 15.138.

729 mota dea est, operique fauet: O. rounds off the proem as in 15–16, where Venus, *mota*, gives a sign of her favourable reaction to O.'s appeal, and bids him finish his *coeptum* ... *opus*.

729–30 naualibus exit | puppis: habent uentos iam mea uela suos: as in 18 *dum licet et spirant flamina, nauis eat*, O. revives the ship metaphor to launch his poetic vessel on a new voyage, marking the importance of this national foundation day. The first use of *naualia* in Latin verse is Prop. 1.20.17–18 *olim Pagasae naualibus Argon | egressam*, but cf. *Met.* 3.661, 11.455, and analogies from ships repaired or retired in *naualia* at *Am.* 2.9.21, *Tr.* 4.8.17.

731 i, pete ... populus, suffimen: the normal prose word is *suffimentum*, cf. Cic. *Leg.* 1.40, and Festus 427 Lindsay, cited on 743. For the root verb, *suffire*, 'to fumigate', see 5.676. The process is *suffitio*. The vocative *populus* found here is preserved in a prayer at Livy 1.14.7, and may have been the only form in use; cf. Luc. 2.116, and on other vocatives in *-us* Priscian, *GLK* II 305.16, F. Neue and C. Wagener, *Formenlehre der lateinischen Sprache* edn 3, I (Leipzig 1892) 131–3.

uirginea ... ab ara: the altar in the shrine of Vesta, where the materials were stored.

732 Vestae munere purus eris: *purus* is seldom used without qualification of a mortal; in O. only *Am.* 3.8.23 *ille ego Musarum purus Phoebique sacerdos*, in ironic contrast with a soldier polluted by blood. Cf. however the ritual *manibus ... puris* of 3.335, 5.435 *manus puras fontana perluit unda.*

733 sanguis equi suffimen erit: the first reference to the longest preserved ingredient in this brew. Along with the ash of the embryo calf from the Fordicidia (see 640) the chief Vestal mixed the blood she had saved from the sacrifice of the *October equus*, the trace-horse of the winning team, slaughtered and sacrificed the preceding year at the race of 15 October. This is attested in three passages of Festus, 117, 190–1 and 246 Lindsay (i.e. Verrius Flaccus, author of the *Fasti Praenestini*, consulted by O. for *Fasti* and the probable source of Plut. *Qu. Rom.* 97). The tail of this horse was cut off (hence Prop. 4.1.20 *curto ... equo*, quoted 721–862n.), its blood drained on the altar in the Regia and the ashes of the burned tail (and blood?) kept by the Virgo Maxima in the shrine of Vesta until the Parilia. Both animal residues were then combined and bulked out with a larger quantity of beanstalks (more likely their ash), an ingredient mentioned in no other source. (See Von Eitrem (1915) 240, 449.)

734 culmen inane fabae: this is probably what Cato, *Agr.* 37.2, Varro, *RR* 1.23.3, Pliny, *NH* 18.120 refer to as *fabalia*, n. pl. On the distinction *culmen/culmus* cf. Varro, *LL* 5.37 *culmi appellantur quod in summo campo nascuntur, et summum culmen.* (See 919.)

735–82 O. addresses a shepherd, introducing and rounding off an appropriate prayer (747–76) with instructions. Parallels and even models for these instructions can be found in Varro, *RR* 2.2.7–9. But O.'s poetic language is Virgilian, adapted from *Georgics* III, whose content is selectively Varronian, and the *Eclogues*.

735 oues saturas ad prima crepuscula lustra: *satur* is regularly used by O. for cattle fed when they were penned or stabled at nightfall, 3.879, 5.498, *Met.* 2.120. *lustrare* is a synonym for *piare*, but has a wider sense of surveying a region (by sight or travel) as in *Met.* 1.213. Passages like 1.669 *pagum lustrate, coloni*, 2.31–2 *secta quia pelle Luperci* | *omne solum lustrant* show how purifying and going over an area or massed group (cf. English 'scouring') could coincide.

736–8 Purifying the pens: *unda* is water taken from a running source as in 655; similarly *uirga* in the quasi-etymological word-play *uirgaque uerrat* is not a branch, but a twig-broom. *prius* is common to both verbs: the *ouile* should be sprinkled and swept before the flock is penned in.

Varro, *RR* 2.2.7 notes that the ground of the sheep pens should be bare and sloping, *ut euerri facile possit et fieri purum*; the same procedure contributes to both physical and ritual cleanliness.

737–8 frondibus et fixis decorentur . . . ramis | et tegat . . . corona fores: the parallel decoration of the pen with branches and its doorway with garlands is varied by switching the syntax from passive to active, and transferring the participle (*fixis/ornatas*) from the decoration to the decorated.

739–40 caerulei . . . puro de sulpure fumi, | tactaque fumanti sulpure balet ouis: what is the point of 740? Hardly 'let the sheep be stung with sulphur until it bleats'. Bleating is characteristic of sheep (cf. *OLD* s.v *balare* b) so the significant element is *tacta*: almost 'let the bleating sheep be stung'. For sulphur in ritual purification cf. *Met.* 7.261 *terque senem flamma, ter aqua, ter sulp(h)ure lustrat*, Juv. 2.157–8 (728n.). Bömer compares the ritual fumigation of Odysseus' palace after the killing of the suitors, *Od.* 22.481–2, 23.50ff., and Vegetius' recommendation of fumigation for mules in *Mulomed.* 3.12 (Von Eitrem (1915) 251, with 206, 248). There is more sound-play on *fumi/fumanti*, *puro/sul-pure* (assuming O. did not write and pronounce *sulphure* to increase assonance on *fu*.)

741 ure maris rores: *rores* is the reading of Z; cf. forms of *ros* *maris* at *AA.* 3.690, *Met.* 12.410. The context seems to require perfume rather than mere firewood: hence the fragrant herb rosemary is more appropriate than *maris oleas* (AU) (of oleander wood, masculine as opposed to the fruitful feminine olive wood in Soph. *Trach.* 1196), read by A–W–C and Schilling. Here *taedam* is not a torch as such, but pine wood burnt for its resinous fumes.

herbasque Sabinas: the evergreen juniper, cf. Pliny, *NH* 16.80, 24.102. (See Von Eitrem (1915) 209–10.)

742 et crepet ... laurus adusta focis: cf. 1.343–4 *ara dabat fumos herbis contenta Sabinis | et non exiguo laurus adusta foco*, Tib. 2.5.81–2 *succensa sacris crepitet bene laurea flammis, | omine quo felix et sacer annus erit.* O. echoes Prop. 2.28.36 *laurus adusta foco*, and 4.3.58 *et crepat ad ueteres herba Sabina focos.* With *crepet*, 'crackle', cf. 781 and Virgil's use of *crepitare* for flames at *Georg.* 1.85, *Aen.* 7.74. *crepare* is also used for the crack of the wooden sistrum at *Met.* 9.784.

In 739–42 O. conveys all the sensory aspects of the ritual: sight, smell and sound.

743 libaque de milio milii fiscella sequatur: Festus 472–3 Lindsay *suffimenta sunt quae ⟨faciebant ex faba milio⟩que mellito, mulso spar⟨so⟩* cites ritual cakes of millet at a vintage festival; Dion. Halic. 2.23.5 includes them in the primitive rustic feasting of a contemporary Curia. But this is the only explicit evidence for millet at the Parilia either as ground meal or cakes. *fiscella*, 'little basket', is the diminutive of *fiscina* (754 below). The forms are interchangeable in the agricultural writers, in Virgil (*Ecl.* 10.71 *fiscella*, *Georg.* 1.266 *fiscina*), in O., and Columella's hexameters (10.307 and 402), but *fiscina* may be more dignified, since it is admitted in oratory (Cic. *Flacc.* 41). On diminutives in *Fasti* see Introd. 4(i).

744 rustica ... est hoc dea laeta cibo: see 372n.

745–6 adde dapes mulctramque suas, dapibusque resectis | ... tepido lacte precare: *suas*, 'proper to the goddess', is common to both *dapes* and *mulctra* but takes the plural rather than, as is normal (G–L 285), the number of the nearest noun. The sacred food is divided into the goddess's part and that of men, portioned out for sharing: *resectae*, from *resecare* (cf. 2.520 *primitias Cereri farra resecta dabant*, Cato, *Agr.* 50.2, and R. Schilling, *Rites, cultes, dieux de Rome* (Paris 1979) 59–63). The pail contains the warm milk offered to the goddess: cf. Tib. 1.1.36 *et placidam soleo spargere lacte Palem*, 2.5.27, and Varro, *RR* 2.11.5 for the shepherds' offering of milk in a chapel of Rumina (goddess of lactation) near the Palatine. This offering to Pales is probably what Pliny had in mind at *NH* 14.88 *Romulum lacte non uino libasse indicio sunt sacra ab eo instituta, quae hodie custodiunt morem.*

siluicolam: only here in O., cf. *Aen.* 10.551 *siluicolae Fauno* and Cat. 63.72 *siluicultrix* of Cybele. O. coins *monticolae Siluani* at *Met.* 1.193. *colere* is often used of deities dwelling in or favouring a place: cf. Cat. 36.11–14, Virg. *Ecl.* 2.62, *Aen.* 1.15–16 *Iuno fertur* ... *unam* | *posthabita coluisse Samo*, and Livy's formula of *euocatio* at 5.21.3 *Iuno regina quae nunc Veios colis.*

747–76 This is the only prayer in book IV which O. dictates, rather than reports. And to whom? To the Roman (shepherd) people named in 731. Denis Feeney suggests he may be imitating the authority as well as the manner of Cato, *Agr.* 141 *sic dicito 'Mars pater te precor quaesoque uti sies uolens propitius'* etc. The prayer is divided more or less equally between requests for pardon of inadvertent past offences 747–62, and for future material benefits 763–76.

747 'consule' ... 'pecori pariter pecorisque magistris: for *consule* with dat. as a stronger form of *faue* in prayer to a deity cf. *Met.* 2.300 *rerum consule summae. magister pecoris* was the normal title; cf. Varro, *RR* 2.2.20, 2.10.5. *magistri* ('shepherds') appears in *Ecl.* 2.33 *Pan curat oues ouiumque magistros* (with the same *polyptoton* as here), *Aen.* 12.717 and *F.* 3.61 *armentorumque magistris* of Romulus and Remus' followers.

748 effugiat stabulis noxa repulsa meis: an apotropaic prayer. For *noxa*, 'guilt', bringing harm in return cf. 1.359 *noxae tibi deditus hostis* of the offending goat sacrificed to Bacchus, 6.129–30, a magic thorn *qua tristes pellere posset* | ... *noxas*, and *Aen.* 1.40–1 *ipsos* ... *submergere ponto* | *unius ob noxam* ... *Aiacis Oilei*, the only instance in the *Aeneid.*

749–50 siue sacro paui sediue sub arbore sacra | pabulaque ... carpsit: the shepherd combines his own unwitting offences with similar acts committed by straying sheep: first grazing his flock (*pascere*) on sacred soil, or sitting under a sacred tree (see Thomas (1988) 261–73). On *-ue* and *-que* substituting for conditional or negative conjunctions in second or third units, cf. K–S II 48 and Kenney (1996) on *Her.* 19.116. To be consistent with the prayer form of 749 and 751 (where MSS are divided between -*ue* and -*que*) the conditional disjunctive -*ue* should also be read at 750.

pabulaque ... inscia carpsit ouis: *pabula carpere* = *pasci*, but the sheep is by nature *inscia* – the only instance in O. where it is applied to an animal. *busta*, 'tombs', 'burials', were of course sacred, protected by custom, law and inscriptions; it was an abomination for mortals to steal from them, and men feared the desecration of their own or kinsmen's tombs by animal life. Cf. Hor. *Odes* 3.3.40–1 *dum Priami Paridisque busto | insultet armentum.*

751 si nemus intraui uetitum: on sacred groves see 649, and for Roman awe of groves cf. *Aen.* 8.349–52 *iam tum religio pauidos terrebat agrestes | dira loci, iam tum siluam saxumque tremebant. | 'hoc nemus ... | (quis deus incertum est) habitat deus ...'*

751–2 fugatae | ... nymphae semicaperque deus: wooded land was the haunt of the nymphs (*Dryades*) and *semicaper Faunus* (5.101, cf. *Met.* 14.515 *semicaper Pan*); the periphrase here avoids the need to specify. For the association of Faunus and the nymphs cf. Virg. *Ecl.* 5.59 *Panaque pastoresque tenet Dryadasque puellas*, *Georg.* 1.10–11 *agrestum praesentia numina Fauni | (ferte simul Faunique pedem Dryadesque puellae)*, 2.494, Hor. *Odes* 3.18.1 *Faune nympharum fugientum amator*, *Met.* 1.192–3 *sunt mihi ... rustica numina, Nymphae | Faunique Satyrique.*

In popular belief Faunus/Pan was aggressive: seeing Pan could 'panic' a mortal (so too Faunus, in Dion. Halic. 5.21) and he would sexually assault man or beast. Nymphs too were perpetually on the run from pursuing Fauni and satyrs, but the shepherd is moved here by a sense of his own profanation.

753 si mea falx ramo lucum spoliauit opaco: *opacus* is regularly associated with woods and groves: 2.409, 3.263, 6.425, *Met.* 10.567. In dry Mediterranean lands shepherds feed branches to cattle and sheep, cf. *Met.* 2.288–9 *quod pecori frondes ... ministro*, *AA* 1.299–300. If a sheep was too sick to graze or move (*aegrae ... oui*) the shepherd would cut the nearest branch and strip the leaves from it (hence *unde*) to offer in a shallow basket. But to cut from a sacred grove was sacrilege, cf. Pliny, *NH* 17.267 *idem arbores religiosas lucosque succidi permisit, sacrificio prius facto*, referring to Cato, *Agr.* 139.

755 da ueniam culpae: the request applies to all the previously mentioned offences. Cf. *Met.* 1.386 *detque sibi ueniam, pauido rogat ore* (the pious Pyrrha), 11.132–3 *da ueniam, Lenaee pater: peccauimus ... sed* *miserere precor*. The phrase *da ueniam* has this *sedes* at *AA*. 2.38, *Her*. 4.156, 7.105, 17.225, 19.149, *Ex P*. 1.7.22, etc.

755–6 nec, dum degrandinat, obsit | ... fano supposuisse pecus: the *dum* clause qualifies *supposuisse*, not the main verb. *degrandinare* occurs only here, but *grandinare* though rare is classical: for the formation cf. *debacchari*, 'to stop raving', *deferuescere*, 'to stop heating' or 'stop seething', as in Varro, *RR* 2.2.11 *aestus dum deferuescant*, or *detumescere*, 'to stop swelling'. *fanum*, of any roofed shrine, seems to have been felt too humble for epic diction: absent from Virgil, it occurs in O. only here and 5.485, 6.659, *Ex P*. 3.1.132 (yet *profanus* occurs in both poets). Roman wall paintings often show small *fana*, sometimes with a shepherd and goat or sheep approaching.

757–8 turbasse lacus ... | mota quod obscuras ungula fecit aquas: compare the Lycian peasants, turned into frogs by Latona for their malicious fouling of a pool at *Met*. 6.363–5 *ipsos etiam pedibusque manuque | turbauere lacus imoque e gurgite mollem | huc illuc limum saltu mouere maligno*. For *ungula* ('hoof', opposed to human *unguis*), cf. 3.456 *cum leuis Aonias ungula fodit aquas*, *Met*. 1.742 *ungulaque in quinos dilapsa absumitur ungues*.

In Italian belief *nymphae* (etymologically associated with *lymphae*, 'water' (Varro, *LL* 5.71, 7.83)), were divine protectresses of springs and pools; cf. *Aen*. 7.137–8 *nymphasque et adhuc ignota precatur | flumina*, 8.71 *nymphae, Laurentes nymphae, genus amnibus unde est*.

759–62 The offences mentioned above were not directly against Pales; but she is asked to intercede with woodland and water divinities for past offences and to protect the supplicant from the risk of future ones: to *fontes fontanaque numina* (on *fontanus* see 655n.) correspond *Dryadas* ... *labra Dianae* in 761: while *sparsos per nemus omne deos* is picked up by *Faunum* in 762.

761 nec ... uideamus labra Dianae: cf. *Ibis* 479; it was the fate of Actaeon in *Met*. 3.143–250 to be punished for seeing Diana bathe (cf. esp. 3.175 *per nemus ignotum non certis passibus errans*). But the household and agricultural term *labra* ('basin', Virg. *Georg*. 2.6, *Aen*. 8.22, 12.417) domesticates Diana's bath.

762 medio cum premit arua die: cf. Theocr. 1.16–17 'we fear Pan: this is the time when he lies exhausted on the land'.

763–76 The prayer moves on to practical requests: for healthy circumstances (763–8), and finally for material profit (769–76.)

763 pelle procul morbos: cf. Cato's prayer in *Agr.* 141.2–3 *uti tu morbos uisos inuisosque ... prohibessis ... pastores pecuaque salua seruassis*; more general is Tib. 2.1.17–18 *di patrii, purgamus agros, purgamus agrestes: | uos mala de nostris pellite limitibus.*

ualeant hominesque gregesque: the pair parallels *pecori ... pecorisque magistris* at 747.

764 uigiles, prouida turba, canes: on the importance of sheepdogs cf. Varro, *RR* 2.9.1 *canis est enim custos pecoris eius quod comite indiget ad se defendendum ... oues maxime: has enim lupus captare solet*, Virg. *Georg.* 3.404–7. With *prouidus* cf. 2.60 *cauit sacrati prouida cura ducis*, *Met.* 7.712, 12.18. British shepherds tend to have one skilled dog, Romans speak of packs: cf. 5.141 *turba Diania.* (On the formulaic use of *turba* see 142n.)

765 neue minus multos redigam: some loss is to be expected.

766 neue gemam referens: *referre* points the contrast with *redigere* of able-bodied flocks, but O. subordinates the obvious verbal parallel to the emotional reaction. Anaphora of negative *neue* balances the preceding anaphora of positive *ualeant.*

rapta lupo: dative. Not 'snatched by the wolf' but as with *erepta* 'rescued from the wolf'. Wolves attacked both in the field and in the pens by night; Virg. *Ecl.* 3.80, *Georg.* 3.407 and 537–8, Tib. 2.5.88 (quoted 721–82n.).

767 absit ... supersint: as in the two preceding couplets negative and positive formulations are balanced. With *herbae frondesque* cf. Virg. *Georg.* 3.528 *frondibus et uictu pascuntur simplicis herbae.*

768 quaeque lauent artus quaeque bibantur aquae: Virgil recommends washing the sheep as protection against disease (*Georg.* 3.445–7), and watering them twice a day (3.329–30, 335); cf. Varro, *RR* 2.2.10 and 12.

769–74 In the last part of the prayer the shepherd indicates that his profit will bring material thanks for the goddess. For himself he asks abundance in milk and cheese (769–70), stock breeding (771–2) and wool (773–4).

769 referat mihi caseus aera: O. adapts Tityrus' complaint that his profit from his cheese was all spent on Galatea, Virg. *Ecl.* 1.33–5 *quamuis ... ingratae premeretur caseus urbi | non unquam grauis aere domum mihi dextra redibat.* On sheep's cheese see Varro, *RR* 2.11.4. (For *aera* plur. = 'bronze coins' cf. 1.220–1.)

770 dentque uiam liquido uimina rara sero: milk curds were sieved to make cheese, cf. *Met.* 12.436–7 *fluit ueluti concretum uimine querno | lac solet* and the Cyclops' *liquefacta coagula* at 13.830. Here O. has transferred *rara* from the sieve holes in his model, Tib. 2.3.16 *raraque per nexus est uia facta sero*, to the wicker itself.

771–2 sitque salax aries, conceptaque semina coniunx | reddat: *salax* is derived from *salire*, 'to mount' (Varro, *RR* 2.2.14), like *rapax*, *uorax*, *ferax*, etc. But it developed a wider reference. On preparing the rams for their responsibilities see Varro, *RR* 2.2.13 *hordeum si est datum, firmiores fiunt ad laborem sustinendum.* The solemn *coniunx* overdignifies the ram's necessary polygamy.

multa sit agna: for the collective singular cf. 2.529 *multa ... tabella*, 6.792, *Rem.* 32 *multa corona*, *AA* 1.48 *multo pisce.*

773–4 lanaque proueniat ... | mollis et ad teneras quamlibet apta manus: adverbial *quamlibet* is rather colloquial, found only once in *Met.*, at 10.119 *quamlibet ignotis*, only here in *Fasti.* *teneras ... manus* shows concern not for the wearer of the wool (as in *Met.* 15.116–19 *oues ... | mollia quae nobis uestras uelamina lanas | praebetis*) but for the woolworkers (*puellae*). The sentimental elegiac poet has taken over from his shepherd; it was the job of slave-women to soften (*mollire*) wool by washing and carding (3.817, *Met.* 2.411, *Her.* 3.70), but he hopes it will come to them without roughness or thorns. (On shearing and wool production cf. Varro, *RR* 2.11.5–9.)

775 quae precor eueniant: cf. *Ex P.* 2.1.55 *quod precor, eueniet.* The formula often opens prayers, as in Cato, *Agr.* 141.1 *cum diuis uolentibus quodque bene eueniat*, Cic. *Mur.* 1 *quae ... precatus sum ut ea res ... populo plebique Romano bene atque feliciter eueniret.* The dependent subjunctive continues in 775 *et nos faciamus* (not the more predictable variant *faciemus* of D). Tactfully the shepherd links Pales' blessings to his ability to repay her.

ad annum: cf. the (damaged) phrase *principio an[ni pastoricii* in the *Fasti Praenestini* (721–862n.). Tib. 2.5.82 calls this *felix et sacer annus* and it is fair to assume the goddess's annual festival was seen as opening the shepherds' year. With *grandia liba Pali* the prayer neatly recalls the reader's and goddess's attention to the offering that has just been given (743–4).

777–8 haec tu conuersus ad ortus | ... uiuo perlue rore manus: as part of the *populus* the shepherd has been told he is purified by Vesta's *suffimen* (732). Now O. belatedly adds requirements for the prayer. He must face the East (cf. *Aen.* 8.68–9 *aetherii spectans orientia solis | lumina,* 12.172 with Servius' comment, Vitr. 5.4), and sprinkle his body with fresh water (cf. Von Eitrem (1915) 81, 247ff.). With *uiuo ... rore* (not actual dew) cf. 2.250 *uiuis fontibus, Met.* 3.27, *Aen.* 6.230 *spargens rore leui et ramo felicis oliuae.*

778 dic quater: since there is no parallel for fourfold repetition in prayer (and this is a very long prayer!) Heinsius preferred *dic ter et in*, a reading found only in one secondary MS. Schilling conjectured *dicque ter*, but *-que et* in 771–2 does not support this awkward placement of *-que*. Von Eitrem (1915) 127, 247–8 notes the predominance of *ter* in ritual: this is the only instance in his index of fourfold action.

779 tum licet: *licet* is emphatic, 'only then', and governs the verbs of both couplets, *potes* and *traicias*.

apposita, ueluti cratere, camella: Gk κρατήρ ('mixing bowl', from κεράννυμι) entered the earliest Latin poetry in the form *creterra* (Naev. *Tr.* 42); cf. 2.251, 3.537, *Met.* 5.82, 8.669, etc. *camella*, the popular term for a wine-jar, is found in Laberius, *Mim.* 60, and Petr. 64.13, 135.4, 137.10.

780 lac niueum potes purpureamque sapam: the festive drink (the chiastic word-order juxtaposes the colour contrast, as in 714 above) is not wine but a mixture (called *burranica*, Festus 33 Lindsay) of milk and *sapa*, a triple-strength concentrate of unfermented *mustum* (on which see 888, 894). On the boiling down of *sapa* see Pliny, *NH* 23.62; it is used to flavour cheese in Petr. 66.7.

781–2 per ardentes ... aceruos | traicias: this seems to occur after twilight (735) so the heaps must be imagined as glowing in the dark.

crepitantis: cf. the simple verb *crepet* at 742. There is onomatopoeic assonance on *s* and *t*.

strenua membra: as often in O. the adjective is used adverbially; *Am.* 1.9.10, *Med.* 64, *Tr.* 1.10.34.

783–806 Another excursus of *aitia*. It is characteristic of Roman didactic poetry to exploit all possible accounts rather than suppress any by favouring one particular explanation. Compare Miller (1992) 12–21 on the six etymologies of the Agonia (1.309–21) or O.'s variant accounts of Vesta, 6.267–92, or Virgil's four incompatible reasons for burning stubble, *Georg.* 1.86–93. As Barchiesi (1991) 1–21 and Hardie (1991) 47–64 both indicate, multiple aetiologies are few in Callimachus and resolved by the poet's verdict, whereas O. and Plut. *Qu. Rom.* leave the choice offered by their sources unresolved. Here, however, O. organizes the six explanations so as to steer his transition from shepherd festival to city foundation (focused on 798–801).

783–4 moris mihi restat origo; | turba facit dubium: *turba* = *multitudo* (not admissible in dactylic metre). With *dubium* (masc. acc. sing.) understand *me* from preceding *mihi.*

coeptaque nostra tenet: as in 721–2 the poet draws attention to the poetic process: but *coepta* aptly evokes Romulus' beginnings at the same time as the poet's incipient narrative.

785–6 omnia purgat edax ignis uitiumque metallis | excoquit: for *ignis edax* cf. *Aen.* 2.758, *Met.* 9.202, 14.541; for fire as moral purifier, *Aen.* 6.742 *infectum eluitur scelus aut exuritur igni*; as physical cleanser, *Georg.* 1.87–8 *siue illis omne per ignem | excoquitur uitium.* O. fuses elements of both passages to describe purification by fire. For fire tempering steel cf. *Met.* 14.712 *durior et ferro quod Noricus excoquit ignis.*

786 idcirco: like Lucretian *ideo* (1.816, 1054, etc.) a favourite link in didactic argumentation; cf. Virg. *Georg.* 1.231, 3.445, *Aen.* 5.680. O. favours its use in refutation: 6.418 *non tamen idcirco*, *Met.* 11.449, *Tr.* 1.5.55, 2.243, 265.

787–8 an, quia ... | sunt duo discordes, ignis et unda, dei: the creative conflict of fire and water goes back to Empedocles, as does *Met.* 1.9 *non bene iunctarum discordia semina rerum*; for fire against water in O. cf. *Met.* 1.432 *cumque sit ignis aquae pugnax*, and the standard *adunata* at *Tr.* 1.8.4 *unda dabit flammas et dabit ignis aquas*, *Ibis* 31 *desinet esse prius contrarius ignibus umor.* But why the unexpected *dei*? Is this an echo of Hephaestus' defeat of Simois and Xanthus in *Il.* 21.342–82?

789–90 iunxerunt elementa patres: for *elementa* = Gk στοιχεῖα, cf. Pythagoras at *Met.* 15.237 *quae nos elementa uocamus*, and 239–40 *quattuor aeternus genitalia corpora mundus | continet.* His list includes *unda* (241) and *ignis* (243). This theory provides no reason to combine (*iungere*) these elements, but 791 goes on to do so.

791–2 an, quod in his ... est, haec perdidit ..., | his noua fit coniunx, haec duo magna putant?: the first three clauses all depend on *quod* and serve to explain *haec ... putant.* Roman thought linked the first belief directly with marriage practice. Varro, *LL* 5.61 cites *ignis et aqua* as causes of birth, which are therefore offered at the threshhold in wedding ceremonies: cf. Festus 77 Lindsay, Plut. *Qu. Rom.* 1. (For fire and water as causes of spontaneous generation see *Met.* 1.432–3 *uapor umidus omnes | res creat, et discors concordia fetibus apta est.*) The *interdictio aquae et ignis* banning exiled Romans was based on the necessity of fire and water for survival.

793–4 sunt qui Phaëthonta referri | credant et nimias Deucalionis aquas: here the distancing of *sunt qui credant* (a consecutive type of relative, 'such that they believe', confirms that O. rejects the connection in advance. He refuses to attribute the Roman cult practice to influence of (Greek) myths. For the Gk acc. form *Phaëthonta* (∪∪ – ∪) cf. *Met.* 2.342, *Tr.* 3.4.30. The genitive *Deucalionis* here is not found in *Met.* Recalling the near-destruction of the world by fire (*Met.* 2.150–303) and flood (*Met.* 1.263–415) O. also returns the familiar reader to the phase of creation from wetness and warmth (*Met.* 1.415–33) that has just been cited in the previous explanation.

796 scintillam subito prosiluisse ferunt: this explains only the bonfires, as commemorating the accidental role of straw in the primitive creation of fire from sparks, which could be deliberately fostered by such materials kept as tinder. Cf. Virgil's account of the discovery of fire by striking sparks from flint at *Georg.* 1.135, also *Aen.* 1.174 *silici scintillam excudit Achates*, 6.6–7.

797 stipulis excepta secunda est: *excipere*, used of welcoming or receiving, even catching something in progress, like fire, takes on the role of *(con)cipere* at *Met.* 1.255 *conciperet flammas*, 7.17.

798 hoc argumentum flamma Parilis habet?: for *argumentum*, in the sense of 'explanation', 'reference', cf. *Met.* 4.761–2 *animi felicia laeti | argumenta*, 8.745 *uoti argumenta potentis*; its basic meaning is 'narrative', but the narrative may be explanatory, and so become an *aition.* The word *Parilis* is the last backward allusion to the shepherds' festival. Subsequent explanations look towards the foundation.

799–800 an magis ... pietas Aeneïa fecit | innocuum ... cui dedit ignis iter?: O. creates his own link through the idea of an *innocuum iter*. For Aeneas' *pietas spectata per ignes* (37, cf. *Met.* 14.109) O. returns to *Aen.* 2.632–3, where moved by *pietas* Aeneas returns home to rescue his father *ducente deo flammam inter et hostis | expedior: dant tela locum flammaeque recedunt*. For quadrisyllabic *Aeneïa* (– – ∪∪) in this *sedes*, cf. *Aen.* 7.1, 10.156, 494, *Met.* 14.441, 581.

801 num tamen est uero propius? 'Can it be nearer the truth that ...?': O.'s hesitant *num* marks the originality of his proposal.

801–5 Through this long sentence extending into the third distich the poet links the founding of Rome (801) as a sort of synoecism with the migration of household gods, shepherds and flocks (805). The notion of Aeneas' divine safe-conduct in his enforced migration eases the new interpretation, which is helped along by giving prominence to the domestic Lares. Like Aeneas' Trojan *Penates* they are ordered (by whom? there was no tradition of a divine command) to be carried to new homes. Cf. Bremmer and Horsfall (1987) 49–62 on Caeculus and the Foundation of Praeneste, citing Serv. on *Aen.* 7.681 *inuocato Vulcano ut eum filium comprobaret, omnis illius multitudinis chorus est flamma circumdatus, quo facto commoti omnes simul habitauerunt et Vulcani filium crediderunt.*

803–4 mutantesque domum tectis agrestibus ignem | et cessaturae supposuisse casae: unless O. attributes the firing of the huts to the Lares there must a change of subject from pass. *transferri* in 802 to act. *supposuisse* (subj. *mutantes ... domum*). O. also contrasts the rural *tecta agrestia* = *casa* of 803–4 (both dat. after *supponere*) with the *noua tecta* of Rome. *supposuisse* (in same *sedes* 756) is often used of kindling, especially funeral pyres, *Aen.* 11.119; cf. *Met.* 6.456, of firing a cornfield.

805 per flammas saluisse pecus, saluisse colonos?: *salire*, picking up *transilire* from 727, is repeated to revive the man–sheep partnership of 747 and 763 in a comic image of both men and sheep leaping across the flames; but the shepherds have now been transformed into *coloni*, 'settlers', like the farmer of Carseoli (692) who will also till the land. Ovidian references to Romulean Rome usually maintain the idea of a mixed pastoral–arable economy.

806 quod fit natali ..., Roma, tuo: both the keyword *natali* (sc. *die*, cf. *Met.* 2.497, 9.285, *Am.* 1.8.94 *natalem ... tuum*, 3.1.57) and the apostrophe to Rome (the only vocative of *Roma* in *Fasti*) redirect the readers and stir their patriotic response. With *nunc quoque* (cf.

494, 710) O.'s reconstructed synoecism is established as the preferred *aition.*

807–8 ipse locum casus uati facit; urbis origo | uenit: in 417 *exigit ipse locus raptus ut ... edam*, the site of Enna, or the religious context, compelled O. to narrate, but here he inverts the phrase. Chance has created his theme for him: whether by arising in his selection of *aitia* for bonfires or by happening on this feast-day, the foundation has come upon him (perf. *uenit* with long first syllable) to determine his subject and treatment (*locus* in the rhetorical sense) of it. At the same time *urbis origo* echoes the last incidence of *origo* (783), introducing the list of *aitia* for the bonfire-jumping.

ades factis, magne Quirine, tuis: Quirinus, identified with the deified Romulus in the legend of 2.475–512 (cf. Livy 1.16) can inspire the poet to narrate his own heroic deeds.

Harries (1991) has argued persuasively that the inspiring presence of Romulus–Quirinus should be seen as affecting O.'s diplomatic and pro-Romulean narrative, which transfers all responsibility from Romulus for the unfortunate incident of his brother's death (see 837–56n.). From the beginning of Roman literature Ennius, Rome's greatest early poet, told of Remus' death, citing Romulus' threat to kill him: 94 Skutsch *nam mi calido dabis sanguine poenas*; Livy offers a more diplomatic version, 1.7.1–2 *ibi cum altercatione congressi certamine irarum ad caedem uertuntur; ibi in turba ictus Remus cecidit*, then appends the *uulgatior fama* in which Romulus killed his brother and justified the act. See further 837–56n.

On the development of the tradition of the twins see J. Cornell, *The beginnings of Rome* (London 1975) 1–11, 27–32, who draws analogies between the Roman tradition of twins exposed and reared by a shepherd, and the earlier accounts of Aeneas' sons Silvius and Latinus (see 42–3n., which follows the version in which Silvius is Latinus' father, not brother) or the brothers who reared Caeculus, founder of Praeneste (see 801–5n.). He concludes (p. 32) 'The pastoral context and association of young shepherd warriors recur in the legend of Cyrus of Persia, and G. Binder has shown ... that [the warrior-band] is an integral feature of many exposure stories.' Bremmer (1987) 34–8 discusses both the tradition of the twin founders and the killing of Remus in the light of parallel myths. Most radically T. P. Wiseman (1995) 103–28 argues that the twin Remus, and his violent death, was a politically inspired creation of the plebeian struggle for parity with the patricians at the turn of the fourth century BC.

809 frater Numitoris: Amulius, see 53–5n. But O. is continuing the narrative from his earlier description of the twins' conception, birth and upbringing in 3.41–70. There he had ended: *Romuleoque cadit traiectus Amulius ense* ... | *moenia conduntur, quae, quamuis parua fuerunt,* | *non tamen expediit transiluisse Remo.*

809–10 et omne | pastorum gemino sub duce uulgus erat: with the singular form *gemino* ... *duce* cf. *Met.* 4.514 *gemina* ... *prole,* 6.111 *gemino* ... *fetu;* but the singular is not confined to twins, cf. 6.736 *gemino* ... *angue, AA* 2.644 *gemino* ... *pede.* In Livy 1.6.3 the desire to attribute higher status to Rome's founding population subordinates the shepherds as an afterthought to citizens of Alba and Latium: *Romulum Remumque cupido cepit in iis locis ubi expositi ubique educati erant, urbis condendae. et supererat multitudo Albanorum Latinorumque; ad id pastores quoque accesserant.*

811 contrahere agrestes 'to concentrate the scattered country people'; cf. Venus' alleged role in forming human communities at 94 *illa rudes animos hominum contraxit in unum.* One may suspect that much of 23–63 and 85–108 (Romulus' calendar as homage to Venus) was written with this section in mind.

811–12 et moenia ponere utrique | conuenit: ambigitur moenia ponat uter: according to Livy 1.6.4 the decision to entrust the choice of founder to the gods came because they were twins, so there was no basis of seniority. By using *moenia ponere* (twice) for the contested action (instead of Ennius' and Livy's focus on naming and founding the city) O. foreshadows the approaching incident.

813 'nil opus est' ... 'certamine' ... 'ullo: perhaps a deliberate reaction against Livy 1.6.4 *foedum certamen,* 7.2 *certamine irarum.*

814 magna fides auium est: experiamur aues 'the reliability of birds is great: let us try out the bird omens'. For association of *auis/es* with auspices and augury (*OLD* s.v. *auis* 1a), cf. 1.180 *uisam primum consulit augur auem,* 1.513, 5.151–2 *fratri* | *prima Palatinae signa dedistis aues.*

experiamur: elsewhere in O., e.g. *Met.* 2.392 *uires expertus equorum, Tr.* 3.2.27 *di, quos experior* ... *iniquos,* the verb *experiri* denotes experiencing rather than deliberate testing.

815–16 alter init . . . saxa Palati; | alter Auentinum mane cacumen init: Cicero eliminated Remus and the whole foundation story from *Rep.* 2.2ff. Livy (1.6.4), Dion. Halic. (1.86.2) and Augustan tradition (e.g. Prop. 4.6.44) assign the Palatine to Romulus. O. is ambiguous: no doubt he remembered that Ennius 74–6 Sk *in †monte† Remus auspicio sedet atque secundam | solus auem seruat. at Romulus pulcer in alto | quaerit Auentino, seruat genus altiuolantum* puts Romulus on the Aventine.

nemorosi . . . Palati: cf. *Met.* 14.822 *summo nemorosi colle Palati, AA* 1.105 *nemorosa Palatia. nemorosus* is found in Virgil only at *Aen.* 3.270. The form is rhythmically appealing: cf. Prop. 4.9.3 *pecorosa Palatia. cacumen* is not used elsewhere of the Aventine cliffs (*Auentini saxa propinqua* in 6.518), but of its prehistoric woods at 3.329 *Auentinae cacumina siluae.*

817 sex Remus, hic uolucres bis sex uidet ordine: so also Livy 1.7.1, who specifies the birds as vultures. Ennius 85–91 Skutsch has first an unspecified bird-group appear, then with the sunrise twelve birds settle in places of good omen, as a result of which Romulus recognizes that he has been given royal authority *auspicio.*

817–18 pacto | statur, et arbitrium Romulus urbis habet: *pacto* is abl., as in *Met.* 2.818 *stemus . . . pacto . . . isto*; but the impers. pass. is unique in O. For *arbitrium* with obj. gen. cf. 5.212 *arbitrium . . . floris, Met.* 12.628 *arbitrium litis.* The nearest analogy is 3.316 *arbitrium . . . in sua tecta* of Jupiter's supreme power.

819 apta dies legitur qua moenia signet aratro: O.'s innovation is to separate the taking of auspices and the famous twelve vultures from the day of foundation. Where predecessors had set both events on the Parilia, O. marks this as the day chosen (*inde mouetur opus*) for the task. If the procedure of the twins is considered as the taking of auspices for the foundation, the postponement would require new auspices; but the fact of double *spectatio* itself disqualifies the occasion for this purpose.

The selection of the founder should be seen as separate from the two augural procedures required on the Parilia. The first, the consultation for divine approval of the day of foundation, should take place on the day itself (cf. Varro, *LL* 5.143; a city is to be founded *die auspicato*), but is suppressed in O.'s text. Instead O. moves directly from the (secular) choice of the Parilia to the day itself and the second augural procedure, the auspication of the *pomerium*. This requires first the sacrifice to the altar set up in 823, then the driving of the furrow tracing the *pomerium* (825–6). Only then can Romulus ask the gods to inaugurate it (cf. the prayer of 827–32, especially 830 *auspicibus uobis*). He then receives an *omen impetratiuum* of thunder (833–5, cf. *augurio*) confirming Jupiter's support in response to his prayer. (I am indebted to Jerzy Linderski for explaining O.'s text in terms of the complex sequence of three divine consultations, and hope to provide a fuller discussion elsewhere.)

For *dies* fem., properly as here of formal dates and deadlines, cf. 376, but O. uses it interchangeably with the masc. (379, 387, 465, 622, 673).

signet aratro: cf. 825 *designat moenia*. Like Virgil (*Aen.* 5.755 *urbem designat aratro*) O. echoes the ritual term *designare* used by Cato (*Orig.* fr. 18 *HRR*, quoted by Servius ad loc.). Cato describes the Etruscan ritual in which the founder yoked an ox and cow, with the ox on the right, the outer side, and the cow on the left inside, to plough a furrow anticlockwise, marking the city wall in such a way that the ploughed earth fell inwards. The plough was lifted to interrupt the furrow wherever a gate was desired *ut glebae omnes intrinsecus caderent, et ita sulco ducto loca murorum designabant aratrum suspendentes circa loca portarum*. Varro, *LL* 5.143 and *RR* 2.1.10, and Plut. *Qu. Rom.* 27 are less specific; only O. adds that the team should be white. Cf. 825–6 and see Frazer (1929) III 379–84.

820 sacra Palis suberant: O. brings the readers back to his opening words in 723 *Pales, faueas pastoria sacra canenti*.

821–4 The ritual *fossa* described here is not included in Cato's or Varro's accounts of the Etruscan rite (cited in preceding note): only Plut. *Romulus* 11 describes this procedure and identifies it as the *mundus*. There is sufficient coincidence with O.'s account of the *mundus* (he does not use the name, or specify its actual situation on the Palatine) to suggest a common source in a lost text of Verrius or perhaps Varro. (See Frazer (1929) III 384–8, especially on Plutarch's material.)

But like Dion. Halic. 1.87–8, Plutarch is apparently trying to reconcile two versions: in *Romulus* 10.1 he has Romulus digging a foundation trench when Remus provokes him and is killed either by Romulus or Celer (cf. Dion. Halic. 87.4); then *after* Remus' death,

Plutarch describes the *mundus* (mistakenly placed in the *comitium*), and moves on (like Dion. Halic. 1.88) to the ploughing of the outline of the walls around it (Wissowa, *RK* 194).

821 fossa fit ad solidum: *solidus* is a common epithet of earth in O., e.g. 2.648 *solida ... humo*, 6.404 *solida ... tellus*, *Met.* 10.180, 15.262 *solidissima tellus*. Here however *saxum*, 'bedrock', must be understood as in *Met.* 6.573. The *mundus* was an offering to Ceres, so grain (*fruges*) is appropriate, cf. Festus 126 Lindsay. Plut. *Rom.* 11.2 specifies 'whatever is used within the law or necessary by nature' and adds that the soil for the fill was contributed by each man from his own country.

823 fossa repletur humo, plenaeque imponitur ara: the anaphora of *fossa* reinforces the ritual symmetry, as in 133–5; as the first half of 823 completes 822, so *plenae* (sc. *fossae*) recapitulates *repletur*, 'an altar is set up on the filled trench'.

824 et nouus accenso fungitur igne focus 'the new hearth enjoys the kindled fire'. For *fungor* in this sense cf. *functa cibo* (332n.). *accendere* is *vox propria* for altar fires; cf. 1.76 *accensis ... focis*, *Met.* 7.260, 10.279, 12.12. With the kindling of fire on the new altar marking the sacred site, the city gets its first hearth. (This is not the sacred and symbolic hearth of the vestals.)

825–6 premens stiuam designat moenia sulco; | alba iugum niueo cum boue uacca tulit: 825 recalls Cato's ritual language (fr. 18 *HRR*, cited 819n.), but in 826 O. takes more poetic freedom.

iugum ... tulit: perhaps = *pertulit*, 'carried', 'bore to the end', as in 2.737. The plain verb stands for its compound, see 535n. O. is particularly fond of applying *niueus*, the emotive synonym of *albus*, to cattle: *Met.* 1.652, 2.865, 10.272, etc.

827 regis: the first time Romulus has been called King.

827–8 Iuppiter... ades: auspices came from Jupiter, and thus he could be addressed as patron of the city even before his role was marked by any temple.

828 genitor Mauors Vestaque mater: O. is more sparing in his use of the archaic form in *Fasti* (only here, 3.171 and 6.53) than in *Met.* As in the *Aeneid* (*Mauors* 7 times, *Mauortius* 5 times) *Mauors* stands freely for Ares in *Met.* VI–VIII as well as for Romulus' divine father (*Met.* 14.804). With Romulus' address compare Mars' intercession for

Romulus at 2.481–90; his role as *genitor*, 3.1–78; and 57 and 130 above. At 6.353–78 Mars intercedes with Jupiter to save Rome when it is besieged by the Gauls in 390, followed by Venus, Quirinus (deified Romulus) and Vesta. In contrast Virgil, seeing the (civil) warfare of Mars as the threat to Rome in *Georg.* 1.489–90, appeals only to Vesta and Romulus to save the city.

829 quosque . . . deos: with this inclusive phrase cf. Virg. *Georg.* 1.21 *dique deaeque omnes*, imitated in Prop. 3.13.41 *dique deaeque omnes quibus est tutela per agros.*

aduertite cuncti: for this use of *aduertite* instead of e.g. *ades, adeste* cf. *Aen.* 4.610–12 *di* . . . | *accipite haec, meritumque malis aduertite numen* | *et nostras audite preces*, *Met.* 8.482 *Eumenides, sacris uultus aduertite uestros*, *Ibis* 67 *huc, precor, huc uestras omnes aduertite mentes.* It is also used to demand human attention: *Aen.* 5.304, 8.440, Ov. *AA* 1.267.

830 auspicibus uobis hoc mihi surgat opus: O.'s version of the foundation would require the taking of new auspices at this time (see 819–20). A human *auspex* (or the more specialized *augur*) was responsible for taking the *auspicia* sent by the gods; the identification of the gods themselves as *auspices* seems to originate with Virg. *Aen.* 3.19, 4.45 (spoken by a Carthaginian). In O. *auspex* is limited to this passage and 1.26, 615 *auspicibusque deis.* For *surgat opus* cf. the play on founding city and poem in Prop. 4.1.57 *moenia namque coner pio disponere uersu*, 67 *Roma faue, tibi surgit opus*, and Ovidian variations on the poetic *opus*, in 5.111 *ab Ioue surgat opus*, *Am.* 1.1.27 *sex mihi surgat opus numeris*, *Tr.* 2.559–60 *surgens ab origine mundi* | *in tua deduxi tempora, Caesar, opus.*

831 longa sit huic aetas dominaeque potentia terrae: construe as if *aetas potentiaque*; *-que* is displaced from the word it connects. The city destined to be mistress does not yet exist, hence *dominae* . . . *terrae* stands for the more usual *domina* . . . *urbs* in e.g. *Rem.* 291 *domina* . . . *in urbe.* This may also explain *aetas* instead of (*longum*) *aeuum*, the usual wish for a city as an organic growth with a finite life-span. Cf. the prophecy of Pythagoras, *Met.* 15.446–8 *hanc alii* . . . *per saecula longa potentem,* | *sed dominam rerum de sanguine natus Iuli* | *efficiet*; cf. other variations on *Romana potentia* (*Aen.* 8.99) in 2.483, 6.359 *haec est cui fuerat promissa potentia rerum*, *Met.* 15.877, and *Tr.* 5.2.35.

832 sitque sub haec oriens occiduusque dies: for the extension of Roman power in space from rising to setting sun see P.

White, *Promised verse* (Cambridge, MA, 1993) 159–68. Bömer (on 5.557–8 *seu quis ab Eoo ... orbe ... seu quis ab occiduo sole*) cites *Rhet. Her.* 4.33 *imperii magnitudinem solis ortu atque occasu metiemur* as the earliest example of this device, cf. *Aen.* 7.99–101 *nepotes | omnia sub pedibus qua sol utrumque recurrens | aspicit Oceanum ... uidebunt*, Hor. *Odes* 4.15.14–16 *famaque et imperi | porrecta maiestas ad ortus | solis ab Hesperio cubili*, *CS* 9–12, Tib. 2.5.57–8. Cf. 2.136 *hoc duce Romanum est solis utrumque latus*, *Ex P.* 1.4.29–30 *Caesaris ... quem solis ab ortu | solis ad occasus utraque terra tremit.*

occiduus stands in for *occidens*, inadmissible in dactylic verse.

833 ille precabatur: parataxis here is briefer and more vivid than a *dum*-clause with pres. indic. of interrupted past time (as in 163 or 533).

833–4 tonitru dedit omina laeuo | Iuppiter, et laeuo fulmina ... polo: as in 2.501 *cum subito motu saepes tremuere sinistrae*, or *Aen.* 2.693, 9.630–1 *caeli genitor de parte serena | intonuit laeuum*, the good omens are on the required left. Contrast the Greek-style positive omen on the right in 664 and the negative left in *Ibis* 99 *ominibusque malis pedibusque occurrite laeuis* and 126. O.'s aural chiasmus of *omina laeuo / laeuo fulmina* is based on variation of syntax, since *tonitrus* and *fulmina* are logically parallel.

835 augurio laeti: cf. Latinus' response to the thunder on the left in *Aen.* 7.259–60 *tandem laetus ait: 'di nostra incepta secundent | augurium que suum'*. Every *augurium* came specifically from Jupiter: cf. 1.611 *augurium ... | et quodcunque suo Iuppiter auget ope.*

fundamina: a typical Ovidian dactylic coinage to replace prosaic *fundamentum*; cf. *Met.* 5.361, 15.433 and the Romulus narrative at *Met.* 14.808–9 *quoniam fundamine magno | res Romana ualet.*

ciues: the title is significant; unmentioned since they were *pastores* and *agrestes* in 810–11, Romulus' followers have now become Roman citizens (see 855).

836 exiguo tempore: with miraculous speed and ease, cf. *exiguo conamine* 325; but given the tradition that the wall was inadequate O.'s treatment of the miracle may be ironic.

837–56 The death of Remus. O.'s account differs radically from that of Ennius, and the version preferred by Livy (807–8n.). Recent scholars have judged the elaborate presentation of his death as a tragic accident borne by Romulus with Stoic self-control to be either a self-exculpatory tale by Romulus–Quirinus himself (Harries (1989)), or deliberately unconvincing (Barchiesi (1994); see 850n.), since it conflicts with O.'s supposed unsympathetic treatment of Romulus at 2.133–4 *facit hic tua magna tuendo | moenia, tu dederas transilienda Remo*, 143 *te Remus incusat*. But, as H. J. Krämer has shown ('Die Sage von Romulus und Remus in der lateinischen Literatur', *Synusia: Festgabe W. Schadewaldt* (Pfullingen 1965) 367–76), O. has shaped his tale to intensify the same elegiac pathos that he develops in the poignant tales in *Metamorphoses* of the deaths of Phaethon, Procris or Hyacinthus, caused unwittingly by those who loved them.

837–44 In this eight-line sequence (balanced by Romulus' grief and speeches in 845–52), the name of Celer introduces the fatal moment of Remus' killing: the units diminish from the four-line sentence of 837–40 with relative clause and included quotation, to the distich 841–2 coupling Remus' attitude and speech, to 843 containing both provocation and retaliation, and the expanding image of his fall in 844.

837 Celer urget opus: the man's role and name (which coincides with Romulus' bodyguard of 300 *Celeres* in Livy 1.15.8, cf. Dion. Halic. 2.13.2) may go back to Valerius Antias; cf. fr. 2, *HRR* I 238.

quem ... ipse uocarat: contracted plupf. indic. (*uoca(ue)rat*).

838–40 'sint'que ... curae' ... 'ista tuae, | neue quis ... | transeat: the connective *neue* shows that *ista* is subject only of *sint ... curae*, and the subj. is an independent prohibition. For dat. *curae esse alicui* (here possessive *tuae* replaces *tibi*) cf. *Met.* 1.250 *sibi enim fore cetera curae*, *AA* 1.624 *uirginibus curae grataque forma sua est*; yet O. uses it with no distinction of meaning from the common *cura mihi* or *tibi est*, at e.g. *Met.* 5.516, 11.297, etc.

839 aut factam uomere fossam: not the dedicatory pit of 820–2 but the ritual furrow turned by the plough outlining the walls.

840 dede neci: his words (cf. *Her.* 14.125 *dede neci*, *Met.* 12.459 *neci ... dederat*, 15.110 *danda neci*, *Ex P.* 4.7.46, *Ibis* 552) echo Virgil's instructions to the beekeeper faced with rival 'kings' in *Georg.* 4.90. Given its context O.'s language may imply that Romulus somehow knew his instructions would cause the death of his brother and rival, but more probably it marks the poet's own recognition of the political utility of Remus' death *ne prodigus obsit, | ... melior ... sine regnet in aula* (*Georg.* 4.89–90).

841 quod Remus ignorans: *ignorans* is more common with a dependent clause; cf. *Met.* 10.637 *quid facit ignorans*, 11.719 *qui foret ignorans*, 13.913. The adjs. *inscius/nescius* would have required an awkward and ambiguous genitive.

841–2 humiles contemnere ... | coepit et ... dicere: *contemnere* is often closer to 'show contempt', 'insult', than 'despise'.

'his populus' ... 'tutus erit?': the harm of Remus' action lay in the Roman belief that it destroyed the magic or protective power of the walls (see H. J. Rose, *Handbook of Greek mythology* (London 1928) 331 n.53 and 314–16, M. Grant, *Roman myths* (London 1971) 110 and n. 64). But the logic of the story is flawed. A wall one can leap over is clearly symbolic or ritual, not defensive, which makes Remus' innocence absurd: the legend must have originated in an act of aggression by the excluded brother. *uulgatior fama est ludibrio fratris Remus transiluisse muros* says Livy 1.7.2, and the reader may read some element of lighthearted humour into *ludibrio* if s/he chooses; O. gives no such handle.

843 rutro Celer occupat ausum: for the digging tool, a guarantee of unpremeditated violence, cf. Varro, *Men.* 291 *rutro caput displanat* and the σκαφεῖον of Plut. *Romulus* 10.1. *rutrum* occurs nowhere else in hexameter or elegiac poetry. For *occupare* introducing a fatal blow, cf. 1.575 *occupat Alcides* (with 577–8, cited in 844n.), *Met.* 1.721, 8.399 *occupat audentem*, 12.342–3. *occupat* usually anticipates and prevents a hostile action, and so seems in conflict with *transiluit*, as if Celer forestalled his leap. Perhaps it has been chosen to stress Celer's rash anticipation of Romulus' intent.

844 ille ... duram sanguinolentus humum: cf. 6.602 *concidit in dura sanguinolentus humo*, 1.577–8 *ille cadit ... | et lato moriens pectore plangit humum*; in epic (cf. Virg. *Aen.* 10.731, 11.669, or the death of Argus, *Met.* 1.718–19) a death notice includes references to blood and to striking the ground. *sanguinolentus* is found in prose and elegy (15 times in O., always in this *sedes*), but is absent from Virgil or *Met.* As at 654 *duram* contributes pathos.

845–8 Again a narrative element – Romulus' reaction – is extended over four lines, three of which convey his grief, giving a different colour to his defiant comment in the Livian tradition. The pattern is repeated in 849–52, before the funeral is completed.

845–6 lacrimas introrsus obortas | deuorat et clausum

pectore uulnus habet: the enjambment is expressive of emotion checked back. It recurs with O.'s parallel use of *deuorare* for Hecuba's grief at *Met.* 13.539–40 *et pariter uocem lacrimasque introrsus abortas | deuorat ipse dolor*; but Romulus is not passively reduced to dumb misery like Hecuba. We may interpret his control either as a religious duty or, as 847 suggests, as epic heroism. If O. considers the dedication still in process, then his dedicator must refrain from grief even at the closest bereavement, as did the consul Horatius dedicating the temple of Jupiter Capitolinus in Livy 2.8.6–8. Measured against the Stoicizing Aeneas, Romulus outdoes him. Where Aeneas or Hercules weeps and steels his heart (cf. *Aen.* 3.492, 4.30 *lacrimis . . . obortis*, also 4.449, 10.465, 11.41 at the burial of Pallas), Romulus suppresses his tears until the proper time (849).

847 flere palam non uult: *palam* is rare in high poetry, twice in Virgil, 9 times in O. (all in elegiacs except *Met.* 9.638).

exemplaque fortia seruat: not by following heroic models (as in *Aen.* 12.439) but by producing them. With this concern for exemplarity cf. 6.647 *sic exempla parantur.*

848 'sic'que 'meos muros transeat hostis': cf. Livy 1.7.2 *sic deinde quicunque alius transiliet moenia mea.*

849–54 The funeral expands focus from Romulus to Faustulus and the community he has founded.

849 nec iam suspendere fletum | sustinet: O. innovates *sustinere* with a dependent inf., cf. 2.416 *perdere cognatae sustinuere manus,* 3.605 *nec credere sustinet* and *OLD* s.v. 6. With *suspendere fletum* cf. *Am.* 1.7.57 *suspensaeque diu lacrimae.*

850 pietas dissimulata patet: cf. 6.90 *atque ira pietas dissimulata foret*; *dissimulare* is 'to conceal what is real' (in 6.90 the filial love of Hebe discoloured by conflict), *simulare* 'to pretend what is false'. Thus O. claims *pietas* for Romulus, as for Aeneas (799) and as Augustus claimed *pietas* in executing Caesar's murderers. Barchiesi (1994) raises the possibility that the line could also be read as *dis simulata patet,* 'is exposed to the gods as pretence', but this should be ruled out. Although ingenious, such word-play would give a sense incompatible with the previous statement.

851 osculaque applicuit . . . suprema: the final kiss to the dead; cf. *Met.* 6.278 *oscula dispensat natos suprema per omnes,* 9.503–4 *toroque | mortua componar, positaeque det oscula frater.* The adj. *supremus* itself often implies burial, as in *Aen.* 6.213 *suprema ferebant,* 11.76 *supremum ... honorem.*

feretro: the bier on which a corpse was carried (*efferri*) to cremation (cf. *Aen.* 6.222, 11.64, 149, *Met.* 3.508, 14.797).

852 'inuito frater adempte, uale': *inuitus,* the protest of one who fears misunderstanding, marks the regret with which Aeneas alludes to his action that caused Dido's death (*Aen.* 6.460), reinforcing Romulus' other words which echo Catullus' grief for his brother (68.20, 92 *heu misero frater adempte mihi,* cf. 101.6). There is no need to suspect Ovidian irony at Romulus' expense.

853 arsurosque artus unxit: the unprepared overflow into the next distich stresses Romulus' continued acts of mourning. The epithet increases the pathos of his service; the model seems to be *Aen.* 11.77–8 *iuueni supremum maestus honorem | induit arsurasque comas obnubit amictu* (another echo of the preparation of Pallas for burial). Virgil does not seem to include anointing in funeral narratives; from O. cf. 3.561 *mixta bibunt molles lacrimis unguenta fauillae, Her.* 10.122 *nec positos artus unguet amica manus, Ex P.* 1.9.47 *funera non potui comitare nec unguere corpus.*

853–4 fecere ... | Faustulus et ... Acca: O. looks back to his narrative of the twins' fostering by the shepherd (addressed by name in 3.56), but the main purpose of this allusion must be to prepare for the appearance of Remus' shade to Faustulus and Acca in 5.453, and for the founding of the Lemuria (interpreted as Remuria) in his honour on 9 May. That episode opens by returning to the grief of Romulus at this burial (5.452 *et male ueloci iusta soluta Remo*), but it is now Remus, not Celer, who is too hasty.

A tradition reported by Dion. Halic. 1.87 (cf. Plut. *Rom.* 10.1) claimed that Faustulus was killed before the actual foundation, in a battle between the followers of Romulus and Remus.

854 maestas ... soluta comas: *comas* is acc. of respect; see 661.

855 nondum facti ... Quirites: the story of Romulus' own death and deification as Quirinus begins and ends with the allusion to his subjects, the Roman citizens, as *Quirites* at 2.479, 505. Thus *Quirites* in 855 points to the last transformation of the primitive shepherds, already narrated but still to occur. (See also 835n.)

856 ultima plorato subdita flamma rogo est: it was customary at Rome to utter a ritual call (*conclamatio*) to the dead before the next of kin lit the pyre. For *plorare* (avoided in high poetry; cf. Axelson (1945) 28–9) used of ritual mourning cf. *Am.* 3.9.1, *AA* 1.75, *Her.* 21.171. With *subdita flamma* cf. *Met.* 9.233–4 *quo flamma ministro | subdita*, of Philoctetes' service at the cremation of Hercules. The narrative ends on a melancholy note of anticlimax.

O.'s version of the drama from 811 to 856 can be read without irony as an instance of unintended tragedy – a pathetic tale, however historically disingenuous. The legend is likely to have had an ugly origin, something like that of Cain and Abel, but our poet has stressed every aspect that can restore some dignity to it.

857–8 urbs oritur... | uictorem terris impositura pedem: for the Homeric image of the conqueror placing his foot on the fallen warrior's neck, cf. *Aen.* 10.495 *laeuo pressit pede talia fatus*, 736 *super abiectum posito pede nixus et hasta.* This becomes a metaphor for the victory of Peace at 1.702 *iam pridem uestro sub pede bella iacent*, or Love at Prop. 1.1.4 *caput impositis pressit Amor pedibus*, or Rome at *Ex P.* 4.7.48 *impositoque Getes sub pede multus erat.* For Rome as victor, but Jupiter as determinant of her victory cf. 6.360 *hanc* (sc. *Romam*) *terris impositurus eras?*, a reprise of the theme of *Romana potentia* from 4.831.

857 (quis tunc hoc ulli credere posset?): for the acknowledgement of disbelief, cf. 1.518 *quis tantum fati credat habere locum*, 2.8 *ecquis ad haec illinc crederet esse uiam*, 2.414, *Met.* 1.400, 6.421, 15.613, *AA* 2.43, *Her.* 18.123, and 203–4, 793–4nn. The distinctive element (cf. 2.8) is the past tense and emphatic *tunc*, contrasting past incredulity with modern insight, as well as primitive beginning with grandiose present.

859 cuncta regas et sis magno sub Caesare semper: Rome is addressed (as in 806) to round off the section. The postponed *semper* of the poet's pious wish turns *Caesar* from individual to dynastic name.

860 plures nominis huius: for the dynastic turn of phrase compare Carmenta's prophecy in 1.531–2 *et penes Augustos patriae tutela manebit | hanc fas imperii frena tenere domum.* Does this suggest a revision from exile? The earliest reference could be to Gaius and Lucius Caesar, conceived as co-heirs before the death of Lucius in AD 2, but it is more likely that the lines reflect the situation after AD 4 when

Augustus adopted Tiberius, giving him the status of Caesar and parity of authority. At this time Augustus also ensured a plural succession in the next generation of Caesares by making Tiberius adopt Germanicus alongside his own son Drusus.

Wishes that the world remain flourishing *sub Caesare* recur at 6.455 and in *Ex P.* 1.2.99 *utque fuit sub eo, sic sit sub Caesare terra*, but the plural is usual in the exile poetry, both before and after Augustus' death, cf. *Caesares* at *Tr.* 1.2.104, 2.206, 4.2.1, *Ex P.* 1.4.55, 1.7.21, 2.2.108, 2.6.18, 2.8.4, 3.6.16 (*Augustos* ... *deos* at 4.15.3).

861 quotiens steteris domito sublimis in orbe: for *orbis* ... *domitus* cf. *AA* 1.177, 3.114, *Tr.* 3.7.51, and 256 above. *steteris* ... *sublimis* is not just another variant on *Am.* 1.15.26 *Roma triumphati dum caput orbis erit*; instead Rome is seen standing on the globe set beneath her feet, like Fortune in *Tr.* 5.8.7–8 *dubio Fortunae stantis in orbe* | *numen*, towering head and shoulders over all.

862 umeris inferiora tuis: for the image cf. Virg. *Aen.* 10.763–5 *Orion* | *umero supereminet undas*. O. offers no parallel, and the spatial language of *Tr.* 4.8.47–8 *nil ita sublime est* ... | *non sit ut inferius suppositumque deo* makes a different and less hubristic point: as Rome stood above the world in power, so she originated with Jupiter / the gods and depended on their greater power to maintain her, cf. Hor. *Odes* 3.6.5–6 *dis te minorem quod geris imperas.* | *hinc omne principium, huc refer exitum.* This element of subordination to the gods, however, is missing from 861–2.

863–900 (22 April H N)
23 April A VIN FP The Vinalia Priora

The *Fasti Praenestini*, somewhat damaged, still preserve enough text to guarantee the general form of the *aition* O. provides for the Vinalia (see 879–96n.):

> A VIIII Vin(alia) f(astus) Io[ui ....
> m[...
> ded[... uini omnis noui libamentum Ioui]
> consecratum [est, cum Latini bello preme-]
> rentur ab Rutulis, quia Mezentius rex Etru[sco]rum
> paciscebatur, si subsidio ueniss[e]t, omnium annorum
> uini fructum.

Thus the *Fasti Praenestini*, O.'s probable source, make this day *fastus* although it is a festival, and other *fasti* make it *nefastus*: see Michels (1967) 183, and Introd. 3(i)(*a*).

863 Dicta Pales nobis: idem Vinalia dicam: for the antithetical use of *idem*, cf. 1.129–30 *modo namque Patulcius idem | et modo ... Clusius ... uocor*, 2.5 and 7 *ipse ego uos habui faciles in amore ministros | ... | idem sacra cano signataque tempora fastis*. Janus is both the opening and closing god: O., addressing his *elegi*, contrasts their previous profane service as vehicles of love with their present sacred function. As in 721–4 O. acknowledges his role as recorder of the festival.

What, then, is the antithesis between O.'s celebration of Pales (and her feast) and his new task of celebrating the Vinalia? Why would the same poet not honour both occasions, and why does O. change categories from deity (Pales) to festival (Vinalia)? He changes to the festival in order to reconcile the claims of two deities, Jupiter and Venus, to this festival (cf. 877–8). The day itself, 23 April, like 1 April, honours more than one deity, and O. wishes to celebrate it both as *Veneris festum*, the anniversary of the temple of Venus Erycina by the Colline gate, and as the Vinalia (Priora), a feast of Jupiter which like the Vinalia Rustica of 19 August (Varro, *LL* 6.20) seems to have acquired additional associations with Venus.

The contrast implied by the adversative *idem* is the opposition between the wineless festival (cf. 745, 780nn.) of Pales, the deity of milk and cheese, and the festival whose raison d'être is celebrating and sampling the new wine.

864 una ... media ... dies: 22 April.

865–76 The anniversary offering to Venus Erycina *ad portam Collinam*. This was not Erycina's first shrine at Rome: Erycina, formerly Aphrodite of Mt Eryx on the NW coast of Sicily, was invited to Rome in 217 BC on the proposal of Fabius Maximus (Livy 22.9.7 and 10.10), and her first temple *in Capitolio* was dedicated in 215 (Livy 23.30.13). Such an act in the early and adverse years of the Hannibalic war was almost certainly motivated by diplomacy and the desire to ensure the loyalty of the 'Trojan' community of Segesta in formerly Punic western Sicily. The foundation of her second temple, by the Colline gate, is associated by O. with the capture of Syracuse in 212 BC, and the temple itself is attested by Livy as standing in 202, when the games of Apollo were threatened by flood, and it was proposed to move them to the higher ground near this temple (Livy 30.38). But a temple of Erycina *ad Collinam* is dated by Livy 40.34 (cf. App. *BC* 1.428, Strabo 6.2.5 p. 272) to a vow of 184 BC, and its dedication to 23 April 181 BC. Since the *Fasti Praenestini* also record an anniversary of Erycina *ad portam Collinam* on 24 Oct. there is reason to hypothesize a destruction and rebuilding of the temple *ad portam Collinam* and a confusion between the anniversary of the first and second dedications. (See C. Koch, *Hermes* 83 (1955) 28, 38.)

In any case O. has here given the cult of Venus, patroness of the month, priority over the more important cult of Jupiter, of which he shows himself fully informed, and has given prominence to a cult and class of women usually ignored or despised.

865 numina ... Veneris: or *ueneris*? The periphrase may not be purely ornamental, since it encourages ambiguity between Goddess and sexual charm. The Romans did not use capitalization to distinguish proper names (cf. 676n.), but given that both 866 and 867 asking for *formam populique fauorem* are concerned with sex appeal, O.'s meaning might be better represented by lower case in our text.

uulgares: like *professae* (used in this sense here only in O.) these are not simply the humble women living out of wedlock described in 134 above *quis uittae longaque uestis abest.* These are *meretrices*, whether freelance or perhaps enslaved, many of them non-citizen. Anecdotal evidence shows that in Roman law of O.'s day they were supposed to register (*profiteri*) and obtain a licence from the aedile: Tac. *Ann.* 2.85 and Suet. *Tib.* 35 report that early in Tiberius' principate the noble Vistilia chose to register as a prostitute rather than be prosecuted for adultery.

866 professarum quaestibus: *quaerere* and *quaestum facere*, though referring to earning of all kinds when the subject is male, were a standard prosaic euphemism for female prostitution (glossed over in *OLD* s.v. *quaestus* 1b).

867 poscite ture dato formam: thus far O.'s presentation of the prostitutes' offering coincides with that of the respectable ladies to Fortuna Virilis; cf. *tura, paruo ture rogata* 145, 150, and *forma* 157. But the *mores* and *bona fama* of 157 are replaced here by *populi ... fauorem*, and 868 *blanditias, dignaque uerba ioco*, popular appeal, and charm of both manner and speech. It is perhaps significant that O. elsewhere applies *populi/publicus fauor* (*Ex P.* 3.4.29, 4.14.56) only to himself, but e.g. Plut. *Romulus* 5, or *Pompey* 2, shows that well-known courtesans were in some sense popular celebrities. (And still are: one acknowledged courtesan, La Cicciarella, even stood for office in a recent election in Rome.)

For *blanditiae* as the gift of Venus cf. *Am.* 1.4.66 *blanditiae taceant sitque maligna Venus*, and for the combination of *blanditiae* with *uerba*, *Am.* 2.19.17, 3.11.31, *AA* 2.466, *Her.* 13.153. In Plautus *blanditiae* are exclusively associated with courtesans except at *Poen.* 136 where the slave's reference to his master's *blanditiae* is infected by the dramatic context, in which two novice courtesans make offering to Venus at the *Aphrodisia* (256); here Plautus may exploit Roman interest in the new cult of Erycina, but the setting is Greek and their offerings mark entry into their profession.

869–70 cumque sua ... myrto | tectaque composita iuncea uincla rosa 'give your mistress pleasing mint with her own myrtle plant and bonds of reed covered with an arrangement of roses': as with the offerings to Venus on 1 April and the flowers gathered by Proserpina's attendants (see 435–442n.), these wreaths combine roses, chosen for visual beauty, with myrtle (see 15, 139) for foliage and mint for perfume (Gk *sisymbria* occurs here only for *menta* (*Met.* 8.663, 10.729, Pliny, *NH* 19.160, 20.146)), all set on a base of reeds.

871–2 Collinae proxima portae | ... a Siculo nomina colle tenent: cf. *Rem.* 549–50 *est prope Collinam templum uenerabile portam: | imposuit templo nomina celsus Eryx*. Here O. turns the identification of the temple into a riddle. The temple of Venus *Erycina* (cf. Cat. 64.72, Hor. *Odes* 1.2.33) is named with play on the goddess's original cult site Eryx, *Siculo ... colle*, but the goddess is only identifiable as Erycina when Eryx is named in 874. For the poetic plurals *templa*, *nomina* cf. 159–60.

873 Syracusas Arethusidas: the city is named only here in O., but cf. the adjective *Syracosius* in 6.277, *Ex P.* 4.3.39 and *Ibis* 547. Here its heavy form (∪ – – –) before the caesura is offset by the unique (and highly dactylic) matronymic; the end-syllables do not offer a pure rhyme, since the *a* of the Latin acc. is long, but short in the Gk *-idas*, and preceding a vowel. O. alludes to the rebellion and fall of Syracuse (a Roman ally since 263) during the Hannibalic war. It was recaptured in 212 BC by M. Claudius Marcellus (cos. 222, 215,

214, 210 and 208), hero of the victory of Clastidium over the Gauls in 222 BC, when he won the Spolia Opima. The most famous ancestor of Augustus' first heir Marcellus, who died in 23 BC, he is celebrated in Hor. *Odes* 1.12.45–6, and subject of a life by Plutarch. That O. names him as *Claudius* rather than Marcellus may be a conciliatory gesture towards Tiberius.

Arethusidas: on Arethusa, nymph and fountain, cf. 422–3n.

abstulit armis: translated by Bömer 'destroyed with force of arms' as if it were *sustulit*, by Schilling 'conquered', the verb is treated by Skutsch on Enn. 244 *auferre domos* 'as a synonym of *cepit*'. But surely it can be translated more literally: 'took away', 'took back' (from alliance with Hannibal).

874 et bello te quoque cepit, Eryx: as the richest sanctuary in Sicily Eryx was an object of fierce fighting until the end of the first Punic war (Plb. 1.55, 58). We do not know when it was overrun by Hannibal in the second. The mythical founder figure Eryx was a son of Venus (cf. *Aen.* 1.570, 5.23–4 *litora* ... *fraterna Erycis* and see G. K. Galinsky, *Aeneas, Sicily and Rome* (Princeton 1969), *Enciclopedia Virgiliana* II 364–5 s.v.)

875 carmine uiuacis ... Sibyllae: cf. *Met.* 14.104 *uiuacisque antra Sibyllae*; the adj. *uiuax*, 'long-lived', recalls the story of her unhappy and ageing immortality told in *Met.* 14 and Petr. *Sat.* 48. As at 257 *carmen* ... *Sibyllae* stands for the Sibylline books (Livy 22.9.7ff.) consulted under pressure from Fabius Maximus in 217 for the foundation of the first temple of Erycina on the Capitol. Since they survived the legendary Sibyl who sold them to Tarquin one might see *uiuax* as the ironic hypallage of an epithet properly belonging to *carmine*.

876 inque suae stirpis ... urbe: for Rome as the city of Venus' son Aeneas see 118, but here *stirps* surely includes Venus' descendants through Aeneas, the Aeneadae of 162. Cf., for the *stirps* of a god, *Met.* 1.159, 2.633, 11.312, etc.

maluit ... coli implies that Venus in coming to Rome had abandoned the mother shrine of Eryx (tacitly rejecting the claim of Sicilian Eryx to be founded by a son of Venus, 874n.); the same implication was left undeveloped in O.'s treatment of Cybele's coming to Rome in 248–56.

877–8 cur igitur Veneris festum Vinalia dicant | quaeritis ... ?: O. has established that the day is *Veneris festum*; now he gives the *aition* for the name *Vinalia* and its dedication to Jupiter (cf. *Io*[*ui* in *Fasti Praenestini* line 1), although in fact the origins of the Vinalia, whether in cult or in myth, go back earlier than the cult of Erycina from the end of the third century. Cf. Varro, *LL* 6.16 *Vinalia a uino: hic dies Iouis, non Veneris*, Festus 322 Lindsay, Pliny, *NH* 18.287 *uinalia priora quae ante hos dies sunt ix kal. Mai. degustandis uinis instituta*, and Plut. *Qu. Rom.* 45, which mistakenly attributes the libation of wine and the Mezentius *aition* to the Veneralia, reporting that '[on this day] a great quantity of wine is poured out from the temple of Venus'.

879–96 O.'s account of the impious demand of the Etruscan tyrant Mezentius that he should himself receive the first of the new wine of Latium (properly owed to Jupiter) can be reconstructed in the *Fasti Praenestini* quoted at 863–900n.: the story derives from Cato's *Origines* fr. 12 *HRR* = Macrob. 3.5.10. There is, however, a logical inconsistency implicit in treating Mezentius' demands, whether for the whole vintage (as in Pliny, *NH* 14.88 *uini mercede quod tum in agro Latino fuisset*) or for a proportion (*primitiae, omnis uini libationem*, Festus 322 Lindsay, cf. *Fasti Praen.* cited in 863–900n.) as impiety, if this story is being presented as the *aition* or origin of the Latin offering of *primitiae* to Jupiter. It seems far more in keeping with ancient religion that these *primitiae*/ἀπαρχαί (cf. Hdt. 4.71 etc.) should have been an inherited custom, not the pious innovation of Aeneas, as here.

But while O. follows Cato and Varro in making Mezentius demand the *primitiae* from Turnus and the Rutuli as the price of his alliance, Plut. *Qu. Rom.* 45 has Mezentius demand the vintage directly from Aeneas and the Latins, and Dion. Halic. 1.65.2 follows another tradition in which Mezentius outlived both Turnus and Aeneas, and demanded the vintage from Ascanius.

Virgil retains Cato's characterization of Mezentius as *contemptor diuum* (7.648, 8.7) and alludes to the story in *Aen.* 11.16 (see below) but omits Mezentius' hubristic demand from the narrative of the *Aeneid*. Evander's narrative to Aeneas (8.481–95, cf. 500–1, 569–71) sets the alliance of Turnus and Mezentius before the narrative time of the *Aeneid* and changes its nature by substituting a more detailed portrayal of Mezentius' hubris towards his own people and converting him into an exile. Thus Mezentius is already a relatively powerless fugitive when he enters the *Aeneid*. However, besides Aeneas' pointed allusion to the spoils of the dead Mezentius as *primitiae* in *Aen.* 11.16 Virgil seems to recall Mezentius' traditional offence against Jupiter in the reiterated references to Jupiter at 10.689 *Iouis ... monitis*, 743–4 *ast de me diuom pater atque hominum rex | uiderit* and Aeneas' prayer in 875 *sic pater ille deum faciat.*

879 Latiae gener ... Amatae: the stress on competition to be Amata's son-in-law could echo Virgil, acknowledging Amata's passionate involvement in *Aen.* 7.56–7 and 12.54–64, where she treats him as *gener* and swears she would rather die than see Aeneas as her son-in-law. But O. may also be following an early annalistic version in Fabius Pictor and Calpurnius Piso (see Servius on *Aen.* 7.51) in which Latinus was already dead when the rivals fought, and Amata did away with two of his sons because they wanted to give Lavinia to Aeneas.

880 Etruscas Turnus adoptat opes: the paradosis *adorat* is not convincingly supported by the examples cited at *TLL* s.v. I 821.40–7 for *adoro* of supplication of gods, etc.; apparent parallels like *Ex P.* 2.2.53 *hanc ego, non ut me defendere temptet, adoro* differ from 880 in expressing the person supplicated. In favour of *adoptat* (G) is the synonymous *adsciscere* of 882 and the fact that O. twice elsewhere (*Med.* 6, *AA* 2.652) seeks word-play on *adoptiuus* and *opes*. Virgil's use of *optare* in *Aen.* 8.503 *externos optate duces* seems a fair parallel.

881–2 ferox Mezentius armis | ... uel equo magnus uel pede maior erat: with the line-ending cf. *Aen.* 8.481, 10.768 and *M. arma* at 10.150, *M. armat* at 10.204. Virgil uses *ferox* of Mezentius only once, inside the simile where the boar–Mezentius *infremuitque ferox et inhorruit armos* (10.711). O.'s praise of his superiority on foot reflects Mezentius' *aristeia* in *Aen.* 10.689–785 before he is wounded in the groin and reduced to fighting on horseback.

883–4 suis adsciscere temptant | partibus: *adsciscere* of military and political alliance is common in classical prose from Cic. *Verr.* 2.5.21 on; elsewhere in O. it is closer to 'graft' or 'adopt', cf. 6.172, *Ex P.* 4.9.127, *Tr.* 1.8.34.

885–90 Mezentius is given six lines; two affirming his worth, two asking his price, and two proposing the outcome.

886 armaque, quae sparsi sanguine saepe meo: like Virgil's warrior, O.'s Mezentius invokes his weapons, but only as witnesses (*testor*) along with his wounds of his fighting record, not as his gods in combat (10.773). The blood spilt on his weapons seems to recall *Aen.* 10.908 *undantique animam diffundit in arma cruore* (the account of his death that ends the book). There is fierce alliteration on *ar*, *s* and *sa*.

887–8 In secular terms, Mezentius' rhetoric is persuasive: *qui petis auxilium* puts Turnus in the weaker position, *non grandia* ... | *praemia* frames his fee as modest, and his language avoids words suggestive of *primitiae*. But this is a sacrilege: Cato (*ap.* Macr. 3.5.10) calls this *quas dis primitias offerebant.*

de lacubus ... musta: for the -*u*- form of abl. *lacubus* cf. *Met.* 12.278 (of a vat for tempering hot steel), Silius 7.211. But the form is not a poetic licence: it occurs in the agricultural writers Varro, *RR* 1.7.7 and Colum. 1.6.13 (see Prisc. 2. 365). *arcubus*, *artubus* are regular in prose to avoid confusion with the abl. forms of *arx* and *ars*. On the new unfermented *musta* see 780n.

889–90 In contrast with the expansive development of the previous couplets Mezentius' last words compress his guarantee into three asyndetic units: the speed of his response and his assurance of victory in return for their gift, conveyed by chiastic antithesis of substantival infinitives, reserving for the pentameter the new element of the rival Aeneas and his supposed frustration. The prosaic *opera*, 'services' (cf. Axelson (1945) 59), occurs only here in O. outside the erotic elegies (*Am.* 2.10.26, *AA* 1.366, 2.673; but cf. *Rem.* 165 *siue operam bellis uellet dare*). The effect is to reinforce Mezentius' gross materialism.

890 quam uelit: irony, since Aeneas' wish that the first-fruits be denied to Mezentius is moved by piety beyond Mezentius' understanding.

891–2 Another condensed distich covers four events: the consent of the Rutuli, the arming of each man in turn (suggesting the single combat familiar from Virgil) and Aeneas' counter-vow on behalf of his side. *induit*, though a genuine repeated event, not an epanalepsis, is characteristically picked up from the 5th foot of the hexameter to open the pentameter.

893 'hostica Tyrrheno uota est uindemia regi: the archaic form *hosticus* for *hostilis* occurs in Augustan poetry only at Hor. *Sat.* 1.9.31, *Odes* 3.2.6, and O.'s poems of exile: *Tr.* 3.10.66, *Ex P.* 1.3.65. For *palmes* of the vine tendril cf. 128, also 1.152 and 354, 3.238, Virg.

Ecl. 7.48, *Georg.* 2.364; as synecdoche for the vine cf. *Georg.* 2.89–90 *uindemia* ... | *quam Methymnaeo carpit de palmite Lesbos*, *Met.* 14.663, 15.710.

894 Iuppiter, e Latio palmite musta feres': in offering the Latin vintage O.'s Aeneas clearly speaks as representative of the Latins. In Virgil's account Aeneas and his allies have to defeat the combination of Latins, Rutuli and Mezentius before he is able to impose a fair alliance on the Latins; but O. restores the earlier version reported by Livy (1.1.6–7) in which Aeneas and the Latins are allied when they face Turnus and Mezentius. O. has even given Aeneas credit for the pragmatic piety of the Latins, for according to Macrobius' quotation from Cato, *Orig.* fr. 12 *HRR Iuppiter si tibi magis cordi est nos ea tibi dare potius quam Mezentio, uti nos uictores facias*, it was they, not Aeneas, who won divine support by making this vow to Jupiter.

895 uota ualent meliora: cadit Mezentius ingens: in two half-lines O. implies both the single combat between Aeneas and Mezentius that ends *Aen.* x, and the victory of the Latins over the Rutuli which comes only with the death of Turnus at the end of *Aen.* xii. *ingens* is another Virgilian echo (cf. *Aen.* 10.842 *ingentem* ... *ingenti uulnere uictum*, and the simile of 10.762–3 *ingentem quatiens* ... *hastam* | ... *quam magnus Orion*) but 896 *atque indignanti pectore plangit humum* while false to Virgil's Mezentius, who welcomes death, emulates Virgil in combining the motif of striking the ground (see 844) with the indignant deaths of both Turnus and Camilla (12.952, 11.831).

897 uenerat Autumnus calcatis sordidus uuis: cf. *Met.* 2.29 *stabat et Autumnus c. s. u.* As in the ecphrasis of the sun-palace of *Met.* 2.23–30, the season is personified and visualized with wine-stained feet as if treading grapes in a vintage fresco or relief, or isolated in a mosaic. For Autumnus (the time of increase, *auct-* from *augere*) as vintage time, cf. Virg. *Georg.* 2.5–6 *grauidus autumno* | *floret ager, spumat plenis uindemia labris*, 2.521–2.

sordidus is rare in elevated poetry: only twice in Virgil (*Ecl.* 2.28, *Aen.* 6.301); in O. *Met.* it is limited to 2.29 and the humble piece of bacon of Baucis and Philemon at *Met.* 8.648. It occurs six times in the elegiac poetry.

898 redduntur merito ... Ioui 'are rendered to Jupiter who has deserved it': adverbial *merito* is characteristic of vows fulfilled *lubens merito*; but O. prefers more independent formulae, like *meritus* ... *honor* at 5.596. Other participial forms such as 3.268 *meritae* ... *deae Tr.* 1.10.43 *meritae* ... *Minervae, Tr.* 4.2.12 *meritis* ... *deis*, support the idea that *merito* is dat. with *Ioui* both here and in *Tr.* 4.2.56.

Why does O. speak of the offering of wine in the autumn (time of the Vinalia Rustica of 19 August), when he is celebrating the earlier Vinalia? These events belong to the August festival: autumn would be the right time for the offering of *mustum* (as in 887), whereas the actual wine would not be ready until spring. Indeed Festus (322 Lindsay) assigns the vow itself to the August Vinalia Rustica.

It seems that O. is anticipating the narrative he would need for the August celebration. It is possible that at the time of composing his entry for the spring Vinalia O. had already decided that he would not or could not go beyond the first half of the year.

899–900 dicta dies hinc est Vinalia: Iuppiter illa | uindicat: *hinc* is aetiological, from this vow (894) or occasion. *illa* (neut. pl. with *Vinalia*) offers suppressed word-play with *uindicat*, as if echoing *Vinalia dicam/dicant* from 863, 877, or better, *uina* and *dicare*, 'the dedication or vowing of wine'. On legal *uindicare*, 'to claim as one's own' (short inner syllable, from *uindex, -icis*), see 90n.

festis gaudet inesse suis: the subject of *inesse* is again *Vinalia/illa*: besides special festivals like the September Ludi Magni, all Ides were sacred to Jupiter.

901–42 (24 April B C) 25 April C ROB NP The Robigalia

The *Fasti Praenestini* are fully preserved, and read:

> C VIII Robigalia np Feriae Robigo uia Claudia ad milliarium V ne robigo frum[e]ntis noceat. Sacrificiu[m] et ludi cursoribus maioribus minoribusq(ue) fiunt. Festus est pu(e)rorum lenoniorum quia proximus superior meretricum est.

902 in medio cursu tempora ueris erunt: for the second half of the pentameter cf. 1.496; and O.'s markers for the beginning and end of spring, 2.150 *primi tempora ueris erunt*, 5.602 *finem tempora ueris habent*. O.'s dating of the middle of spring is a month too late (cf.

Ideler (cited 677–8n.) 150–1): the midpoint of spring according to Caesar's calendar, used by Varro, *RR* 1.28 and Pliny, *NH* 18.59, was the equinox on 25 March. But O.'s error may come from his source: in Columella 11.2.36, 21 April is treated as the midpoint. However, O. seems to make the same error in dating the setting of Aries in 903, and a quite different kind of error in 904 by replacing the (evening) setting of Sirius with its rising. This is all the more surprising as Virg. *Georg.* 1. 217–18 clearly marks the entry of the sun into Taurus in late April as the time when the Dogstar sets: *aperit ... annum* | *Taurus et auerso cedens Canis occidit astro.* (Merkel (1841) lxxiii-iv considered treating 901–4 as displaced from book III, but saw this was incompatible with the present form of 901.)

903 frustra pecudem quaeres: O. imagines the reader searching the sky for constellations, like the farmers of Hesiod and the *Georgics*; cf. 1.313 *octipedis frustra quaerentur bracchia Cancri*, 5.143 *bina gemellorum quaerebam signa deorum*, 5.493–4 *si mediis Boeotum Oriona quaeres,* | *falsus eris*, 6.195 *si quaeritis astra.*

Athamantidos Helles: for the constellation Aries, identified with the ram who carried Phrixus and Helle, see 715.

O.'s dating of the evening setting of Aries is more than a month later than the apparent setting, calculated as 20 March, and three weeks after the true evening setting of 5 April. While O.'s intermittent astronomical references are both inaccurate and arbitrary, he does try to note either rising (real or apparent) or setting of most signs of the zodiac (Cancer 1.313, Capricorn 1.651–2, Pisces 3.400, Scorpio 3.712 (cf. 163–4n.), Taurus 4.717).

904 signaque dant imbres: cf. 1.316 *signa dabunt imbres exoriente Lyra* and 385 where O. transforms the calendar predictions of rain into a personal experience. On the association of this phase with rain cf. Colum. 11.2.37 *tertio cal. Maias mane capra exoritur, Austrinus dies interdum pluuiae. Pridie cal. Maias canis se uespere celat: tempestatem significat.* Pliny, *NH* 18.280–92 notes the hazards that mildew created for the flowering or seed-forming crops when these rains coincide with extremes of cold by night.

exoriturque Canis: this is perhaps the strangest of O.'s astronomical inaccuracies. It is not just that he has misreported as a rising Sirius' evening setting (which Colum. 11.2.37 above and Pliny, *NH* 18.285 assign to 30 and 28 April respectively: cf. Ideler (cited 677–

8n.) 164, Bömer on 5.723). O. incorrectly reports the rising of this star again on 22 May at 5.723 *nocte sequente diem canis Erigoneïus exit*, with a back reference to the *aition* of 939. In fact both true and apparent early risings of Sirius (19 July, 2 August) occur in high summer, bringing the notorious discomfort of the summer period that constituted 'the Dog days', celebrated by poets from Hesiod through Aratus to Virgil (*Georg.* 2.353 *Canis aestifer*), and Horace (*Odes* 1.17.17–18 *Caniculae* | *uitabis aestus*, 3.13.9 *flagrantis atrox hora Caniculae*). How could O. have let this pass?

905–6 Nomento Romam cum ... redirem, | obstitit ... candida turba: returning from Nomentum about 15 miles NE of Rome (probably from a villa such as Seneca and Atticus owned at Nomentum), O. would follow the Via Nomentana and enter by the Porta Collina. The *candida turba* would consist of the Flamen Quirinalis and his attendants.

907–8 flamen in ... lucum ... ibat | exta canis flammis, exta daturus ouis: the *Fasti Praenestini* (901–48n.) set the grove of Robigus (called *Robigo* by O.) at the fifth milestone on the Via Claudia, which joined the Flaminia outside Rome, across the Mulvian Bridge: how then would O. have intersected with the priest's journey to the grove, if his own route was on the Nomentana? Mommsen's explanation, that O. made a diversion to visit his gardens near the Via Claudia (cf. *Ex P.* 1.8.43–4) commits the documentary fallacy of treating a poetic text as a record. As with the old man of Carseoli and the bonfires of the Parilia (689–90, 691, 725–8nn.), O.'s involvement in this obscure boundary ritual is simply a 'device of presentation' (cf. North (1989) 141). Yet one can still ask why he introduced the reference to Nomentum. We might compare the unexplained diversion from the narrative of Cybele's journey upstream from Ostia for the episode at the Almo (337–40n.).

antiquae ... Robiginis: fem. *robigo* seems to be used for the god here, which goes against both Varro, *RR* 1.6.0, invoking the aid of *Robigus* for his crops, and the *Fasti Praenestini* quoted above, where *Robigo* is dative. Festus 325 Lindsay distinguishes between masc. *Robigus*, the god to whom the offering was made, and fem. *robigo* (as in 911, so Virg. *Georg.* 1.150–1 *mala ... robigo*, and Colum. 10.342 cited below), the disease against which the god protected the crops. The exceptional feature of this cult was the sacrifice of a dog with the more predictable sheep: cf. Colum. 10.342–3 *hinc mala robigo, uirides ne torreat herbas,* | *sanguine lactentis catuli placatur et extis* (see 936–9).

909 accessi: obviously the rite was not usually witnessed. We might suppose that the Robigalia, like the Ambarvalia, involved a purification along all the boundaries, and O. joined the procession when it crossed the Nomentana, accompanying it across country to the *lucus*. *ne nescius essem* (cf. 58) justifies O.'s act as a scholarly inquiry; *cognoscere* and *docere ritus* (cf. *Met.* 15.5 and 483) are the essence of religion but also of didactic poetry, cf. 1.631 *si quis amas ueteres ritus, adsiste precanti*, *Am.* 3.13.5 *grande morae pretium ritus cognoscere.* In contrast, at 6.511 *cognoscere ritum* is seen by Bacchantes as a violation of their women's rites.

910 edidit haec flamen uerba, Quirine, tuus: in addressing the god Quirinus whose *flamen* is concerned, O. seems to mock the device of apostrophe; his report of the priest's words to his primary divine master and patron treats the prayer to Robigo as if it were a minor disloyalty.

911–32 In both length and content this prayer recalls the only slightly longer prayer to Pales at 747–76, and more remotely within the poem, but closer in its agricultural concerns, the prayer offered by the poet in person to Ceres and Tellus at 1.675–96, with the following sequence to 704.

911 'aspera Robigo, parcas Cerialibus herbis: cf. 921 and the prayer to Ceres at the *feriae Sementiuae*, 1.687–8 *crescat scabrae robiginis expers* | *nec uitio caeli palleat ulla seges*. For other prayers with *parce*, *parcite* cf. 2.451, 6.160; for *parce* with infin. as a form of prohibition, see 204.

912 et tremat in summa leue cacumen humo: the emphatic word here is *leue*, 'smooth' (the *-e-* is long), as opposed to *asperum.* The growing stalk (cf. 127 *herbae rupta tellure cacumina tollunt*) must sway freely above the ground, not weighed down by mildew.

913 sata sideribus caeli nutrita secundi: as with *uitio caeli* in 1.686, *caelum* covers variations of temperature and humidity, but the constellations were also thought to affect growth. In a passage based on Varro, Pliny, *NH* 18.273 rejects the popular belief that *robigo* is caused by dew burnt into the grain by fierce sun, and adds a complex excursus (280–92) blaming diseases like mildew and *carbunculus* on the conjunction of cold, wet skies with the rising and setting of certain constellations or the full moon; at 285 he asserts as the *uera causa*, the real explanation of mildew, that *canis occidit, sidus et per se uehemens et cui praecedere caniculam necesse sit.* For the role of *sidera* see also 18.208. Generally O. keeps *secundus* close to its original sense of 'following' (either 'second', or 'favouring' winds, tide, etc.) but cf. *Met.* 7.619 *fulgore ... tonitruque secundo, Her.* 16.377 *dis ... secundis.*

914 dum fiant falcibus apta: for the *falx* as symbol of harvest cf. *Am.* 1.15.12, 3.10.12, *AA.* 2.322, *Her.* 1.53. *aptus* is rather a maid of all work in O. (cf. 774, 789, 819, 866, of which only the last is the obvious choice of word); here it seems to stand for *matura.*

915 uis tua non leuis est: for the positive *uis* of a god, cf. 105, 1.133 etc.; for destructive *uis, Met.* 8.875, 9.161.

quae tu frumenta notasti: *frumenta,* as Axelson (1945) 138 notes, is prosaic, occurring only in *Georgics,* once at *Aen.* 4.406, and here alone in O.'s works; the metonymy *Ceres* (see 395–6, 645 and 917) and its variants are far more common. *notare* often represents disfiguring by scratching (2.698, *Met.* 1.509), here the reddened discoloration; cf. *Met.* 4.329 *pueri rubor ora notauit,* 6.46, *Her.* 4.32 *candor ab insolita labe notandus.*

916 in amissis ... habet: one of several prosaic constructions of *habere,* 'consider', 'count as', with prepositional phrases. Cf. *habere ... inter:* 5. 347–8 *non est | illa coturnatas inter habenda deas, Am.* 1.11.2, *Her.* 6.118; *habere ... pro: Ex P.* 1.9.49 *pro numine ... habebas.* Contrast *Met.* 1.585 *luget ut amissam.*

917 nec uenti ... Cereri nocuere nec imbres: on the harmful effect of *uenti/imbres* on grain crops cf. Virg. *Ecl.* 3.80–1 *triste ... maturis frugibus imbres, | arboribus uenti,* the storm of *Georg.* 1.333ff., *Met.* 5.483–4 *nimius modo corrupit imber | sideraque uentique nocent,* on wind and rain as parallel hardships *Georg.* 2.293 *non flabra neque imbres, Aen.* 4.249 *caput et uento pulsatur et imbri, Aen.* 9.60 *uentos perpessus et imbres,* Hor. *Odes* 3.30.3 *quod non imber edax, non Aquilo impotens.* For the metonymy of *Ceres* = 911 *ceriales herbae* = the growing wheat, repeated at 931, see 395–6, 645.

918 marmoreo ... adusta gelu: cf. *Tr.* 3.10.10 *terraque marmoreo est candida facta gelu* and 47 *inclusaeque gelu stabunt in marmore puppes* for *marmor* of the frozen surface; for *-uro* of cold cf. *Tr.* 3.4b.48 *adstricto terra perusta gelu,* 5.2.66 *glaebaque canenti semper obusta gelu. adurere* in Virg. *Georg.* 1.93 *penetrabile frigus adurat* is echoed by *Met.* 14.763–4 *nil* *uernum nascentia frigus adurat | poma*; behind the poetic usage lurks *uredo*, a regular farmer's term for blight.

nec sic . . . pallet: for the discoloration of sick wheat cf. 1.688 *nec uitio caeli palleat ulla seges.*

919–20 si . . . Titan incalfacit . . . locus est irae . . . tuae: O. adopts the theory rejected by Pliny, *NH* 18.273, that mildew is provoked by *rorem inustum sole acri.* But both *Titan* (see 180) and the reference to Robigo's divine anger strike a mock-epic tone, contrasted with the prosaic *culmos . . . incalfacit udos.* The word *culmus*, 'stalk', occurs only here in O. (distinguish *culmen* 734); *incalfacere* (cf. *calfacit* 698) only here and at *Met* 15.735. The reverent address *diua timenda* elevates the divinity of Robigo to match *diuae* previously addressed (Venus at 162, Ceres and Tellus at 1.696, both rounding off prayers; Ceres has already been shown in fear of Robigo at 911, 917). By addressing his appeal to malevolent Mildew as opposed to the benevolent *Robigus* who protects against it, O. provides a stronger foil for the shepherd's prayer to beneficent Pales.

921–32 The second half of the prayer moves to the larger context, celebrating peace and contrasting beneficial farming with evil warfare, the proper object of Robigo's attack: the line of thought resembles that of the prayer to Ceres and Tellus in 1.667–96 with its sequel of reflections on the conflict between warfare and farming.

921–2 parce, precor, . . . aufer | neue noce cultis: in content this simply rewords 911–14, in form it intensifies *parce* 911 with alliteration on *p* and *r* (for *parce, precor* cf. Tib. 1.8.51, Hor. *Odes* 4.1.2, and see Appel (1909) 120); O. creates further sound-play from *scabrasque manus a messibus*, reworking *aspera* and *falcibus apta*, and the reprise of harm done to the crops from 911 and 917. Personification of Robigo comes from the suggestion of infectious skin disease in *scabrae manus*, and the image of handling continues in *amplectere* (923) and *carpes* (925). To this O. adds the psychological twist of *posse nocere sat est.* Insatiability in the exercise of power or revenge is characteristic of female deities like Juno: *Met.* 4.427 *idque mihi satis est? haec una potentia nostra est?*

923 durum amplectere ferrum: as an apotropaic finale to the prayer (cf. Hor. *Odes* 1.21.13 with Nisbet and Hubbard on *dei auerrunci* diverting plague against Rome's enemies) O. proposes other victims to Robigo, exploiting the dual reference of her name to both kinds of red rot, mildew and rust (also called *ferrugo*). The idea of sending the *pestis* from crops to weapons is a new twist on the favourite antithesis of agriculture and war, common to Virgil (*Georg.* 1.494–6, 508, *Aen.* 7.635ff.), Tibullus (1.10.49–50 quoted at 927), and O. (*F.* 1.697–700): this is often associated with the reforging of agricultural tools into weapons. Not only the epithet *durus* for war, weapons and warriors, but the contrast of *tener* and *durus* is characteristic of bucolic and elegy, cf. *Ecl.* 10.44 *duri* ... *Martis in armis*, Tib. 1.10.49–50 *duri* | *militis, Am.* 1.4.44 *nec tenerum duro cum pede iunge pedem*, 3.4.1, *dure uir, imposito tenerae custode puellae.*

924 perde prior: Robigo need not be content with unused power as in 922; the harm done by weapons justifies pre-emptive attack.

925 utilius gladios ... carpes: the polite 'advisory' future takes the place of the imperative (cf. G–L 243), and the argument from advantage (human, not that of Robigo) plays off the opposite notion of harmfulness (from 917, 922), while *carpes* in the double sense of 'pluck' and 'consume' maintains the image of the corroding hand.

926 nil opus est illis: otia mundus agit: as in 1.68 *otia terra ferax, otia pontus habet*, 285–8, and 701–4, O. stresses the peace of the Roman empire, this time without repeating his praise and gratitude to Augustus for *otia nostra* at *Tr.* 2.224, 235 *non tibi contingunt quae gentibus otia praestas.* This had been a theme of panegyric since Horace's *Carmen saeculare* 57–60; cf. *Odes* 4.5.17–20 and 15.1–20 esp. 17–19 *custode rerum Caesare non furor* | *ciuilis aut uis exiget otium,* | *non ira, quae procudit enses.*

927 sarcula... bidens et uomer aduncus: O. adds *sarcula*, an agricultural term brought into poetry by Hor. *Odes* 1.1.11 (cf. 1.699, *Met.* 11.36) to the tools of his model, Tibullus' praise of peace at 1.10.49–50 *pace bidens uomerque nitent, at tristia duri* | *militis in tenebris occupat arma situs.* The terms *bidens* and *uomer* come into poetry with Lucretius and Virgil: cf. Lucr. 5.208–9 *consueta bidenti* | *ingemere, Georg.* 2.400 *aeternum frangenda bidentibus*, and Lucr. 1.313–14 *uncus aratri* | *ferreus* ... *uomer, Georg.* 2.223 *uomeris unci.* O. replaces *uncus* by *aduncus* (common of noses, beaks and talons from Ennius onwards), cf. 2.295 *nullus anhelabat sub adunco uomere taurus, Am.* 3.10.32, *AA* 1.474, 725, *Rem.* 172, *Ex P.* 4.10.6.

928 ruris opes: with *inquinet* (another term of pollution, cf. 3.496, *Met.* 14.56) the idea of tools as *ruris opes* (cf. *Tr.* 3.10.59 *ruris opes paruae, pecus et stridentia plaustra*) is a variation on Virg. *Georg.* 1.160 *duris agrestibus arma*, 165 *uirgea ... Celei ... supellex.*

930 adstrictum longa sentiat esse mora: the warrior's sword has rusted, providing a desirable obstruction to war. Taken with *sentiat* the *longa mora* would be the delay in drawing the sword. It is better taken instrumentally with *adstrictum* as the period of disuse; cf. *AA* 2.456 *ne lenta uires colligat ira mora, Tr.* 1.3.8 *torpuerant longa pectora nostra mora.* For *adstringere* of binding together cf. 2.577 *pice, AA.* 2.47 *ceris*; this is also the sense in Virg. *Georg.* 1.91 *uenas adstringit hiantes.*

931 at tu ne uiola Cererem: for *at tu* in commands, marking a change of tone or address, cf. 3.621–2 *at tu ... regni commoda carpe mei*; 6.97 *at uos ignoscite, diuae*, Virg. *Ecl.* 5.88 *at tu sume pedum, Aen.* 8.643 *at tu dictis, Albane, maneres*, 9.290 *at tu ... solare inopem.* With *ne uiola* cf. 2.506 *nec uiolent lacrimis numina nostra suis.*

932 absenti possit soluere uota tibi: on the farmer's *uota* see 641–2n. Normally (see 192, 663, 808, 828) deities are begged to be present to aid and grant vows: *absenti* is a deliberate paradox.

933 uillis mantele solutis: an echo of *Georg.* 4.377 = *Aen.* 1.702 *tonsisque ferunt mantelia uillis.* Such napkins, or napped cloths, were used in ritual, cf. Varro, *LL* 6.85 *mantelium ubi manus terguntur*, Lucil. 1206 Marx *mantela merumque*, Festus 118 Lindsay.

934 meri patera turis acerra: the *patera* was a shallow cup used for libations; cf. *Aen.* 1.729 *impleuitque mero pateram*, 4.60 *ipsa tenens dextra pateram ... fundit, Met.* 9.160, 15.575. For the *acerra* or thurible cf. *Aen.* 5.745 *plena supplex ueneratur acerra, Met.* 13.703 *custodem turis acerram, Ex P.* 4.8.39–40 *de parua ... dis libat acerra | tura.* Both wine and incense are offered in 935, with the more conventional *fibrae* (= *exta* 908) of the sheep (*bidens* fem., not to be confused with the masc. hoe or fork of 927). Cf. offerings of *pecoris fibrae* at 2.681, *Met.* 11.248, *Tr.* 1.9.49 *ouium fibrae.*

936 turpiaque obscenae ... exta canis: the shock is held over for the pentameter. *turpis* covers the physically ugly and morally shameful; *obscenus* describes sexual behaviour (3.675, 695 explicit jokes, 6.337 incest or rape, *Met.* 10.465 genitalia) or aesthetically offensive behaviour (carrion-eaters, dogs and birds: *Am.* 2.6.52 *obscenae quo prohibentur aues*). The terms seem interchangeable at *Tr.* 2.211–12 *turpi carmine ... | arguor obsceni doctor adulterii.*

O. has already reported dog sacrifice at 1.389 *exta canum uidi Triuiae libare Sapaeos*; Bömer (1956) cites the evidence of Colum. 2.21.4 *ne sementem quidem administrare nisi prius catulo feceris* for sacrificing a puppy in agricultural cult, while Plut. *Qu. Rom.* 52 and Pliny, *NH* 29.58 cite the sacrifice of a bitch to Genita Mana. But the main occasion of dog-sacrifice at Rome was the *Augurium Canarium*. This was a ritual to placate the Dogstar, whose date varied with its sighting, close or even coincident with the feast of Robigus. Given that Pliny, *NH* 18.285 attests a direct connection between Dogstar and mildew (cited 913), the evidence converges to suggest that these rituals were, if not identical, closely associated, despite their different locations.

There was even a Greek equivalent, reported by Ap. Rhod. 2.522ff.: the dawn sacrifice of a dog by the Cean priests at the time of the Dogstar Sirius, when there are 40 days of Etesian winds. The same Cean sacrifice to the Dogstar is mentioned by Call. *Aitia* 75.32 Pfeiffer ('Acontius and Cydippe') without specifying the victim. Thus Hellenistic models gave O. incentive to make much of the unusual Roman offering, and the *aition* which he presents in 939–42 refers this sacrifice to the tale of Maira, the Dogstar.

As in the *Augurium Canarium* for the Dogstar, the dog sacrificed to Robigo/us was almost certainly red-haired; cf. Festus 358 Lindsay *rutilae canes . . . immolantur ut ait Ateius Capito, canario sacrificio pro frugibus deprecandae saeuitiae causa sideris caniculae*, cf. 39 Lindsay: *rufae canes* were sacrificed near the Porta Catularia *ut fruges flauescentes ad maturitatem perducerentur*.

937–8 tum mihi 'cur detur sacris . . . quaeris?' | . . . 'causam percipe' flamen ait: the regular pattern of question and answer (see 193–6) is ingeniously inverted. The priest's reply in the main clause contains O.'s reported question, but in 938 the afterthought *quaesieram* is essentially a stage direction, commenting on *quaeris*, like the parenthesis in 691.

937 noua uictima: on O.'s justification of different sacrificial victims in 1.333–456 see Introd. 3(i)(*c*). The explanation here is more magical and less moral: a sympathetic affinity between supernatural being and victim, comparable to the practice required by *ius diuinum* of sacrificing females to female deities, black animals to the Manes etc. (See W. Warde Fowler, *Religious experience of the Roman people* (London 1914) 179.)

939 est Canis, Icarium dicunt, quo sidere moto: cf. *Am.*

2.16.4 *Icarii stella proterua canis*. Only the word *Icarius* evokes the Attic culture-myth of Bacchus and his host Icar(i)us, and the dog raised to the stars and so reported by Eratosthenes, *Catasterismoi* 14 p. 79, and Hyginus, *Astr.* 2.4 and *Fab.* 130; cf. also Apollodorus 3.14.7 with Frazer's note, Pausanias 10.38.1, and Servius on Virg. *Georg.* 2.389. In the myth Icarius gave wine to his guests, who mistook their drunken unsteadiness for poisoning and killed him; he was found by his faithful dog Maira, who fetched his daughter Erigone. She hanged herself in grief (according to Hyg. *Astr.* 2.4 *canis mortuae spiritu suo parentauit*) and all three were rewarded by catasterism. Erigone was identified with Virgo, and with her the dog is prominent in Aratus: 'the dog, star-enwrought yet not clearly marked in his form ... the tip of his terrible jaw is marked by a star that keenest of all blazes with a searing flame, and him men call Seirius' (327–32 tr. Mair). O. had translated Aratus, and knew Callimachus well, but omitted this myth from the *Metamorphoses* as he did many catasterisms.

940 tosta sitit tellus ... seges: elsewhere (*AA* 2.231) O. calls this star *sitiens canicula*, with *sitire* causative.

praecipiturque: the crop is premature. This seems to be a technical usage; cf. Colum. *De arb.* 9.2 *quae praecipiuntur aestu* and 11.2.69 *humorque ea non patiatur praecipi aut infuscari* (*TLL* x 2.451.54–78).

941 pro cane sidereo canis hic: for the idea of substitution compare Numa's verbal duel with Jupiter at 3.339–44.

942 quare pereat nil nisi nomen habet 'it has no cause to be killed except its name': *pereat* (GM) offers a more pointed and syntactically neater comment, with the dog as subject throughout, than the indefinite *fiat*, 'why this happens', of A and U. Contrast the justified retribution of 712 *quo ... modo ... perdidit ipsa perit.* The etymology may be an *aition* and still unfair.

943–8 (26–30 April, D F, E C, F NP, G C, H C)
28 April F FLOR NP The Floralia

The *Fasti Praenestini* read:

> Ludi Florae. feriae ex s(enatus) c(onsulto) quod eo di[– – – – – – – –] et [ara] | Vestae in domu imp(eratoris) Caesaris Augu[sti po]ntif(icis) ma[x(imi) | dedicatast Quirinio

et Valgio co(n)s(ulibus). eodem | die aedis Florae quae rebus florescendis praeest | dedicata est propter sterilitatem frugum.

943 Tithonia: another variation for naming the dawn (373 *Pallantias*, 389 *Eos*, 714 *Memnonis mater*, 721 *Aurora*). Once Aurora is identified as the wife/woman of Tithonus, O. recalls the connection of her neglected husband (cf. *Am.* 1.13.35–40) with the house of Aeneas: Tithonus is identified as brother of Anchises' father Assaracus, introduced in 34, 123 above.

944 sustulit immenso ter iubar orbe suum: another periphrasis for the passing of three days. The light of day (only at 1.78 is *iubar* a light or ray other than the sun) is here identified with dawn, as it is with the morning star at 2.149–50 *quintus ab aequoreis nitidum iubar extulit undis* | *Lucifer*; at 5.547 it is *dies* that lifts the sun.

945–8 O.'s notice of the Floralia is brief, deliberately suspended until he invokes Flora's presence on the last day of the festival, 2 May (5.183–4 *Mater, ades, florum* ... | *distuleram partes mense priore tuas*). Given the length of book IV, caused by April's abundance of major festivals, given too the relative dullness of May, which has no real festivities, there is no need to read political significance into O.'s courteous gesture of making way for the *grandius opus* of honouring Augustan Vesta. The *Fasti Praenestini* had given her the same precedence. Indeed the Floralia had not been included in calendars before its inclusion in the *Fasti Praenestini*: it had been a movable feast, *conceptiua, non stata*, like the *feriae sementiuae* which O. looked for in vain in the January calendar (1.657–62). Like other mobile festivals, such as the Compitalia (varying between the end of December and January), the Floralia also crossed the boundary between months (cf. 5.185 *incipis Aprili, transis in tempora Maii*).

We know, from 5.283–94 and 329–30 and Pliny, *NH* 18.286, that the Floralia were first celebrated in 238 BC *ut omnia bene deflorescerent*, but not made annual until 177 BC. Flora was in a sense a goddess of pollination, and Pliny sees her cult as answering the same anxiety for the successful development of the crops as the cult of Robigus four days earlier. But as O. will make clear (5.262–7), Flora ensured the successful setting not just of grain but of the fruit of plants, orchards, olives and vines.

945 uariis florum dea nexa coronis: etymologically Flora was associated with *flos*, hence garlands, and drinking-parties (cf. 5.335 *tempora sutilibus cinguntur tota coronis*, 341–2 *nulla coronata peraguntur seria fronte | nec liquidae uinctis flore bibuntur aquae*. With *uariis* of contrasting colours cf. 429–30 *tot* ... *colores* | ... *dissimili flore* and O.'s indication at 5.356 that Flora was depicted *cultu uersicolore*.

946 scaena ioci morem liberioris habet: cf. 5.331–2 *quare lasciuia maior | his foret in ludis liberiorque iocus*. In O., as in comedy and Catullus, *iocus* (sometimes coupled with *ludus*) often has the sexual connotation of 'fun and games': *AA* 2.724, 3.328, 580. The *ludi scaenici* for Flora offered a more earthy kind of theatrical occasion than the traditional tragedy and comedy offered to Ceres, Cybele and other gods. This was the official occasion for mime, a highly improvisational form of musical comedy. In the generation from Sulla to Caesar Rome had developed literary mime with verse libretti, fragments of which survive. But most mime was bawdy, full of stage business and highly visual; it featured actresses who often stripped on stage. This may account both for Livy's and Virgil's silence about Flora and her festival and for O.'s warm welcome to the goddess. (See Fantham (1992b) 49–52.)

947 exit et in Maias sacrum Florale Kalendas: cf. 5.189 *circus in hunc* (sc. *mensem*) *exit clamataque palma theatris*. For other uses of *exire in* cf. *Rem.* 653, *Tr.* 4.3.41, with the sense of 'vanishing', and *Am.* 3.12.41, *Ex P.* 3.3.101, where it implies 'extension' or 'outcome'.

948 tunc repetam: at 5.183–90 introducing a major treatment of Flora and the Floralia (191–378).

grandius urget opus: previously used to denote a more serious genre like tragedy (*Am.* 3.1.70 *a tergo grandius urget opus*). See Introd. 2(i).

949–54 O. honours the new Palatine Vesta. On 6 March 12 BC (3.419ff.), on the death of Lepidus, the disgraced holder of the office of Pontifex Maximus, Augustus finally had himself elected Pontifex Maximus and added the cult of Vesta to that of Apollo, worshipped within the Palatine precinct of his home since 29 BC.

949 aufer, Vesta, diem: a strange command, even if we translate *auferre* as 'win', 'carry off the prize'. But the notion of an Augustan divinity pre-empting other rites has already appeared figuratively at 673–4 *hanc* ... *Cytherea diem properantius ire | iussit*. A hierarchical society like Rome expected more important figures to displace others: O.'s readers might be less sensitive than some modern critics (Barchiesi (1994) 121–5) to Augustan ceremonies being privileged over ancient fertility rituals.

949–51 cognati Vesta recepta est | limine; sic iusti constituere patres. | Phoebus habet partem: Vestae pars altera cessit: cf. *Met.* 15.864–5 *Vestaque Caesareos inter sacrata Penates* | *et cum Caesarea, tu, Phoebe domestice, Vesta.* If O.'s readers could be relied upon to identify Augustus as Vesta's *cognatus*, this implication of his divine descent must have been publicly acknowledged. O. has already invoked this kinship for Augustus in 3.425–6 *ortus ab Aenea tangit cognata sacerdos* | *numina; cognatum, Vesta, tuere caput!* As a descendant of Aeneas, Augustus descends from Jupiter through Venus and so is *cognatus*, 'collateral kinsman', of Vesta (Fraschetti (1988) 956–7). As Aeneas' descendant he also has a hereditary claim to tend the fire which maintained by its perpetual flame continuity with the ashes of Troy; cf. 1.528–30 *Iliacos accipe, Vesta, deos.* | *tempus erit cum uos orbemque tuebitur idem,* | *et fient ipso sacra colente deo.*

In what special sense was Vesta received in Augustus' home? Dio 54.27.3 reports that since the Pontifex Maximus had to live in a public residence 'Augustus made a portion of his own house (οἰκία) public property' (he would make the entire house public after the rebuilding of AD 3, Dio. 59.15.5–6). This public status of his domestic precinct and blending of his private and public identities made it possible to represent his private shrine of Vesta and the Penates as public cult, although the public cult continued in the forum temple (Fraschetti (1988) 946–9). But it seems that this was confirmed by a dedication. The *Fasti Praenestini* for 28 April (see on 943–8; *patres* designates the Senate, as in 261) report a dedication to Vesta on the Palatine *ex senatus consulto*, and the Fasti Ceretani specify that it was a statue: *fer(iae) q(uod) e(o) d(ie) sig(num) Vest(ae) in domo P(alatino) dedic(atum est)*. This would have been a novelty, since Vesta was not represented by a statue in the forum Temple (cf. 6.295–6); but it would have been easy to set up e.g. a Greek cult statue of Hestia.

The *Fasti Praenestini* as shown above are damaged where the objects dedicated were identified. Editors agree on an altar (*ara*), but Degrassi and others could not accept Mommsen's supplement *aedicula* (shrine), on the grounds that it could not have displaced the forum temple, which in fact remained a centre of public cult. However, Guarducci has continued to claim ('Vesta sul Palatino', *MDAIR*

71 (1964) 158–69, cf. 'Enea e Vesta', *MDAIR* 78 (1971) 89–118) that the Sorrento Base and some Tiberian coins honouring the deified Augustus illustrate a small shrine of Vesta in the precinct to the SW of Augustus' house, and that this is the reference of 4.949–54. Given the dedication date, the shrine would have to have been built in less than two months between 6 March and 28 April. Her argument is archaeologically attractive, but not necessitated by either the needs of cult or O.'s text.

952 quod superest illis tertius ipse tenet: *illis* is dat. after *superesse*; *quod* is the space left unused. *tertius ipse* exalts Augustus (*ipse* is regularly used for *dominus*, whether legal or moral: *OLD* 12) on a par with his divine housemates. In this O. goes no further than his celebration of Augustus' elevation to the position of Pontifex Maximus, where Augustus is (or has? the question is theological) an *aeternum numen*; cf. 954. On O.'s skilful treatment of the Augustan ideology associated with Vesta see Herbert-Brown (1994) 66–80.

953–4 state Palatinae laurus, praetextaque quercu | stet domus: as Augustus reports (*Res gestae* 34.2) when he was given the name Augustus by decree of the Senate on 16 January 27 BC *et laureis postes aedium mearum uestiti publice coronaque ciuica super ianuam meam fixa est*: the door of his Palatine home was surmounted by the oak wreath awarded for saving a citizen's life and flanked by laurel bushes. Hence Apollo's promise to Daphne-as-laurel in *Met.* 1.562–3 *postibus Augustis eadem fidissima custos | ante fores stabis*. This wreath and inscription is found on some of Augustus' coinage. *praetextus* here may exploit the association with magisterial dress, cf. 5.567 *Augusto praetextum nomine templum.*

stet domus: the physical and the dynastic house are fused in this parting loyal vow: so the physical house is revered in *Ex P.* 3.1.135 *cum domus Augusti Capitoli more colenda*: for the sense of dynasty compare the late (exilic) passage of 1.532 *hanc fas imperii frena tenere domum*, and *Tr.* 3.1.41, 4.2.10 *perpetuo terras ut domus illa regat*, *Ex P.* 4.6.19–20 *sitque . . . sacrae mitior ira domus.*

aeternos tres habet una deos: cf. 3.421–2 *ignibus aeternis aeterni numina praesunt | Caesaris.*

The book ends on an exalted and pious note: questions of the poet's sincerity are irrelevant, and there is no cause to claim subversive intent in such a carefully worded tribute.

BIBLIOGRAPHY OF WORKS CITED

I. EDITIONS

Burman, P. (1727). *P. Ovidii Nasonis Fastorum libri sex cum notis variorum.* Amsterdam.

Merkel, R. (1841). *P. Ovidii Nasonis Fastorum libri sex.* Berlin; 2nd edn (1850–2) Leipzig; 3rd edn (1884) Leipzig.

Peter, H. (1874). *P. Ovidi Nasonis Fastorum libri sex.* Leipzig; 3rd edn (1889); 4th edn (1907) Leipzig.

Paley, F. A. (1881). *P. Ovidii Nasonis Fastorum libri sex.* London.

Hallam, G. H. (1886). *The Fasti of Ovid.* London and New York.

Ehwald, R., and Levy, F. W. (1924). *Fastorum libri VI. Fragmenta.* Leipzig.

Landi, C. (1928). *Fastorum libri VI*, in *Corpus scriptorum Latinorum Paravianum* 51. Turin; 2nd and 3rd edns. by L. Castiglioni (1950, 1960) Turin.

Frazer, J. G. (1929). *Publii Ovidii Nasonis Fastorum libri sex*, edited with a translation and commentary, 5 vols. London.

(1931). *Ovid: Fasti.* (Latin–English); 2nd edn by G. Goold (1989) Cambridge, MA.

Bömer, F. (1957, 1958). *P. Ovidius Naso: Die Fasten*, 2 vols. Heidelberg.

Le Bonniec, H. (1969, 1970) (trans. and comm.), *Les Fastes*, vol. I Catania, vol. II Bologna.

Alton, E. H., Wormell, D. E. W., and Courtney, E. (1978). *P. Ovidi Nasonis Fastorum libri sex*; 2nd edn (1985) Leipzig.

Schilling, R. (1993, 1995). *Ovide: Les Fastes*, 2 vols. Paris.

II. ARTICLES AND BOOKS

Albrecht, M. von (1968). 'Zur Funktion der Tempora in Ovids elegischer Erzählung (Fast. v, 379–414)', in von Albrecht and Zinn (eds.) *Ovid* (*Wege der Forschung* 92) Darmstadt, 451–67.

Allen, K. (1922). 'The Fasti of Ovid and Augustan Propaganda', *AJP* 43: 250–66.

Alton, E. H., Wormell, D. E. W., and Courtney, E. (1977). 'A catalogue of the manuscripts of Ovid's *Fasti*', *Bull. Inst. Cl. Stud.*, University of London, 24: 37–63.

Appel, G. (1909). *De Romanorum precationibus, RVV* VII 2. Giessen.

Arbesmann, P. R. (1929). *Das Fasten bei den Griechen und Römern, RVV* XXI. Giessen.

Axelson, B. (1945). *Unpoetische Wörter* (Skrifter utgivna av Vetenskaps-Soc. i Lund 29). Lund.

Barchiesi, A. (1991). 'Discordant Muses', *Proc. Camb. Phil. Soc.* n.s. 37: 1–21.

(1994). *Il poeta e il principe: Ovidio e il discorso augusteo.* Rome–Bari.

Barsby, J. (1978). *Ovid* (Greece and Rome New Surveys in the Classics no. 12). Oxford.

Barwick, K. (1925). 'Ovids Erzählung vom Raub der Proserpina und Nikanders HETEROIOUMENA', *Philologus* 80: 454–66.

Bayet, J. (1971). *Croyances et rites dans la Rome antique.* Paris.

Beard, M. (1987) 'A complex of times: no more sheep on Romulus' birthday', *Proc. Camb. Phil. Soc.* n.s. 33: 1–15.

Binder, G. (1988). *Saeculum Augustum* II: *Religion und Literatur.* Darmstadt.

Bömer, F. (1957). 'Interpretationen zu den *Fasti*', *Gymnasium* 64: 112–35.

(1964). 'Kybele in Rom: Die Geschichte ihres Kults als politisches Phenomen', *Mitteilungen des Deutschen Archäologischen Instituts* (*Röm. Abt.*) 71: 130–51.

(1987). 'Wie ist Augustus mit Vesta verwandt?', *Gymnasium* 94: 525–8.

(1988). 'Über das zeitliche Verhältnis zwischen den *Fasten* und den *Metamorphosen* Ovids', *Gymnasium* 95: 207–21.

Borgeaud, P. (1996) *La Mère des Dieux.* Paris.

Boyancé, P. (1954). 'Cybèle aux Megalésies', *Latomus* 13: 337–42.

Braun, L. (1981). 'Kompositionskunst in Ovids Fasti', *ANRW* II 31.4: 2344–83.

Bremmer, J. N. and Horsfall, N. M. (1987). *Roman myth and mythography* (*BICS* Supplement 52). London.

Brugnoli, G. and Stok, F. (1992). *Ovidius 'parodesas'.* Pisa.

Cameron, A. (1995). *Callimachus and his critics.* Princeton.

Classen, C. J. (1962). 'Romulus in der römischen Republik', *Philologus* 106: 174–204.

Coarelli, F. (1983–5). *Il foro romano: periodo repubblicano e augusteo*, 2 vols. Rome.

Courtney, E., ed. (1993). *The fragmentary Latin poets*. Oxford.

Degrassi, A. (1955). 'Esistette sul Palatino un tempio di Vesta?', *MDAIR* 62: 144–54.

(1963) *Inscriptiones Italiae* XIII 2: *Fasti et Elogia*. Rome.

Dumézil, G. (1970). *Archaic Roman religion*. Chicago.

Eitrem, S. von (1915). *Opferritus und Voropfer der Griechen u. Römern*. Kristiania.

Fantham, E. (1983). 'Sexual comedy in Ovid's *Fasti*: sources and motivations', *Harv. Stud. Class. Phil.* 87: 185–216.

(1986). 'Ovid, Germanicus and the composition of the *Fasti*', *Papers of the Liverpool Latin Seminar* 5: 243–81.

(1992a). 'The role of Evander in Ovid's *Fasti*', *Arethusa* 25: 155–71.

(1992b). 'Ceres, Liber and Flora: Georgic and anti-Georgic elements in Ovid's *Fasti*', *Proc. Camb. Phil. Soc.* n.s. 38: 39–56.

(1995). 'Recent readings of Ovid's *Fasti*', *CP* 90: 367–78.

Fauth, W. (1978). 'Römische Religion im Spiegel der "Fasti" des Ovid', *ANRW* II 16.1: 104–86.

Feeney, D. C. (1992). 'Si licet et fas est . . . : Ovid's *Fasti* and the problem of free speech under the Principate', in Powell (1992) 1–25.

(1998). *Literature and religion at Rome: cultures, contexts and beliefs*. Cambridge.

Foley, H. P. (1993). *The Homeric Hymn to Demeter: translation, commentary and interpretive essays*. Princeton.

Fox, M. (1996). *Roman historical myths*. Oxford.

Fränkel, H. (1945). *Ovid. A poet between two worlds*. Berkeley.

Fraschetti, A. (1988). '*Cognata numina*: culti della Città e culti della Casa del Principe in epoca Augustea', *Studi Storici* 29: 941–65.

(1990). *Il Principe e Roma*. Rome–Bari.

Gagé, J. (1930). 'Romulus–Augustus', *Mélanges d'archéologie et d'histoire: Ecole française de Rome* 47: 138–81.

(1935). *Res gestae divi Augusti*. Paris; 2nd edn (1977).

Gallo, I. and Nicastri, L., eds. (1991). *Cultura, poesia, ideologia nell'opera di Ovidio*. Naples.

Graillot, H. (1912). *Le culte de Cybèle, Mère des Dieux, à Rome et dans l'empire romain* (Bibl. des Ecoles Françaises de Rome). Rome.

Gruen, E. (1990). *Studies in Greek and Roman culture and policy*. Leiden.
Guarducci, M. (1964). 'Vesta sul Palatino', *MDAIR* 71: 158–69.
Hardie, P. (1991). 'The Janus episode in Ovid's Fasti', *Materiali e discussioni per l'analisi dei testi classici* 26: 47–64.
Harmon, D. P. (1986). 'Religion in the Latin elegists', *ANRW* II 16.3: 1909–73.
Harries, B. (1989). 'Causation and the authority of the poet in Ovid's *Fasti*', *CQ* 38: 164–85.
(1991). 'Ovid and the Fabii', *CQ* 41: 150–68.
Haslam, M. (1993). 'Callimachus' *Hymns*', in Harder et al. (eds.) *Hellenistica Groningana* I: *Callimachus*, 122–5. Groningen.
Heinze, R. (1919). 'Ovids elegische Erzählung', *Sitzb. Akad. Leipzig*, Phil.-hist. Kl. 71, 7 = *Vom Geist des Römertums* (Stuttgart 1960) 308–403.
Herbert-Brown, G. (1994). *Ovid and the Fasti: a historical study*. Oxford.
Herescu, N. I., ed. (1958) *Ovidiana: Recherches sur Ovide*. Paris.
Herter, H. (1941). 'Ovids Persephone-Erzählungen und ihre hellenistische Quellen', *Rheinisches Museum* 90: 236–68.
Higham, T. F. (1958). 'Ovid and rhetoric', in Herescu (1958) 32–48.
Hinds, S. (1982). 'An allusion in the literary tradition of the Proserpina myth', *CQ* 32: 476–8.
(1987a). *The metamorphosis of Persephone: Ovid and the self-conscious muse*. Cambridge.
(1987b) 'Generalizing about Ovid', *Ramus* 16 = *The Imperial Muse*, 4–31. Boreal, Victoria, Australia.
(1992). '*Arma* in Ovid's *Fasti*', *Arethusa* 25: 81–149.
Hunter, R. L. (1992) 'Writing the goddess: form and meaning in Callimachus' Hymn to Athena', *Materiali e Discussioni* 23: 9–34.
Johnson, W. R. (1979). 'The desolation of the Fasti', *CJ* 74: 7–18.
Kellum, B. A. (1990). 'The city adorned: programmatic display at the *Aedes Concordiae Augustae*', in Raaflaub and Toher (1990) 276–308.
Kennedy, D. F. (1992). 'Augustan and anti-Augustan: reflections on terms of reference', in Powell (1992) 26–58.
Kenney, E. J. (1969). 'Ovid and the law', *Yale Classical Studies* 21: 242–63.
(1973). 'The style of the *Metamorphoses*', in J. W. Binns (ed.) *Ovid*, 116–53. London–Boston.

(1974). *The classical text: aspects of editing in the age of the printed book.* Berkeley.
(1984). *The ploughman's lunch: Moretum, a poem ascribed to Virgil.* Bristol.
(1996). *Ovid: Heroides XVI–XXI.* Cambridge.
Knox, P. (1985) 'The Epilogue of the *Aitia*', *GRBS* 26: 69–75.
Latte, K. (1960). *Römische Religionsgeschichte.* Munich.
Le Bonniec, H. (1958). *La culte de Cérès a Rome.* Paris.
(1989). *Etudes ovidiennes: introduction aux Fastes d'Ovide.* Frankfurt am Main.
Lefèvre, E. (1976). 'Die Lehre von der Entstehung der Tieropfer in Ovids Fasten 1.335–456', *Rheinisches Museum* 119: 39–64.
(1980). 'Die Schlacht am Cremera in Ovids Fasten 2.195–242', *Rheinisches Museum* 123: 152–62.
Liebeschuetz, J. H. W. G. (1979). *Continuity and change in Roman religion.* Oxford.
Littlewood, R. J. (1981). 'Poetic artistry and dynastic politics: Ovid at the Ludi Megalenses (*Fasti* 4.179–372)', *CQ* 31: 381–95.
Luce, T. J. (1990). 'Livy, Augustus, and the Forum Augustum', in Raaflaub and Toher (1990) 123–38.
McKeown, J. (1984). '*Fabula proposito nulla tegenda meo*: Ovid's *Fasti* and Augustan politics', in Woodman and West (1984) 169–87.
Michels, A. K. (1967). *The calendar of the Roman republic.* Princeton.
Millar, F. (1993). 'Ovid and the *Domus Augusta*: Rome seen from Tomoi', *JRS* 83: 1–16.
Miller, J. F. (1980). 'Ritual directions in Ovid's Fasti: dramatic hymns and didactic poetry', *CJ* 75: 204–14.
(1982). 'Callimachus and the Augustan aetiological elegy', *ANRW* II 30.1: 371–417.
(1983). 'Ovid's divine interlocutors in the *Fasti*', in C. Deroux (ed.) *Studies in late Latin literature and Roman history* III 156–92. Brussels.
(1991). *Ovid's Elegiac Festivals.* Frankfurt–Bern.
(1992). 'The *Fasti* and Hellenistic didactic', *Arethusa* 25: 11–31.
Nagle, B. R., tr. and ed. (1995). *Ovid: the Fasti.* Bloomington, IN.
Newlands, C. (1992). 'Ovid's narrator in the *Fasti*', *Arethusa* 25: 33–54.
(1996). *Playing with time: Ovid and the Fasti.* Ithaca, NY.

North, J. A. (1989). 'Religion in republican Rome', in *Cambridge Ancient History* VII 2. Cambridge.

(1995). 'Religion and rusticity', in T. J. Cornell and K. Lomas (eds.) *Urban society in Roman Italy* 135–50. London.

Nugent, S. G. (1990). '*Tristia* 2: Ovid and Augustus', in Raaflaub and Toher (1990) 239–57.

O'Hara, J. J. (1996a). *True names*. Ann Arbor, MI.

(1996b). 'Vergil's best reader? Ovidian commentary on Vergilian etymological wordplay', *CJ* 91: 255–76.

Palmer, R. E. A. (1974). *Roman religion and Roman empire*. Philadelphia.

Peters, H. (1875). 'Über die doppelte Redaction der Ovidischen Fasten', *Neue Jahrbücher fur Philologie und Paedagogik* 111: 499–505.

Phillips, C. R. (1992). 'Roman religion and literary studies of Ovid's *Fasti*', *Arethusa* 25: 55–80.

Porte, D. (1978). 'Les Fastes d'Ovide et le sourcil latin', *Latomus* 37: 851–73.

(1984). 'Claudia Quinta et le problème de la *lavatio* de Cybèle en 204 av. J.-C.', *Klio* 66: 93–103.

(1985). *L'étiologie religieuse dans les Fastes d'Ovide*. Paris.

Powell, A. (1992), ed. *Roman poetry and propaganda in the age of Augustus*. London.

Price, S. (1984). *Rituals and power*. Cambridge.

Raaflaub, K. A. and Toher, M., eds. (1990). *Between republic and empire*. Berkeley–Oxford.

Richardson, N. S. (1974). *The Homeric Hymn to Demeter*. Oxford.

Sabbatucci, D. (1988). *La religione di Roma antica: dal calendario festivo all'ordine cosmico*. Milan.

Santini, C. (1974–75). 'Toni e strutture nella rappresentazione delle divinità nei *Fasti*', *GIF* 25: 41–62.

(1975). 'Motivi astronomici e moduli didattici nei *Fasti* di Ovidio', *GIF* 27: 1–26.

Scheid, J. (1992). 'Myth, cult and reality in Ovid's *Fasti*', *Proc. Camb. Phil. Soc.* 38: 118–31.

Schilling, R. (1954). *La religion romaine de Vénus*. Paris.

(1979). *Rites, cultes, dieux de Rome*. Paris.

Scullard, H. H. (1981). *Festivals and ceremonies of the Roman republic*. Ithaca, NY.

Stok, F. (1990). 'L'alternativa dei *Fasti*', *GIF* 42: 177–98.

(1991). 'L'ambiguo Romolo dei *Fasti*', in Gallo and Nicastri (1991) 183–212.

Summers, K. (1996). 'Lucretius' Roman Cybele', in E. Lane (ed.) *Cybele, Attis and related cults: essays in memory of M. J. Vermaseren*, 337–66. Leiden.

Syme, R. (1978). *History in Ovid.* Oxford.

Tarrant, R. J. (1983). 'Ovid: *Fasti*', in L. D. Reynolds (ed.) *Texts and transmission*, 266–8. Oxford.

Thomas, R. F. (1988). 'Tree violation', *TAPA* 118: 261–73.

Treggiari, S. M. (1992). *Roman marriage: iusti coniuges from the time of Cicero to the time of Ulpian.* Oxford.

Vermaseren, M. J. (1977). *Cybele and Attis: the myth and the cult.* London.

Wagenvoort, H. (1956). *Studies in Roman literature, culture and religion.* Leiden.

Wallace-Hadrill, A. (1982). 'The Golden Age and sin in Augustan ideology', *Past and Present* 95: 19–36.

(1987). 'Time for Augustus', in M. Whitby et al. (eds.) *Homo viator: classical essays for J. Bramble*, 221–30. Bristol and Oak Park, IL.

Warde Fowler, W. (1908). *The Roman festivals of the period of the republic.* London.

(1914). *Roman ideas of deity* (repr. 1969). New York.

(1920). *Roman essays and interpretations.* Oxford.

White, P. (1988). 'Julius Caesar in Augustan Rome', *Phoenix* 42: 334–56.

Wilkinson, L. P. (1955). *Ovid recalled.* Cambridge.

Williams, G. W. (1978). *Change and decline: Roman literature in the early empire.* Berkeley–Los Angeles–London.

Wiseman, T. P. (1979). *Clio's cosmetics.* Leicester.

(1984). 'Cybele, Virgil and Augustus', in Woodman and West (1984) 117–28.

(1994). *Historiography and imagination.* Exeter.

(1995). *Remus: a Roman myth.* Cambridge.

Wissowa, G. (1912). *Religion und Kultus der Römer* (2nd edn). Munich.

Wlosok, A. (1975a). 'Amor and Cupid', *HSCP* 79: 165–79.

(1975b) '*Geminorum mater amorum* (Ovid, Fasten 4.1)', in *Monumentum Chiloniense: Studien zur augusteischen Zeit. Festschrift für Erich Burck*, 514–23. Amsterdam.

Woodman, A. and West, D., eds. (1984). *Poetry and politics in the age of Augustus*. Cambridge.

Wormell, D. E. W. (1979). 'Ovid and the *Fasti*', *Hermathena* 127: 39–50.

Zanker, P. (1988). *The power of images in the age of Augustus*. Ann Arbor, MI.

INDEXES

Italic numbers refer to pages of the Introduction, non-italic to line-numbers in the Commentary.

1 Latin words

2 General

This index is selective; not all incidental geographical and personal names are listed. Earlier poetry and prose sources are indexed only where influence or allusion in *Fasti* is claimed.

www.ingramcontent.com/pod-product-compliance
Ingram Content Group UK Ltd.
Pitfield, Milton Keynes, MK11 3LW, UK
UKHW041635140825
461867UK00011B/396
* 9 7 8 0 5 2 1 4 4 9 9 6 0 *